THE
SHEPPERTON STORY

THE SHEPPERTON STORY

THE HISTORY OF THE WORLD-FAMOUS FILM STUDIO

GARETH OWEN

First published 2009

The History Press
The Mill, Brimscombe Port
Stroud, Gloucestershire, GL5 2QG
www.thehistorypress.co.uk

British Library Cataloguing in Publication Data.
A catalogue record for this book is available from the British Library.

ISBN 978 0 7524 4970 8

Typesetting and origination by The History Press
Printed in Great Britain

CONTENTS

Dedication

This one is for Mum

In memory of Richard Best BEM
and Robert S. O'Keefe.

ACKNOWLEDGEMENTS

The author wishes to express his thanks to the following people who helped make this book possible, some of whom sadly passed away before its completion:

Lesley Pollinger and all at Pollinger
    Limited
Steve Abbott
Sir Ken Adam
Sir Anthony Havelock-Allan
Angela Allen MBE
Anthony Andrews
Ken Annakin OBE
E.M. Smedley-Aston
Lord Attenborough CBE
George Baker
Robert S. Baker
Roy Ward Baker
Terry Bamber
Kenneth Branagh
Clifton Brandon
Dora Bryan OBE
Malcolm Burgess
Martin Cahill
Jack Cardiff OBE
Ian Carmichael OBE
Dick Clement
Kevin Connor
Eric Cross BSC
Michael Deeley
Shirley Eaton
Mark Eden
Matthew Field

Bryan Forbes
Damian Fox
Freddie Francis
Alan 'Fluff' Freeman
Andrew Freeman
Geoff Freeman
Lewis Gilbert CBE
John Glen
John Goldstone
Dulcie Gray CBE
Guy Green
Kenneth Griffith
Val Guest
Guy Hamilton
Peter Handford
Julie Harris
Tony and Iris Harwood
Geoffrey Helman
Brian Henson
Gordon Hessler
Jenny Hillyard
Peter Howitt
Alan Hume BSC
Peter Hyams
Duncan Kenworthy OBE
Basil Keys
Irene Lamb
John Lee BSC

Valerie Lesser
Richard Lester
Bert Luxford
Jonathan Lynne
Ronnie Maasz BSC
Peter Manley
Sir John Mills CBE
John Mitchell MBE
Sir Roger Moore KBE
Ossie Morris OBE BSC
Ronnie Neame CBE BSC
Keith Northrop, Goodman Derrick
Muriel Pavlow
Neil Purvis
Graham Rinaldi
Steven Saltzman
Marc Samuelson
Elaine Schreyeck
Peter Graham Scott
Sir Ridley Scott
Tony Scott
Tony Searle
Jeanie Sims
Ed Sloper, CP Cases
John Temple Smith
Norman Spencer
Victor Spinetti
Anthony Steel
Michael Stringer

Stoke Poges Memorial Gardens
Tamar Thomas (Kenneth Branagh's
    office)
Wendy Toye CBE
Queenie Thornton
Robert Wade
Ken Wallis MBE
Kay Walsh
Paul Welsh
Sebastian Wormell, Harrords Archive
Jaz Wiseman
Dave Worrall and Cinema Retro Archive
    (www.cinemaretro.com)
Susannah York
An extra special thank you to:
David Blake
Leslie Gilliat
Roy Pembrooke
Noreen Ackland
Richard Best
Robin Harbour
Doris Spriggs
John Herron and all at Canal+ Image
    (UK) Ltd
Andrew Boyle
John Aldred for going the extra mile, and
    being invaluable!
And to Rupert Boulting for access to his
    father's and uncle's archives.

Whilst every effort has been made to credit the correct source for photographic material used in this publication, the author apologies for any omissions.

FOREWORD

BY LESLIE GILLIAT

I was both delighted and flattered when Gareth Owen asked if I would write the foreword to this history of Shepperton Studios. It contains hundreds of amusing anecdotes, scores of rare photographs and covers just about every film made there since Shepperton came into existence – that's over 800 films.

Furthermore, the book has not only brought back many fond memories for me, of filming at Shepperton, but includes many details about the early history which were previously unknown to me, and I'm sure a great many others.

I first worked at Shepperton (then Sound City) in 1937 on a Will Hay film called *Old Bones of the River*, which was on location from Gainsborough Studios. My next visit wasn't until 1951, when, having left Denham Studios where I worked as production manager on *No Highway*, I joined my brother Sidney and Frank Launder to work on *Lady Godiva Rides Again*. That was followed by another twenty films at the studio including *Gilbert and Sullivan*, *The Green Man*, *Only Two Can Play*, *The Amorous Prawn* and the *St Trinian's* films, to name but a few.

In fact, some of my most enjoyable memories of the studio are of working on the *St Trinian's* films. The new girls for each film always knew the words of the school song before filming even started, and were terribly well behaved in real life! From the production point of view, the wardrobe was one of the cheapest ever known on a film. Between films, I always stored the school costumes in a film vault, though the holes in the straw hats became larger with each film!

I loved working at Shepperton and still fondly recall many old friends and colleagues who worked there with me over the years – Lew Thornburn, Frank Kelly, John Cox, Charlie Hillyer, Bert Easy, Harold Taylor, Bill Rule just to mention a few, and you'll read about them within these pages.

I nearly became much closer to the studio in 1959 when, after a very difficult stint as the British Lion representative on *The Third Man* television series, I was offered the job of studio manager by David Kingsley of British Lion, which then owned the studio. I felt I wasn't the right person for the job, and anyway I wanted to carry on making films and not work behind a desk. The job went to Andy Worker, and I'm sure he carried out a much better job than I would have done. However, a Gilliat did become much more involved with Shepperton when my brother Sidney later became chairman.

Of course, there is much, much more to the Shepperton story too, and my congratulations go to Gareth for writing such an interesting, accurately detailed and important history of one of the greatest film studios. I'm sure, once you've read it, you will all agree with me.

Leslie Gilliat
September 2008

INTRODUCTION

Tucked away in a quiet corner of the Middlesex countryside, near to the massive Queen Mary reservoir, is a former estate now known as Shepperton Film Studios.

The studios themselves are, in fact, about a mile outside of Shepperton village; an unspoilt, Thames-side settlement, close to the major motorway networks and about thirty minutes from both central London and Heathrow Airport.

Shepperton, like most other UK studios – Pinewood, Elstree, Ealing, Denham and Bray – is centred around a one-time country house, Littleton Park Manor. Though unlike the other major studios, Shepperton was not initially controlled by a company with production, distribution and/or exhibition interests. It could be said that Shepperton was a truly independent studio, with an independent spirit.

The magic of the grand, stately home has been enjoyed by many famous stars and film makers over eight decades, such as Humphrey Bogart, Orson Welles, Sir John Mills, John Wayne, Charlie Chaplin, Deborah Kerr, Peter Cushing, Sir Alec Guinness, David Lean, Lord Attenborough, Lord Olivier, Carol Reed, Dame Margaret Rutherford, The Boulting Brothers, Peter Sellers, Sigourney Weaver, Kenneth Branagh, Tom Hanks, Robert Downey Jr, Launder & Gilliat, Sir Michael Caine, Dame Edith Evans, Sylvester Stallone, Robert De Niro, Russell Crowe, Nicole Kidman, Brad Pitt, Kirsten

The south view of Little Park Manor and gardens, c. 1920. (Jenny Hillyard, granddaughter of Sir Edward Nicholl)

Dunst, Colin Farrell and Brendan Fraser – to name but a few. They brought films such as *The Third Man, Richard III, The Tales of Hoffman, Dr Strangelove, The Day the Earth Caught Fire, I'm All Right Jack, Flash Gordon, Mary Shelley's Frankenstein, Alien, Robin Hood: Prince of Thieves, The Crying Game, Gladiator, Troy* and *The Da Vinci Code* to life.

Whilst proud of its past, Shepperton Studios is also very much geared to the future, with extensive refurbishment and investment, state of the art post-production and digital effects facilities and, of course, healthy bookings in the diary. But how did it all start? How did this little area in south-west London became synonymous with the best in film production? To answer that question, we must go back a few hundred years to the beginning of what is now the studio's central building, The Old House.

The author sitting on Sir Alexander Korda's memorial bench, which bears his coat of arms. Korda was the most influential film-maker in Shepperton's history.

CHAPTER 1

EARLY DAYS

The story of Littleton Park Estate goes back to AD 700, when the earliest mention was made of Westminster monks running it. In the Domesday Book, Robert Blunt was listed as the tenant in chief, before Baron William Blunt took ownership in 1166. The estate's ownership changed hands nearly twenty more times before, in 1689, Thomas Wood, a ranger at Hampton Court, built Littleton Park Manor based on a design by architect Sir Christopher Wren, who famously designed St Paul's Cathedral.

It subsequently remained in the Wood family until 1901, when Richard Burbidge bought the estate. He was a fascinating figure.

Born in Wiltshire in 1847, Richard Burbidge ventured to London at the age of thirteen to make his fortune; rather like Dick Whittington, to whose legend he was compared several times. He gained an apprenticeship to a grocer and wine merchant in Oxford Street. No sooner had his apprenticeship come to an end, however, than he had set up in business on his own in Marylebone. Around this time, the idea of the 'department store' had begun to develop, and Burbidge was not slow in estimating its possibilities. He gave up his own premises and accepted a position at the Army and Navy Stores, before going on to become a manager at Whiteley's in Queensway, Bayswater (then London's largest store, and now a major shopping centre). His advancement was rapid, and the experience he gained invaluable.

In the 1880s, Charles Digby Harrod established his London Department Store, and business went from strength to strength. In 1889, he decided to retire and sold the store to a new limited company, Harrods Limited. Annual profits had reached £16,000 – a huge

Sir Richard Burbidge, former managing director of Harrods. (Courtesy of Harrods Archive)

sum in those days, when the weekly average wage was just over £1.60. The first year of the new company was distinctly rocky, however, and without Mr Harrod in charge, the store was losing customers. As a short-term measure, Harrod was persuaded to come out of retirement until a suitable replacement could be found. Enter Richard Burbidge.

Burbidge was considered a workaholic, and the perfect replacement for Harrod. In 1891 he took over the reins. Burbidge knew the department store business inside out but, more importantly, he had the vision and enthusiasm to take Harrods to undreamt-of heights. More than anyone else, it was Burbidge who made Harrods the greatest store in the world.

C.D. Harrod had built up a business based on high quality and good value. Burbidge added razzamatazz and Harrods fast became London's 'most fashionable rendezvous for shopping'. In 1898 he installed Britain's first escalator and in the early 1900s created the palatial new Harrods building with its eye-catching terracotta façade and luxurious interior décor, outshining any other shop in London. Burbidge's charm was legendary and Harrods made him a very wealthy man, enabling him to buy a country home, Littleton Park in Shepperton.

When the Woods owned Littleton Park, they erected a number of monuments in the grounds, commemorating different victories of the English Army. There was also a large urn on a plinth inside the Gothic summerhouse commemorating the last visit of King William IV to the estate, dated June 1836. His Majesty was a frequent visitor, staying with the Woods en route from London to Windsor. It is said that he enjoyed relaxing in the summerhouse next to the River Ash which runs through the grounds. Queen Victoria's son, the Prince of Wales (later King Edward VII), also became a frequent visitor and enjoyed hunting on the estate.

In 1874, while the house was being repaired, a disastrous fire occurred and everything was destroyed except the servants' quarters and the stables. Hogarth's famous picture, 'Strolling Players in a Barn' – which had come to Littleton directly

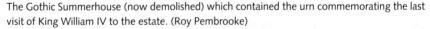

The Gothic Summerhouse (now demolished) which contained the urn commemorating the last visit of King William IV to the estate. (Roy Pembrooke)

The Victorian boat house. (Jenny Hillyard)

from the artist – was also destroyed in the flames. The remaining structures were turned into a small house and remained so until Burbidge bought the property, and set to work on rebuilding it. Burbidge was a collector of building materials and decorations, and would often store them with the view that he might need them one day. Many were now moved into Littleton.

The aforementioned summer house and a boat house were previously used by Queen Victoria at Buckingham Palace. He paid £3 5s for the summer house and £5 for the boat house. He also found homes for statues of Bacchus and 'Kneeling Slave' by Watts from the 1851 exhibition; marble figures from Burlington house were placed inside the house, as were panels representing historic naval and military events, also from Burlington. A ceiling from the committee room at the House of Commons; along with panelling from the 'Ancient House' at Colchester; doors and windows from Exeter Hall YMCA; entrance doors and a mantelpiece from the *Morning Post* offices in the Strand; the swing walnut door from the Olympic Theatre; doors and panelling from the late Lord Strathspey's house in Kensington – used in the billiard room and music room in Littleton – all became part of the house. Burbidge also brought over the annexe from Westminster Abbey as used at the time of King Edward's coronation, and part of the annexe used in connection with King George's coronation. All the beams throughout the house and the old timbers were used in the annexe of these coronations.

Several pavilions were dotted around the estate and a well-appointed Japanese garden took pride of place amongst the many wonderful Chestnut trees and rhododendrons. It was said, of the many hunts held on the estate, that one could ride for miles without leaving the park. A large two-acre kitchen garden with orangery

The grand entrance hall to Littleton Park house. Above the fire place on the right is painted a list of owners of the estate dating back to AD 700. (Jenny Hillyard)

and greenhouses proved ideal for growing peaches, grapes, apricots and figs, with every type of fruit tree indigenous to Britain in the gardens outside. The greenhouses boasted central heating, electric lighting and even a 'wireless receiving set'.

Astleham Manor also formed part of the property and was used as a keeper's cottage by Burbidge until 1911, when the Metropolitan Water Board acquired the land on which the house stood. He had the manor house moved brick-by-brick to a place near Littleton, where it became known as Astleham's Cottage. Rumour has it that Dick Turpin was in some way connected with the house.

For twelve years, Burbidge revelled in the rebuilding of his home, and filling it with interesting and beautiful items. For example, he found some statues that had once been at Burlington House and then moved to the Embankment before being junked in a yard near Battersea Park. Burbidge rescued them and built a hall to accommodate them at Littleton.

Burbidge paid frequent visits to the Caledonian market where all sorts of weird and wonderful building materials and ruins could be found. He saw the potential in these 'derelicts' and bought them cheaply. He also bought a fountain that had originally been at the meat market for Whiteley's department store when he was manager there, and later moved it to his Kensington stores and then on to Harrods. He called it his mascot, and the directors of Harrods later agreed to give it to him – which he subsequently moved to Littleton.

There was an abundant supply of the purest of water with the estate's own artesian well, believed to be over 600ft deep. Other water was pumped from the river by means of a water wheel to a tank holding some 26,000 gallons.

The side entrance hall with carved marble figures. Directly in front is the fireplace, with owners of the estate listed above. (Jenny Hillyard)

Burbidge loved to give annual garden parties at Littleton for his staff from Harrods and dinner parties for buyers. It was also reported that he often lent Littleton to a Mr Hepworth for 'the taking of films', which he was lately greatly amused by when he saw them. Little did he know that, a few decades later, films made there would be entertaining millions!

The River Ash, running through the estate, was said to be a great source of joy to Burbidge: he liked to go out in one of his boats on summer evenings, or to one of his summer houses and listen to the nightingales. He called it his 'silent hour'. He also enjoyed riding around the grounds and farm on a quiet cob before breakfast. He loved all the tame things that found sanctuary in his premises: squirrels, kingfishers, moor-hens, herons, badgers and so on. He was also a good judge of horses, and some of his ponies won many prizes – 'Sensation' and 'Midnight Queen' being his two favourites. There was also fishing, shooting tennis, cricket, football and a nine-hole golf course to keep him amused.

Burbidge – being a regular church-goer – did much for the church on the estate too. He paid for the restoration of the chancel, the purchase of oak screens and stalls, contributed heavily towards the cost of the organ, and gave a piece of land for the enlargement of the churchyard, keeping a portion where he built a vault for the family. In the church itself, hung twenty-four shot-torn colours of the Grenadier Guards, placed there in 1855 by Colonel [later General] Wood. Sadly, in 1905, Burbidge's wife died. He was distraught. He buried her in the vault he had so recently built.

The deeds to the manor were considered so beautiful in their own right that Burbidge lent one of them to the Victoria and Albert Museum in 1915. Meanwhile, the Great

War had broken out in 1914. Burbidge continued in his efforts to combine business with genuine philanthropy. He stated that any single men employed by him at Littleton, who signed-up with the services, would receive half-wages from him for the duration of hostilities. He then developed a new idea for the ladies. 'It was suggested as the war had left a large number of gentlewomen with reduced income', reported Harrods' 4 January 1916 edition of *The Sphere*, 'Richard Burbidge inaugurated a scheme for the training of such ladies for a business career'. The scheme proved a massive success. Burbidge's other activities during the conflict included being appointed by the Prime Minister to act on the commission examining Post Office employee wages. He was also a member of the General Purposes and the Executive Committee of the Board of Control of Regimental Institutes, which regularised the supply and management of Army canteens. He was also Honorary Treasurer of the Tariff Commission, and sat on the Shop Committee appointed by the Home Office prior to the introduction of the National Shops Act. Additionally, he served as chairman of the Executive and Emergency War Committees in connection with the provision of invalid kitchens.

There were many other societies and clubs that benefited from Burbidge's support and guidance, and he was the first to be asked to lend his aid to the Ministry of Munitions. Burbidge also provided premises for many of the groups he supported, including King Albert's Civilian Hospital Fund and Lady French's Fund.

Fifty-six years after heading to London to seek his fortune, Richard Burbidge was rewarded with a baronetcy in 1916 and became Sir Richard Burbidge. Sadly, he died suddenly the following year, on 31 May 1917. He had been in his flat above the store talking to his daughter, when he complained of feeling tired and would go to bed. His daughter had barely reached her home in Kensington when she received a telephone call. Her father had died sitting in his armchair, just as she had left him. It was said he was 'worn out by his labours'.

The River Ash adjoins the manor's grounds, where a statue of Old Father Thames sits on a large rock. (Roy Pembrooke)

The model railway housed in the old conservatory of the house. (Jenny Hillyard)

As well as Harrods, his mark had been left at the much-improved Littleton Park, and in 1917 the 900-acre estate and all it held within was sold to Member of Parliament and shipping magnate Commander Sir Edward Nicholl.

'I believe,' says Sir Edward's granddaughter Jenny Hillyard, 'that Sir Edward visited Harrods one day and said "I'm looking for a place to hang my hat, any suggestions?" and as they had Littleton Park on their books, so to say, they suggested it. Sir Edward bought it and its contents lock, stock and barrel.'

'I used to go there as a child,' says Oscar-winning costume designer Julie Harris, 'when it was owned by Sir Edward, as I was playmate with his two children, Leslie and Dodo – who incidentally, married a film producer, Frank Bundy, later on. I remember this amazing aviary – the conservatory, later used for filming – and also a miniature railway running around the grounds, and another inside the conservatory. There was the River Ash, wonderful gardens and woods, and a boathouse – which the two children used to lock me in! It really was a children's paradise, and I very much looked forward to my visits there. Of course, I never dreamt what was to come – a film studio, and my career in the business, and there in particular, later on.'

Sir Edward named one of the Navy's ships after the estate, the SS *Littleton*. A scale model was later built and displayed in the old house. Sadly, it disappeared after the rock group The Who took over the house. It is now believed to be in a museum somewhere in the north of England.

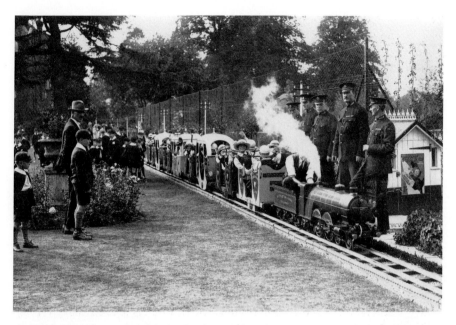

The miniature railway in the grounds of Littleton Park was a great favourite of visiting children. (Jenny Hillyard)

Meanwhile, a few miles away in rural Buckinghamshire a once-stately home was sold to another MP, Lt Col Grant Morden. Heatherden Hall was later to become Pinewood Studios. The story of both studios often intertwines over the years ahead, and indeed, combines in the early twenty-first century.

Back in the early 1900s, there were two dozen or so film studios operational in the London area. The boom in, and demand for, films was significant in the early part of the century, and by 1913 there were 600 cinemas in greater London alone. Most of the studios were nothing more than disused factories, conservatories, ice-rinks and just about any other sturdy structure that would convert to a glass-roofed one for maximum light. With the introduction of artificial light, however, purpose-built studios began popping up. Demands increased beyond the basic floor space needed to including cutting rooms, prop and scenic storage, office space, dressing rooms and so on, and many of the make-shift studios disappeared in favour of the new purpose-built ones. The London smog was also a factor in desiring artificial light, and so came superior studios on the outskirts of London: Beaconsfield (opened in 1922), Bushey (1913), Crystal Palace (1913), Ealing (1911), Elstree (1913), Isleworth (1914) and Twickenham (1913), in addition to many in and around central London itself, such as Clapham and Islington. Most of these sites, it should be added, were built to accommodate silent films, and so the advent of sound saw many undergoing expansion or conversion, and in some unviable cases, closure.

In 1927 the Cinematograph Film Quota Act was passed. It had long been noticed that the majority of films being shown at British cinemas were American and, with their success, the box-office proceeds returned to America. The British Government was keen to reverse this trend and the Quota Act introduced, which purported to enhance and increase British Film Production by requiring a certain number of British films to be produced and shown at cinemas. Undoubtedly, the act extended the lives of many British studios, as a great number of films were produced to meet quota levels. Simplicity was the key, as editor Richard Best (who worked on several 'Quota Quickie' films in the 1930s) recalls:

> They were generally about an hour, cost £1 per foot of film, and therefore budgeted at a modest £6, 000 each. The stories were usually straight-forward, uncomplicated ones, with pretty reasonable scripts. There wasn't any heavy camera coverage, post-synchronisation or sound effects. Library tracks would be used for effects and music. Many famous names of the future made their start in 'Quota Quickies' including Vivien Leigh, Wendy Hiller and Rex Harrison.

But the requirement to make and exhibit British films to offset the Hollywood invasion did not always work out as planned.

'It was often remarked,' says Freddie Francis, who began his career with the motion picture camera on early Quota Films, 'that only the cleaners at the Plaza ever got to see the films, as they were often run early in the mornings, to fulfil the requirements of the quota act. American films ran in the evenings!'

Nevertheless, the sudden increase in production also meant there were too few qualified film-makers to fill the vacancies, and 'many gifted amateurs suddenly found themselves making films' added producer Sir Anthony Havelock-Allen. As well as being an invaluable launch-pad for many up-and-coming technicians, the films also instigated the careers of many of the silent movie directors. They also played a major part in Shepperton's inception and the 'Quota Films' became an important part of the studio's early history. The story of Shepperton Studios proper starts a few years later, in 1929, when Norman Loudon bought Littleton Park Manor and its surrounding sixty acres of grounds.

Loudon, who ran a successful camera company, became active in the 'flicker book' business in 1927, and was based in London's Earl's Court. The booklets contained close-up photographs of people such as sportsmen performing an action (batting, kicking etc) shot in slow motion with a 35mm camera. When the fifty pages were 'flicked' in quick succession by a forefinger and thumb, 2½" x 4" photos produced the impression of two or three seconds of continuous movement – much like the old 'What The Butler Saw' machines in fairgrounds. The books were very popular with children, as they were inexpensive to buy, and Loudon carved a successful business. However, the feature film business was fast becoming the form of entertainment and, perhaps mindful of this, in 1928 Loudon purchased Littleton Park House from Sir Edward Nicholl. He then added seventy acres of surrounding land to his deal, including woods and a stretch of the River Ash. The total price worked out to £5,000. He was keen to enter the world of film, and now he had his ideal premises.

Two years later, in 1930, Loudon registered Flicker Productions Ltd with a capital of £3,500. He was underway!

CHAPTER 2

THE '30s: SOUND CITY, OPEN FOR BUSINESS

In 1932, Loudon formed Sound City Film Producing and Recording Studios with a capital of £20,950. Financing for the operation came primarily through Loudon himself, and through him offering moneyed individuals the opportunity to invest in film production. A few months later, the first sound stage was constructed on the site, measuring 110ft by 80ft.

The stage employed the latest sound system, and was very much indicative of Loudon's desire to be state-of-the-art – fully embracing talking pictures – as was further demonstrated by his choice of company name. A second stage was soon added, measuring 80ft x 40ft. This first year two features, and five short films for MGM, were produced. Great use was also made of the conservatory and ballroom in the house in their production.

One of the shorts, *The Safe*, was written by W.P. Lipscombe, a silent film actor who had achieved some success in writing short comedies.

Shepperton's first full-feature film was a comedy entitled *Watch Beverley*, directed by Arthur Maude, a native of Pontefract in Yorkshire who had entered the film industry as a writer, director and actor in 1914 at the age of thirty-three. Two more Shepperton directorial assignments followed for him the next year: *The Wishbone* and *She Was Only a Village Maiden*, both for Loudon's Sound City Films.

A rising star in the company was the producer of *Watch Beverley*, Ivar Campbell (who produced under the supervision of Loudon). Born in New Zealand, Campbell travelled to Britain, joined the stock exchange and then became a film producer in his late twenties thanks to the 'Quota Quickies' and his financial know-how. Obviously intrigued by the film-making process, he decided his next (and only second) job in the film industry would be as director, and as he had the confidence of backer Loudon, *Reunion* was the result, a sixty-minute feature. He wrote, directed and/or produced another twenty or so more films before losing his life in the Second World War.

Norman Loudon's production programme, meanwhile, continued apace and saw Campbell employed as director on fantasy *Eyes Of Fate*, drama *Side Streets* – a forty-six-minute drama written by actor Philip Godfrey – and *Golden Cage* (all 1933), the latter based on the play by Lady Trowbridge, and notable for its casting of Anthony Kimmins. At the time, Kimmins was a young writer who later went on to great things as a director, writer, and producer, including three 'Quota Quickie' films the very next year.

Ivar Campbell's assistant director on *Reunion*, John Baxter, was another rising star, carving himself a career as a director in his own right. In 1933, he directed *Song of the Plough*. Future cinematographer and director Guy Green was a clapper boy on the production:

> Oh I remember vividly that long walk from Shepperton railway station to the studio, having already left London at 6a.m. The studio hadn't been open for very long at all, and had completed only a handful of films, mainly in the old conservatory. They had recently built a new sound stage however.
>
> I remember going for my interview with Norman Loudon and his financial side kick Ivar Campbell, and they agreed to take me on for a weekly salary of £4.
>
> My first engagement was as a clapper loader on *Song of the Plough* which was filming on a nearby location, in a field. The director was John Baxter and the cameraman Glen Jennings. There was an atmosphere of the 'old boys club' about it. I heard from Glen Jennings many years later, and we both had very fond memories of our early days at the studio.
>
> David Lean was moonlighting on the editing of this film with another. I never met him on the stage floor, however our paths did cross later on when we both worked on *One Of Our Aircraft Is Missing* and on subsequent projects.

Lean wasn't terribly impressed by the project as he explained in a Moviemen interview, 'I worked on a lot of bad pictures, and bad pictures are very good for one's ego, because the worse they are, the more chance you have of making them better.' Lean would often work on two films at a time: at one studio during the day, and then another at a second studio all evening, as was the case with *Song of the Plough*.

Baxter's second film, crime thriller *Doss House*, was, appropriately, an observation of human suffering set in a down-and-out hostel. It was gritty, hard-edge, realistic drama, long before the sixties ushered in the kitchen sink genre to greater effect, and whilst initially courting murmurings of gloom and disaster, it was surprisingly successful. Baxter was to become an influential producer and director during Shepperton's early years and with his partner, from his former casting agency, under the banner Baxter & Barter, made another half dozen films including *Birds of a Feather* (1935) starring Sir George Robey, *Hearts of Humanity* (1936) with Eric Portman, and the musical *Talking Feet* (1936).

'Talking Feet was my first experience of a musical,' says sound assistant John Aldred:

> It was on this production that I was introduced to the system of playback, playing back an acetate 78 disc to the stage on a given cue. I overheard a conversation between Sludge (the camera maintenance man) and John Byers (head of the sound department), wondering if I was too young for playback. John Byers leapt to my defence by saying, 'If he can operate home movie he can operate

An early Sound City studio brochure from 1934, listing the facilities at the studio and profiling some of the films made there in its short history. (Gareth Owen Collection)

playback!' So I became an experienced playback operator. Filmed in the 1932 stage the film really consisted of a series of music acts, joined together with a thin story line. I believe it introduced an up-and-coming young actress named Hazel Court.

The Sound City facility was also attracting outside production companies; the Wainwright Brothers, Embassy Pictures and Argyle Talking Pictures soon became tenants on site.

Director Harry Hughes brought *The Improper Duchess* to the studio. It was Ronnie Neame's first assignment as cinematographer at Shepperton. He recalls:

The Improper Duchess was a film made by City Films – not to be confused with Sound City or Two Cities – and starred Yvonne Arnaud. I lit that film with a youthful enthusiasm! I remember it fondly actually because Yvonne Arnaud presented me with an inscribed silver cigarette case after shooting ended.

Loudon's own productions rolled fast. *Paris Plane* was a crime thriller from the son of Nelson Keyes, John Paddy Carstairs. No sooner had Carstairs embarked upon his directorial project at Shepperton, when director Maurice Elvey moved across from Twickenham with his project, starring Conrad Veidt and Peggy Ashcroft, *The Wandering Jew*, to take advantage of the studio woodlands. Produced for Gaumont British, the film was hailed in *Variety* as 'a beautiful production, a historic triumph – and most likely a commercial error.' The film is interesting in that Jesus Christ is not directly depicted by image nor by voice. During the early scenes, Christ is apparently located just outside the right-hand edge of the film's frame; Veidt and the other actors turn in profile to the camera and stare at something off-screen. When Christ speaks to Veidt, we do not hear an actor's voice; instead we see words (in a very ornate type font) superimposed directly in front of Veidt's face, spelling out Christ's malediction. There is an eerie glow from just beyond the frame, apparently representing Christ's aura. Pontius Pilate, played by Basil Gill, was completely cut in the US version of the film.

Basil Dean, over from his Ealing Studios, was busy producing *Three Men in a Boat*, the second filmic version of Jerome K. Jerome's comedy about three men holidaying on the River Thames, and made good use of Shepperton's grounds and the River Ash running through, before going out on location a few miles down the road on the Thames. The film *Drake of England* also completed some photography at the studio, as first assistant director E.M. Smedley-Aston recalls:

It was my first time at Sound City. We shot scenes for Drake on the backlot. We couldn't use the lot at BIP [British International Pictures Studios at Elstree] you see as water was needed, so we used the River Ash for the scene at Tilbury when Good Queen Bess welcomes Drake's safe return. Elizabeth was played by Athene Seyley and Drake by a slightly arthritic Matheson Lang!

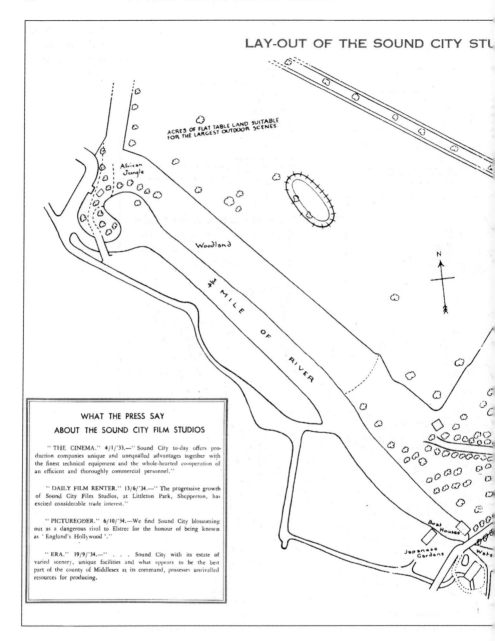

LAY-OUT OF THE SOUND CITY STU

ACRES OF FLAT TABLE LAND SUITABLE
FOR THE LARGEST OUTDOOR SCENES

African
Jungle

Woodland

¾ MILE OF RIVER

N

WHAT THE PRESS SAY
ABOUT THE SOUND CITY FILM STUDIOS

"THE CINEMA." 4/1/'33.—"Sound City to-day offers production companies unique and unequalled advantages together with
the finest technical equipment and the whole-hearted co-operation of
an efficient and thoroughly commercial personnel."

"DAILY FILM RENTER." 13/6/'34.—"The progressive growth
of Sound City Film Studios, at Littleton Park, Shepperton, has
excited considerable trade interest."

"PICTUREGOER." 6/10/'34.—We find Sound City blossoming
out as a dangerous rival to Elstree for the honour of being known
as 'England's Hollywood'."

"ERA." 19/9/'34.—" . . . Sound City with its estate of
varied scenery, unique facilities and what appears to be the best
part of the county of Middlesex at its command, possesses unrivalled
resources for producing.

Boat
Houses

Japanese
Gardens

Arthur Woods was the film's director, and Claude Freise Greene the lighting cameraman. Camera assistant Ronnie Neame recalls working on this film with great fondness, partly because it led to promotion:

I was friends with Arthur Woods when the subject of *Drake Of England* came up; we had previously worked together at Elstree on *Radio Parade*. We were certainly familiar with the surrounds of Shepperton too, as at the weekends,

Plan of the studio
and its grounds.
(Gareth Owen
Collection)

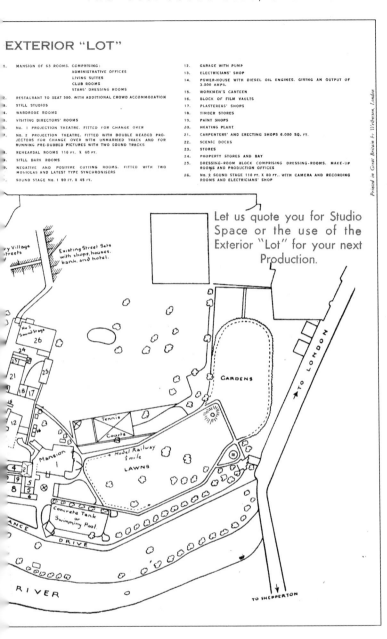

EXTERIOR "LOT"

1.   MANSION OF 63 ROOMS, COMPRISING:
          ADMINISTRATIVE OFFICES
          LIVING SUITES
          CLUB ROOMS
          STARS' DRESSING ROOMS
2.   RESTAURANT TO SEAT 300, WITH ADDITIONAL CROWD ACCOMMODATION
3.   STILL STUDIOS
4.   WARDROBE ROOMS
5.   VISITING DIRECTORS' ROOMS
6.   No. 1 PROJECTION THEATRE, FITTED FOR CHANGE OVER
7.   No. 2 PROJECTION THEATRE, FITTED WITH DOUBLE HEADED PRO-
     JECTORS FOR CHANGE OVER WITH UNMARRIED TRACK AND FOR
     RUNNING PRE-DUBBED PICTURES WITH TWO SOUND TRACKS
8.   REHEARSAL ROOMS 110 FT. X 60 FT.
9.   STILL DARK ROOMS
10. NEGATIVE AND POSITIVE CUTTING ROOMS, FITTED WITH TWO
     MOVIOLAS AND LATEST TYPE SYNCHRONISERS
11. SOUND STAGE No. 1 80 FT. X 45 FT.

12. GARAGE WITH PUMP
13. ELECTRICIANS' SHOP
14. POWER-HOUSE WITH DIESEL OIL ENGINES, GIVING AN OUTPUT OF
     3,000 AMPS.
15. WORKMEN'S CANTEEN
16. BLOCK OF FILM VAULTS
17. PLASTERERS' SHOPS
18. TIMBER STORES
19. PAINT SHOPS
20. HEATING PLANT
21. CARPENTERS' AND ERECTING SHOPS 6,000 SQ. FT.
22. SCENIC DOCKS
23. STORES
24. PROPERTY STORES AND BAY
25. DRESSING-ROOM BLOCK COMPRISING DRESSING-ROOMS, MAKE-UP
     ROOMS AND PRODUCTION OFFICES
26. No. 2 SOUND STAGE 110 FT. X 80 FT., WITH CAMERA AND RECORDING
     ROOMS AND ELECTRICIANS' SHOP

Printed in Great Britain by Wotherson, London

Let us quote you for Studio Space or the use of the Exterior "Lot" for your next Production.

Arthur, who owned a small aircraft – a rarity in 1933 – would take me flying, and do I mean flying! We would position ourselves high above the enormous reservoirs between Shepperton Studios and Staines (now the busy approach to Heathrow) and indulge in stunts!

We would dive at the water below, pulling up at the very last moment. Then loop-the-loop, bringing my stomach to my mouth. We became a falling leaf, the plane twisting and turning as it fell to earth. Unquestionably we were quite mad!

Drake of England. Queen Elizabeth I meets Francis Drake at Tilbury Docks, aka Sound City Studios and the River Ash. (Courtesy Ossie Morris BSC)

Claude Freise Green was engaged as cinematographer and me, as usual, as his assistant. There weren't such people as camera operators in those days as the cinematographer would light the set and operate himself. But he would always have an assistant on hand. The story portrays Sir Francis Drake, the British Vice-Admiral, who insisted on finishing a game of bowls before engaging the Spanish Armada.

Freise was a willing drinker at the best of times, but now he was drinking more heavily. As soon as he arrived on set he would ask the prop men to bring his 'medicine' – either whiskey or gin. He never gave the impression of being drunk, although he always wore dark glasses to hide his bleary eyes. It was amazing to me how he managed to judge the lighting in tinted glass. Then after lunch he would drop off to sleep in his chair and that was when I had to take over, virtually becoming the lighting cameraman and generally keeping things going until he awakened.

While he was sleeping, the rest of us would finish the shot and then move onto another setup, leaving him behind. Someone once placed a cardboard sign at the front of his chair that read 'A Penny For The Blind'. When he awoke he would become angry with me for taking over, but I had no other choice.

One afternoon, he collapsed and had to be rushed into hospital – the film was without a cameraman.

'You know you can do it', said Arthur Woods.

'I don't think I've got the experience,' I replied.

'Nonsense! You've been doing it for the last three weeks haven't you?'

'I suppose so, but Friese was there.'

'Was he?'

This conversation took place over lunch in the Shepperton restaurant when Arthur and I were sitting with the new BIP boss, P.C. Stapleton, who settled the matter. 'I want you to take over', he stated. 'There are eight weeks of shooting left. I won't give you a raise in salary but I will give you a bonus at the end. What do you say?'

'Thank you sir.'

My bonus for seven weeks' work was £40. I learned a lot about lighting along the way and was not only the youngest cameraman in the country, but the cheapest too.

It was with *Colonel Blood*, directed by W.P. Lipscombe, that things really started looking up for Sound City. Norman Loudon produced the big-budget drama, set at the time of Charles II, which was said to be budgeted at £60,000.

The epic told the tale of one of Britain's most daring criminals, Colonel Thomas Blood, and his attempt to steal the Crown Jewels. The film saw a superior recreation of the Tower of London on the newly constructed studio tank, and the Crown Jewels themselves re-created. No expense was spared, and Loudon, it seemed, was keen to rival Alexander Korda who was producing the lavish *The Private Life of Henry VIII* at Elstree, which went on, on its first day of release at Radio City Music Hall in New York, to set a world record for a single day's box office revenue of $18,400 (£9,000) and worldwide some £500,000. Sadly, Loudon's production did not match the success of Korda's, nor – it could be said, thankfully – did it escalate over budget to the same degree, with the final cost being put at a colossal £93,710.

The studio was expanding too, as assistant director E.M. Smedley-Aston recalls: 'Building had started on two studio blocks containing two medium-sized stages. Initially one was let to Richard Wainwright and John Stafford – two independent producers.'

1934 was a busier year for the studios, and a year that marked the first association of the aforementioned Alexander Korda. Fresh from his success with *The Private Life of Henry VIII*, Korda had persuaded his backers, the Prudential Assurance Company, to bank-roll his lease of Worton Hall Studios in Isleworth, and his production programme continued. It was with the film *Sanders of the River* that Korda first visited Sound City.

John Aldred, who later became one of the country's top sound technicians, adds that:

> … my father was a dental surgeon and one of his patients was Norman Loudon. My father told Loudon about my interest in films, and that I wished to be involved in the business when I left school. He did in fact give me a job, but that was a couple of years later, as I will mention. Another patient was John Byers,

The administration block and original 1932 studio. (Roy Pembrooke)

who headed Shepperton's small sound department, and he was shown my mini cinema at the top of the house, complete with screen tabs, coloured lights, and sound from 78 records. He promised to keep in touch and offered to show me around the studio.

I duly arrived on my bicycle from Ashford, a distance of about 3 miles, and was taken on a studio tour by John Byers. The only film in production that day was *Sanders of the River* out on the back lot, where the River Ash flowed through the studio grounds. A complete native village had been built on the river bank, and the whole unit was present although there was little activity. It was explained to me that they were all waiting for the sun to come out, as all the previous day's scenes had been filmed in sunshine. If the sun did not come out, they would wait around until it got dark and film some night scenes with large arc lamps. I remember seeing Zoltan Korda for the first time, and he looked too scruffy to fit my idea of a film director.

The art director was Vincent Korda (who spoke no English) and he had designed and built the large river boat which was supposed to come upstream and stop at the village. It was not self propelled but drawn by a cable attached to a tractor that was hidden in the bushes. Strangely, I don't remember seeing a sound truck anywhere, or a camera.

Originally envisioned as a modest 'Quota Quickie', the Edgar Wallace story *Congo Raid* soon developed into a full-blown feature, thanks to a five-picture deal Alexander Korda had just signed with United Artists, after acquiring shares in the company through an agreement with Douglas Fairbanks Sr. Alex's brother, Zoltan, was given directorial duties and in late December 1933 had set out with his director of photography, Osmond Borradaile, and a small crew to Africa where, according to Barradaile, they were to 'capture footage of remote, spectacular and inaccessible locations largely unknown to motion picture audiences.' Studio work got underway the following year at Worton Hall in Isleworth, but in the event it proved too small a facility to house the Congo-set adventure. Sound City, on the other hand, offered the perfect solution, albeit minus the tropical sun, and the aforementioned wonderful jungle scenery was re-created along the banks of the River Ash.

'As a teenager I went along to see a night shoot,' adds costume designer Julie Harris. 'I'm not sure if it was one of the Nicholls family that arranged it, but I know I was invited by someone, and there was quite a change since my days visiting as a playmate of the Nicholls children. I'd never been on any kind of film set, let alone one that was to be set on fire! It was truly amazing to watch with all of the extras, and crew running about. Maybe that's when the "film bug" bit me?'

However, the grandeur of *Sanders of the River* (which spent almost six months on the lot at Sound City alone) saw its budget spiral to £149,789 – an extraordinary amount for the time – and whilst Korda's backers may have been encouraged by the healthy box office on *Henry VIII*, they were less than pleased when this production barely recovered its costs.

Ronnie Neame recalls that:

Paul Robeson's stand-in on the film was Mzee Jomo Kenyatta, who in 1964 went on to become President of Kenya (the country was supposedly named after him) when it received independence from Britain. I remember Prince Michael represented Britain at the hand-over ceremony. The British flag was lowered and the Kenyan flag took its place. Story has it that Prince Michael said to Kenyetta, 'Do you think you can manage this?' It was all very friendly!

Alexander Korda's production of *Sanders of the River*. (Gareth Owen Collection)

John Aldred notes that:

> He was elected by the black native extras to be their representative, or shop
> steward, on the film. It was he who said how much they were to be paid, what
> hours they could work, and what rest periods they needed. I also remember, as
> part of my studio tour, being shown the cutting room block, the three review
> theatres, and watching the rushes of Sanders through a projection port. I was
> quite concerned that the sound was out of sync, but the projectionist said he
> could do nothing about it and that the editor would sort it out later.
>
> I was home again, on my bike, by lunch-time!

There is an interesting story about the theme music for *Sanders* called *Ay-ee-yo-ho*,
composed by Mischa Spolianski (who had never been to Africa). Many years later,
when Zoli was again filming in the African Congo, he heard a group of fishermen
paddling their canoes upstream and singing *Ay-ee-yo-ho*. The tune from *Sanders* had
passed into African folklore.

Another film which popped in for a few days filming on the back-lot was *Mister
Cinders*. Ossie Morris recalls:

> I was a young clapper boy on that, and it was actually a BIP production up at
> Elstree, but we needed a few scenes on a river and off we all went to Sound City.
> A German by the name of Otto Kanturek lit the film, and I remember it was
> written by George and Kenneth Western, who both acted in it too, and never
> did another thing after! Jack Davies also had a hand in the script and he went on
> to write some terrific screenplays, including many for Norman Wisdom. It was
> a good training ground for Jack and I.

Another rising talent at the studio was scenario writer Frank Launder. Over at John
Maxwell's BIP Studios in Borehamwood, Launder had written a dozen or so film scenarios
and scripts, starting off in the silent days, and then had a brief spell in charge of publicity,
before transferring across to Sound City. His first Shepperton film was a comedy starring
Will Fyffe called *Rolling Home*, directed by American Ralph Ince, which saw a wonderful
dockland set constructed on the river as well as a country village set on part of the back-lot.
It was Launder's first of many films at Shepperton, and in his later career he returned as a
producer, director and writer, most famously with the *St Trinian's* series of films.

Anthony Kimmins also enjoyed a successful (and his first) year as a director, with three
'Quota Quickie' films produced for Sound City. *How's Chances, Bypass to Happiness* and
Once in a New Moon, which was based on a book by Owen Rutter called *Lucky Star* and
witnessed the construction of an entire Sussex village on the lot.

Producer Michael Balcon's Gainsborough Pictures (which he formed in 1924) was
absorbed into the Gaumont-British Picture Corporation in 1928, and the corporation,
through its two studios at Shepherd's Bush and Islington, embarked upon an ambitious
programme of films. In 1934 Balcon produced *The Iron Duke* with George Arliss, featuring
distinguished actors Gladys Cooper and Emlyn Williams, and directed by Victor Saville. It

Mister Cinders. (Courtesy Ossie Morris BSC)

was the story of how the Duke of Wellington defeats a French scheme to discredit him. All of the battle sequences were mounted at Shepperton, some in the garden at the front of the Old House, and the rest of the interiors at Shepherd's Bush. It was suggested, however, that Arliss was too old at nearly seventy, playing Wellington in his mid-forties. That aside, the film performed well.

The garden and lot were now being used quite extensively by films from other studios for specific sequences. For instance, Saville's next film, *The Dictator*, with Emlyn Williams as King Charles VII in the romantic drama, completed photography and post-production at Sound City and saw a wonderful model of Tower Bridge constructed on the lot. Michael Balcon completed part of *Lady in Danger*, directed by and starring popular comic Tom Walls, alongside a stretch of the river; as did director Monty Banks with his 'Quota Quickie', *Falling in Love*. Prolific producer Julius Hagen oversaw the completion of his Twickenham-produced musical starring Stanley Holloway, *Lily of Killarney*, which re-created the Irish countryside on the estate.

1935 was a little quieter than the previous two years, with just six films shooting, the reason being that Sound City was closed for redevelopment and expansion by Loudon. Many of his staff found themselves redundant, and many labourers who had found security in work at the studio found themselves without employment.

At the end of 1935, the studio now boasted a lot 'of over sevnty acres of unrivalled exteriors, that has everything the film producer wants, from Bond Street to the jungle' – according to a brochure issued.

With two sound stages in operation and two more planned, there was also: 6,000 square feet of new workshops; two mobile sound vans; four cameras; Back Projection; two viewing theatres; 3 channel dubber; and finely equipped cutting rooms. Additionally the studio offered an enormous stock of existing sets: permanent street sets and country villages; along with three-quarters of a mile of river and a concrete pool 17,000 square feet for exterior and trick work. Magnificent offices and living accommodation in the Mansion for artistes and production staff.

Reaching the studio, it proclaimed, was easy as 'the newest of London's arterial roads, the Chertsey Road, will practically pass the gates of Sound City from Hammersmith. Electric trains from Waterloo or Earl's Court to Shepperton Station. Studio 5 minutes from station.'

Ivar Campbell next directed *Radio Pirates* whilst American director William Beaudine, who was prolific in silent cinema, filmed *Two Hearts in Harmony*. He stayed on in Britain to direct a few Will Hay comedies before returning to America, where he remained very busy directing features and television shows, clocking up more than 250 directorial credits before his death in 1970.

Producer Basil Keys says how:

I got my first job in the business on that film as a third assistant director. A lowly gopher, in all but name. I remember the studio fondly, with its giant conservatory, and it's strange that to this day I always remember Norman Loudon as being a 'big man' – certainly not in size but in terms of him being a very solid character. He also had a very pretty secretary named Miss Preston.

I didn't hit it off too well with Beaudine and, probably because I was vastly incompetent back then, was fired. That did me the power of good if I'm honest and certainly shook me up!

The press were certainly impressed by Sound City. *The Cinema* said, 'Sound City today offers production companies unique and unequalled advantages together with the finest technical equipment and the whole-hearted co-operation of an efficient and thoroughly commercial personnel.' *Picturegoer* said, 'We find Sound City blossoming out as a dangerous rival to Elstree for the honour of being known as England's Hollywood.'

1936 saw an expanded and much improved Sound City. The facility now boasted seven stages, covering over 70,000ft of floor space. Two stages had dimensions of 150ft by 120ft, two were 120ft by 100ft, one was 100ft by 80ft, and two were 70ft by 40ft. Furthermore, it was said that 'stages can be utilised to give a total length shot of 268ft' (this was if A and B, or C and D stages were combined). All were air conditioned, and four were fitted with water tanks.

Two RCA recording systems and one Visatone with silent track were offered, as were the latest Debrie cameras, camera crane, modern lighting, tubular scaffolding, back projection, playback, wind machine, twelve cutting rooms, three viewing theatres, vaults, post-recording theatre, RCA and Visatone dubbing equipment.

Workshops were 'fully equipped with the most modern machinery and equipment for facilitating the work of carpenters, plasterers, painters and electricians.' Furthermore it was advertised that 'part of the premises is licensed as a hotel and includes restaurant accommodation for all purposes.'

Loudon was more intent on renting out his facility than continuing to fund his own programme of films, although he was not without his competition. In Borehamwood, American producer Joe Rock took over the former Neptune Studios on a long lease. He hired Gerry Blattner, son of the former lessee Ludwig Blattner, as his manager. Consolidated Studios at Elstree, meanwhile, were bought by producer Julius Hagen, head of Twickenham Film Distributors, for his JH Productions, to add to resources for making 'Quota Quickies' at his Twickenham Studios. Hagen also acquired the newly built Riverside Studios in Hammersmith, London.

Supply of and demand for film was unprecedented. 907 million cinema admissions were recorded (and rising), 111 new cinemas were opened, and eighty-eight new film production companies were registered during this year. Realising the value of film as a medium, and the growing importance of its history, the Government set up the National Film Archive.

It turned out to be an extremely busy and important year at Shepperton. Loudon's tactics proved spot-on. George King directed three films for MGM: *Sweeney Todd*, *Reasonable Doubt* and *The Crimes of Stephen Hawke*. E.M. Smedley-Aston was King's assistant director:

I had actually been made redundant by Gaumont-British where I'd been Raoul Walsh's assistant on OHMS. Luckily I got the job as first assistant with George King, who used the Stafford stages at the studio. George's product was mainly 'Quota Quickies' and featured a selection of stars ranging from Tod Slaughter to Zazu Pitts. He was good to work for and after eight films together I was made production manager. I left him in 1938 to work with Sam Wood on *Goodbye Mr Chips*.

Ronnie Neame was a camera operator on the last two features:

Many people dismiss the 'Quota Films' as being unimportant; well I disagree. They may not have been held in the same regard as 'first features' but many people owe their careers to starting on these films.

George King was a lovely director to work with – very competent and easy to get on with, but also economic and always on budget and schedule which was important with these films. It was actually through working on *Reasonable Doubt* that I first met Gabriel Pascal, who was the producer. He was born in Transylvania – he was one of a band of Hungarian exiles that centred around Alex Korda, and was quite a character. With all due modesty he thought I was a 'young genius' and when he was setting up *Major Barbara* at Denham a few years later, he called for me to light it!

Two films followed from Redd Davis with *King of the Castle* and *On Top of the World*, whilst another quota film, *Grand Finale*, also lensed at the studio. It was one of several produced by Anthony Havelock-Allen for Paramount. He reveals that:

> My entry into the film business was through a friend called Captain Richard Norton, who subsequently became the first Managing Director of Pinewood Studios a few years later. He was a banker who found himself left out when the American bank [for which he worked] was closed due to the 1928-29-30 slump. They had, prior to that, raised some money via flotation for British & Dominion Films. As one of the directors of the bank, Norton sat on the Board of B&D. I was in the gramophone business, but Norton said that he felt the film industry was the business for me. I was fairly well connected in theatre, and had been a cabaret manager so had a wide knowledge of stars, near-stars and so on. It was as a casting director that I began my career at B&D. However, when B&D studios at Elstree burnt down in early 1936, we were three years into a contract with Paramount to make quota films, and so quickly relocated to other studios – Sound City being one – in order to complete the contract.
>
> The studio was efficient and well-regarded, and I certainly enjoyed my brief time working there.
>
> The quotas had to be not longer than, and not shorter than, one hour and fifteen minutes. They weren't particular liked, apart from by the people who got their starts. Vivien Leigh made two, though denied it! Rex Harrison first appeared in one as did Wendy Hiller and Margaret Rutherford. I also gave George Sanders his first starring role in a quota film. Additionally, Terence Rattigan and Robert Morely wrote scripts for us, before they became famous.
>
> Virtually all the quota films have since been lost, as they were shot on nitrate. Nobody was interested in taking the time or money to change them or preserve them.

Richard Best was a young assistant editor on *Grand Finale, Murder by Rope* and *Showflat* and has fond memories of his arrival at the studio:

> After the fire at B&D, I was moved to Shepperton on the 'Quota Films' with Lister Laurance, the editor, and Anthony Havelock-Allan. B&D wasn't really an old studio, but compared to Shepperton it was very old-fashioned. I did feel Shepperton had a maternal and grander feel about it, and didn't appear to be so much of a cottage industry as B&D at Borehamwood.
>
> The entrance to the studio was through the original drive of the old house; it was quite a splendid way in actually, as it wound up through the grounds towards the house. Sadly that's all gone now.

As you approach the house, to the front door, the conservatory stood to the immediate right, outside. Once inside the door, one was in a very large hallway. It had, of course, been used for shooting and still was as I remember walking through and there was a caravan parked up, from which Googie Withers came out! Later it became the black and white café, so called because of the colour of the tiles on the floor. That was the real meeting place for folks like us. Beyond that was the old ballroom, with a highly polished springy wooden floor which was the studio restaurant.

The three films were shot pretty much back-to-back. I was a young assistant on these so wasn't too involved with the directors, though I was around when they came into the theatre to see the rushes. I knew of George Pearson, who had directed a lot of silent films, and later on his daughter became Ronnie Neame's secretary.

All the 'Quota Films' were shot economically, and all completed within a month of starting. Everything was done at Shepperton, apart from the dubbing which, for part of it at least, we had to go to Warner Bros at Teddington – no doubt because time was short and Shepperton's dubbing space quite limited at that time.

'He was a strange little chap,' adds director Freddie Francis about George Pearson, 'and always wore his coat and hat on set. He never really came to terms with talkie pictures, and would often call out directions mid-scene to the actors.'

Production continued apace. Wainwright Productions, who had now painted their name on the block they occupied, filmed *The Crimson Circle* with director Reginald Denham, whilst John Argyle produced *Happy Days Are Here Again* for director Norman Lee. One of Loudon's former protégés, John Baxter, produced and directed *Hearts of Humanity*, and then directed *Men of Yesterday*. The following year Baxter was responsible for three more films, including *The Song of the Road*, which was distributed by Sound City Films, as were *Merry Comes to Town* and *The House of Silence* – a nifty little thriller, similar in plotline to *Jamaica Inn*.

They marked Loudon's final foray into film production though. One wonders if perhaps Loudon was looking towards distribution as a possible means of expanding his film interests? But with the above-mentioned films being 'Quota Quickies' and B-films, the mechanics of the box office would mean that only a tiny percentage of the total income from the film programme they were part of, would find their way back to Loudon.

Meanwhile, great use was made of the old house and gardens for Tim Whelan's 1936 film version of the George Elliot's *Mill on the Floss*. Two films, *Sporting Love* and *The Robber Symphony*, were partly based at the studio. The latter was a truly European film from German actor Freidrich Feher, who also wrote the script, directed, produced and composed the music for the two-hour fifteen-minute epic. *Sporting Love* was based on a Stanley Lupino film and was photographed by Eric Cross:

I very much enjoyed my early films at Shepperton. It was a grand studio, with the lovely house dominating. It was, of course, state-of-the-art with its facilities and equipment and to a certain degree made Elstree and the others seem a bit old-fashioned in comparison. The atmosphere was very exciting. I'm afraid that now I'm 101 years old, I can't remember too many specifics of this actual film but I do know it was a very happy time, so that really says it all for me!

Rounding off 1936 were quota films, *Second Bureau* and *Such is Life*, whilst producer Richard Wainwright made two features, *Wolf's Clothing* with Gordon Harker, Claude Hulbert and Lilli Palmer, and *Secret of Stamboul* starring Valerie Hobson, James Mason and Kay Walsh.

'I remember all my films in the 1930s with affection and fear,' commented Kay Walsh. 'Affection because of the warm-hearted old pros in the casts and fear because of having broken out of the chorus at a time of appalling unemployment and presenting myself as an actress – I had no training and dreaded being rumbled!'

1937 was perhaps one of the busiest years yet, with twenty-five films moving into production at the studio. A number of directors made multiple films. James Fitzpatrick lensed *Auld Lang Syne*; a forty-four-minute B-feature, *The Bells of St Mary's*; and a slightly longer one-hour film, *Last Rose of Summer* – all for MGM. John Baxter directed *Academy Decides*, *Talking Feet* and the aforementioned *Song of the Road*. George King remained busy with Sound City Films' *Merry Comes to Town*, *Wanted* and a 'Quota Quickie' crime thriller entitled *Under a Cloud* for Paramount.

John Aldred remembers working on *Wanted*:

It was early in 1937 when I received a phone call from Shepperton Studios to say there was a vacancy in the Sound Department for a floor assistant, and I arranged for an interview the following day. John Byers, head of the sound department, took me to see the Studio Manager, Percy Bell, to discuss details. Having established my qualifications, making home movies, I was told I could start work on a new film the following Monday at a salary of £1 per week. 'If you are any good', said Percy Bell, 'We'll start paying you the following week!' So keen was I to get inside a film studio that I accepted the position.

This was to be the most important decision of my life, because it transpired that I was to stay in various studio Sound Departments for most of my career. My father decided that I was too young to be cycling seven miles to work each day, meanwhile, so I found lodgings in Shepperton village for 25s per week. The sound camera operator, whose name was Stan, became most intrigued as to how I could afford to pay more for my lodgings than I was earning!

The film, my first, was *Wanted* with American actress Zazu Pitts and English comedian Claude Dampier, directed by George King, and shot on C Stage. My job was to assist the boom operator, Jack Davies, in laying out cables for microphone and telephone.

The shooting stage was a hive of activity, with carpenters and plasterers building sets and electricians rigging lamps. Due to the fragile nature of the roof, everything had to be built up from the floor including scaffolding for the lighting. The studio floor was awash with cables, which always seemed to be getting in everybody's way. The picture camera was a DeBrie Super Parvo, which was the camera most in use at Shepperton at that time, and one of my tasks was to look after the camera motor cable when the camera was tracking.

There was so much to take in that I cannot remember the name of the cameraman, or anything about George King. The schedule I believe was four or five weeks. I was most intrigued by the yellow make-up required on hands and faces, Max Factor 26 for women and 28 for men, in order to suit the contrast range of the Kodak Super X picture negative. Then on my second day I was taken at lunchtime to see the rushes from the previous day. I could not understand how they could have been developed, printed and synchronised so quickly!

I soon became well acquainted with the morning and afternoon tea trolleys, which even in those days were a feature of all British film studios. I was expected to make sure the sound crew received their refreshment.

My father came to fetch me after work on Friday, and asked me what I had been doing. 'Well', I said, 'I've been on strike!' It all happened on the third day of shooting, when the management (Percy Bell) refused to meet a delegation from the electricians who wanted more money. So they refused to switch on the lights, and the rest of the crew could do nothing. Apparently it was all settled by the following morning. It was during this production that I was persuaded to join the union, the ACTT (now part of BECTU) for a subscription of 6 old pennies per week. Happy days.

George King was then re-united with Tod Slaughter for *Ticket of Leave Man*, in which Slaughter played a crazed killer named the Tiger, famed for theft, murder and his anonymity. 'To my great surprise,' says E.M. Smedley-Aston, 'Halliwell's Film Guide credits me as the producer on the film. I had in fact just been promoted to production manager, and George King was very much the producer!'

Tod Slaughter next starred in the MGM film *It's Never Too Late To Mend*, which David MacDonald directed. 'That was a happy reunion,' adds E.M. Smedley-Aston, 'and it was directed by David MacDonald – I being his first assistant director rather than production manager. We'd worked together at Gaumont on OHMS both assisting Raoul Walsh.'

The film was based on a novel by Charles Reade, and set in a Victorian prison. It is said that after seeing a stage version of the story, Queen Victoria introduced a raft of prison reform bills. MacDonald's second film of the year, also for MGM, was a forty-four-minute war story entitled *When the Poppies Bloom Again*, starring Nancy Burne.

Double Exposures was a crime feature from director John Paddy Carstairs. 'The schedule was five working days, quite unrealistic for a feature film,' says sound assistant John Aldred:

I can remember it as being the worst example of the current crop of 'Quota Quickies', and I do not think it ever reached a cinema. Earlier in 1937 I remember there had been an attempt to make a film of the 'Rinso Music Hall', a popular programme from Radio Luxembourg. The budget must have been extremely low, because they ran out of money on the third day of shooting whilst Teddy Brown was playing his Xylophone!

The Last Adventurers was a romantic drama, and concerned a skipper's daughter who falls for a humble fisherman rescued by her father. It starred Niall McGinnis, Roy Emerton, Linden Travers and Kay Walsh.

'This was shot in the original 1932 studio, and also on location at Grimsby,' reveals the film's sound assistant John Aldred, and he remembers vividly the so-called advances in technology with this film:

The sound equipment was Visatone, an English system manufactured by the Marconi Wireless Company. This seemed to be far more difficult to manage, and the equipment looked more primitive than the RCA channel.

The motor system on the camera was completely different to that on my previous film too, and I was assigned new duties in charge of synchronisation. Both sound and picture camera motors were run up to speed on a DC supply, and then locked on to a small three-phase generator in the sound track. The Debrie camera was frequently reluctant to 'lock in', and sometimes took almost 80 feet of film. The maintenance engineer, a man called Pryke whose nickname was 'Sludge', always seemed to be working on camera motors!

The Grimsby location was a first for me, so I was not quite sure what to expect. There was a lot of waiting around in the harbour for the sun to shine, but we seemed to have managed quite well in the week that we were there. On the last day we were resigned to recording sound effects, which were basically trawlers going in and coming out of the harbour. One boat was asked by hand signals to blow its siren, which it did right opposite the microphone. This caused the mirror of the galvanometer to come right off and disappear on to the floor of the truck! We never did find it, and it was our last Galvo. The completed picture finally appeared in cinemas as a second feature.

1938 was a leaner year in Shepperton's history, as indeed it was at Denham and Pinewood, and at the end of the year it closed its doors and the renters moved their production to Denham. The end of the 'Quota Quickies' had been signalled, and with it a quite dramatic downturn in production. The receivers were appointed by Westminster Bank at British producer JH Productions, headed by Julius Hagen, and its Twickenham Studios were sold cheaply to Studio Holdings Trust and then leased back to Hagen thanks to a bit of clever juggling on the producer's part.

Alexander Korda – of whom we will soon learn more – was studio chief, in charge of finance and a 'creative producer' at Denham, and floundering. He found himself £1 million in the red with recent films failing to replicate the massive success of *The Private Life of Henry VIII*. Yet despite flagship studios and companies finding the going tough, there still seemed to be a great optimism and enthusiasm in the industry. Odeon cinemas increased in size to cover 220 sites and Highbury Studio was built in Islington, London, by producer Maurice J. Wilson, who announced he was to lease it for independent productions. A few miles away, MP Studios, formed by producer J. Banberger, took over the former Consolidated Studios at Elstree, which were mainly used for production of 'Quota Quickies'. Merton Park Studios was formed, and British screen and stage star Jack Buchanan bought Riverside Studios in Hammersmith, London.

Shepperton had its staple group of directors, including James Fitzpatrick (who directed three films), George King (who directed three films) and John Baxter (one film, *Stepping Toes*), as well as a couple of new faces: Reginald Denham with crime thriller *Kate Plus Ten* (Denham had previously directed *The Crimson Circle* in 1936 at the studio), and Marcel Varnel with a Gainsborough film, *Old Bones Of The River*.

'*Stepping Toes* was shot on C stage with RCA equipment that I assumed was rented with the stage as a package,' says John Aldred:

> Once again I was the playback operator, and the assistant director Lance Comfort insisted that I operate on the set and not hidden away in the sound garage. I was immediately surrounded by the Dagenham Girl Pipers, who had never before seen my equipment or me. The set resembled the stage of a theatre, where various acts came and went. One scene comprised twenty mini-pianos arranged in tiers, with the top pianos disappearing from view. I commented on this and was told to just operate the playback as it was not our problem.
>
> All the acetate discs I was playing had been recorded before the production began. I do remember one other production shooting on neighbouring D stage, and the crews intermingled around the tea trolleys, otherwise the place was pretty quiet. This was to be my last picture at Shepperton for seventeen years as I was made redundant, and did not return for over a decade! Incidentally, in 1938 not everybody possessed a car, including actors and extras, so the usually method of getting to Shepperton Studios was by train from Waterloo followed by a short bus ride. This system gave rise to the following popular ditty that was circulating around the studios at the time:
>
> ASSISTANT DIRECTOR'S LAMENT
> 'What shall I do, what shall I do,
> An actor's missed the train.
> The crowd's got lost,
> In love I'm crossed,
> And we're working late again!'

Marcel Varnel's film, meanwhile, shot primarily at Islington Studios, but as camera assistant Leslie Gilliat explains, there was a very good reason for going to Shepperton, although sadly one visit ended with a fatality:

> I was based at Gainsborough Studios in Islington, when we were making the Will Hay comedy *Old Bones of the River*. It was a comedy take on *Sanders of the River*. However, Gainsborough lacked one important feature – a river! And

so, along with filming on the River Thames around Isleworth we also moved across to Shepperton. The whole place was deserted and the stages were empty. We only used the back-lot, and built our village next to the River Ash, much like they did for Korda's *Sanders of the River*. We brought in a number of African extras, and they were a lot more expensive than the white people as there weren't too many of them around. Sadly, there was a very tragic accident during the filming, when one of the extras – wearing a grass skirt – danced a little too near the fire and burnt to death.

The fact that stages were empty was a great concern to Norman Loudon. His bread-and-butter 'Quota Quickie' films had ceased, and he was faced with possible financial ruin. However, he decided that he needed to diversify. He had a film studio and a

Will Hay in *Old Bones of the River*, one of the few times Gainsborough Films ventured to Shepperton. (Courtesy Graham Rinaldi Collection)

great deal of land. At the studio's Annual General Meeting, Loudon announced plans to build a zoo and pleasure park in the studio grounds. It drew gasps of amazement.

Designs were drawn up and a full-scale model of the project was constructed on L stage – taking over the entire stage! Many thought Loudon foolish. Nevertheless, a draft prospectus was prepared, for investors, demonstrating how the planned zoo would be set out, and how it could run alongside the fully operating film studio. Sound City Zoo and Wonderland was certainly an ambitious project. Along with animal enclosures, a safari-type feel would be introduced by recreating natural habitats on the lot – rivers, jungles, deserts and mountains. Children's rides were planned, and everything would be flood-lit at night.

The following year was to see great advances in the zoo project; however, it – and indeed production itself at the studio – was soon to come to an abrupt end.

Only five films went before the cameras in 1939, one of them, *Spy for a Day*, was directed and produced by Mario Zampi and starred Duggie Wakefield. According to young studio hand Roy Pembrooke, they caused quite a stir when 'Some of the crowd artists dressed in German uniforms very foolishly walked down Shepperton High Street during their lunchtime!'

Zampi also produced *French Without Tears* with much the same crew, including editor David Lean, who was very much seen as a 'director in waiting' and more often than not attended the shooting ready to lend advice to the director, and thus edited the film at night. The completed film was 'sneak previewed' at the Astoria, Finsbury Park. It was probably one of the first, if not the first, to adopt the practise. The audience were given cards and asked to comment. One of the cards that best pleased the producers read 'bloody good!'

Kay Walsh was married to Lean at that time, and recalls:

I remember one lively and noisy dinner, at which Mario Zampi was extolling the glories of Mussolini. I loved Zampi, despite this. He was so noisy and untalented, but so keen and ambitious that he sizzled. David and I were living in digs in Shepperton and I recall Anatole DeGrunwald bursting in the next day to tell us of Chamberlain's broadcast and saying 'war's declared'.

War was indeed declared.

CHAPTER 3

ALEXANDER KORDA AND WORTON HALL

There are two other significant stories that are part of the Shepperton Story – namely Alexander Korda, the Hungarian immigrant who rose to become Britain's most famous movie mogul, and a quaint old estate in a London suburb known as Worton Hall.

Alexander Korda was born in 1893 in Pustaturpásztó, and there, with his two brothers Zoltan and Vincent, enjoyed a comfortable childhood.

His prolific rise to fame in the film business started when he moved to Paris and took lowly jobs at the Pathé studios. With the advent of the Great War a few years later, young Korda found himself in great demand within the business when his poor eyesight saw him declared unfit for active service. Film was recognised as a very powerful propaganda tool, and Korda was well versed in the business and able to put himself forward.

After the war, Alex had two dozen film credits to his name – many being great successes. He moved to Vienna, then on to Berlin and ultimately to Hollywood – to the new centre of movie making. He rapidly became a sought-after director, but by 1929 Alex was becoming bored with Hollywood, which he felt lacked any new challenges and he became homesick for Europe. Added to that his next picture, *The Squall*, had to be a talkie. He wasn't happy. He was intrigued with the new development, but disliked it immensely. He returned to Europe.

The newly opened Paramount studios at Joinville and Saint-Maurice saw Alex as a valuable asset and it was during his time there that Paramount embarked upon a British film programme to fulfil the Quota Act requirements. David Cunnynghame was the production manager charged with setting up the programme at B&D Studios in Borehamwood. Cunnynghame had worked with Alex previously in Paris and duly asked him to move across the Channel to London and direct one of the new programmes at Borehamwood. In September 1931 he filmed *Service for Ladies*, a romantic comedy with Leslie Howard. The film took six weeks to complete – a full week over schedule – mainly due to Alex insisting scenes be reworked to improve them and because he often arrived late on set, after the 'night before'.

Alexander Korda (pre-Knighthood) in the 1930s.
(Gareth Owen Collection)

During his second film, *Women Who Play*, Alex was
struck down with flu and the reins were handed over
to Arthur Rosson about three weeks later. Meanwhile,
Service for Ladies opened to rave reviews and box office
gold. Alex's confidence was boosted greatly and plans
for his own film projects advanced, and London Film
Productions was formed in 1932.

Paramount gave the company a contract to make
five 'Quota films', and with it David Cunnynghame
left Paramount to become a full-time member of
Alex's new company. The famous 'logo' which graced
all of the London Film Productions was filmed for
their very first production: London's famous Big Ben
clock striking 11a.m. It is claimed that 11 a.m. was
just coincidental to the time of the sun coming out
one day in July 1932.

Alex's greatest success came with a film about
Henry VIII. He courted many British companies for
finance, but all ultimately turned him down. In February 1933, Alex set off to Italy to
try and source money. Two months later he persuaded Ludovico Toeplitz, director of
the Cines Studios and son of Giuseppe Toeplitz, president of the Banca Commerciale
d'Italia, to finance the film.

Production began at B&D Studios on *The Private Life of Henry VIII*. The film was
one of the most expensive films ever made in Britain. Initially the budget was to
be between £55,000 and £60,000. The final budget was shown to be £93,710.
Everything about the film was lavish. Even the food in the banqueting scenes was
brought in daily from Claridges. It was the biggest film, and biggest risk, of Alex's
career. It paid off – the reviews were ecstatic. The prestige it brought to the British
Film Industry was unheard of. And box-office takings were very healthy!

Now keen to find a studio of his own to produce further British films, Alex set his
sights on Worton Hall Studios in Isleworth.

The old English mansion, with terraces and rolling lawns, paddocks, vineries,
wooded glades, orchards, farm land and fields, had been acquired by the Samuelson
Film Manufacturing Company Ltd in 1914 for the purpose of establishing a film
studio. G.B. Samuelson sensed great opportunities for the film business after selling a
newsreel detailing the state funeral of King Edward VII and in 1913 he financed his
own film project – filmed at Will Barker's Ealing Studios – about the reign of Queen
Victoria. *Sixty Years of a Queen* was well received and fuelled Samuelson's desire to
become fully involved in the film business, as director George Pearson – his soon-to-
be business partner – recounted:

Its [*Sixty Years of a Queen*] success was remarkable, and its reception led to Samuelson's decision to have his own studio, and to make his own films. Walter Buckstone, an expert cameraman, arranged a meeting between Samuelson and myself. Samuelson was a young man with amazing enthusiasm and boundless energy; his excitement regarding his venture was infectious; that meeting ended with my appointment as Film Producer at Worton Hall.

The ground floor of the old house was converted into an office space with a theatre, editing room, wardrobe room and canteen. The grand ballroom and dining room were maintained for filming purposes whilst the upper-floor rooms were used as private accommodation for staff and visitors. A glass studio of 50ft x 40ft was constructed within the grounds, and the whole cost of setting up a film facility was just over £1,000.

On 1 July, dignitaries and celebrities – including Will Barker, who had established Ealing Studios a few years earlier – were motored to Isleworth, a leafy suburb of London, for the grand opening ceremony, which was performed by actress Vesta Tilley cutting through a ribbon across the studio door with a pair of golden scissors, whilst the band played her favourite music hall song, *The Girl Who Loves A Soldier*. Lunch was served in a large marquee on the lawn in front of the house, before Walter de Freese, presiding over the affairs of the day (and who was also the husband of Vesta Tilley), proposed the toasts. De Freese's background was in the music halls, but he predicted cinema as the new medium of mass entertainment. Managing Director George Berthold Samuelson declared that his new studio would produce films to rival the best America could offer.

'It was a great day for all of us,' recalled George Pearson, 'and it was with obvious emotion Samuelson spoke of his intention to make films worthy of England, and in that purpose he continued with an enthusiasm that knew no bounds.'

The company consisted of G.B. Samuelson, chairman and managing director; Harry Engholm, director and secretary who, after a career in journalism, joined Will Barker as a scenario writer; the aforementioned George Pearson, producer and director; Fred Paul, actor; and Stage Manager Jack Clare.

Although it opened on 1 July, Samuelson's first production got underway some three

George Pearson. (Gareth Owen Collection)

weeks earlier when the Sherlock Holmes story, *A Study In Scarlet*, went before the camera on 8 June. Produced by Samuelson, directed by Pearson and written by Engholm, the film was listed by the British Film Institute in 1992 as being amongst the lost films it most wanted to find. It was significant in that it was the first British-owned Holmes film to go into production, yet no one knows what happened to it.

'The film called for ambitious locations,' according to Pearson, 'but we hoped to find passable replicas of the Rockies and the Salt Lake Plains in England. We discovered what we needed at Cheddar Gorge [in Somerset], and the Southport sands [Merseyside].'

On 4 August, news of war came. That evening, Pearson met Samuelson on the steps of Will Barker's Soho Square office. They could hear the crowds yelling, cheering and singing; they were moving towards Buckingham Palace, in the belief that the German Navy would be at the bottom of the North Sea in a week. Samuelson was tremendously excited, 'Come on George, we'll take a room for the night at Frescati's … write a script … "The Great World War" … and start filming tomorrow.'

In a hectic fashion, filming indeed commenced and two weeks later, on 17 August, it received its trade show premiere. The film brought cheers from the patriotic crowd.

As one might gather, the Great War did little to dampen Samuelson's production programme. In fact, it helped step-up production at the studio and they made films non-stop that played to packed houses. So hectic was the schedule of productions that Samuelson initiated, that George Pearson was physically exhausted to the point he feared he could not continue working with such output:

> By April 1915 I had directed eleven films; I was tired mentally and bodily. I felt
> I could not keep pace with Samuelson's enthusiasm and tireless energy. Already

Worton Hall Studios in its infancy. (Courtesy Doris Spriggs Archive)

there were rumours of fresh subjects, *Deadwood Dick* and *Infelice*, another novel for adaptation. I could not face them. I pondered long on the prospect of resignation; it seemed the only possible solution.

It was then that he left Worton Hall to become chief director at Gaumont's Shepherd's Bush studios. The gap he left was filled by Fred Paul and he subsequently took charge of *Infelice* and six episodes featuring the *Adventures of Deadwood Dick*.

Whilst war raged in Europe during 1915, the studio was expanded and a great number of two reeler-films moved into production, many based on popular stories, such as *Lady Windermere's Fan* (1916); *Little Women* (1917); *The Admirable Crichton* (1918); along with original stories *John Halifax, Gentleman* (1915); *A Cinema Girl's Romance* (1915); *The New Clown* (1916); *Her Greatest Performance* (1917) and many others. Samuelson directed several himself, whilst Paul starred, directed and wrote a number. When not keeping the facility busy with his own productions, Samuelson also cannily leased out part of the complex to other companies. Riding on a wave of success, Samuelson could seem to do no wrong. However, in 1920 the post-war slump occurred, costs spiralled and foreign films flooded the British market. It was not an ideal time to be in the picture business. It was then announced, in the trade press, that his company had been taken over by General Film Renters.

Samuelson continued in production and continued stretching himself – perhaps in countenance to the lavish Hollywood movie invasion of British cinemas (which in turn saw the creation of the 1927 Quota Act) – and his ambitious production programme in 1925 of some twenty-nine films, and eleven the following year, was proving financially problematic for Samuelson and his company. The cinema box office didn't return the riches he had hoped, and in 1927 he made only one film, *Land Of Hope And Glory*. Other producers – potential renters of his studio – were also feeling the pinch of the Hollywood machine and so G.B. Samuelson faced the inevitable – he could no longer afford to sustain his own production activities, nor maintain an empty studio. He sold Worton Hall Studios to British Screen Productions in 1928.

Samuelson continued to write and direct for other companies for a few years, including US company Majestic which led to United Artists (their distributors) offering Samuelson (and his company of the same name) a three-picture deal. Ironically, the year after he sold-out, 'talkies' arrived in Britain, and with them came a new lease of life for Samuelson's beloved studio.

The new owners, British Screen Productions, had George W. Pearson at the helm – not the same George Pearson who helped Samuelson form Worton Hall Studios, but another. It seemed fortuitous, though, that the name should still be linked with the studio. Sadly, their tenancy was short lived, as in 1931 former city banker Captain Richard Norton moved in with his programme of 'Quota Quickies' for United Artists, as well as a few other independent renters. Norton subsequently moved back to B&D Studios in Borehamwood to continue his Quota production programme, though with Paramount Pictures.

Two years later, the studios were sold to J.W. Almond and Edward Gourdeau, who fully modernised the complex and introduced the new Western Electric Sound

System. However, by the following year of 1934, there was to be another new owner; the great Alexander Korda. He took out a lease, with an option to buy the facility, for £35,000 per year. Korda was riding high on the great success of *The Private Life of Henry VIII* and decided it would be beneficial to have his own studio, rather than continue as a tenant at B&D in Borehamwood. He wanted a home and chose Worton Hall – albeit, it would transpire, as a temporary measure.

Impressed by his success, Sir Connop Guthrie – who sat on the board of the Prudential Assurance Company – agreed a deal with Korda to back his film programme and lease of the studio.

Aside from the importance of Korda's ownership in the late 1930s, and between 1946 and 1952 – when the studios closed – there was an inextricable link between this studio and Korda's Shepperton Studios, as many films found themselves based between the two facilities. Douglas Fairbanks Sr had been so impressed by *The Private Life of Henry VIII* (and undoubtedly the returns to his company, United Artists) that he offered Korda an interest in UA. Together, Korda and Fairbanks then formed Criterion Film Productions in 1935, with producer Marcel Hellman, Hungarian-born director-producer Paul Czinner and Captain A. Cunningham-Reid. The following year, they exercised Korda's option to buy, and purchased Worton Hall Studios.

Criterion produced four films. Independently, in 1935, the legendary Buster Keaton starred in a film for producer Sam Spiegel, who had arrived in England fleeing the Nazis in Berlin; his first film in Britain was to be *The Invader* with Keaton. Eric Cross was the film's cameraman. He recalls:

> Keaton, by this time, was an alcoholic. His salary [of £12,000] was spent almost entirely on drink. Keaton paid a 'minder' to keep him off the booze during the shoot; though what wasn't known is that he also paid him again, to slip him a bottle! It was quite mad.

The film took less than a month to shoot, and was plagued by disagreements and disasters. At one point, Spiegel hired some showgirls for the dance sequence in the story – no doubt more for their looks than anything else, as when it came to filming it became apparent that none could dance a step!

Korda had ambitions of creating a grander studio for his grander films. He had continued to produce films under his distribution deal with UA separate to his Criterion deal, and began looking at a site in Denham, Buckinghamshire, called The Fisheries. It consisted of 165 acres of land, a grand house and a river. The following year, whilst continuing production at Worton Hall, it was announced that Denham was to be the site of the new London Film Studios.

On 26 March 1936, *Whither Mankind* commenced production at Worton Hall. The film was later re-titled *Things to Come* and was H.G. Wells' vision of mankind's future after a massive air war, which had been in pre-production during most of 1935. Korda planned to take the whole world by storm with this gigantic feature. Worton Hall was expanded to accommodate the film and a gigantic new silent stage was built measuring 250ft x 120ft. It was the largest of its kind in Europe. Michael Powell

Things to Come. The giant silent stage was built especially for this production, and later relocated to Shepperton as H Stage. (Courtesy David Blake Archive)

later described it in his autobiography as standing 'like a white elephant in the giant shrubberies'.

A few weeks later, on 16 April, another Wells story was put into production at Worton Hall – *The Man Who Could Work Miracles*. Some exteriors were filmed in Denham's grounds, despite the studio still being under construction. For the terrific special effects requirements on both these films, Korda brought over Ned Mann from Hollywood, along with his effects team. He became known as 'The Mann Who Could Work Miracles' around the studio!

Korda's relationship with United Artists was, whilst important, never a really happy one. He complained that their worst cinemas were retained for British films, and films – more importantly, his films – were dumped in houses that played both good and bad pictures. The grosses of Korda's productions were falling below break-even point, and those included the Criterion productions. It was decided that Criterion would cease production at Worton Hall and Fairbanks Jr would return to Hollywood. A strain was obviously put on his relationship with Fairbanks Sr.

Other productions at Worton Hall had included a film from acclaimed movie maestro Erich von Stroheim, and film titles such as *Captain's Orders* (directed by Ivar Campbell), *Too Many Husbands* (directed, produced and adapted from the stage by Ivar Campbell), *Special Edition*, *Mistaken Identity* and a Googie Withers film, *You're The Doctor*.

In early 1939, with Korda firmly ensconced at Denham, a deal was struck by Producer Maurice Wilson, who had made a number of comedies with the likes of Stanley Holloway and Tommy Handley, to lease the studio. However, his tenure was short-lived due to the outbreak of the Second World War.

Worton Hall Studios from the air. Note the 'Please! Studios' painted on top of the silent stage in the hope aircraft might avoid flying directly overhead. (Courtesy David Blake Archive)

One of the Criterion productions at Worton Hall. (Courtesy David Blake Archive)

CHAPTER 4

THE WAR YEARS

In September 1939, the British government temporarily closed all places of entertainment. Studios were rapidly requisitioned and initially used to store vital provisions such as sugar and other foods, and for a brief period it looked likely that British film production would be abandoned altogether. Rationing, shortages of materials and indeed personnel – it is suggested two-thirds of technicians were called up, and a few others hot-footed it to Hollywood before they could be! – proved a major threat, not least when coupled with lack of operational studios.

Beaconsfield Studios and Walton-on-Thames were requisitioned by the Ministry of Works, Beaconsfield for use by Rotax as an aircraft engine magneto factory; Walton-on-Thames was also used for aircraft production by Vickers-Armstrong (Spitfire fighters and Wellington bombers), following a direct hit on the Vickers plant. Bushey Film Studios was used as an ARP (Air Raid Precautions) depot and to store nitrate films away from danger in London. BIP Studios (later Associated British Picture Corporation, ABPC) at Elstree were requisitioned by the Royal Ordnance Corps. Amalgamated Studios were used by the Ministry of Works for storage. MP Studios at Elstree were requisitioned by the Armed Forces. Pinewood Studios provided

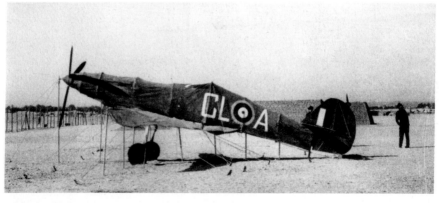

A dummy Hawker Hurricane made at Shepperton, deployed in the Western Desert. (Roy Pembrooke)

accommodation for Lloyds of London, the Royal Mint and the Crown, Army and Royal Air Force film units. Teddington Studios were closed. Ealing, under Michael Balcon, remained open and embarked upon a programme of morale-boosting films. Worton Hall Studios were requisitioned by the Ministry of Works and their primary use was in camouflage preparation, and many former studio scenic artists found gainful employment at the site once again. Shepperton, meanwhile, was taken over and used as a site to make decoy scenery and dummy aircraft.

The war years are probably the most documented in British film history. They marked a golden period when British cinema broke free of Hollywood shackles and discovered an identity of its own. Denham Studios escaped requisition by virtue of Gabriel Pascal's film *Major Barbara* running over schedule. He was determined that his film would be completed, regardless of the prying British Army officers and Luftwaffe.

Several individuals' efforts ensured that the film industry was kept alive, however. It has been said that Anthony Asquith's mother was able to place an appropriate word or two in prominent cabinet minister's ears. Lady Yule and J. Arthur Rank proved their commitment through a programme of films produced by their British National and distributed through GFD. Michael Balcon, now in control at Ealing, trumpeted the importance of film to the war effort, and pleaded with technicians to stick to their craft (a reserved occupation) and not feel guilty about dodging front-line duties. He later wrote in *Kinematograph Weekly*:

> Realise the potential importance of your work and be proud of it. Don't be ashamed of it … While this fight for recognition goes on it is essential that the hardcore of the industry be preserved. Stick to it! The time will come during this war when a man behind a film camera will command the same respect as a man behind a gun.

Alex announced the formation of a new company, Alexander Korda Film Productions, and planned a new programme in America; though without abandoning production

A dummy DUKW (amphibious truck). The DUKWs were used in the D-Day period. (Roy Pembrooke)

A replica QUAD artillery tractor with 25-pounder field gun. (Roy Pembrooke)

in Britain completely. Certainly after losing control of Denham to Rank, and with few box-office successes coupled with war, Alex felt that his adopted country was no longer the place to continue working. Over the course of 1940, he wound down activities in Britain and prepared to move to Hollywood.

His penultimate film of the year, *The Thief of Baghdad*, had started work in the UK. Wendy Toye remembers it with great fondness:

> My first encounter with the Korda brothers was when I'd been engaged to choreograph all of the movements in *The Thief of Baghdad*. Mary Morris played a little character covered in blue paint, and had to sit on a throne behind which were six arms, and we couldn't have just three people as the width of the throne was too great, so we had the right arm of one person and left arm of another … and to get these to work in sync was quite tricky.
>
> I went to a meeting at Shepperton, where the rehearsals were taking place, and we sat in the grand boardroom there – me at one end of the table and the three brothers Alex, Zoli and Vincent at the other. Alex said 'we need these arms to go clip-clop' whilst demonstrating with a fast up-and-down movement of his horizontally spread arms. Zoli said 'no they must go zeem-zoom' and made a more gracious fanning action with his arms. Vincent then chipped in 'no, they must wave up and down' … we spent about half an hour just talking about how the arms should move. It was tremendously funny.

The film was completed in America and Alex's last film in Britain was *Old Bill and Son*, at his beloved Denham. Plans for further propaganda films were aborted and on 19 June, with his British company now closed, Alex set off for Lisbon on the first leg of his trip to Hollywood.

The 'colony' of ex-pats came in for significant criticism, having seemingly 'abandoned' their country in its time of need. Michael Balcon was chief amongst the critics. 'They are badly needed here,' he wrote in *Picturegoer and Film Weekly* magazine,

Sir Alex and Lady Korda on investiture day in 1942.
(Gareth Owen Collection)

'by an industry that fed them in happier times and which now lacks their talents.'

Balcon swung Ealing Studios into overdrive and devoted everything to the continuing war effort, although whilst his films were popular in Britain they had little impact in Hollywood. And that is where the British government wanted to strike – at the hearts of American cinemagoers and thus hopefully bring America into the war.

What was unknown, however, was that Alex Korda was contributing greatly to the war effort from Hollywood. At Churchill's request, British Security Co-ordination was set up in America in 1940. Alex was asked if he could assist, with his contacts. Alex's West Coast office had already been operating as a cover for some British Intelligence officers for some time, as indeed did his London Films' offices around Europe before the war.

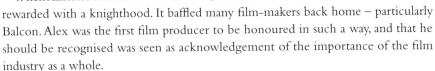

When America entered the war in 1941, Alex was rewarded with a knighthood. It baffled many film-makers back home – particularly Balcon. Alex was the first film producer to be honoured in such a way, and that he should be recognised was seen as acknowledgement of the importance of the film industry as a whole.

'And what you might not know,' says continuity supervisor Angela Allen, 'is that back home the British spies were actually trained at Shepperton before they went off into Europe. No one knew that – or at least, it wasn't made public knowledge until fairly recently. So Shepperton's war-time role was perhaps slightly more important than we'd been lead to believe. I dare say there are still a few more things we don't know about what went on there!'

In Hollywood, Alex Korda made only four films: *That Hamilton Woman*, *Lydia*, *To Be Or Not To Be* and *Jungle Book*.

Back in Britain, and despite the war and the threat of cinemas being bombed mid-performance, attendances rocketed. It was calculated that everybody in Britain under the age of forty went to see at least fifty-three feature films a year! The threat of death was an everyday risk. Even when a title appeared warning of an air raid it would say, 'The show will go on and if you wish to leave please do so quietly'. In fact, 160 cinemas were destroyed during the course of the war, but it did nothing to dampen the enthusiasm and thirst for British projects over American.

Technicians lacked modern equipment, and had to make do with old cameras and sound equipment; but they learned to improvise and problems served only to become a spur to inventiveness. Shepperton played its part too, although not through film production. Dummy and decoy airfields were seen as a valuable diversion for attacking Luftwaffe, and in October 1939 two dummy airfields – one for daylight and one for night – were given the go-ahead. The man responsible for this work, Colonel John Turner, set up his base at Sound City.

The Queen Mary Reservoir, next to the studio, suffered many bombs and mines being dropped, no doubt due to its importance in supplying drinking water in this area of Greater London. In October 1940, the studio took a direct daytime hit during a raid. It claimed two casualties: Edward Swindells, fifteen, and Geoffrey Hebdon, seventeen, two evacuees from London who hadn't long started work at the facility. Roy Pembrooke reveals:

> I was working in the stores department at the time, and was walking back from the Old House one day when I heard the most enormous bang. My first thought was the reservoir had been hit, but as I approached the stores, which was opposite C stage, I saw that the studio had been hit, and the two boys were lying on the ground, covered in camouflage paint – as there was a big store of it there. One of them was pronounced dead at the scene, and the other boy died soon afterwards at the local hospital. It was the first time I'd seen a dead body. It haunted me for many years: had I been five minutes earlier returning, it could have been me too.

A plaque commemorating their loss stands in Littleton Church. Another bomb fell on the studio the next day and buried itself under D-stage, mercifully failing to detonate. It was dug out by the (Army's) Royal Electrical and Mechanical Engineers.

Roy Pembrooke remembers the studio wartime precautions:

> At the top of the Old House, a man was on duty during working hours and it fell to him to put a flag up and blow a whistle as a warning of German aircraft approaching, and all personnel dashed to cover as quickly as possible. There weren't any air-raid shelters or bunkers – we took our chances!
>
> Every night of the war there were at least ten members of the staff on fire duty when, as you might guess, the hotel bar was a useful haven between air raids.

A, B, C and D stages were used by Tate & Lyle to store sugar. However, when the nearby Vickers aircraft factory was bombed, A and B stages were cleared to make way for the workers from Vickers. Queenie Thornton explains:

> I was a young sheet metal worker with Vickers, one of the few women, amongst many men, engaged in making sections of Wellington Bombers at the studio from 1943 onwards. We worked around the clock on the stages, and I actually preferred the night shifts. I found I could sleep better during the day as there weren't any air raids to disturb us. I do remember quite a few raids coming over the studio though, and we'd take shelter wherever we could. The next year one of the bombs hit.

The air-raid memorial plaque which stands in Littleton Church, in memory of the two boys who died at the studio during an air raid. (Roy Pembrooke)

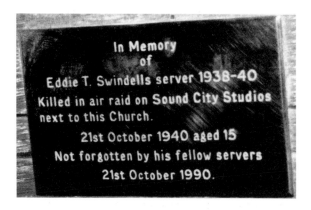

In Memory
of
Eddie T. Swindells server 1938-40
Killed in air raid on Sound City Studios
next to this Church.
21st October 1940 aged 15
Not forgotten by his fellow servers
21st October 1990.

The importance of the Wellington's role during the Second World War is emphasised by Wing Commander Ken Wallis MBE, who piloted several raids over Germany in the aircraft:

> The Wellington was an amazingly tough aircraft, designed by Barnes Wallis. I understand some 11,500 were made – more than any other bomber. They were in service at the start of WWII and still in service at the end. Sadly the enormous contribution made by the bombers has all but been forgotten. The aircraft hit the enemy hard during the darkest days of the war, and certainly played a significant part in our later victory. Shepperton's part in their manufacture was indeed significant too.

Norman Loudon and his studio manager, Percy Bell, remained *in situ* at the studio, and co-ordinated the day-to-day running of the complex with Colonel Turner.

In continuing the 'dummy' activities, the studio produced a whole array of diversionary materials – weapons, buildings, landing barges, tanks, aircraft (made out of canvas and wood and then camouflaged) and even people. They kept German intelligence guessing where troops were being gathered for the D-Day invasions, and provided both invaluable time for the Allies to prepare and terrific diversions of German air-bomber power. Roy Pembrooke adds:

> They were used in the Middle East too, to deceive the Germans and Italians, and in fact played a major part in our victory during that campaign. When the Americans came into the war, the guns of an Ack-Ack site in nearby Addlestone were taken to help defend New York, and they were replaced by dummy guns made at Shepperton.

The role of the studios was acknowledged by the RAF too, as Pembrooke continues:

> Many of our aircraft flying over enemy territory were nominated and given names of films stars who had worked at the studios.

A mock anti-aircraft gun site, as manufactured at the studio. (Roy Pembrooke)

Morale was kept high amongst workers at Shepperton, as Queenie Thornton recalls:

> When we stopped for supper, around midnight, some of us would put on a show in the canteen. We'd dress up and sing a few songs … even dance. We tried to keep as jolly as we could with everything going on in the war. It was a very welcome diversion really. After taking part in these shows, around 2a.m. I'd often feel quite sleepy, so I'd find a nice big sheet of metal and settle down behind it for a snooze!

Shepperton Studios played an important role in the war. It, and the lives lost at the studio during this time, will never be forgotten.

CHAPTER 5

THE '40s

In late 1944, The British Lion Film Corporation purchased Worton Hall from Criterion Film Productions. Formerly based at Beaconsfield, the company was keen to find an up-scaled base for its now up-scaled activities. British Lion formed Worton Hall (1944) Ltd and was the major shareholder.

In the autumn of 1945, the government announced plans to revert studio space to film production activities. Producers anticipated being 'back in business' within months. Loudon announced that Sound City would re-open in September with three stages operational – two large and one small. The first film to move in, curiously, was a J. Arthur Rank Production. *London Town* could not be accommodated at Denham due to Gabriel Pascal's epic *Caesar and Cleopatra* which had been in production for well over a year, and Pinewood was still in the process of being vacated by the Army, RAF and Crown Film Units. The film was a big-budget musical and having seemingly little confidence in a British director to handle such a brash, colourful and vigorous film, Rank brought over Wesley Ruggles from America. It was a decision, it must be said, that was much influenced by star Sid Field too, who insisted on a 'Hollywood' director.

The film was derided by critics, and many questioned why Rank went to the expense of bringing in an American director when British directors were equally capable of making 'bad musicals' on their own! *London Town* failed to make any impact in America, and it suffered a severe re-edit (and shortening) before its US release, with its title changed to *My Heart Goes Crazy*.

Ruggles complained that he had faced many obstacles. He claimed Shepperton was 'in a shambles' after the war and hadn't been used for years. Furthermore, 'returning British technicians, unaccustomed to making big-budget musicals at the best of times, were rusty.' Making a lavish extravaganza, it was said, in a country where clothes rationing was still in force, and where many materials – no matter the cost – were simply unavailable, 'was bound to be a forlorn task'.

In *Kinematograph Weekly*, 7 June 1948, Rank called *London Town* one of his 'biggest mistakes'. It lost the organisation a fortune.

In early 1946, the first film moved into production at Worton Hall was a screen adaptation of the stage play *The Shop at Sly Corner* by Edward Percy. It follows an

London Town was an expensive musical produced by the Rank Organisation, though their own Pinewood Studios was too full to accommodate it! (Gareth Owen Collection)

antique dealer, who was also a fencer, and how he kills a blackmailer in order to shield his daughter. Oscar Homolka played the antique dealer with Derek Farr, Kathleen Harrison and Muriel Pavlow in support. Pavlow recalls:

> What I remember about that film is that I fell in love on it. It reached the stage of my having costume fittings and I still didn't know who was to be my leading man. Then the producer's wife came up to me and told me it was to be Derek Farr. The first scene we played together was the one where my character (Margaret Heiss) comes in, sees him, throws herself into his arms and kisses him – and that we did! We announced our engagement two weeks later and were married three months after that. I remember the publicity woman on the film, upon our shyly telling her about our engagement, saying 'this is wonderful, don't tell anyone else, this is wonderful!'

The character of Margaret Heiss was a musician, and in particular played the violin.

> Oh goodness. We employed some interesting camera set ups for those sequences as I really couldn't play at all. Mind you, I did practise a lot before filming started, much to the annoyance of my parents whom I was living with at that time!

And what of her co-star?

> Oskar Homolka was lovely. Though he would always try and upstage me – and everyone else. I knew that if I tried to fight this experienced actor on that score I would come off the worse; and I just enjoyed working with him after that. He was a 'cuddly bear' sort of man but had a very penetrating glance. Nothing escaped him.

George King, the director, had made a number of 'Quota Films' prior to the Second World War at Shepperton. The tight schedules and limited camera movements on those films were long-forgotten and Muriel Pavlow described him as 'very easygoing, without any pressure to rush anything … but with his eye ever on the budget!'

A couple more films followed, *Piccadilly Incident* and *White Cradle Inn*, before there was to be a big change at British Lion.

In late 1945, en route from Hollywood, Korda announced his ambitions of wanting to buy Sound City at Shepperton. It was a better studio than Denham, and even possibly rivalled Pinewood. Upon his return to Britain he instigated discussions to purchase first British Lion, and in doing so assume control of Worton Hall once again. He swooped again a few months later, in April 1946, when British Lion purchased a 74 per cent stake in Sound City for £380,000. Korda controlled both Worton Hall and Shepperton, and by virtue of controlling British Lion, a third complex with their Beaconsfield Studios. The latter remained on lease to the Ministry of Works, which in turn spent £146,000 refurbishing it as a base for The Crown Film Unit.

Meanwhile, Rank sold Amalgamated Studios in Borehamwood (which had been used by the Government as a storage facility and not used as a film studio) to the Prudential Assurance Company which had suffered severe losses through their partnership with Alex Korda at Denham. The impressive new facility was in turn sold to MGM who re-named it MGM British Studios. Rank then acquired the much smaller Gate Studios in Borehamwood for GHW Productions and their Religious Films output.

It remained business as usual at Worton Hall, with much daily crossover business from Shepperton, and vice versa. Doris Spriggs was a young assistant secretary in the studio's front office and recalls her days there with great fondness:

> I was the second secretary to Gerry Blattner, the studio manager. I would handle the work orders, set strikes, transport etc. The studio had one car, one lorry and one driver. The rest was hired in as and when required.
>
> I'd also collect the time sheets, clocking in cards and so on, and had the task of paying the extras direct. I remember there was a huge safe in the office in which all the money was kept – it would have been quite a haul for a would-be thief!
>
> I actually followed in the footsteps of my father, as he worked at the studio just after the Great War, for G.B. Samuelson, and he later told me a few stories about some of the films and film stars he'd worked with. He worked in many capacities

– a bit of lighting, painting and he even once appeared in a film. It was that sort of atmosphere. I remember him telling me that the company would throw big parties at the Café Royal in London after a production; no expense was spared!

London Films produced *Mine Own Executioner* at Worton Hall, directed by Anthony Kimmins. An impressive cast was assembled, headed by Burgess Meredith, Kieron Moore, John Laurie and Dulcie Gray. Gray notes:

It was a thoroughly enjoyable film to make, and I very much enjoyed working with Burgess though I know he was having a bad time with his wife, Paulette Goddard, they really weren't getting on and in a way his character in the film was in a similar situation. Though I remember a doctor Burgess consulting told him that he was allergic to his wife's hair! Burgess said 'do you think that is suitable grounds for divorce?' – he was quite serious too.

The story centres on post-war London, and how a clinical psychologist Milne (Meredith) is close to burnout. He has his own marital difficulties as well as an overloaded schedule. Gray continues:

Kieron Moore [the co-star] was such a lovely actor, and very, very Irish, though I think he was really put into many films that weren't terribly suitable for him. Certainly in this and *Man About The House* [which filmed at Shepperton in the same year] he was very good, but I don't think he ever achieved his full potential which I felt very sorry about. He had a bit of a tough time afterwards and sadly died very young. I was very fond of him.

Doris Spriggs, Worton Hall Studios assistant, at the site outside her former office, with the author, in 2007. (Photograph by Andrew Boyle)

Richard Best was engaged as editor on the film, and recalls it with great fondness:

Anthony Kimmins was a wonderful man to work with, as were the producers. I know Tony was credited as a producer, but the men who ran the production were Jack Kitchen, a Canadian who had been an editor earlier in his career; and Alf Black, who was the son of the owner of the Palladium, and had been in the Army Film Unit with me. It was of course made for London Films. Except for one of two locations, the whole film was shot at Worton Hall.

But what of the studio itself, at that time?

The studio was very small still. You only had to stand in the middle of the garden and you could see it all! When you entered the gates, there was a little building on the left – which I guess would have been a gate-keeper's cottage at some point – and that was the cutting room area. There was a little lawn, and then the house on the right with stages on the left; dominated by the great silent stage. You never got the impression of being in a big studio. Even British National [at Borehamwood] was small, but in comparison, Worton Hall was tiny. It was a very intimate studio shall we say. But, we did have dubbing facilities. However, space was at such a premium that in the theatre, the projector was angled out onto a mirror to be reflected onto a screen – as the 'throw' wasn't long enough. The theatre was used to view rushes too. It was a very happy little place to work.

Two very special visitors to Worton Hall during the shoot of the *Mine Own Executioner* were the young Princesses, Elizabeth and Margaret. Guy Hamilton, the film's first assistant director, takes up the story:

Anthony Kimmins was 'Uncle Tony' to Princesses Elizabeth and Margaret, and wrote all of their speeches during the war. He arranged the visit. I remember on one of the stages we had a nightclub set, and there was a great big crane on the set to cover the dance floor; it was decided that should be the set they visit. Gerry Blattner, the studio manager, met them both on arrival and I was given the job of hiding in the bushes with a switch – the switch that controlled the red and green lights above the stage door.

So, when they approached the stage I switched the light to red and Gerry said 'Oh the light is on red which means that no one, including yourselves your Royal Highnesses, can enter' ... a couple of seconds later I switched it to green and Gerry said, with great delight, 'oh it's now on green and we may enter' ... that was my bit over!

They then went onto the stage, and we all swung into motion ... up went the crane and action was called, and cameras turned-over. Though, I can reveal that there wasn't any film in them – we didn't have enough lights on stage, so it would have been a waste of film!

From there they went to meet Ned Mann who had this wonderful model bridge (almost like the one over the River Kwai) and a train that ran over it. They then went into the screening theatre and saw a piece of film of the train in action, which I know they found fascinating.

Both Princesses were then presented with plastic daggers (and plastic was a relatively new thing back then) and I'll always remember that as they left the theatre Margaret goosed her sister with her dagger, and Elizabeth jumped about six inches!

Worton Hall's history was subsequently inextricably linked with that of Shepperton Studios. Films would base between the two, or start at one and complete work at the other.

In June 1946, Alex bought a mansion at Hyde Park Corner, 144–146 Piccadilly, which had belonged to King George VI when he was Duke of York, and constructed a very expensive headquarters. The rooms were filled with antiques, oriental carpets and chandeliers, the obligatory screening room was installed, and a canteen for the staff and chauffeurs. Alex's home was, in fact, a suite of rooms at Claridges Hotel. He made a point of never carrying money, as he had no occasion to use it! Along with a new top-of-the-range Rolls-Royce, Alex bought an ex-navy Fairmile torpedo boat which he had converted into a luxury yacht.

His newly acquired studios received similar 'extravagances' and were re-equipped under the supervision of Vincent Korda. Vincent's son, Michael Korda, recorded his first visit to Shepperton in *Charmed Lives*, where he said:

Princess Elizabeth and Princess Margaret were escorted around Worton Hall Studios by Anthony Kimmins during the production of *Mine Own Executioner*. (Courtesy Doris Spriggs Archive)

Having passed through a small village [Laleham] we stopped at what might have been the gates of a small factory. The studio policeman swung up the small barrier and saluted, and we drove around the perimeter road of my Uncle's new domain. We passed the huge sound stages, the prop warehouses, the special effects stage, the new red brick row of cutting rooms and screening rooms, the carpentry and plasters departments, the generating plant, the covered walkway leading to the dressing rooms, finally sweeping into the courtyard of an old English Manor House surrounded by carefully designed gardens and a huge lawn. Shepperton Manor was his home from home, and he liked its mosaic tiles, the mullioned windows, the baronial staircase, the minstrel's gallery, and the large conservatory.

Alex, meanwhile, set about planning his new production programme for the coming few years, most of which centred on the bankable stars of the day: Paulette Goddard, David Niven, Orson Welles and so on.

In August 1946 *Bonnie Prince Charlie*, starring David Niven, had started its location shooting. It was to be the first in the programme from London Films.

However, it never completed photography. Location shots were in the can, but Korda was unhappy with the script and the director, Robert Stevenson. The studio work was delayed and David Niven went on to another film. It was not until 1947 that David Niven became available again, and meanwhile Korda himself directed *An Ideal Husband*, for which Hyde Park Corner was re-created on the back-lot at Shepperton. Studio hand Roy Pembrooke says:

In the space of sixty days a complete, life sized replica of the arches at Hyde Park Corner was built. Many hundreds of yards of ground was levelled and covered with tarmac. A section of the world famous Rotten Row was built. An encampment sprang up overnight to stable seventy of the Royal Horse Guards' horses used in the scenes. Water was laid on to stalls and fodder brought to the grounds. A field kitchen to cater for 500 extras was erected together with marquees for dressing rooms. Electric and all domestic services and telephones were supplied from the Lot installation.

Soon after its completion, he turned his attentions to the ill-fated *Bonnie Prince Charlie* once more. The original producer, Ted Black, was sidelined and Korda himself took on the script re-write, before engaging Hugh Stewart to handle production matters. A new director was needed, as Richard Best explains:

We were at the end of *Mine Own Executioner* when Anthony Kimmins received a call from Korda to take over the film from Robert Stevenson. We were on the verge of winding up, so that wasn't a problem, but Tony was really jumping in at the deep end as there wasn't much time for preparation at all. But then, Tony came back and said to the production manager, Ken Horne, and me that he'd asked if we could both go with him for support. He just wanted someone on the unit who he knew and could talk to – obviously, there wasn't anyone amongst the unit Hugh Stewart had pulled together he was familiar with. We both went to Shepperton. The editor was a lady named Grace Garland, so really that side was all sown up. But nevertheless, we were given an office near the stage where I was given set plans and suggestions for camera angles for the shooting. I had to read the script and work out where the camera should be. Whether Tony took any notice of my six weeks of instructions I don't know, but I then received a phone call from MGM to work on *The Guinea Pig* so had to leave.

But I do remember that one day I was sitting in rushes, and Korda said 'I would like you to come and see the film I have just directed, *An Ideal Husband*, as I think you are over-shooting here.' He made a theatre booking, and ran his film for us. It was, of course, a very different film and reliant on dialogue and you can shoot a lot in a well planned scene. Bonnie was an action film and you shoot it to cut. He was a very great man, but I don't think his argument was valid on this occasion.

Over-shooting was an argument Korda had with many of his directors, and it actually later resulted in Guy Hamilton being given his opportunity to direct, but more of that later.

'Part of the filming of Bonnie,' adds Doris Spriggs, 'was at Worton Hall, though never credited. The silent stage was used for the giant Scottish bog sequence, which became the Battle of Culledon.'

Vincent Korda, incidentally, having approved the set of the Scottish moor in the Highlands, asked for more 'Fissles'. It wasn't until he produced a sketch of a thistle on the back of an envelope that people realised what he meant. When Alex ventured on to the set, disapproving of the colours of the Royal Tartan as being 'awful', Vincent retorted, 'that's the way the bloody things are'. Alex asked, 'why do they have to be so much in orange and green? I hate it, all that purple stuff. It looks like a biscuit tin. And vat are those tings with spikes?' 'Fissles', replied Vincent.

Korda's aforementioned film *An Ideal Husband* went on the stage floor at Shepperton before the re-grouped *Bonnie Prince Charlie* and became the studio's first big Technicolor film. There had actually been labour problems at the studio just ahead of filming commencing, and Alex rushed to the studio to resolve them personally. Three weeks later there was a threatened strike of the make-up artists over pay. Alex again oversaw its settlement. These problems, and many others besides, were always tackled by Alex Korda personally. He liked to be totally hands-on, but as a result many more important issues didn't receive the attention they deserved. Furthermore, during the make-up strike saga, Alex often left his cast and crew hanging around on the stage to go off to meetings, causing many to ask if he really had nothing better to do.

In 1947, Britain was plunged into a financial crisis as a result of international 'dollar drain'. That summer, the British Government announced drastic measures to reduce imports and increase exports. Hollywood films were seen as a major 'import' and substantial profits from British cinemas were returning to America. The ad volorem tax was imposed on 6 August and required a 75 per cent duty on American film earnings in Britain. The tax was not to be calculated on actual earnings, but predicted earnings. The film industry on both sides of the Atlantic was furious.

Three days after the tax was imposed, the Motion Picture Association of America (MPAA) suspended all shipments of films to the UK. However, there were already around 125 American films awaiting release at the time. To off-set a sudden rush into exhibition of the awaiting American films, a new Quota Act was established requiring 25 per cent of all cinema screenings to be of British films.

The British Government assumed that an industry deprived of American dominance would react swiftly to increase its indigenous output. However, post-war Britain did not have the capacity to replace the 80 per cent dominance held by the Americans. Little did they think that films take months to prepare, and then possibly a further six months between commencing photography and being released for distribution into the system. Rank embarked on a prolific programme of forty-seven films, whereas other (independent) UK studios faced crisis unless there was a massive injection of finance to independent producers.

By March 1948, Harold Wilson in his capacity as president of the Board of Trade reached a new agreement with the Motion Picture Association of America to lift the 75 per cent customs duty on film imports and to arrange for controlled remission of funds to the US. There was a sudden massive influx of previously unreleased American films, and the cinemagoers opted for the rich, lavish Hollywood offering over those coming from UK film-makers.

Rank faced near ruin, with debts of some £16 million, and whilst British Lion had shown a profit of £61,000 in 1946-47, the company was shouldering heavy production losses. By 1948 the largest independent production and distribution company was also facing collapse.

Rank embarked upon severe cost-cutting exercises, and despite bringing great prestige to the organisation – and, at least, satisfactory box office figures – many producers who had found a home under Uncle Arthur's umbrella soon found themselves out in the cold. British Lion and Alex Korda, meanwhile, were seen as independent spirits and as such many of those leaving Rank would soon join forces with Korda. However, despite raising £1 million through share offerings, Korda was floundering. After the disappointing premiere of *An Ideal Husband*, Alex was working on facts and figures for Sir Wilfred Eady, the Permanent Secretary at the Treasury.

The Government began considering how they might intervene with an official loan system for the independents. On 12 February, British Lion applied to the Finance Corporation of Industry (FCI) for an advance of a further £1 million. Harold Wilson, the president of the Board of Trade, had stated it was the Government's policy to support British production, especially in light of the ad volorem tax. He wrote in support of the British Lion application to the FCI. The following day a memorandum was circulated within the Board of Trade expressing concern that:

> … if it is ever allowed to get about that the Government are prepared to put up money for films or are even thinking of putting up money themselves, we shall never be able to get the atmosphere which will put our film industry on a sound

basis … the problem therefore seems to be to find an existing organisation (if there is one) or if not, to set up a new one which can venture into this new field with sufficient authority and determination to enable them to make a success of it.

The National Film Finance Company was formed. In November 1948, British Lion agreed a £2 million loan (twice the original figure) from the Government through the NFFC, with a fixed 4 per cent interest. Before the loan was to be forthcoming, an investigation was to be conducted into the company's accounts and proposed programme. The investigators reported back that £2 million was insufficient, and the loan was increased to £3 million secured by a mortgage debenture.

Bonnie Prince Charlie was premiered and received scathing reviews. This prompted Alex to take out newspaper adverts to defend his film. 'Some of the London critics', he wrote, 'have written about it not with a pen, but with a hatchet.'

Production at Shepperton, meanwhile, continued apace. *Anna Karenina* was the eleventh filmic adaptation of the Tolstoy story, and it received the full Korda make-over. Despite its grand settings and starring Vivien Leigh and Ralph Richardson, it was poorly received. Ralph Richardson fared much better in his second project for Korda at the studio, Carol Reed's *The Fallen Idol*. Partly filmed at Worton Hall too, the story was of how an ambassador's son (Bobby Henrey) almost incriminates his butler friend (Ralph Richardson) in the accidental death of his shrewish wife. Carol Reed and Graham Greene, who penned the story, both won Academy Award nominations. One reviewer commented:

Worth it just for that last shot of the little boy on the stairs, whose mother has just come home and is calling to him. Exquisitely crafted – beautifully acted, written, directed, and filmed. They don't make films like this anymore. When you see something like this you realize that intelligence has really left cinema.

Dora Bryan was spotted by Carol Reed in Noel Coward's stage play *Peace in our Time* and offered her a small role in *The Fallen Idol*. She recalls:

This was the first real filming I did. I remember – as I lived in Piccadilly – getting up in the small hours to be at the studio by 7am. There weren't any cars – it was all public transport. On my first day I had on high heeled shoes, a little red suit and a plastic mac. There was no one around to ask directions, so there was I trudging through fields of thick snow in the depths of winter. I was forty-five minutes late but fortunately no one said anything. I didn't have a script and really didn't know what part I was playing until I met Carol Reed on set that morning. He told me what sort of feeling he wanted and gave me a few lines of dialogue. I was to play a prostitute!

I didn't have a costume, and was told just to wear what I had on. I was horrified to think I was playing such a character in my own clothes. I became the tart with a heart of gold, in high heel shoes and a plastic mac – which they

Ralph Richardson led the cast in Carol Reed's superior thriller, *The Fallen Idol*. (Courtesy David Blake Archive)

let me wear – saying 'hello dearie'. Carol was the type of director who would say 'do what you think Dora' as there wasn't really a script, we made it up as we went along. One of the favourable critics said of me 'this girl who's name I can never remember … ' so I wrote to them and said 'My name is Dora Bryan'. I felt quite satisfied after that.

Harold Huth produced and directed melodrama *Night Beat* with Anne Crawford, Michael Hordern and Sid James for British Lion at Worton Hall. Guy Hamilton explains:

In 1947 I was put under contract with London Films as an assistant director, and my first film was *Night Beat* at Worton Hall. It was a delightful studio with the old house forming the centre; and in only having the medium and two small stages (plus the silent stage, which was soon to move to Shepperton) they could really only accommodate one film at a time which I thought was wonderful. It made life so much easier as, say for instance, we needed a can of paint; someone could dash to the stores and grab one and they'd know who to charge it to. With the bigger studios you'd need a chit and then have it counter-signed and so on. It made everything run smoothly!

The Last Days of Dolwyn stemmed from Alex Korda's association with producer Hugh Stewart on *An Ideal Husband* when, one day, Korda asked him if he had any ideas for films. Stewart told him a story of how a 1890s Welsh valley was flooded for a new reservoir to provide water for an English town. Shortly afterwards, Korda commissioned Emlyn Williams to write a screenplay. The film went before the cameras at Worton Hall studios in 1949. Emlyn Williams wrote, directed and also starred with Edith Evans and, making his screen debut, Richard Burton. Great use was made of the giant silent stage in recreating the Welsh village to be flooded and Pop Day, the acclaimed matte artist, was given the job of making it all look real.

'The silent stage at the studio,' adds former studio secretary Doris Spriggs, 'used to have painted on the roof in large white letters "Quiet Please" because of aircraft flying to and from Hounslow Heath and Heston! I remember that Richard Burton lodged in what was a council house directly next door to the studio gate, and cutting rooms.'

Soon afterwards, with Shepperton's roster ever-increasing, Korda was keen to house the larger productions totally. He knew that some films only visited Isleworth to take advantage of the huge silent stage, and gave the order to dismantle the structure and move it to Shepperton.

'There's an interesting little bit of trivia here,' says Clifton Brandon, who worked on many films at Shepperton as production manager, 'because if you look at the back of the silent stage today, you can see some faded lettering. It doesn't spell anything

Richard Burton's first leading role was in *The Last Days of Dolwyn*. (Courtesy David Blake Archive)

The Worton Hall silent stage became known as H Stage when it was moved to Shepperton. (Roy Pembrooke)

though, however at Worton Hall it did spell "London Film Productions". When reassembling the structure at Shepperton, nobody bothered to tell the labourers, and so they put it together with the letters all jumbled up!'

Further improvements at Shepperton included the addition of the 'Big Ben' cafeteria which could accommodate the growing size of film units to the tune of 1,000 people!

Following Korda from Denham, where they had been working as two of Rank's Independent Producers – a loose association of producer/director teams which Rank gave complete autonomy for their subjects – were Michael Powell and Emeric Pressburger.

They had spent several years with Rank and Independent Producers, but in 1944 the death knell was sounded. Gabriel Pascal had cost Rank dearly with productions *Caesar and Cleopatra* and *London Town*, which were hoped would help Rank break the US market, but it diverted funds from his UK productions. Soon after the Second World War and the introduction of the ad volorem tax, the Independent Producers were disbanded, and several moved over to join Korda. In his autobiography, Powell wrote:

In those days before the war, we were little men and Alex was a big one. We did not aspire to be great. It was not our scene. We were ingenious, resourceful, inventive and courageous, but we were not great. Alex was great. I never knew another like him for wit, authority and charm. I have met great artists in the cinema – not D.W. Griffith alas! – but I have met Walt Disney, Charlie Chaplin, Alfred Hitchcock and Fritz Lang. These were all great artists, great film-makers, but Alex was a great man; and although it looked as if it might be difficult to make good pictures with him and his associates, the atmosphere was one of enthusiasm and of great picture-making, and a million miles from the bourgeois tantrums of John Davis, whose tall shadow was falling across his master, Arthur Rank.

Powell and Pressburger's first film with British Lion was at Worton Hall. *The Small Back Room* starred Jack Hawkins, David Farrar, Michael Gough and Kathleen Byron. The script was based on Nigel Balchin's novel and focussed on a bomb expert with a lame foot and a drink problem, risking his life dismantling a booby-trapped bomb. Noreen Ackland, the assistant editor, recalls a near disaster in post-production at Worton Hall:

> *The Small Back Room* had Cliff Turner as the editor and he was suffering from shell-shock after the war, and would do all sorts of odd things; he'd disappear for days and days and then he'd take vital sequences in his top pocket and was really in quite a state. Reggie Mills and I, having just finished on *The Red Shoes*, were asked to go and take it over. Although it was my first job at the studio, I had been there a little earlier as my husband Dick had been working there [on *Mine Own Executioner*]. I have to say that I found it to be a very old fashioned and small studio; the cutting rooms weren't as lavish as the ones we'd had on *Red Shoes* at Pinewood!

A wonderful comedy from Howard Hawks, and starring Cary Grant and Ann Sheridan, stopped off at Worton Hall to complete some studio shooting. *I Was a Male War Bride* saw Cary Grant as a Frenchman, and then Frenchwoman, trying to return with his new wife to America from war-torn France. The other production at the studio was *Saints and Sinners*, directed by Leslie Arliss.

Shepperton remained busy with a handful of films. Herbert Wilcox directed his rather confusing four-periods-of-war drama *Elizabeth of Ladymead* for British Lion, and Gregory Ratoff directed *That Dangerous Age* for London Films, based on Illa Sugutchoff's play *Autumn* – the writer was probably more famous for his play, *The Man Who Broke The Bank At Monte Carlo*. Next, Romanian-born Jean Negulesco brought *Britannia Mews* in. It was not a happy experience for the film makers, as editor Richard Best reveals:

> This was an American financed film, and in my many years in the film business as an editor I have to say I have never seen so much coverage on a film. The shooting was unbelievable.
>
> In many ways it was only a two-hander film; a love story that turns sour and then another love story that turns out with wedding bells.
>
> Every sequence was covered with a long, a medium, two-shots, close-ups … throughout the scene not just for the salient points. There was no guidance for me as an editor as the director didn't shoot to cut. It was obviously under instruction.

Assistant Director Guy Hamilton recalls:

This was one of the films from Fox. Korda was keen to see his studio used by other productions, and the Hollywood major was the first to move in. It was, I felt, a boring film to make. Negulesco was a typical director from Zanuck's stable. They brought great cranes onto the set and had so many wide-angle camera set-ups that it became farcical. He covered every single scene so heavily it was quite ridiculous.

It was done that way so as Zanuck's LA-based editor could cut the film any which way. If he wanted to remove Maureen O'Hara from the film for instance, he could do it as he'd have enough shots without her in to re-cast another actress.

Richard Best adds:

Oh yes. I discovered that every single day a second set of rushes was sent to 20th Century Fox in Hollywood, for Darryl Zanuck and the film's producer, William Pearlberg, who had set up the film and returned to America. Within three weeks Negulesco disappeared to Paris, to meet Zanuck. He took the footage that we had assembled and when he returned he announced that Zanuck had declared it a 'dead duck'. He was going to have it cut in Hollywood as well. You can imagine what that did for my morale.

Guy Hamilton remembers:

One afternoon, and it was getting late, that Negulesco was unhappy about a scene with Dana Andrews. Dana had to shoot a gun, and the director felt there wasn't enough of a 'puff' of smoke from the gun, nor was there enough blood on the victim. The unions were very powerful in those days, and when the clock struck 5.30pm that was it; everybody went home. It was fast approaching this, and I thought it was getting silly as we'd have to come back the next day for this one shot. So I said to Negulesco – I kidded him actually – that he'd only need one or the other: more puff or more blood, because the camera would only hold on one of the two, it wouldn't and couldn't hold on both. So we agreed, more 'puff'. We re-shot, so to say, and at about 5.20pm had it in the can.

A few days later, Negulesco received a cable from Zanuck. I was called to his trailer. 'Zanuck wants to know where shot so-and-so with the extra blood is.' He was working to a complete dot-to-dot sequence with his editor out there and was terrified if he didn't get each shot it might affect his edit later. Quite a mad way of filming.

Richard Best continues:

Anyway, we completed the film, and I put a cut together. It was never worked on though, as all my other films had been, for a week or two to get it perfect.

It was just declared finished and we were all shipped off to Hollywood – with 12,000 feet of film.

We were summoned to a 9p.m. showing in Fox's theatre. To my horror the American editor's copy was screened.

I remember when the director first saw my cut of the big fight sequence in the Mews, he said to me that it was 'too brutal' and needed calming down a bit. That seemed very odd to me, but I made the cuts. Meanwhile, when Zanuck saw this cut copy (which had the 'brutal fight' toned down), the only comment – and I mean only – was that he felt the fight was not strong enough! I felt vindicated over my cut!

When I returned to Britain, I asked for my name to be removed from the film, as I didn't feel I could take a credit for 'editing' a film that was effectively cut by someone else, simultaneously. I've never known that situation before or since, it's quite ridiculous.

Despite this unhappy film at the studio, Guy Hamilton remembers Shepperton only with tremendous affection:

I'll always remember my approach to the studio in my 'early days'. You'd approach the main gate – which is sadly no longer there – and the four stages would dominate the skyline.

A and B stages were linked with a huge long corridor, as were C and D stages. There would usually be two films shooting at any one time, each taking a pair of the stages. The star dressing rooms were in the Old House, and many times was the case I'd assist a star who'd had a drink or two too many, to a room upstairs to sleep it off overnight. That practise was soon brought to an end by the insurers, who realised that if they stumbled out of bed at night not knowing where they were, they might have fallen down the grand staircase and broken their necks!

There might be four or five cars in the car park, as cars were a luxury then. Most people would make there way to Staines on the train and there would be coaches at the station to relay everyone to the studio; and similarly back at the end of the day.

Whilst Alex Korda increasingly based himself out of his Piccadilly office, with only occasional forays to the studio, his presence was always in evidence, as Guy Hamilton recounts:

I loved him. He was truly unique and a joy to work with. He rarely ever spent time at Shepperton unless absolutely necessary, preferring instead to base himself at 146 Piccadilly where, incidentally, he had an open telephone line to the studio.

But there was always a 'threat' that he might descend, as in the restaurant there was always a large round table in the corner that was reserved for him. No one was allowed to use that table as it was 'Sir Alex's table'.

I do remember though one time when Alex was due to visit. As first AD working at the studio, I joined the throng of Management personnel, Heads of Department and so on. It looked like the state opening of Parliament. Ten minutes after his arrival, Alex was on his way home again, down the endless A–B corridor towards his Rolls-Royce. Being a foggy December – and with an epidemic of 'flu having invaded the studio – Lew Thornburn, the studio manager – who was a wonderful character – ordered the corridor sprayed with disinfectant and polished to the nth degree. It really was immaculate. Fit for a king. Alex turned to Lew, who was walking alongside him though maybe half a step behind, and in his thick Hungarian accent said:

'Lew'

'Yes Sir Alex?'

'This corridor smells of cat's piss, do something about it'.

Exit Alex.

Korda was not averse to calling his film makers to see him in London, when he wasn't totally pleased, either, as Guy Hamilton reveals:

I was summoned on a Saturday morning together with one editor, one cameraman, one assistant art director etc. to view the rough cut of Emeric Pressburger's first and only directorial effort. Obviously retakes were on the cards. The three Korda brothers walked in. The lights went out and we watched in silence till the end. Alex lit a cigar and addressed us.

'Boys, I could eat a tin of trims and shit a better picture.'

CHAPTER 6

THE THIRD MAN

Perhaps one of the studio's most important films, and certainly one of Korda's great successes, came with *The Third Man*, which was a co-production with David O. Selznick who had agreed a multi-picture deal with Korda. In return for American distribution rights, Selznick would provide a substantial part of the budgets and the Hollywood stars without charge.

After the Second World War, there was a great market for films in Europe, and Alex was swift to act in selling the British Lion catalogue to as many countries as he possible could. The films performed well and earned well. However, therein lay a problem – getting the money out under post-war regulations and restrictions. Austria was one such country. Alex had considerable monies there, but he simply could not remove them.

According to author Graham Greene, it was Korda who first instigated the idea of a film set against the background of the four-power occupation in Austria. Greene was to spend two weeks in Vienna researching the story before, on his penultimate day, a meeting with a British Intelligence officer offered up stories of the 'Underground Police' who patrolled the city's enormous system of sewers, and the black market trade in adulterated penicillin. He had his story.

Orson Welles soon became the firm favourite for Harry Lime. Selznick agreed on condition that American actor Joseph Cotten played Martins. Trevor Howard was then signed as Major Calloway, and completing the cast was Alida Valli, Bernard Lee and Wilfrid Hyde-White.

Shooting commenced in Vienna on 22 October and would run through until 11 December, when it transferred to London. Re-commencing on 29 December, filming finally finished on 31 March 1949.

It seemed odd to shoot on location in the autumn with short days but, of course, most of the shooting on *The Third Man* was to take place at night, and the rain associated with the season helped the atmosphere tremendously and saved the local fire crews coming out!

Shooting was organised into three units, each with its own lighting cameraman. Robert Krasker was in charge of the night unit, Stan Pavey the sewer unit and Hans Schneeberger the day unit – all directed by Carol Reed. Guy Hamilton, the film's assistant director, explains:

The night unit would finish around 4am, and you'd sleep until 8a.m. By 9a.m. it was light and the other units started. It would start getting dark around 4p.m., so we'd break and get a few hours sleep, and then be up by 7p.m. for the night unit again. For nearly two months we snatched a few hours sleep here and a few hours there – and had lots of Benzedrine. Carol directed it all.

Orson Welles proved to take his part just a little too seriously, and became every bit as elusive as Harry Lime. At one point Vincent Korda was dispatched to Rome to find the actor and bring him back to London. They arrived to discover he had moved to Florence. They followed. There, they were told the actor had just left for Venice. Again, they followed … and so continued this game of cat and mouse. Eventually they caught up with Welles in the south of France, got him drunk and bundled him into an aeroplane. In London, he signed his contract and then duly disappeared to Rome again! He was eventually found but meanwhile Guy Hamilton had been doubling for him wearing a big black coat and hat in the shadowy sequences filmed in Vienna.

The reason for Welles' elusiveness can be attributed to a deal he signed in 1946 with Korda – which was for three pictures, none of which materialised.

'I knew I was going to do it,' Welles later said, 'but I was going to make Alex pay for all those movies I hadn't done [films which Korda had previously promised to employ the actor in] … and I'm going to make it just as unpleasant as possible.'

Guy Hamilton doubled for Orson Welles in the atmospheric night-time street shots. (Courtesy Canal and Image UK Ltd)

When Welles did eventually turn up in Vienna, some weeks after production had begun, his first scene was in the sewers. Carol Reed noticed some water cascading down from one of the ducts and suggested to the actor it would be wonderful if Harry Lime was to run under this duct – the water on his face would provide wonderful scope for drama. Welles was furious that he should be expected to work in such filthy conditions. It was therefore decided to build the sewer back at Shepperton. There was very little else left for Welles to film in Vienna.

'He had a couple of shots walking to and from the Prater wheel,' adds Guy Hamilton, 'and I think I'm correct in saying that was the sum total of Orson's work in Venice.'

Welles was to prove reliably difficult as regards the studio schedule. He insisted that he was so busy, he could only possibly give the production one week at Shepperton. All of the sets he was involved in therefore had to be constructed at the same time.

Production actually started off, in Britain, at Worton Hall Studios. It featured Major Calloway treating Martins to a drink in the Kartnerstrasse beer cellar, before filming Harry Lime's flat where Martins interrogated the porter about Harry's accident. Paul Hoerbiger, who played the porter, could not speak English and learnt his lines phonetically. Production then moved to Shepperton on 6 January.

Vincent Korda designed the sets, of which seventy-five were built in total. On B stage, Vincent oversaw the completion of the main sewer set and ensured the construction department worked day and night to complete all the sets required for Welles' pending arrival. Two units worked solidly for the whole week and, miraculously, Reed completed all of Orson Welles' scenes.

A and B stages contained a mass of small sets adjoined to one another, yet no one watching the film would think it was filmed anywhere but on location in Vienna; such was the genius of Vincent Korda. Reed's greatest masterstroke came with the film's music. Fifty-odd years on, everyone has heard the magical zither twang its way through *The Harry Lime Theme*. Forty million copies of the tune have been sold with many top groups performing cover versions.

It was Anton Karas who was playing the zither at a welcome party organised

The famous Prater Wheel in Vienna, with Joseph Cotton. (Courtesy Canal and Image UK Ltd)

Production designer Vincent Korda. (Gareth Owen
Collection)

by Karl Hartl in Vienna and Reed, fascinated,
couldn't get the music out of his head. He asked
Guy Hamilton to track down the musician. It
took several weeks, but Hamilton found Karas,
and engaged him for the film's soundtrack.

Reed also asked Karas to play live in the
cutting room theatre, to inspire atmosphere
and to encourage the editing team – playing
days, evenings and sometimes into the night.

The film was perfection in every aspect. But
then, disaster struck. Assistant editor Noreen
Ackland was working on *Gone to Earth* for
Powell and Pressberger when Carol Reed knocked on her door regarding *The Third
Man*:

> The crew were on location up in Shropshire and I was charged with looking
> after the rushes, so I would forward them on and when they came back after
> being viewed I'd get them ready for editing. However … Carol barged into my

The Shepperton scoring stage, here recording the music for *The Third Man*. (Gareth Owen
Collection)

cutting room and he said, 'Noreen I've just been in touch with Michael Powell and he said I can borrow you whilst they're away on location – will you bring a notebook and pencil, and come in the theatre with me?' I trotted in and he ran a sequence – in Alida Valli's bedroom – and he gave me the notes on how he wanted it cut. Then we came onto the final reel in the sewers, and Carol got it just how he wanted it and said, 'will you take this with you, lock it in your cupboard and take the key home because I don't want it touched.'

At that time Ossie Hafenrichter and his two assistants had been working on the film, flat-out for many weeks, days and evenings, and the bins were overflowing with film. I went home and early the next morning I received a 'phone call, asking me to go in immediately as there had been a fire. What had happened was Ossie had left his moviola switched on, with all this film strewn about. They said a moviola fault had caused the fire.

Luckily the 'sewer' reel, locked in my cabinet, was still intact.

The fire started about 3am, and Carol's first instructions were to get me and Frankie in to order the re-prints as the film had a screening booked at the Cannes Film Festival which was only a couple of weeks away.

Loads of other assistants were drafted in to try and meet the deadline, and I was ordering up all the re-prints from what was left – we had the cutting copy of the sound reel (the picture reels had been lost in the fire), but the negative of the sound had been cut which made it very difficult. The picture negative was safe at the labs, but to put the complete film together we had to make a dupe of the sound, and match the mods to the picture negative and cut it that way. It was a terrible way to have to do it.

Fortunately, the routine practise of logging the key numbers of the rushes helped enormously in ordering reprints.

I slept in the Old House for a few hours each day, whilst my assistant Frankie lived nearby so she went home. It was almost a calamity but we worked around the clock and got it ready! The film went on to win the third Cannes Film Festival.

John Glen was a young messenger at the studio, and recalled the role he played in helping to restore the film when it was damaged in the fire. He says that 'virtually every editor that was free was drafted in to re-cut the film from scratch. Some eight reels of film had to be reprinted from the negative, and it was down to the meticulous care of one of the senior editors, Geoff Bottril, that they were able to salvage the film from the jaws of oblivion. He had written down the film's code numbers in a book which proved invaluable when it came to re-printing the movie.'

Glen continues:

We worked all the hours God sent to get back on schedule. The key numbers were a code on the negative and were printed through onto the positive prints. This enabled the negative cutters to match exactly the film editor's work print containing hundreds of cuts. We were able to reassemble the reels by following the numbers Geoff had written in his book. Carol Reed was a regular visitor to the numbering room, and would sometimes bring me a beer.

One Saturday evening, I was in the bath getting ready for a night out, when I heard a knock on the front door. It was the associate producer [Hugh Perceval]. I rapidly got dressed and met him on the doorstep. 'We need you at the studio,' he said. 'Can you number some film for us? It's urgent.' Half-an-hour later, a Rolls-Royce pulled up and took me to Shepperton, where I worked until about 2a.m.

Glen also proved invaluable in providing the footsteps for the soundtrack:

Echoing footsteps often had to be recorded in a special chamber and carefully synchronised. Jack Drake, the Sound Editor, found a stairwell with a promisingly hard surface outside the Westrex theatre in Shepperton. I went into the theatre and watched a continuous loop of film of Cotten's footsteps, memorised their exact speed, then dashed outside to the stairwell and walked along the hard surface. The echoing footsteps that Jack Drake recorded are the ones accompanying Joseph Cotten in the film.

Orson Welles in *The Third Man*. (Courtesy Canal and Image UK Ltd)

Awards and acclaim came flooding in for the film, and Karas' music became some of the most cherished in cinema history. Though it is amusing to realise that Sir Arthur Jarratt, chairman of British Lion, sent Reed a telegram saying, 'Dear Carol, saw *The Third Man* last night. Love it. I think you've got a big success there. But please take off the banjo.'

Following his tremendous success, and subsequent wealth – Korda gave Karas 50 per cent of publishing royalties, though technically he was not obliged to – Karas performed *The Harry Lime Theme* only occasionally. Most emotionally, he played it at Carol Reed's funeral in 1976.

It wasn't the end of *The Third Man* though, as a few years later British Lion, National Telefilm Associates (USA) and the BBC backed a television series based on the adventures of Harry Lime. Between 1959 and 1965, seventy-seven half-hour episodes were filmed. Michael Rennie played Lime. Leslie Gilliat takes up the story of the series' shaky start at Shepperton:

> The finance deal was with the BBC and British Lion (which owned the screen rights to the character and story) and as there was some American money, half were filmed in America, and half in the UK – Shepperton. In America they were shooting them in four days, whereas here the first one took nine days and the second took eight days … panic set it with British Lion who thought they'd lose the series as the Americans wanted to close down production here and go back to the USA. David Kingsley, the Managing Director of British Lion, asked if I could go over and see what was happening.
>
> I arrived at the Shepperton Board Room, opened the door and saw twenty-two people sitting around the table including Mort Abrams and Felix Jackson (the American producers), Ronnie Waldman from the BBC and so on.
>
> 'Ah', said David Kingsley, really dropping me in it. 'This is Leslie Gilliat and he's here to tell you where you've been going wrong.'
>
> The idea for the UK shoot was to film for four days with one day off. I was getting a little hot under the collar and told them that I'd worked through all the progress reports and worked out the exact number of hours that they'd spent on each episode. If you take those hours and compare with what we'd shot in London, it wasn't nine days but nearer to five (in hours employed). They shouted 'nonsense' and so I asked if the progress reports weren't accurate.
>
> I was volunteered to take over the production, and was duly lumbered for four or five months! It was like a sausage machine.
>
> The first series complete, a second series was commissioned at Elstree and they asked me to join them. Fortunately I was busy elsewhere!

CHAPTER 7

THE LION'S ROAR

In 1950 *The Cure for Love*, directed, written by and starring Robert Donat, started photography at Worton Hall for British Lion. Studio assistant Doris Spriggs remembers:

> My abiding memory of Robert Donat and *The Cure for Love* was that he was a chronic asthmatic. I remember being asked to go over to his dressing room during the shoot, as he had a very bad asthma attack in there and had pulled the washbasin off the wall!

Sadly, it was another such an attack, in June 1958, which claimed Donat's life. He was just fifty-three years old. Dora Bryan remembers the film as having a much-extended schedule due to Donat's ill health:

> Robert really was ill a lot of the time and we'd sometimes hang around all day in the hope he might be well enough to work. His dressing room was like a hospital, it was very sad.
>
> It didn't help that it was a long hot summer, though I do remember that Gladys Henson and I got Robert hooked on ice-cold coca cola, with ice cream on the top. It was delicious!
>
> I was in Traveller's Joy at the theatre at the time, and when offered ten days on this film, I leapt at it. Ten days developed into ten weeks, and at £100 a day it really was terrific work!

The small studio remained busy and Launder & Gilliat (having defected from Rank's Independent Producers) were credited for making their superior comedy *The Happiest Days of Your Life* with Alistair Sim, Margaret Rutherford and Joyce Grenfell leading the cast, and using both Shepperton and Worton Hall.

'Well that's not quite correct,' says Associate Producer E.M. Smedley-Aston:

> We made it at Riverside Studios in Hammersmith, as Sidney Gilliat was working on *State Secret* at Worton and Shepperton was, as far as I can recall, full.

It was a very happy picture with an all-British crew, apart from a Hungarian art director (Ivan King) a Yugo-Slav editor (Oswald Hafenrichter) and a Russian composer (Mischa Spoliansky). There may have been a few scenes at Worton and Shepperton, and post-production, but the bulk was Riverside for London Films and British Lion.

The company's head, Alex Korda, was certainly enjoying both critical and box-office success, but there were cracks beginning to surface in the company in relation to the Government loan. London Films recorded a hefty loss of £127,000 in the year 1949-50 and British Lion had lost almost £1.4 million the year before.

Herbert Wilcox next directed *Into the Blue*, a comedy co-written by Nicholas Phipps who later went on to write the *Doctor* comedies starring Dirk Bogarde. The story follows a cheerful stowaway, Michael Wilding, on a yacht and how he helps the owners catch smugglers. Constance Cummings, Jack Hulbert, Edward Rigby and Odile Versois co-starred.

'Oh what a film,' exclaimed Continuity Supervisor Elaine Schreyeck:

We went over from Newhaven to France by boat – we were all sick on board too! – and then we journeyed up the Seine on the boat! We shot at Le Havre to start with, and then further inland before arriving in Paris on Bastille Day, where the celebrations were in full flow. We then moved down to Founteinbleau, before ending up in Monte Carlo – where we all stayed at the Hotel de Paris, the finest there is – and shot extensively around the harbour. I've never experienced such a wonderful location shoot before. We then returned to the studio where, to be honest, there was very little work left to do and I think we all felt it was somewhat of an anticlimax after our time in France!

The Black Rose boasted an impressive cast of Tyrone Power, Orson Welles and Jack Hawkins for Henry Hathaway's medieval drama, filmed expansively in England and North Africa. 20th Century Fox's Ben Lyon ensured excellent production values, with great masses of surging extras and plenty of swashbuckling flurry. Listen out for Peter Sellers dubbing the voice of the oily Lu Chung played by Alfonso Bedoya. The director returned to Shepperton in 1954 with another medieval romp, of which more later. Hathaway was not, however, a favourite of the Shepperton workforce, as Guy Hamilton reveals:

Henry Hathaway took a deep rooted objection to all work stopping twice a day as the tea trolley was wheeled onto the stage. We were all generically christened 'You limey tea drinking sons of bitches' and he meant it!

Bluey Hill, a famous 1st AD, took him to view a set under construction on the next stage. The plasterers were all drinking tea. As the set was required Monday, Hathaway exploded 'tea drinking sons of...etc.'

The result: an immediate down tools and strike. Management and union leaders were called in. No resumption of work would be made until

Mr Hathaway apologises, they said.

'No way' he said.

It was left to the powers that be at 20th Century to explain to Henry that the production would come to a total halt. 'You can't mess with limey Unions' they said.

The finale was stage managed. A grumpy Hathaway accompanied by management and union reps walked onto a stage full of gloating plasterers and painters.

Hathaway: 'I apologise for having spoken perhaps a little hastily.'

Shop Steward: Mr 'Athaway, on behalf of myself and the Brothers, we accept your graceful apology and I think that we can now … etc, etc.'

Honour is satisfied – the party headed for the stage door but not before Henry turned and got in one parting shot: (in full American accent) 'PLASTER FASTER, YOU BASTARDS!'

Powell and Pressburger set to work on *Gone to Earth*, which along with *The Third Man* was one of the two films Selznick backed with Korda. Jennifer Jones (Selznick's wife), David Farrar, Cyril Cusack, Sybil Thorndike and Esmond Knight starred.

'Esmond Knight was blind, and he was in the film as Jennifer Jones' father,' recalls Assistant Editor Noreen Ackland:

The location was a little place called Sleap, and Esmond was being driven there in a unit car. Unfortunately, they'd got lost along the way. A short time afterwards they spotted a village policeman, and the driver pulled the car over for Esmond to wind his window down.

'Excuse me officer'

'Yes?' he asked

'Could you tell me the best way to get to Sleap?'

'Well, I always sleep on my side, I don't know about you' he replied, and trotted off down the lane!

Esmond loved telling that story.

Jennifer Jones would always be found standing on her head for a good five minutes every morning. That was a curious sight for visitors. She was, of course, meditating and relaxing ahead of the day's shooting.

I remember that on one particular morning at 9a.m. her husband, Selznick, had made an appointment to view the film thus far in the theatre at Shepperton. The projectionist got it all laced up and ready to roll, but it wasn't until 2p.m. that he turned up. He walked in, snapped his fingers and said 'run it' without a word of apology for his lateness. I guess that was typical of his behaviour in Hollywood. It didn't go down too well in Shepperton!

The Lost Hours is a rather good memory-loss thriller starring Mark Stevens, Jean Kent and Garry Marsh. During a London reunion of a Second World War RAF unit, an American pilot gets into a fight with one of his buddies, who is drunk and belligerent.

Poster artwork for *The Lost Hours*. (Courtesy Robert S. Baker)

The next day the pilot wakes up in a strange hotel room with blood on his suit, and cannot remember how he got there. Then he discovers that the friend he fought with the night before has been murdered, and he is a prime suspect. Directed by David MacDonald, the film was produced by Robert Baker and Monty Berman at Worton Hall. Baker also had a hand in the story:

> I came up with the scenario which was then fleshed out into a script by Steve Fisher and John Gilling. This was the first picture I made with an American leading man; I later went on, with Monty, to do a whole series of 'B pictures' with American leads, for Eros Films.
>
> We'd invariably strike a deal with an American distributor to take the film, and thereby cover the cost of the American artist. Our pictures were made on very, very tight budgets and on four week schedules, so every penny needed to be accounted for and this was a very satisfactory way of bringing on board a 'name' but without hiking up the budget.
>
> It was our one and only ever film at Worton Hall – and I dare say we chose it because we couldn't get in to a cheaper studio! I will say that we were very

happy at the studio, and everything went very smoothly, though there was a general feeling it was all 'winding down'.

State Secret was a book by Roy Huggins which had caught the attention of Frank Launder and Sidney Gilliat. It is the story of an American physician who is brought to an Eastern European nation under false pretences and when his patient, the current dictator, dies, he is slated to be killed as part of the cover-up. He escapes with the unwilling aid of a cabaret singer (Glynis Johns) – the only person he can find that speaks English – across high mountains. Korda invited his old business partner, Douglas Fairbanks Jr, to take the lead. Glynis Johns, Herbert Lom and Jack Hawkins co-starred.

Leslie Gilliat reveals more:

> Alex Korda wanted us to film in Austria. He was quite determined it should be Austria. It was absurd as *State Secret* was a completely different type of film to *The Third Man* and needed completely different locations, but Alex had it in his mind. I duly arranged to go out on a recce.
>
> The whole location was a nightmare though. The various zones – British, American, Russian etc after the war – were operational and moving between

Frank Launder and Sidney Gilliat, the formidable film-making duo, were responsible for many of Shepperton's most famous classic titles. (Courtesy Leslie Gilliat)

them was not at all easy. Italy would be a better location, I thought, and unbeknown to Alex I arranged a recce. I then prepared two budgets: one for filming in Austria and another for Italy. The one for Austria was three-times the amount of the Italian one.

After much arguing, Alex turned to me and said 'Make the bloody film in Italy then'.

Gilliat set about scheduling the film. All was set ... until Fairbanks joined the production! Gilliat continues:

Douglas Fairbanks was an odd character. I remember Lew Thornburn [who was in charge of production at the studio] telling me that when Fairbanks was at Worton Hall before the war, he was on a daily expense allowance and always made a point of claiming back the 6d tip he left after his lunch! Before we left for the location shoot, he asked me to alter the schedule as there was some trouble in Greece and he wanted to go out there to 'fly the American flag' and see if he could sort things out.

The Italian locations were tough, and I remember I wrote the most bizarre movement orders. For one location, we travelled by car a certain amount of the way, then it was the chair lift before a two-hour walk! People lost a lot of weight walking up there each day.

The weather was a major problem, as were the low temperatures. Guy Hamilton was first assistant director on the film, and recalls wryly the one piece of advice he was given ahead of leaving Britain, 'They said, "Bring a warm sweater!"'

Douglas Fairbanks Jr and Jack Hawkins in *State Secret*. (Courtesy Leslie Gilliat)

Guy Hamilton, Sidney Gilliat and Douglas Fairbanks Jr on the location of *State Secret*. (Courtesy Leslie Gilliat)

Leslie Gilliat recalls:

I remember during one of the night shoots in a town location, we got slightly ahead and at around 3a.m. needed a double for one of the characters … the character herself wasn't needed until we got back to the studio, just a good double! But where to find anyone at 3a.m.?

The brothels, came a suggestion. So off I went to a brothel, and had my driver/interpreter line everyone up, but it was no good … and so we moved onto the next one. I'll never forget it; there were policemen, journalists, soldiers and so on all sitting in a little room on chairs and as the one at the end got up and went off with his 'lady' all of the others in the queue would budge along a seat. I found a suitable girl, but she requested a ridiculous fee. I couldn't beat her down and so requested she get dressed and ready to go. Realising she'd be a little time, I asked the driver to drop me back and then go back for the girl. A few minutes later he returned, but the car was empty. I asked him where the girl was, and he said she'd refused to come as she liked her work too much!

It was a terrific film though, and I believe is being re-made in America. But if and when you see it next, you'll notice a little trick we had to do. We were fast running out of time, and Fairbanks had a pretty hefty overage in his contract; and we couldn't afford to pay that. There was one more scene we needed him for, which involved a commentary playing over him walking down a long corridor, through doors and so on to his office – that part was already in the can.

I grabbed Fairbanks and got him to record this commentary, knowing that once I had this then I didn't really need him anymore. We then filmed the sequence, using the camera as if it was Fairbanks, so what the viewer saw through the lens is what Fairbanks' point of view would be. That way we were able to release him on time, and still get the shot we needed – and nobody knew! Until now.

Twins Roy and John Boulting first moved into Shepperton with a superb thriller, *Seven Days to Noon*. They were to become very important figures in the future of British Lion and Shepperton Studios. Barry Jones played gentle Professor Willoughby, who worked for the Government in the development of atomic bombs. He steals one of these bombs and delivers the Government an ultimatum. Desist from developing these devices or he will explode one in the centre of London. The film won an American Academy Award for Best Original Story.

'I hate the word daring,' said Roy Boulting in a 1985 interview, 'but it was a bold project for the time. I had offered the project around City financiers and film companies but they all said it would be too expensive and impossible to make, I mean for a start we had to evacuate London.'

The brothers then turned to Alex Korda who, within hours of reading the script, gave the go-ahead. The film was brought in on time and on budget; 'evacuating' London was done by shooting in the deserted streets soon after dawn.

In a letter dated 20 April 1993 to Camera Operator Ray Sturgess, about an article Sturgess was writing for a trade journal, Producer Roy Boulting shared a few of his thoughts on the film's atmosphere which Sturgess helped create with his stunning photography of an empty London:

Seven Days to Noon, starring Sheila Manahan and Barry Jones. (The Boulting Brothers Archive)

The Boulting Brothers, Roy and John,
Shepperton's other formidable film-making duo
(Roy on ladder). (The Boulting Brothers Archive)

In the finished film, it was a climactic moment: London threatened, its citizens evacuated, the city empty. Your images, vivid, beautifully composed and mostly shot in a gentle, early morning light that only served to intensify the forlorn beauty and vulnerability of this ancient city, provided a sequence that audiences all over the world found extraordinarily moving. 'There are no stars in *Seven Days To Noon*' wrote one critic in America, 'the only star is London herself'. And for those who know her, they will see her as they have never seen her before. It is something not to be missed!

Similar sentiments – some even detailing your sequence shot by shot – were expressed by film critics everywhere, from Toronto to Timbuctoo. But, with respect, it has nothing to do with 'production value'. That is something one hears about in Wardour Street, where money and grosses and percentages are a preoccupation of purely material minds. Your work in *Seven Days* was a creative contribution informed by poetic sensibility.

Director John Boulting took a small, Hitchcock-style cameo in the film – dressed as a vicar, standing in a London tube train into which Barry Jones stepped in an attempt to avoid pursuing policemen.

The Wooden Horse was a superior British war-set adventure. An impressive cast included Leo Genn, David Tomlinson, Peter Burton, Michael Goodliffe, Anthony Dawson, Bryan Forbes, Peter Finch and Anthony Steel. Steel recalled in an interview with the author in 2000:

It all came about by accident really, as when I left the army I met up with two friends of mine, Guy Middleton and Taffy [Hugh] Williams in Berlin. We were having a drink and they mentioned that Olive Dodds at the Rank Organisation wanted to create some new stars for the future. I eventually met with Miss Dodds and she asked if I'd ever thought about being an actor. I said, in all honesty, no! With that, she said she'd let me know. A month or so later I received a letter saying they wanted to offer me a two year contract. As the money was considerably better than what my old Army chums were making, it seemed like a good opportunity. I went into the 'Charm School'. I found it all a bit boring to be honest, as it was mainly acting theory, and said I really wanted some practical experience. They gave me bit parts in a handful of films including *The Blue Lamp* and *Poet's Pub* before I landed *The Wooden Horse*. I'd heard they were looking for an unknown actor to co-star. I met the director Jack Lee and got the part. It was a very successful film which allowed me to renegotiate my contract with Rank!

The movie tells the story of Stalag Luft III where British airmen Leo Genn and David Tomlinson are imprisoned. In a daring attempt the duo, with one more accomplice, Anthony Steel, break out of the heavily guarded camp by digging a tunnel from under their exercise title instrument. The second half of the movie concerns their attempts to reach Sweden, a neutral territory from where they can reach England. Jack Lee recalls:

Ian [Dalrymple – the producer] and I had read it and agreed we should do it. I learned later that Johnny Mills had wanted it too – we bid more for the rights than he did and so won it. Most of it was actually made in Germany, where we built the POW camp. I enjoyed making it even though a lot of it went over budget. The weather was a problem, but I was partly to blame with covering everything too much, and then there was indecision about the ending. We shot it in two different ways in fact.

1951 kicked off with Powell and Pressburger's *The Elusive Pimpernel*. Southern England was scoured for Regency houses, streets, palaces and crescents and many were found on the Marlborough Downs and in the Severnake Forest. Powell wanted a young talented cast to surround David Niven; Patrick Macnee, David Hutcheson and Robert Coote were amongst them, and he then turned his attentions to casting the beautiful women, and special auditions were held for ladies with beautiful bosoms – for the scene where the blindfolded prince is able to identify his lady friends by that certain part of their anatomy!

Powell wanted to shoot the French scenes in France, and in French. Korda had other ideas. Assistant Editor Noreen Ackland remembers:

There were quite a few differences of opinion on this film, as Mickey saw it as a musical. Korda wanted to re-make it as a drama. Then came the news of Margaret Leighton to play Lady Blakeney. Mickey hated Margaret Leighton, and said she wasn't a film actress. He couldn't stand her and made it known. It was Korda's casting, and the chemistry between the leads just wasn't there, though Korda kept insisting Mickey would love her as much as David Niven did – that was a lie. Niven hated her, and it showed!

Mickey was uneasy. He'd lost faith in the project. They eventually fell out over it all, and Korda stopped the shoot.

Powell felt uneasy at continuing working at Shepperton, a studio dominated by the Kordas, and felt that the safest option was to continue with the film as far away as possible, and they moved to British National studios in Borehamwood, and production resumed.

The Lady with a Lamp came from Herbert Wilcox, and starred Anna Neagle in the biopic of Florence Nightingale. A young assistant director on the film was Geoffrey Helman:

Many scenes were, of course, set in hospitals – and there were some quite gruesome sights; after all, war is never pleasant. Amongst the great number of casualties were soldiers' injuries that necessitated amputation. Herbert and Anna, during pre-production, visited the Star & Garter home in Richmond, west London, where there were quite a lot of amputees amongst the veterans. Herbert enlisted the majority of them to play extras in the hospital sequences. I have to admit that the crew felt a little uneasy about it all, and somewhat embarrassed that our director had recruited these disabled veterans as extras. The 'extras' thought quite the contrary and made jokes out of the situation, to try and help us overcome our embarrassment. They had nothing to feel embarrassed about, so why should we? It worked on screen brilliantly.

Incidentally, Herbert Wilcox gave a job on the film to John Brabourne as 'Technical Advisor on medals and decorations'. It was his first job in the industry, and he later went on to great success as a producer of such films as *Sink The Bismarck!*, *HMS* Defiant, *Death On The Nile* and *A Passage To India*.

Pandora and the Flying Dutchman was the first production from Romulus Films. Brothers John and James Woolf (sons of distribution pioneer C.M. Woolf) set up the company following John's departure as joint managing director of General Film Distributors (later Rank Film Distributors) in 1948, along with Independent Film Distributors. Independent would put up to 70 per cent of a film's budget, but ultimately fared badly. It was then the brothers decided to concentrate on producing themselves:

In a 1990 interview, John Woolf recalled:

Jimmy went to America to look for interesting proposals to bring back to England. The first one he found was Pandora which was to be directed by Albert Lewin. So we brought Lewin to Shepperton to make the film with James Mason and Ava Gardner. That's what started us off with Anglo-American productions because British films were then very parochial – the best were Ealing films and even they didn't sell in America.

Production assistant Jeanie Sims adds:

We worked around the clock to complete *Pandora*, as we hoped it would be the Royal Film Performance of that year. We actually lived in the Old House at the studio during this period as they still had the bedrooms and bathrooms there. The restaurant at that time was down on the ground floor and they would send up hot rolls and coffee in the morning for our breakfast. I'd then trot over to the bathroom and, one such morning, I heard Harry Miller [the best sound editor of the day] shouting 'Who's that?'. I called down that it was me. 'Do that again – that walk along the corridor'. I did. 'Stay right there, I'm going to get the sound crew' he said. He discovered that the sound I made walking was exactly the sound he wanted for the timbers on the boat in *Pandora*. And that's what you hear in the film!

They eventually decided to use *The Mudlark* as the Royal Film as it was a 'very British' picture all about Queen Victoria. I don't think it was a very glamorous picture to be honest, but there we are.

Following the great success of *The Red Shoes*, Powell and Pressberger decided, in 1950, to film *The Tales of Hoffman* which was, according to Powell, 'the perfect composed film, the film I had always dreamt about. It was the perfect combination of music, dance, song, acting, design and beautiful women.'

However, it was perhaps the most problematic film Powell and Pressberger embarked upon. Noreen Ackland takes up the story:

We filmed almost entirely on the giant silent stage at Shepperton, and there were some fantastic sets designed by Hein Heckroth. It was such good fun to be on the set, and it used to amuse me immensely when Robert Helpmann kept referring to Leonide Massine as 'that old plodder' because he was getting on in years! They were both of a similar age in fact. Daggers were drawn between those two, but mind you that probably goes back to *The Red Shoes* as in a scene Massine had to produce a knife, and with it he actually cut Helpmann's hand, but maintained it was an accident.

Though perhaps my abiding memory is from the end of the production. We ran the film, and those people who are familiar with it will recall right at the end Pamela Brown, as the poet's muse, had this wonderful piece of dialogue which she spoke beautifully. Mickey and I were quite proud of the finished film, but Alex Korda was horrified. 'No one will sit through this, and wait for that nonsense at the end'. Mickey was very upset and called Korda a philistine and other such names.

Korda was furious. 'You've gone too far this time Mickey', he said, 'and I shall see that you never make another film in this country'.

In fact, Mickey didn't make another film for a long time.

CHAPTER 8

THE LAST DAYS OF WORTON

Whilst Worton Hall continued in the shadow of Shepperton, it still managed to attract the leading film makers. And they didn't come much bigger than John Huston and Sam Spiegel.

Cecil Scott Forrester's *The African Queen* was a story Producer Spiegel was both excited by and cinematically confident of. Huston also saw the film as a sure-fire success; and hopefully one that would give him some financial independence.

'Columbia had bought the rights years before from C.S. Forrester,' explained John Huston in his autobiography *An Open Book*, 'planning to make a film with Charles Laughton and Elsa Lanchester. For some reason they didn't make it. Then Warners bought the property from Columbia for Bette Davis. They, too, never followed through.'

Spiegel and Huston set about pulling all the elements together. It would be a location film, in Africa. Katherine Hepburn was approached for the role of Rose Sayer. She was intrigued and excited by the book – and was also badly in need of another hit film. Huston then approached James Agee, a poet, novelist and film critic to write the screenplay. The screenplay was one thing that seemed to evade Katherine Hepburn, as production drew nearer, however Spiegel produced a first draft to her before she left for Britain, and as she described in her book *The Making of the African Queen*, she was not overly impressed.

> The first part was generally speaking OK. But from the love scene on it seemed to sag. The getting into the love scene seemed too abrupt and – well, no use in going into details. But I thought that there would be serious trouble with it.

Casting continued. Humphrey Bogart was not only an old friend of Huston, he was also an old colleague and Bogart had every confidence in Huston, adding 'before I met Huston, my range was Beverley Hills to Palm Springs.' Bogart and Hepburn were both on board and both now in Britain.

Horizon was to contribute part of the budget, and for the rest Spiegel looked to Britain, and John and James Woolf's Romulus Films.

'Sam Spiegel's company didn't have all the finance, only the American contribution,' recalled Sir John Woolf in a 1990 interview. 'Spiegel and Huston soon fell out because Sam was always running out of money. Sam was supposed to have paid Huston and Bogart out of the American budget, but the money hadn't arrived and I think Huston got very fed up. In the end I had to give the guarantee of completion to the American bankers (Heller and Company) myself.'

In fact, Spiegel never really had any American money at all. His deal with Romulus was seen as a means of paying for the below-the-line cast, crew and expenditure; whilst the so-called American money was to cover Bogart's $125,000 (and 30 per cent of net profits); Hepburn's $65,000 (and 10 per cent of net profits); Huston's $87,500 and Spiegel's $50,000 – that was all deferred. Heller and Company were to cover these costs but refused when Spiegel was unable to offer a completion guarantee. The film looked like falling apart, and Hepburn walked out, although somehow, thankfully, Spiegel managed to hold it together and convince his star to remain with it.

Whilst he had his stars, it seemed his director was fast losing his initial interest in the film and became more and more pre-occupied with elephants. Guy Hamilton was first assistant director and takes up the story:

I found John Huston to be a difficult director to work with as he really didn't have much interest in the film; he was fulfilling a contract with Spiegel and nothing more. His main concern was killing an elephant!

I don't know why but he had a fascination about killing one of these animals, and I remember going to see him in London at a suite in Claridges. I walked in and there was a man from Purdy [the gun makers] there, and the room was full of guns of all shapes and sizes. Huston was choosing his weapons for his 'safari'. Two weeks later we all left for Nairobi and all of the guns were confiscated! Elephants were protected there, and whilst there was a culling programme, one had to obtain a permit and the waiting list was something ridiculous like three years. Huston wasn't happy.

Then someone said to him that he should think about the Belgian Congo, as no permits were needed there. With that, Huston decided to move the location of the shoot.

He hired a little aeroplane and flew over the Congo until he spotted a herd of elephants, and marked the spot. It was in the middle of nowhere – miles and miles from any facilities or settlements. It was mad.

Katherine Hepburn shared Hamilton's feelings: ' … our camp, which was just being completed, [was] south down the Congo River about eight hours by rail and then west into the jungle by car another forty miles and no telephone. I can't describe my emotions', she wrote in her book.

There, as well as the extreme humidity, the cast and crew had to dodge snakes, scorpions, crocodiles, huge ants and tsetse flies. Guy Hamilton continues:

Our art director, Wilfred Shingleton, designed and built raffia huts for us all, which were functional if basic. Showering and bathing was near impossible and consisted of locally recruited women carrying pots of water to an overhead tank, which then provided the showers.

Like many others, I fell sick with chronic dysentery and was sent home a few weeks ahead of the end of the location shoot.

'The bottled water that was brought in for us to drink,' says Continuity Supervisor Angela Allen, 'was later found to be very polluted and everyone was down with dreaded illnesses and diseases – apart from Bogie and John who only ever drank whiskey!'

All were looking forward to returning home. 'Ah! Back home!' continues Hamilton. 'We all knew that Spiegel had yet to finalise a studio deal – and the unit were only a couple of weeks away from returning. He'd been going around all the studios in Britain to see which would offer him the best deal. Eventually, and mercifully, he settled on Worton Hall ... we could start work!'

The studio's largest sound stage had a tank constructed on it, as Hamilton explains:

One of the more amusing incidents during the production involved those awful leeches. When Bogie was pulling the African Queen through the water, he emerged covered in these horrid creatures. They were actually made of rubber and the damn things kept falling off! We recreated the sequence on the stage and a tank. The water was icy cold and my main concern was ensuring Bogie didn't freeze in it, so we had a constant supply of buckets full of hot water, and we'd tip them in. I remember Jack Cardiff [the DoP] kept shouting, 'That's enough – I can see the damn steam'.

Then came the close-ups for inserts. We needed a shot of real leeches you see, and Bogie wouldn't be involved ... so we hired a willing body! The leeches were brought over by a chap from London Zoo, and when he arrived he produced these tiny little things like worms. I was horrified and said that ours were more like giant slugs! 'Oh they're the same thing – these will swell up when they taste blood!'

Ah, well maybe our willing stunt-man would suffer that ... 'Ok' came the reply.

But then these damn creatures wouldn't take a hold and kept falling off. I then hit on the idea of laying our man on the floor or a table and putting the camera on top, looking down. Great! But then, the damn creatures sort of rolled over and went limp.

'Oh that's because of all the hot lamps', we were told.

So how could we get them to stick and draw blood? Lots of umming and aarring went on and it was suggested that maybe we should just draw a small amount of blood?

'Hang on', we said as we pressed needle tips into our stunt-man, 'this won't hurt', and once little drops of blood appeared, we nurtured the creatures into taking a sip. And it worked!

Studio Assistant Doris Spriggs adds:

> Bogart's body double was a chap named George Shock, and I remember paying
> him nine guineas for enduring the leeches! We all watched the sequence being
> filmed one Friday, and when I arrived in on Monday morning I discovered the
> tank – which was huge – had burst the previous night. My office was just inside
> the studio block, and was full of water, oil and all sorts. I'm not exaggerating
> when I say it's lucky it never happened whilst anyone was on the stage as it would
> have resulted in severe injury, or worse as the crane which was standing next to
> the tank was twisted like it was a hairpin, and the huge stage door was broken.
> We were insured and we could shoot other pieces around it whilst waiting for
> it to be repaired; including the waterfall sequence which was done on the tiny
> back-lot, and it included huge wooden buckets which could be loaded (and
> thus deposit) huge amounts of water. It was tremendously effective.

Everyone concerned with the film agrees, despite the ups and down and unpleasantness
of some of the locations, that it was one of the most enjoyable films they have ever
worked on. No doubt it had much to do with the stars.

Huston's secretary, Jeanie Sims, adds:

> On the last day at Worton, Bogie and Katie came in – they were in fact going
> back to America on, I think, the *Queen Mary* – and got absolutely drenched
> completing a part of the waterfall sequence. I remember Bogie coming over to
> me – soaked through – and said 'What is it with that John Huston. All the man

The exterior of the
large sound stage
today. (Photograph by
Andrew Boyle)

said to me was 'would you like to play in *The African Queen*'. The poor man was shivering and ready to leave for America. Both he and Katie had a terrific sense of humour! It kept us all going.

The African Queen was a sensation, and box-office gold. Spiegel was able to look his critics in the eye and smile. Chief among his critics was none other than Alex Korda, who famously said, 'A story of two old people going up and down an African river – who's going to be interested in that? You'll be bankrupt.' Humphrey Bogart went on to win his one and only Oscar for the film.

Cinematographer Jack Cardiff adds an interesting postscript:

On my previous film, *The Magic Box*, which was a prestigious picture for the Festival Of Britain, the producers offered us half salary with the other half coming from the box-office takings. It was a very nice film but not a financial success and didn't make a lot of money. So we never really got the other half of our money. So when the contracts for *The African Queen* were being drawn up, Sam Spiegel offered me a profit cut and I said 'No way!' and turned it down. That's got to be the silliest thing I ever did – it made so much money that I would have been a millionaire.

The final films to make use of Worton Hall Studios were Emeric Pressburger's *Twice Upon a Time* (which completed filming at Shepperton) and Compton Bennett's *The Gift Horse*.

In October 1951, Korda's massive loan from the National Film Finance Corporation in the 1940s was due for repayment. However, Korda declared that he could not afford to make a repayment without curtailing his production programme. Part of that curtailment meant the selling-off of Worton Hall.

The National Coal Board was keen to take over the site as a second Central Research Establishment base. The acquisition commenced in March 1952, and the contract between the National Coal Board and the British Lion Film Corporation was signed in May of that year. British Lion vacated the premises on 30 June, and the following day the acting director of the Central Research Establishment moved into his office in the old Manor House.

'It was a very sad day,' recalls Studio Assistant Doris Spriggs. 'Virtually the entire studio staff was made redundant – apart from studio manager John Bourne and myself. We were the only two kept on and transferred to work at Shepperton. The Coal Board intended to sink shafts across the land for experimental purposes – and that was the end of Worton Hall Film Studios.'

Fast-forwarding to the new millennium, the former studio site is relatively much the same, albeit now as an industrial park. The Old House is exactly as it stood during the studio's heyday, and is now a driving test centre. Many of the buildings on the lot are still in use: two of the former stages are factories; the old canteen and restaurant are workshops, as is the old wardrobe department; the former paint shops and power houses are still in use, and a number of new buildings have been constructed on the

The staff of Worton Hall celebrate Christmas with their much-anticipated annual pantomime. Studio assistant Doris Spriggs plays a fairy godmother (front row, far right). (Courtesy Doris Spriggs Archive)

site of the old silent stage and A stage. Sadly, however, the garden in front of the house is a little overgrown.

The former cutting rooms are in the process of being demolished; however, upon glancing through one of the windows a warm satisfaction can be gained when it is noticed an old film-can rack is still in place!

The occupiers of what was C stage are an equipment storage and transportation case manufacturing company called CP Cases. It's particularly gratifying to see on their website that they are proud of the history associated with their company's headquarters:

> In the 1940s and 50s, our building was a 'sound stage' within the Isleworth Studios complex. Legendary director, John Huston, completed the watery Congo scenes from the film *The African Queen* in our factory building. What a unique sight … Humphrey Bogart (who in 1952 won an Oscar for his performance) hauling the boat, *The African Queen*, through a tank of freezing water – covered in live leeches – not something we subject our visitors to! The Worton Hall site houses a 35,000 sq ft manufacturing facility.

Company Marketing Director Ed Sloper explained that at a recent party to celebrate the wedding of Managing Director Peter Ross, the whole factory was converted into a 'film set' with drapes and décor resembling perhaps much of that from *The African*

The Old House, Worton Hall. Front aspect as it looks today. (Photograph by Andrew Boyle)

Queen – and very appropriately, the film was running on a large screen in the corner of the building throughout!

Whilst the outside structure remains the same – apart from the addition of windows – a mezzanine floor has been added inside, though the original glass roof and sound-proofing are still pretty much in evidence, as is some of the original wooden stage floor and wiring.

There is still an air of 'something special' at the site. Echoes of film-making glory, maybe? Or perhaps just a rather nice place to be? One thing is for certain: its unique place in British film history will not be forgotten.

CHAPTER 9

THE '50s: TROUBLED TIMES

It was a certainly a case of 'leaner times' in the British Film Industry at the beginning of the 1950s. The wartime boom in film production and exhibition had ended. The BBC had acquired Lime Grove Studios in 1949. Denham Studios had closed in 1951 and ABPC sold their Welwyn Studios to a tobacco company the same year. The closure of Worton Hall Studios took place the following year, as did Rank Organisation's Gate Studios at Elstree. But there were still 4,597 cinemas in Britain with 4,220,700 seats – and that meant there was still a pretty big need for films.

In an attempt to assist the business, the Government introduced the Eady Levy, albeit on a voluntary basis. It was a way of redirecting some of a film's profit at the box office back into production. A small levy on each ticket sold, dependent on seat price and a minimum box-office take each week, was calculated to pump up to £3 million back into the industry each year. Named after the British Film Fund's architect, Sir Wilfred Eady, the scheme would see participating cinemas gain relief on their Entertainment Tax.

Ralph Richardson made his directorial debut with *Home at Seven*, a tight little British thriller based on a play by R.C. Sherriff, in which Richardson also starred alongside Margaret Leighton, Jack Hawkins and Campbell Singer.

However, all is not really as it was reported. Ralph Richardson didn't direct at all. Director Guy Hamilton explains:

If my memory serves me right, Alex Korda entertained Carol [Reed] and David [Lean] (Mickey Powell may have been there too) to dinner in his penthouse at Claridges where they were nicely bollocked for taking far too long –15 plus weeks – to shoot a picture.

Long schedules at the time, it must be said, had much to do with the unions. ETU (Electrician Trade Union) rules, for example, meant that gaffers were not allowed to go onto the next set and pre-light following the cameraman's instructions à la the Hollywood system. Consequently, film-makers would move onto a new set, sometimes very large ones, and the whole day would be spent lighting whilst the crew sat around.

Hamilton continues:

Alex tried to circumvent this by sending for Sir Tom O'Brien (Head of ETU) and offering to pay his gaffers £100 if they could change the rules. Sir Tom replied 'You're joking. My member's (of which there were 800,000) average wage is £15 and you want to pay fifty of them a hundred quid a week. Revolution! I'd be hung and thrown out of my own Union.'

Alex said he could shoot a picture in three weeks much to the merriment of those around the table and they challenged him to do so.

Alex picked *Home at Seven* which had starred Richardson on stage.

With two weeks rehearsal, and three weeks shoot, Alex engaged Ralph to direct the rehearsals in the vast composite set built by Vincent Korda, whilst Alex flitted off to America. It was always the intention that he would direct as Ralph was clueless and disinterested in film mechanics.

I was 1st AD and in rehearsal the only person who never knew his lines was Ralph who forever spouted large chunks of text from the play which were not in the film script. Alex returned and sure enough wrapped up the film in 3 weeks – despite having even fired the cameraman and re-shooting the first day's work!

Korda's emphasis was to be on intense rehearsal periods, and then – as Guy Hamilton says – a two week shoot. Alex came in on schedule, but preferring not to suggest he was in the director's chair on such a 'cheap' film, he elected to give Richardson the director's credit!

Following the tremendous success of *The Third Man* it was a dead certainty that Alex would again collaborate with Carol Reed. That came about in *Outcast of the Islands*, a Joseph Conrad story, in 1952. Hamilton confesses:

I really can't remember much about *Outcasts* in the studio, as all the fun was a lengthy location recce with Carol and Hugh Perceval to Singapore, one end of Java to the other, Bali (I nearly turned native and stayed there) up to Cambodia and Hanoi before rejoining Carol in Brunei (where in those days the Sultan hadn't got a pot to piss in. Oil had not yet been discovered. He and the family lived in a miserable little bungalow). John Wilcox, our cameraman, came out from UK joined by a couple of assistants from Singapore and we shot a huge amount of location material and footage with doubles.

ACT [the Association Of Cinema Technicians] then blacked the footage in the labs and Hugh Perceval, John Wilcox and I were summoned to Soho Square to be expelled from ACT for having worked with non union labour out there. This was, we later discovered, all a ploy to get Carol to join the Union. Alex Korda, with a contribution to ACT Blind Babies Fund, saved our skins and future. Carol never joined ACT but it marked the start of my lifelong fight with the unions whose power was finally destroyed many, many years later. They did a great deal more harm than good to the film business, and ACT & NATKE

[National Association Of Theatrical Television and Kine Employees] claimed to 'run' the business – they did their best to destroy the industry.

The union's stranglehold on the British Film Industry was both extremely strong and influential. It was later sent-up in the Boulting Brother's production of *I'm All Right Jack* at Shepperton in 1959.

Herbert Wilcox directed *Derby Day* with Anna Neagle and Trent's *Last Case*, which witnessed the return of Orson Welles to the studio.

'When I heard Orson was cast, I had my reservations because he did have a reputation,' says Continuity Supervisor Elaine Schreyeck:

> He liked a bottle of brandy to start with in the mornings, but you know he was quite amazing because he knew all about cameras, lenses. He once said 'Elaine what lens do they have on?'. I said whatever it was, and he said 'Right, so you're seeing me from here up to here'. He knew exactly how he would appear and so below a certain area (say his belt for example) he knew it wouldn't show so didn't worry about it. I was most impressed. He knew what he could get away with and totally changed my opinion of him!

A young up-and-coming actor by the name of Kenneth Williams was cast in a small role in the film. He obviously got on well with Herbert Wilcox because he was invited to read for a part in *The Beggars Opera* which Wilcox was next producing, along with Laurence Olivier. The actor was later elated to see that famed critic Dilys Powell singled out Williams in her critique of the film!

Geoffrey Helman notes:

> I was second assistant director on Beggar's Opera which also starred Stanley Holloway, Dorothy Tutin, Athene Seyler, Laurence Naismith and a whole load more.
>
> It was particularly notable because it shot in 1952, and was completed in 1953 – the year of Queen Elizabeth's coronation. Many Heads of State and Royals were flown in from all over the world for the event, and of course they had to be 'entertained' during the evenings of their stay. This film was chosen to be screened for the visiting Royals and dignitaries on one of the evenings. A terrific honour.

In another film, when well-off aircraft designer Tom Denning (John Mills) finds his daughter's current boyfriend is a bit of a nasty character he tries to buy him off, but ends up hitting him and accidentally causing his death when he falls. Instead of calling the police he dumps the body in a lonely spot on the road to the north, making it look like a hit-and-run accident. Weeks later there is still no report of the body being found, and Denning starts to go to pieces. He then lets his wife into his secret and the two of them start making enquiries, possibly making things worse. It was a tense and dramatic film, and called, appropriately, *Mr Denning Drives North*.

John Mills says:

People asked if I might have reservations in playing a darker role than those I'd played recently, such as in *Scott of the Antarctic* and *Morning Departure*. Well no, I didn't even hesitate. It was a terrific part, well written, and I was jolly well paid too! What more could I ask?

It was my first engagement at Shepperton, and I found the old house truly delightful and the dressing room suites were quite something – certainly like nothing I'd been used to before with a wonderful bedroom, sitting room and bathroom. It really was luxurious and they really looked after their actors!

I knew Alex Korda of old, and in fact, he and Merle Oberon used to live in the house where I have lived for the last thirty-odd years. I really couldn't sum him up in words. He is beyond mere words, if you understand what I'm saying.

Meanwhile, Zoltan Korda made his penultimate film, *Cry the Beloved Country*, at the studio for London Films and British Lion. Set in South Africa, the story centred on a white farmer (Canada Lee) and a black preacher (Sidney Poitier) who find friendship through linked family tragedies.

The film was widely acknowledged as one of the finest statements for racial understanding. Valerie Lesser takes up the story:

I was offered the job of Assistant Editor on the film, and so I went out to South Africa where I met Zoli Korda for the first time. He was a wonderful person – not quite as wonderful as Alex – but certainly something special. I can't tell you

how hard we worked. I never actually got to see anything of the country, just my cutting room! I was on the film for a year, it all wrapped up and I was due to move on to *The Sound Barrier*, however I was called back and remained for another six months in re-editing.

Zoli could be a very difficult man, but I always got on with him. He was, I must admit, a very dirty person in terms of personal hygiene, he always wore an old battered hat which he'd had since *Sanders of the River* too. There were certain rumours, going around the studio that Zoli and I were

Zoltan Korda and his well-worn hat! (Gareth Owen Collection)

more than 'just friends' shall we say. It stemmed from the fact that he suffered quite badly with arthritis you see, and on various occasions he would say to me 'if I lie down on the floor, will you take your shoes off and walk up and down my back?'. Of course, I did, and someone saw it on one such occasion and immediately jumped to the wrong conclusion!

Alex Korda played a lesser part in the productions than he would have done only a year or so earlier. His health was failing and he, by his own admission, was becoming an old man.

Following Powell and Pressburger, and Launder and Gilliat, David Lean next made the move from the old Rank Independent Producers to join Alex Korda's company at Shepperton, with *The Sound Barrier*. Lean's Associate Producer, Norman Spencer, explains:

> Korda was very happy because, with David, he now felt he had a royal flush; with the likes of Carol Reed, Powell and Pressberger and so on. He was an absolutely wonderful man, hugely charismatic and quite unique in the history of the British film industry. His was erudite, spoke several languages, was extremely well read and knew the film-making process back to front. Several years before when I was a young assistant director working on a film called *Night Without Armour* at Denham, the director fell ill for two weeks, and Alex came down from his office and took over. How many studio chiefs could do that?

'He was a lion of a man', commented David Lean in his official biography, on Alex Korda. 'Grey hair, nearly white, the appearance of being tall – it was something to do with his presence. An enormous personality.'

Lean continues:

> He could take any subject and talk on it for twenty minutes. You can't imagine how wonderfully exotic I found him … it was always fascinating if you spent an evening with him because you never knew who was going to drop in. He had a penthouse flat at Claridge's. I remember one evening being there and who should come in but Anthony Eden, who was Foreign Secretary. Alex knew all these people and would go after titles for people. He once said to me 'You are going to be in the Honours List. You are going to get a CBE, I know that, but for goodness sake don't get married and it'll happen some day.'
>
> Carol Reed had already been made a knight you see, but it took me twenty more years!

In July 1952, British Lion asked the Board Of Trade for financial assistance in building more stages at Shepperton. They agreed, and in early 1953 E, F and G stages were completed and ready for business. Korda and the British Lion Board were confident that they were over the worst. How wrong they were.

Fifteen films were to move into production in 1953. *The Ringer* was the third in Korda's 'experimental' low-budget programme, which he again was set to direct, albeit no doubt without taking a credit. Guy Hamilton recalls:

Having proved his point with his first low-budget film, Alex said up next was *The Holly and the Ivy*. Again I was the 1st AD; and I was asked to stay on for another.

I had been under contract with Alex for some years, and it was coming up for renewal (again). Carol Reed had previously said that he felt Alex ought to give me the chance to direct one day and each time my contract came up for renewal (at Christmas time) I mentioned it, and the response was inevitably that there were too many directors around and not enough good assistants, so it never happened. But this time, with a bit of blackmail and a lot of help from Carol, I was to get my break – to direct the next quickie. Carol suggested *The Ringer* – a trusted old warhorse by Edgar Wallace. He had been Wallace's assistant both on stage and when his plays were transferred to film. Carol said, 'Always make a comedy thriller as your first film – you'll miss some of the laughs, some of the thrills but with luck there will be enough left for you to be allowed to make another film.'

Wise words. The list of first time directors who never made another film is endless. I shall always be deeply indebted to him.

The cast included Herbert Lom, Donald Wolfit, Mai Zetterling, Greta Gynt, William Hartnell, Denholm Elliott and Dora Bryan. Not a bad group of 'contract artists' at all.

Shooting early in the year, the film fell foul of the so-called Shepperton Fog. Guy Hamilton continues:

Being in the Thames Valley, we were very susceptible to mist and fog from the river. In the late afternoons it would seep down into the studio and into the stages! We'd have maybe 50 arc lights to try and 'fight' the fog but the scenes always looked as though they were set in thick London smog. Therefore, on foggy days we'd wrap at 4p.m.

Hamilton wasted no time in his new role as director, and followed up with *The Intruder* for British Lion and Producer Ivan Foxwell. The superior thriller starred Jack Hawkins, Hugh Williams, Dennis Price, George Baker, Dora Bryan and, as a very nasty abusing stepfather, Edward Chapman – who was later better known for his comedy roles, particularly opposite Norman Wisdom. George Baker recalls:

Guy had a small part in the film for which he thought I might be right. My agent, Jimmy Fraser, arranged everything so that I could do the film without working on matinee days, as I was on the West End stage at the time. I was playing a young officer who had to walk into the officers' mess and over to the

Commanding Officer, played by Jack Hawkins, and say 'Group Headquarters would like you to phone them sir.'

Jack was standing by the bar. I had a long walk from the door to the bar. We rehearsed and everything went well. When we were about to film, the doors were closed, the bell rang out, the red light went on and everything fell silent. Turn over. Action. Off I went. Half way through my walk I realised I had not the faintest idea of the words I had to say. I didn't dare stop, so I just walked on. As I approached I saw Jack looking at me. He turned to Guy Hamilton and said 'I'm so sorry Guy, I'm not quite sure what you said … ' My relief was indescribable. Jack had realised my plight and thrown me a lifeline. We were to set up again from the top. As I turned to leave, Jack gave me a wink. The rest of the take was fine. In one of my next little scenes, with George Cole, Guy gave me an enormous close-up. Jimmy Fraser later got permission to show a clip from this film to Bob Lennard, casting director of ABPC. It changed the course of my life for the next few years, and I'll always be grateful.

Carol Reed returned to film *The Man Between* with James Mason and Claire Bloom, whilst Herbert Wilcox turned his attentions to Joseph Conrad's *Laughing Anne*, who was played by Margaret Lockwood, and music-hall star Ronald Shiner played Nobby Clark.

'Ronald Shiner,' adds Assistant Director Geoffrey Helman, 'was one of the highest paid comedians in the country. He made the leap to films in the mid 1930s and didn't look back. When Herbert was thinking about casting him in the film, it became clear that money was of no real importance. Ronald had his mind set on a new Bentley, and he said to Herbert Wilcox that he would star in the film in exchange for a new car. The deal was agreed there and then.'

The year was to mark the twenty-first anniversary of London Films, and indeed Alex Korda was fast approaching sixty. Time to take stock, perhaps? Alex certainly gave the impression that it was perhaps time to wind down his day-to-day involvement in the film business. That notwithstanding, to mark his company's coming of age, *The Story of Gilbert and Sullivan* was commissioned. Robert Morley and Maurice Evans were set to play the two writers behind some of the best-loved operettas. An all-star supporting cast was assembled with Frank Launder and Sidney Gilliat producing – Gilliat also directed. Sidney's brother, Leslie, was associate producer:

The idea was to film with two units, and George More O'Ferrall would direct all of the stage work, and Sidney – my brother – would direct the main part of the film. I sat down for three weeks trying to work a schedule out, because there were certain guest actors who appeared on the stage and then in the main film, and so on. It was a nightmare trying to balance the schedule and contain everyone within a reasonable time period. I finally got it to work and pulled the unit together, however George fell behind but I worked them Saturday and got them back on sync. We had completed about three-quarters of the shoot, with this double schedule, and Alex [Korda] said he didn't like it – the reason being that we had Hein Heckroth as our art director, and he'd painted these most wonderful backdrops and paintings but he didn't quite know how to design all of the sets and as such got the scale all wrong. Alex was quite alarmed and said 'We will start this again from the beginning'. I had to reschedule the whole thing for all of these sets and was getting a migraine a day in the process, though Alex brought in Vincent Korda who was really terrific and whilst Hein kept the credit, you'll see on the film that we give 'Special Thanks' to Vincent.

The Red Beret came from American producers Irving Allen and Albert 'Cubby' Broccoli. Director Terence Young was engaged by the producers to work on the script, whilst they set about casting the leading role of the paratrooper officer. They opted for the biggest box-office draw they could think of, Alan Ladd. Coincidentally, Ladd had just walked out on Paramount when they refused to meet his demands for more money. Through a mutual friend, Broccoli organised a meeting with Ladd. The actor listened to their pitch, and said he was interested. However, the producers soon realised that it was Ladd's wife, Sue, who would ultimately be the one to convince as she was the total controlling force in his life and career.

The Story of Gilbert and Sullivan on the River Ash at Shepperton. (Courtesy Leslie Gilliat)

They made a substantial offer of $200,000 plus 10 per cent of profits to Ladd's agent, Lew Wasserman. He turned them down. It was then they decided to contact Sue Ladd directly. She was furious when they told her Wasserman had refused their offer. She called the producers to the house, along with Wasserman and proceeded to tell the agent that, as he hadn't secured Ladd anything like what they were offering on any other pictures, she wanted her husband to do this film. Sue Ladd was keen to visit Europe, and as this film was scheduled to shoot at Shepperton, she felt it the perfect opportunity – an all-expenses-paid holiday. It was also suggested it be a three-film deal instead of just one. Everyone agreed, although Broccoli and Allen had barely enough money to pay their rent let alone Alan Ladd for three pictures.

Columbia Pictures were keen to work with Alan Ladd, and when they heard he was attached to the project, were keen to step in.

The film was a great success financially, though perhaps less so critically. However, Allen and Broccoli were up and running and greater things were to come for them.

John Huston, following his production of *The African Queen*, chose to film his next project in Britain too, at Shepperton. John Woolf recalled in a 1990 interview:

After *African Queen* Huston didn't particularly want to go back to America. We had just read *Moulin Rouge* by Pierre la Mure and thought it would be a wonderful follow-up. I gave it to Huston to read but he didn't want to do it. We nagged him until eventually he asked us who we envisaged as Toulouse-Lautrec. We told him we thought José Ferrer would be perfect. Huston said that if we could get him, he would think about it again. Ferrer loved the idea, so then Huston agreed to do the picture.

Moulin Rouge was to film on location in Paris before transferring back to the studio. Cinematographer Ossie Morris remembers:

I received a call to ask if I'd go and meet Huston at his suite in Claridge's. I thought it was some sort of mistake, why would Huston want to talk to me? I was in awe of Huston to be honest. We talked about various things and he asked me what I knew about the French impressionist painters. I didn't know that much, but he then asked if I was familiar with Lautrec. I said I wasn't and, naturally, felt I'd blown it. However, a few days later, John Woolf asked me to meet him again. I was offered the picture.

Huston said he wanted the film to look as though Lautrec had shot it. We were filming on Technicolor and the colours really were very bright and garish, so I knew I had to somehow subdue them. I began experimenting on a small stage at Shepperton. I asked the art director to construct a few set façades for me, and then the wardrobe department to dress a few extras in costumes. I then pumped smoke onto the stage and added a fog filter to the camera. We shot some footage. In those days, it would take two weeks before rushes were delivered because of the complicated tri-strip processing techniques. When they came back, I showed John and he said 'I think we're onto something.' I felt quite happy!

Technicolor were not at all happy with what the film makers were doing. Morris adds:

> At a screening of some footage in paris, George Gunn, the customer liaison chief at Technicolor, said that we were desecrating everything that they stood for, and that we were killing definition and colour and he asked we do not proceed using this technique. John listened, and then turned to me, 'what do you think Ossie?' I replied that I thought the technique was what we were after. With that, John turned to the Technicolor people and said 'thank you gentlemen, and fuck you'.

A little while later, the head of Technicolor in the USA wrote to the director and his cameraman, having seen the finished film, offering whole-hearted congratulations for the 'magnificent job' they'd done and for 'enhancing the name of Technicolor'.

The main *Moulin Rouge* set was built at Shepperton, on one of the large sound stages, and that presented a new challenge for Ossie Morris with his colour technique:

> The smoke really had to be very thick, to the point of not really being able to see much with the human eye as the colour system somehow cut through the smoke. The camera could see more than I could. As a result, the electricians – whose union the ETU was run by Communists! – a couple of days in, came out on strike claiming they couldn't work with all the smoke. The studio personnel manager involved the doctor who said that there wouldn't be a problem so long as the sparks could drink plenty of milk. These gigantic tea urns appeared, full of milk, and were taken up into the gantry. They also insisted the stage door be opened at lunchtime as it got quite warm in there too. I was quite against this, as it was one thing pumping smoke in, but to get it to settle and create the desired effect was a time consuming process. And it wasn't as though people were on set during lunch! I realised I couldn't win with the ETU, so agreed to opening the door. However, ten minutes before lunch ended, I'd go back and close the doors to start the fog machines.

There was another person in the 'colour story' on the film. Huston – right at the very beginning – brought in Eliot Elisofon as 'special colour consultant'. He was *Life* magazine's top photographer, and was considered perhaps one of the world's finest photographers. The idea was that he could experiment with colours and filters, put him on the film and give him a credit, and indeed, it was agreed that *Life* magazine would feature the making of the film considerably, thus generating valuable publicity.

Elisofon was described as a 'supreme egotist' and made no bones about believing he was the greatest photographer living. Everyone liked him, but equally found him quite unbearable. It was when his *Life* article and photo spread appeared that things turned slightly sour, however. Morris remembers:

> According to the article, it was said that Eliot photographed the film. Well, he did take stills but didn't 'photograph' the film, that was my job as DoP. It was worded in an ambiguous way – very crafty. And of course, people thought he was actually responsible for the look of the film. Huston went mad and cabled the magazine and it got quite nasty between them. Meanwhile, I wrote to Eliot and said I felt he behaved disgustingly, but he just blamed *Life* magazine. It was all very unfortunate.

'Unfortunate is not the word,' adds Huston's secretary, Jeanie Sims, 'as Ossie was robbed of an Oscar nomination. *Life* magazine did a lot of damage in fact. Ossie was the talk of the business for his photography, but the American Academy failed to recognise him when we all knew he should have got the Oscar, let alone a nomination.'

In the event, the unique use of colour employed was, according to Huston, 'the best thing about the film'.

On several occasions during the film, Huston went in for close-ups of Lautrec's hand drawing. The hand was actually that of artist Marcel Vertés, who had made something of a name for himself in Paris by making very good forgeries of Lautrec!

CHAPTER 10

THE GOOD DIE YOUNG

By 1954, British Lion was massively in the red. Alex Korda felt it like a lead weight around his neck, and confessed he wanted to 'get out' of the company. However, he did whatever was in his power to try and keep the company afloat, to the point of making himself ill in the process.

Production continued at the studio. Wendy Toye, a talented dancer and choreographer as well as theatre director, explains how she was given her big film break by Alex Korda:

Alex saw my short film, *The Stranger Left No Card*, on the recommendation of actor Bill O'Brien as he'd told Bill that he was looking for a short film to accompany a feature. Alex was so impressed that he sent the film to Cannes, and it won a prize! I then met with him and, after talking a little about *The Thief of Baghdad*, he offered me a contract as well as one to the star of the short, Alan Badel. I liked Alex very much and we got along tremendously well. Everything about him was exuberant – his manner, his surroundings, his cigars.

My first directorial assignment for Alex was with *The Teckman Mystery* which was a rather good spy story based on the BBC series by Francis Durbridge.

I realise that I and Muriel Box were the only two women directors working at that time, but I never once felt intimidated nor found it difficult. You see in my work as a theatre director I knew the job and through my work as a choreographer, I knew many of the technicians. I wasn't shy to ask advice either and that really boded me well.

Wendy stayed on to make a second film that year, with a cast including Kenneth More, Shelagh Fraser and Mandy Miller – *Raising a Riot*. Wendy continues:

Oh that was a charming story, based on a book by Alfred Toombs, and produced by Ian Dalrymple and Hugh Perceval. Hugh was so English with a great bristling black moustache and a ginger suit [inside which he had pockets stitched – one for paperclips, and another for rubber bands], and the story goes he was out in the Far East somewhere looking at locations, sitting straight up-right in his old, thick suit, with his briefcase and umbrella between his legs in the intense heat.

Business carried on at Shepperton, and the return of John Huston with *Beat the Devil* provided much comfort to the staff at the facility.

'The man who wrote the book was called Claude Cockburn,' says Huston's secretary, Jeanie Sims. 'He was in fact a member of the Communist Party. In order to get the book published, he used the pseudonym James Helvick. Huston had come across the book whilst we were preparing *The African Queen* and liked it immensely.'

A little time later, Huston gave the book to Humphrey Bogart, who ran his own film production company with Morgan Maree.

'More or less accidentally,' reveals Jeanie Sims, 'Bogie thought John wanted to do it and immediately bought the film rights for $10,000. John then assumed it was Bogie who wanted to do it. It was all quite a mix up and that's how it came into being.'

Huston met novelist Truman Capote, who had written the dialogue for *Indiscretion of an American Wife* and Huston told him how he needed help badly. Capote agreed to help.

'As soon as we arrived on location in Italy on the Friday (with shooting starting the following Monday) we were told there was to be a party,' says Director of Photography Ossie Morris. 'It turned out to be a party to tear up the original script, and that's when we were introduced to Capote!'

'The money for the film was being put up by a conglomerate of backers that included Roberto Haggiag, the Woolf brothers and Bogart himself', revealed Huston in his autobiography:

> In Rome I told Bogie that we were in a desperate situation. 'We haven't got a script, and I don't know what the hell is going to come of this. It may be a disaster. In fact it's got all the earmarks of disaster' I said. 'Why John' said Bogie 'I'm surprised at you. It's only money!' That stiffened my back. You can't argue with somebody like that, so we went ahead to do the best we could.

Jack Clayton, later a distinguished director, was production manager and proved invaluable in helping the director stall for time:

'We didn't want the company to know that the script wasn't ready, so Jack announced that I didn't want the actors to see their lines until just before we shot a scene,' wrote Huston. 'He explained that I was experimenting with a new technique, trying to encourage a more spontaneous approach to the material.'

'It was the case that we'd be filming one sequence and Huston and Capote would be upstairs frantically writing the next,' reveals Ossie Morris.

Although David O Selznick had absolutely no involvement with the film, he was married to one of the stars, Jennifer Jones. That was excuse enough for him to interfere. Almost daily Huston would receive cables, concerning the production and Selznick's recommendations for scenes etc. Some cables ran to ten or twelve pages.

'One day after receiving a particularly long cable,' revealed Huston, 'I sent him a cable back. Page one answered various points he had made. I then omitted page two and jumped to page three. From then on I answered anything he asked me by replying "Refer page two, my cable X date". It drove him right up the wall!'

Peter Sellers made a little known contribution to the film, in post-production. Jeanie Sims explains:

> Peter was a great friend of John's, and was known as a great mimic. I can't quite remember if it was because we had to re-cut for the censor, or whether it was just extra looping that was needed, but Peter was drafted in to perform four of the voices on the soundtrack, including Bogie who had suffered tooth damage in a car accident and couldn't record some of his own dialogue on location.

The film wasn't well received. Huston described it as being 'ahead of its time'. Its off-the-wall humour left viewers bewildered and confused. A few European critics hailed it as a masterpiece, but all these years on it has developed a cult status.

It was a busy year for Guy Hamilton, who directed both *An Inspector Calls* with Alastair Sim as the titular inspector, based on J.B. Priestley's acclaimed stage play, and *The Colditz Story*.

'*The Colditz Story* was totally studio-based,' reveals Assistant Director Peter Manley, 'and we built the castle courtyard, facades and the recreation areas with barbed wire and so on, all on the backlot. It was quite a set.'

'I remember one day, Pat Reid, who had written the book and been a prisoner there,' says one of the film's stars, Sir John Mills, 'walked across the studio with me to

The Colditz Story featuring Bryan Forbes, John Mills and Lionel Jeffries. (Courtesy Canal and Image UK Ltd)

the backlot. When he saw the castle he really did not want to go in, as he thought it so real that he was frightened to step inside. That says so much for the art director.'

Guy Hamilton adds:

We had a wonderful Art Director on that film called Alex Vetchinsky. He was legendary actually. In the recreation of the prison on the lot, we'd obtained a number of photographs actually taken by prisoners. Vetch was able to piece them together to form what was almost an architect's plan of the courtyard, and any gaps that existed he could work out from the surrounding structures what they would likely be. He was a genius. The courtyard was so impressive that I added a few other little sets around it, allowing us to shoot through windows and get some wonderful camera angles.

'Some of the cast had actually been prisoners of war themselves,' continues Peter Manley, 'so there really was a gritty reality to the film that worked extremely well.'

The Belles Of St Trinian's was the first, and some say the best, in the series of the misadventures of the girls' school. Alastair Sim played headmistress Miss Fritton. (Courtesy Canal and Image UK Ltd)

Frank Launder and Sidney Gilliat set up the first in what was to become a tremendously popular series, *The Belles of St Trinian's*. Based on cartoons by Ronald Searle, the wonderful hellcats of St Trinian's girls' school, or rather 'School for Young Ladies', were brought to life with great comic emphasis by the producer and director team, who also wrote the screenplay.

In *The Belles of St Trinian's*, the arrival of a Sultan's daughter, Princess Fatima, at England's famous and prestigious school precipitates even more chaos than usual. Her father's horse, Arab Boy, is due to run at the nearby Gold Cup so Clarence Fritton, bookie brother of headmistress Millicent (both played wonderfully by Alastair Sim), ensures that his own daughter is on hand to report progress. At the same time the Barchester police have planted Sergeant Ruby Gates (Joyce Grenfell) as a teacher, and the Ministry of Education are sending a third inspector down after the previous two disappeared without trace.

Second Assistant Director Joe Marks remembers:

The cast were excellent, and few today could come close to Alastair Sim.

The girls were all very talented young ladies from Italia Conti or the Peggy O'Farrell Agency in East London. They did, however, used to like gambling both on set and off, and we had several poker schools running at once! However, we thought as long as it kept them quiet we shouldn't really mind … though when they once broke hockey sticks over each other, over a bet, then things did get a little touchy!

George Cole, who played Flash Harry, says:

I think this one was the best, with Alastair as the headmistress and the brother. I worked with Launder and Gilliat quite a lot, and they always gave me a good script, though terrible money. If Alastair was in the film it was even worse as he got most of it!

The first film's script had a real understanding of farce, though it was all there in Searle's original cartoons to, as it were, be drawn from. They lost it a bit in the sequels.

Hobson's Choice was perhaps an unusual choice for David Lean's follow-up to *The Sound Barrier*. Lean's Associate Producer, Norman Spencer, says:

It really was an old theatrical chestnut of a play, and I really couldn't see how we could make a decent film out of it. Korda and David were minded otherwise. We met the author, Harold Brighouse, who was rather ancient then, he didn't know what to make of all of the excitement, wished us well and went back home and so David and I started work on the screenplay.

I think another reason David was keen to do this was because he would often say how Noel Coward once told him 'never to come out of the same hole twice' – meaning always do something different. After *Sound Barrier*, this was certainly different!

Casting was the next step. David Lean was keen on Roger Livesey for the part of Hobson, whereas Spencer had his mind set on Charles Laughton. Lean consented to meet Laughton. Within minutes, the director was convinced he had his lead.

'Charlie was a fascinating man', said David Lean in Kevin Brownlow's biography of him. 'We used to finish work at Shepperton and go to a pub and have a beer and chat about things. I found him immensely entertaining and interesting.'

Robert Donat was cast as Willie Mossop, and having played alongside each other in *Henry VIII*, both actors were thrilled. There was one condition to Donat's participation, on the part of the film's insurers – he had to pass a medical examination. As we have read earlier, Donat suffered from chronic asthma attacks, and the insurers were obviously worried as to whether he was fit enough to star. 'It was always when he was tense, or before he started a picture that one of these attacks would hit', recalls Norman Spencer. 'This time is was a very serious attack. In the event, the sheer stress and worry Donat suffered over the impending examination – he badly needed the film for financial reasons – brought on a serious asthma attack. The doctor deemed him unfit. He was devastated.'

Faced with a potential delay in production unless the part was re-cast, rapidly, Lean turned to his old friend John Mills:

I was on holiday in the South of France with Rex Harrison, and our wives, and was out water skiing one day when Rex pointed to a man on the shore, waving

John Mills rated *Hobson's Choice* as his favourite Shepperton film. Charles Laughton (right) played the titular Henry Hobson. (Courtesy Canal and Image UK Ltd)

something at us. It was a telegram from David [Lean] which read 'Dear Johnny. SOS. Deep Trouble. *Hobson's Choice*. Please Come Back.' Of course I knew the play, and loved it. I love comedy. So I joined up! It really is my favourite film. And that haircut I had to have, which was really ghastly, was David's idea. What a genius he was!

After a week on location in Salford, near Manchester, the crew returned to the studio. One of the most famous sequences in the film is the 'moon walk' when a totally drunk Hobson comes out of the pub, and is transfixed by the sight of the moon reflected in a puddle. Art Director Wilfred Shingleton constructed a huge set at Shepperton where cobbles for the street were pre-cast and produced with indentations to ensure the deep puddles which were crucial to the sequence. The film was well received, both by the critics and the box office. In May the Government referred the decision as to whether the Receivers should be brought in at British Lion to a Cabinet Committee. Alex Korda lobbied hard, but alas to no avail. On 1 June 1954, the Government, through the NFFC, applied to the courts to appoint a Receiver. The entire company's share capital had been wiped out, and over £2 million of taxpayer's money – the NFFC loan – written off. As the accountants sat scrutinising every single line in the company's books over the coming months, they would find many 'improper dealings' and 'misappropriation' of funds. The Paris office and South African office had significant sums of money involved, whilst the Rome office of London Films – under the control of Peter Moore, who had in 1950 been accused of embezzlement – was a cause of great concern. When the accountants moved in, Moore resigned and delivered to London a cheque for $50,000 of 'missing funds'.

Korda was not to be kept down, however. He worked out a deal with Robert Dowling in New York for a $15 million fund to finance a new slate of productions for London Films, and through John Woolf negotiated a distribution deal for them in the UK. It seemed that whilst the roar of British Lion had been stifled, Korda was, yet again, set to rise phoenix-like. Norman Spencer explains:

Korda had been, I would say, happier at Shepperton than he was at Denham – which were the studios he built. His career was waning somewhat now with the collapse of British Lion, but he had been working with some of the best film-makers in the business and that was something very special. He never managed to fully recover from British Lion's failure, nor replicate the success he had there, with the likes of *The Third Man*. But he was still very much a 'mogul'.

Meanwhile, Shepperton continued with business as usual, under the management of the administrators and the newly formed British Lion Films, which replaced British Lion Film Corporation.

Henry Hathaway returned to the site of his former success, and hatred, to shoot his next film, *Prince Valiant*, with James Mason, Janet Leigh, Robert Wagner and Victor McLaglen in this Arthurian tale. 'It was a horrendously difficult film to make,

Aerial photograph of Shepperton in the mid-1950s. H stage dominated the top-right corner of the lot. (Gareth Owen Collection)

especially with Henry Hathaway directing!' comments Leslie Gilliat, the film's associate producer:

> We had a wretched Viking boat, which was actually an old lifeboat which our art director had converted, which we had to get up to Scotland for the first location. I had previously been right the way around Scotland with Henry and the cameraman (who he fired three times during the production!), and we settled on locations on the Isle Of Sky, Braemaer, Fort William before moving to North Wales then on to Tenby in South Wales.

I remember when we were up in the Isle Of Skye, the weather was really awful and we had this awful supposed Captain, from Glasgow, who quite obviously knew very little about handling a boat and to our horror, when the boat started rocking in the rough sea, he yelled out 'Abandon ship'. The engine then failed, before this idiot then dropped the sails (which landed on the poor extras) and we were drifting out to sea! We managed to get the engine started again, and the extras began rowing.

1955 was a busy and healthy year for the studios with fifteen productions going on to the stage floor, several with the involvement, in some shape or form, of Alex Korda. *Three Cases of Murder* was one such film. Wendy Toye, who directed *The Picture*, describes:

It was a film of three parts. It was a little story I read some time before, bought the film rights and Sidney Carroll wrote the screenplay for me. Hugh Pryse was cast as an eccentric old man, who was in a picture gallery, and in looking at one particular picture – of a house – started murmuring to himself that it needed a light in the window. He walked towards to the picture and as he drew nearer we heard the footsteps change from the gallery floor to the gravelled path of the house. He knocked on the door, which then opened and he went in. Leueen MacGrath and Alan Badel were inside the house – Alan's character was a taxidermist; all very macabre. Alan took a light that the old man was carrying, killed him and put it in the window. He then came out of the picture, looked back and said 'Oh dear, now we need another light to balance with it in the other window'. Just then a young girl (Ann Hanslip) came alongside him and looked at the picture, she lit a cigarette with a lighter. He saw the lighter, put his arm around her and walked her into the picture – so you knew she would be murdered next!

The idea behind the film, which Alex Korda instigated, was to make Alan Badel a leading man. He was to play a small part in the first segment, a more substantial role in the second segment and then the lead in the third segment – which was my segment. However about halfway through the shoot, I was asked to go up and see Alex in his office at the studio. He told me that whilst he was thrilled with what he'd seen so far, he couldn't sell the picture to the backers without a bigger name – Alan wasn't big enough on his own; so he brought in Orson Welles. But the trouble was that Orson insisted his segment, *Lord Mountdrago* written by Somerset Maugham, should appear third. That was the film in which Alan played an equal ... and so the order was changed and the whole idea about expanding Alan's part in each segment was lost.

David Eady (*You Killed Elizabeth*) and George More O'Farrell (*Lord Mountdrago*) directed the other two episodes. *Cockleshell Heroes* was the name of Cubby Broccoli and Irving Allen's next film. Colonel H.G. (Blondie) Hasler RM, led ten marines into Bordeaux Harbour during the Second World War, where they planted limpet mines on German warships. The tiny boats they used were shaped like cockleshells, hence the title. José Ferrer – who had recently starred in *Moulin Rouge* – both starred and directed. Howard, Victor Maddern, Anthony Newley and Dora Bryan rounded out the cast; the script was written by Bryan Forbes, with assistance from Blondie Hasler.

'José was a wonderfully kind and gentle man,' says Dora Bryan. 'I remember he came to see me in a play in Chichester, and then afterwards came backstage and asked if I'd like to play Myrtle in *Cockleshell Heroes*. Of course, being an actor himself he was sympathetic to us other actors, and it made for a wonderfully friendly and happy production.'

A few on the other side of the camera held a slightly different opinion though, as camera operator Ronnie Maasz recalls:

José was a rather irascible bloke, and he soon fell out with Ted Moore who was lighting the picture, over a little error on a day for night sequence. Ferrer seized on it, and had Ted replaced by John Wilcox who was the second unit cameraman.

We had spent so much time meanwhile in getting close up shots of José Ferrer, to the detriment of the other actors I might add, particularly Trevor Howard – who in fact disappeared for three days to get away from him – and time was running out! Irving Allen was mindful of this, and in fact wasn't too friendly towards Ferrer. I remember one day in rushes, Irving came in, determined to put a rocket up, watched what had been shot and declared 'it is an absolute load of crap'. Ferrer responded by turning around, and saying 'I'm never going to speak to you again you dirty bastard', leapt over the seats and out of the theatre. He didn't speak to Irving again. It was said Irving tried to have him removed

The premiere of *Geordie*. From left to right: Bill Travers, Frank Launder, Bernadette O'Farrell and Leslie Gilliat. (Courtesy Leslie Gilliat)

off the picture but his contract was so watertight it proved impossible. I do know that Ferrer left before the end though, as Irving shot the last sequence, on location in Fulham.

Geordie, starring Bill Travers in the titular role, was a film developed by British Lion, now in administration. Launder and Gilliat were keen to move it in to production. Leslie Gilliat recounts:

> That was touch and go as to whether we'd be able to make it actually, as the receivers were in with Alex. We were fully prepared to start and I had to attend a meeting with Alex and others, and they asked if I could delay the film.
>
> I explained that we couldn't as we had the perfect weather and it was very much a location film. They gave us the go-ahead and for the first ten days it poured with rain!
>
> The chap from Film Finances [the completion bonders] announced he was coming up, and thankfully the sun was shining that day and we shot like mad. He said he could see we were going to be alright and let us carry on.

Summer Madness was the next film from David Lean. He claimed it as being his favourite. 'I have never yet made a picture,' he later wrote, 'with any object in view other than to translate into moving pictures a story, a character, a love affair or a place which appeals to me and I would like to show others.'

'It was a story which Korda suggested,' remembers Norman Spencer, 'which was a play called *The Time of the Cuckoo*. We read it and thought it needed opening up and the greyish lead characters needed re-writing, much to the disgust of the play's author, Arthur Laurents, who demanded his name be removed!'

Korda and United Artists backed the film, which starred Katherine Hepburn in one of her best performances, alongside unknown Rossano Brazzi who was cast in Rome after the director was bowled over by his good looks and charm. Only pre-production and post-production work was to be completed at Shepperton. Before leaving for location work, Korda offered Lean one piece of advice:

> Just remember that if I'd chosen some of the highly respected directors of the present moment, they would seek out all the side streets of Venice and never take a shot of the Grand Canal or the Piazza San Marco because that would be a cliché. They're not a cliché for nothing. For God's sake don't be shy of showing these famous places.

Lean wasn't. He regarded Korda's advice highly.

Peter Handford was sound recordist on the film throughout its location shoot, and recalls vividly that, 'David was a little nervous of his first location film – it was all location. Though when we were out in Venice, he said to me "Peter I'll never work in a studio again" ... the film really opened up a whole new dimension in David's film-making.'

The Good Die Young was the next production to move into the studio. Camera Operator Ronnie Maasz recalls of the film, which was directed by Lewis Gilbert:

> It was my first big feature picture as a freelancer, and I was very over-awed with the star line-up of Laurence Harvey, Richard Basehart, Gloria Grahame … we were mainly Shepperton set, though I do recall we had a couple of nights on the London Underground in central London. It was a very joyous production.

Off on a comedic adventure was Stanley Windrush (Ian Carmichael). We learn that he has to interrupt his university education due to being called up towards the end of the war, and quickly proves himself not to be officer material. This leads him to meet up with wily Private Cox (Richard Attenborough) who knows exactly how all the scams work in the confused world of the British Army. It all combines for a wonderfully funny film, *Private's Progress*, from the Boulting Brothers; directed by John and produced by Roy.

Ian Carmichael remembers:

> I was a jobbing actor in the West End as a review artist, and we review artists were never really cast in films, but then I landed the lead in the play *Simon and Laura*. Muriel Box was about to direct a film version, saw me, and offered me the film – against a lot of opposition. Shortly after that, the Boulting Brothers rang up my agent and said that they had two projects that they'd like to talk to me about: *Private's Progress* and *Brothers in Law*. I went over to Shepperton to meet them, I thought they must have seen the play and had been impressed and was feeling rather proud of my new success with he play. They said 'no, it was because we saw you in a mime-sketch review at the Globe Theatre!'
>
> John directed *Private's Progress* and Roy produced. I thought 'God this is very funny' and rather fancied myself playing comedy. The other thing I liked was that the brothers would never start a film until the script was perfect. There would be no last minute changes, and coloured pages slipping in [used to indicate re-written script], it was all agreed before the camera turned.
>
> I later worked with them in those roles reversed too; there was very little difference as they were both very sensitive and hugely talented, and they worked so well together.
>
> The film gave me my first big role, and John coaxed me to give a 'film performance' as I'd be so grounded in theatre you see, and only ever had a day here and there in films before. It was a terrifically fun film, and one that really launched my career. The Boultings signed me to a five film agreement. There wasn't a set time on the contract, and it wasn't exclusive to the point of me not being able to work for other producers, they just had first call on me.

Kenneth Griffith was another member of the Boulting repertory group, and explained his part in the film as a rather backward character:

Privates Progress. Richard Attenborough (L) and Ian Carmichael (R) receive direction from John Boulting. (The Boulting Brothers Archive)

My phone rang. It was Roy Boulting who said 'Kenneth we're making a film about Britain's contemporary questionable spirit – as reflected in aspects of army life – a comedy. I have to tell you that all of the better parts have gone; but there is a smallish part of a somewhat backward chap. Perhaps you'd like to call round and collect a script?' I did just that. But I then asked if they would consider doing me a favour.

'What favour?' they asked.

'Well I've looked at the part very carefully and the truth is that you could cut every word of dialogue that my character speaks and it wouldn't even affect anything that anyone says.'

'Well?'

'I was wondering if you would allow me to cut all my lines but still place me in the same position in the groupings that I would have had if I was speaking?'

I think it was John who asked why I was always so difficult, and I explained that I wanted to really make the character so backward and shy, that he really couldn't speak – but he did think. With combined exasperation, they agreed. I did ask, however, to keep the last line that my character had: 'Please sir, how do you get a medal'.

The performance edged me into film comedy.

The British Lion Film Corporation was allowed to continue trading in 1954, but when the Receivers moved in, it was without a figurehead.

In March 1955, the managing director of the NFFC, David Kingsley, was appointed a director of the studio, and in 1958 he would subsequently become managing director. But for the ensuing eighteen months, Shepperton would bob along without any real direction being decided. It was run as a 'going concern' and some £1.5 million was recovered through the company to its debtors.

Filming went on, and *The Baby and the Battleship* came from director Jay Lewis.

'That was fun! I received the script up at ABPC at Elstree, and it really wasn't very good,' says Sir John Mills, 'but I did think there was "something" there. So I asked if I could have it re-written. They readily agreed, and I gave it to Bryan Forbes to work on. He came up with a really funny script, and as such we secured Dickie Attenborough and Michael Hordern to co-star with me, and Bryan.'

Having served his apprenticeship at the studio in the 1930s, sound recordist John Aldred returned to the studio, and recalls how it had changed in the intervening years:

I returned to work for John Cox, who was the Head of the Sound Department at that time and during the Korda years. He had already received an Oscar for best sound on *The Sound Barrier*, directed by David Lean. Unlike MGM Studios, which I had just left, Shepperton was extremely busy and I was one of thirteen sound mixers employed at that time. Five of us were allocated to post-sync, sound effects, music, and re-recording, and there were seven production mixers working either in the studio or on location.

In contrast to 1937 when I was last there, the studio had expanded significantly. A new Sound Department had been created with post-sync and re-recording theatres, workshops, and garages for the sound trucks. Another cutting room block had been added, which contained its own review theatre for running rushes. The old 1932 shooting stage was now the music scoring stage, and was also used for sound effects and post-sync. A changeover from photographic recording to magnetic recording had recently been completed. Of course, the huge Stage H, known as the silent stage, had changed the studio landscape, but the main shooting stages A B C and D had not changed at all. The original roofs were still there, but were not strong enough to support any weight, so sets and lighting gantries were built up from the floor as in the 1930s. The restaurant and bar were no longer situated in the old Manor House. A new canteen and restaurant building had been built which could cater for staff as well as hundreds of extras. A new and much larger powerhouse was also in evidence.

A cluster of smaller stages, E F and G, had also been built in 1953 to compensate the loss of Isleworth Studios that had been closed down. These new stages were built primarily to attract television productions, and had their own offices and dressing rooms.

It seemed that, despite the troubles with British Lion and the studio's uncertain future, it still remained busier than its competitors. One of its next successes was from the Launder and Gilliat stable. Leslie Gilliat explains:

> *The Green Man* started off as a play which Frank [Launder] and Sidney [Gilliat] wrote in the late 1930s, but it only ran a short time because of the blitz. Then they heard that Laurence Olivier was looking for a new play, and took this one on – updating it – and it had a very good run in the West End.
>
> It was then decided to turn it into a film, and Alastair Sim was going to direct it. We felt that he needed a good right hand man to work alongside him, and Bob Day was appointed. However, right at the last moment, Alastair cried off and didn't want to direct. So we were in a situation where we had Bob Day thrust forward; but we felt he really wasn't experienced enough to handle the whole film on his own at that time. Basil Dearden stepped in and he and Bob directed the film between them, although he let Bob take the full credit.
>
> The Old House became *The Green Man*, and it was such a versatile building which I used many times, including in *The Great St Trinian's Train Robbery*. It was marvellous as you didn't need to hire generators or anything. It was all there!

A Hill in Korea was written by Ian Dalrymple (who was also executive producer) and Anthony Squire (who was also the producer). Cast member George Baker remembers:

> We were to make the film in Portugal and the whole cast had been signed for eleven weeks; we were then to come home and finish the film at Shepperton. It was cheaper to keep us all there rather than pay airfares back and forth to England. The actual location was miserable; miles from anywhere in the middle of sand dunes. The heat by midday was almost unbearable. We were based in Lisbon and had a two hour drive to work every morning and, of course, two hours back at night.
>
> Director Julian Amyes had cast Michael Caine, with whom he had done a television play in which he had given a wonderful performance; but now here, he was without a single line to speak. I tackled Julian and Anthony about the sense in bringing a good actor over from England for eleven weeks and not giving him a line to speak or a scene to play. The upshot was that we devised a scene which included him and I have always been a little pleased that I suggested the scene and wrote the first lines Sir Michael spoke on film.

We returned to England and Shepperton to complete the film. The art department had built a replica of the temple. The monsoon lashed down from water hoses above our heads. The mud was muddy and the film had been hard work, but rewarding.

Richard III was a production that would secure its star an Academy Award nomination, along with a BAFTA for Olivier, and also for Best Film and Best British Film. It was a triumph for London Films. Olivier recalls, in his autobiography, how joyous a production it was:

Our location work was followed by thirteen weeks at Shepperton Studios. I adored every moment of the picture's making and have always felt quite happy about the result.

The Hide Out was a Rank film, based out of Shepperton, as director Peter Graham Scott recalls:

John Temple Smith offered me the direction of this small British film. It was a cold winter and Mimi [Peter's wife] and I needed a new boiler for our house. The three week shoot provided us with central heating! It was a typical second feature of the period, about the panic caused in London by an outbreak of anthrax traced to a smuggled consignment of stolen furs. Most of it was shot around the docks, but John had secured some second hand sets at Shepperton, so the interiors were played in oddly elegant surroundings, giving the little film, starring Dermot Walsh, Rona Anderson and Ronald Howard, considerable production value.

Ken Annakin directed two films that year, *Three Men in a Boat* (the second filmic version of Jerome K. Jerome's story to lens at Shepperton) and *Loser Takes All*. However, he reveals that he was preparing to shoot another story altogether with Alex Korda around, what was to be, the end of his control of British Lion a couple of years earlier:

Alcock & Brown was (and is) a terrific story. Captain John Alcock and Lieutenant Arthur Whitten Brown, in a modified Vickers Vimy IV made the first non-stop aerial crossing of the Atlantic. They took off from Lester's Field, near St. Johns, Newfoundland on 14 June 1919 and landed 15 June 1919 at Clifden in Ireland. The time for the crossing was sixteen hours, and twenty-seven minutes.

The news of the adventure spread like wildfire and the two men were received as heroes in London. For their accomplishment they were presented with Lord Northcliffe's *Daily Mail* prize of £10,000 by Winston Churchill who was then Britain's Secretary of State. A few days later both men were knighted at Buckingham Palace by King George V for recognition of their pioneering achievement.

It was all set-up. All agreed. Kenneth More and Denholm Elliot to star. Set designs by Vincent Korda. Three more days to prepare, and we were to begin shooting. But the blow fell; Alex Korda's British Lion was bankrupt. The film was cancelled.

After being somewhat disappointed, to say the least, *Three Men in a Boat* was a subject that attracted me, and I had a script written by my friend, actor Hubert Gregg.

Sydney Box, who was now my agent, made a deal with John and Jimmy Woolf to finance the film. There was one condition – I had to cast Laurence Harvey instead of Hubert Gregg in the lead. I knew I was being disloyal, but it was the only way to get the picture made. David Tomlinson was also cast, and I don't think he and Larry Harvey were what you might call bosom buddies, as on the first day, when Larry walked onto the stage, [Tomlinson said] 'Here comes the last of the great whores of the London stage!' And here was I with a ten week schedule ahead of me, with Larry, David and Jimmy Edwards all sitting in a boat!

The film called for a lot of location work, on the River Thames, during one of the worst summers I ever remember. We started shooting in May and I remember, in September, I was trying to get some sunshine shots with three doubles sitting in a rowing boat. Both Jimmy and John Woolf visited the location and tried to force me into shooting in grey drizzly weather. Eric Cross, our lighting cameraman, persuaded me that an open air comedy would look nothing without brightness, but he would shrug his shoulders when pressed by the Woolf brothers. A difficult situation for any caring director.

I had terrific actresses to work with – Shirley Eaton, Jill Ireland and Martita Hunt, a superb comedienne in her own way. I recall a fun cricket match with Robertson Hare, Miles Malleson and A.E. Matthews; they were all great stage actors and could make fun out of any situation you put them into. The match was set on a smooth grassy area within sight of Shepperton's sound stages. We picked-up quite a few shots using the River Ash on the lot, with big Brute lamps lighting for sunshine.

One day, in the commissary at Shepperton, Charlie Chaplin walked in. He was preparing for his film *A King in New York*. Larry jumped up and introduced himself and then guided Chaplin to our table. I recall being so pleasantly surprised that he seemed to be a very normal, polite person – quite serious and not at all like his screen image.

Then came Ken Annakin's second film of the year – *Loser Takes All*. The Mediterranean-set comedy starred Glynis Johns, Rossano Brazzi and Robert Morley. It has been criticised as being a 'misfiring comedy'. Annakin explains:

I worked very closely with Graham Greene on the script in Monte Carlo. He was the easiest person in the world to work with, and we were in complete accord. He was not, however, happy with the movie at the end as Rossano

Sir Alexander Korda in his studio, shortly before his untimely death. Ill health had made him seem older than his years. (Gareth Owen Collection)

Brazzi was a ridiculous piece of casting forced on us by Sir Arthur Jarratt (then heading British Lion). [Brazzi had recently been cast by David Lean in *Summer Madness*]. That part should have been played by Trevor Howard or David Niven. Brazzi brought a phoney romantic air to the ex-accountant role, and although a good actor, he didn't have one ounce of British style comedy in his make-up.

We shot the interiors, including all the casino scenes at Shepperton. George Perinal photographed, but only the interiors. He'd worked a lot at Shepperton and was, by now, feeling old age creeping up, so he liked to stick to lighting studio interiors – we had another cameraman for the location work – at which he was a master.

I remember Graham Greene arriving at Shepperton one day when we were shooting a scene with Felix Aylmer, as the Devil, tempting Brazzi. Graham said it should be more 'screwballish'. I agreed. With Niven or Howerd, Aylmer could have lead the scene into a much more fun and crazy encounter. Alas, it never was.

Also that year, Ealing Studios was sold by Michael Balcon to the BBC for use as television film studios. Highbury Studios in Islington, north London, no longer needed by the Rank Organisation for film production, was given over full-time for television production.

However, the news of Alex Korda's death perhaps overshadowed everything else that was going on at Shepperton, and in the business in general that year. It was the end of an era.

CHAPTER 11

UNDER NEW MANAGEMENT

'Sometimes I think of retiring,' said Sir Alexander Korda in 1955, 'but then I go to my desk again and I know I cannot.'

What was to become his final programme of films included *A Kid for Two Farthings*, *Summer Madness*, *Storm Over the Nile* (a re-make of *The Four Feathers*), Laurence Olivier's *Richard III*, *The Deep Blue Sea* (a filmic treatment of Terence Rattigan's play), and *Smiley* from Anthony Kimmins. Some were made at Shepperton, others where finance dictated.

'*Storm Over the Nile* was predominantly studio,' says Ian Carmichael, who played Tom Willoughby. 'Anthony Steel and Larry Harvey went out on location to Africa briefly, but the rest of the cast was Shepperton bound and great use was made of footage from the original version, also directed by Zoli Korda, *The Four Feathers* which I believe Alex Korda licensed – from himself!'

In July 1955 Alex suffered a heart attack. Despite shrugging it off as 'minor' it took a full three weeks before he was on his feet again, to any degree, and he then retreated to the south of France on his doctor's orders.

Six months later, he was admitted to hospital for 'an examination' as he described it. The following day, January 23rd, it was announced Alex had passed away during the early hours, having suffered a massive heart attack.

When Alex Korda died, the British film industry stood momentarily silent. One of its greatest influences had passed. His great success had, in later life, been overshadowed by many failures. He had lost control of British Lion and Shepperton, yet with his usual charm and charisma, he continued in production, stitching together finance wherever he could get it. Despite only being in his fifties, in his last years he was nevertheless 'an old man'; in appearance and in outlook.

'Alex was unique,' adds Wendy Toye, reflecting on her working relationship with him. 'You can't really describe his genius, nor his charm, in mere words. He was a one-off.'

Norman Spencer agrees:

> Alex possessed immense charm and charisma. He knew the film-making process in-side out. He could step on to the stage floor and take over direction of a film, just as easily as he could head a studio and all of its troubles. When he died, a massive hole formed in the film industry. I can't stress enough how big. And no one has come close to filling it, and I doubt they ever will.

In the words of Michael Powell, simply – 'Alex was a great man'.

His funeral was held at Golders Green Crematorium on 27 January 1956. Four days later a memorial service was held at St Martins-In-The-Fields in central London, lead by Laurence Olivier.

Alex had decreed, that on his death, London Films should be liquidated. He left a mere £385,684 in his will. After tax and death duties it was whittled down by some £158,160. But what happened to his personal millions? It is interesting to note that, from 1950 onwards, Alex had made regular trips to Zurich, Switzerland. His last trip was made three weeks before his death.

In February 1959 – some three years later, and legal wranglings resolved – Sir Alexander Korda's ashes were buried in a private plot at Stoke Poges Memorial Gardens in Buckinghamshire, close to his son Peter's home. A discreet memorial stone, bird bath and stone seat – with the Korda coat of arms carved – form the tasteful, peaceful resting place of Britain's movie mogul. And it is but a mere stone's throw from Denham Studios, where he enjoyed so much success.

1957 witnessed the birth of perhaps Shepperton's nearest 'franchise' of films – with the second of the *St Trinian's* comedies, *Blue Murder at St Trinian's*. After the success of *Belles* in 1954, it was only a matter of time before Launder and Gilliat put another film into production and the famous school song was heard again. Leslie Gilliat reveals:

> Sidney wrote the words to their theme song, which reflected the fun and chaos that would later be unleashed. However, in the first film *Belles of St Trinian's* (which I didn't work on) you couldn't hear the words of the song and I thought this was a great pity. Therefore for *Blue Murder* I asked that the words of the song appear at the bottom of the titles, and have a bouncing ball move across them.
>
> Then of course we had the complaint that everyone watched the bouncing ball and not the credits!

> 'Maidens of St Trinian's
> Gird your armour on.
> Grab the nearest weapon
> Never mind which one!
> The battle's to the strongest
> Might is always right.
> Trample on the weakest

Glory in their plight!
St Trinian's! St Trinian's!
Our battle cry.
St Trinian's! St Trinian's!
Will never die!

Stride towards your fortune,
Boldly on your way!
Never once forgetting
There's one born every day.
Let our motto be broadcast
"Get your blow in first",
She who draws the sword last
Always comes off worst.'

Sidney Gilliat (1954)

We had an Italian location on *Blue Murder*, and so the authorities requested a script for approval, thinking that we were going to portray an Italian as a murderer, given our title!

By the time production was winding up, it became obvious that we would be making another in the series and I thought ahead to all of the costumes – gym slips, skirts, knickers, hats and so on – and of course when you finish a film, you haven't any money to pay for storage facilities. I went to see George Rochell who ran the vaults at Shepperton, and asked him if he had an empty vault. He said, unofficially, yes and so I stored all of the costumes for the next film.

The legendary director Otto Preminger next made two films: the first being George Bernard Shaw's *Saint Joan* from a script by Graham Greene.

An all-star supporting cast was assembled, including Richard Widmark, John Gielgud, Harry Andrews and Richard Todd. However, tyrannical director Preminger searched half the free world to find the perfect Joan of Arc. After a much-publicized contest involving some 18,000 hopefuls, he chose unknown, and untrained, Jean Seberg. She was, in fact, grossly miscast and the critics savaged her performance. Sound recordist Peter Handford explains:

Preminger had a reputation for being a bit of a monster, and deservedly so too! I got along with him fairly well though, because I stood up to him and gave him back as good as he gave me. And it was a difficult production without any added problems from him. However, at the end of the shoot, he came over to me and handed me an envelope. 'You're underpaid' he said and walked off. In the envelope was £200 – a fortune in those days. I've never forgotten – he was quite sweet underneath after all!

Sound mixer John Aldred recalls a near-fatal accident during filming:

> The burning at the stake was almost for real. The flames were a little higher on the
> take than on the rehearsal, and Jean got her hair and eyebrows singed! In addition
> the large crowd were causing problems. They wanted extra payment for waiting in
> line to get paid at the end of the day. The previous day many had to wait one hour
> for their pay. So Otto Preminger quickly filmed all the long shots of the crowd in
> the morning to get his master shots, and sent the crowd home at lunch-time!

Preminger next turned his attentions to *Bonjour Tristesse*. He cast Seberg again,
though giving her a more colourful, and disturbing, role as the manipulative teenage
temptress, Cecile, opposite Deborah Kerr and David Niven.

Lucky Jim was an acclaimed story by Kingsley Amis. The Boulting Brothers were
very keen to produce a film adaptation; however, they were beaten to the film rights,
as Ian Carmichael recalls.

> There was a triumvirate of people – Patrick Campbell, his wife, who I believe
> was a publicist, and Charles Crichton – who secured a film deal with Amis, and
> left the Boultings feeling a bit miffed. However, the triumvirate worked through
> British Lion and secured backing for the film from them. I did talk to John and
> Roy about being offered the lead and whilst they had some reservations about
> the script, they were happy for me to take the film.
>
>   I didn't particularly care for Charlie's way of working. Whereas the Boultings
> would whisper in my ear, he would stand behind the camera and shout. We
> had been shooting for two weeks when I realised the Boultings were really not
> impressed by the rushes that were coming through, and called a meeting of the
> Board of British Lion. Charlie Crichton and his team were removed from the
> production, which the Board were entitled to do, and the next week John and
> Roy took over – with John directing.

Produced by, directed by, starring, written by and scored by Charles Chaplin, *A King
in New York* was for Chaplin a very personal project, and one he chose to base at
Shepperton. Chaplin was a very hands on film maker, some say too hands on. But he
cared deeply about his material, as sound mixer John Aldred confirms:

> Charles wrote and conducted the musical score for the film with meticulous
> care, if rather old fashioned in style. When the film's editor remarked that one
> section of music was too long and did not synchronise with the picture, Chaplin
> refused to make another take. He just said 'Re-cut the picture!' During re-
> recording, his wife Oona sat in the theatre making a patchwork bed cover and
> offering comments. We always stopped for morning and afternoon tea breaks,
> and a tea trolley from the canteen was wheeled into the sound department.
> Charles and Oona lined up with the crew in the queue. In those days a cup of
> tea cost around 2*d* or 3*d* and it amused us when Charles only had a £5 note!

Roy Boulting's next production was *Happy is the Bride* with Ian Carmichael, Janet Scott, Cecil Parker, Terry-Thomas and Joyce Grenfell.

'John wasn't involved,' says Ian Carmichael, 'as Roy directed it for producer Paul Soskin. I hadn't worked with Roy as a director before, only John. I had no need to worry though, it was hugely enjoyable.'

Rounding off the year, meanwhile, was a gentle comedy from producer-director team, Michael Relph and Basil Dearden, *The Smallest Show on Earth*.

Jean (Virginia McKenna) and Bill (Bill Travers) play a young, struggling, married couple. Out of the blue they receive a telegram informing them that Bill's long-lost uncle has died and left them his business – a cinema. They pack their bags and head off in expectation of selling the cinema; however, they discover it's falling apart, and is run by a comically incompetent staff – including Peter Sellers, Margaret Rutherford and Bernard Miles – who seem to have worked there forever. They set out with a plan to sell it, but things don't quite go to plan.

'The exterior of the Bijou cinema in the film,' explains Associate Producer Leslie Gilliat, 'was actually constructed especially for the production in between two railway arches in Kilburn, north London. The whole building – in the story – would shake from its very foundations up when a train went past, and so it was rather comical.'

The Smallest Show on Earth staff – Bernard Miles, Bill Travers, Margaret Rutherford, Virginia McKenna, Peter Sellers and Leslie Phillips. (Courtesy Leslie Gilliat)

In December 1957, Sir Arthur Jarratt was appointed president of the Kinematograph Renters' Society, and resigned his position at the NFFC. David Kingsley, already a director of the studio company, was appointed Jarratt's successor as managing director of Shepperton Studios.

Meanwhile, the studio had, through a second debenture, announced proposals to finance a modernisation plan for A, B, C and D stages. The company had made a modest profit of just over £17,000 at the end of the financial year ending March 1957.

The Bijou Kinema façade was constructed between two railway bridges in Kilburn, north London. (Courtesy Leslie Gilliat)

1958 was an important year in the Shepperton story. It was made known, though not very clearly, that the NFFC wanted to 'get out' of their investment in British Lion and sell the studio. No one stepped forward. It was then that an offer was made to Launder and Gilliat, via their agent Christopher Mann. Effectively the film makers were told that they would be acceptable as purchasers.

Then came a call to the Boulting brothers, as Roy Boulting recalled in an interview shortly before his death:

> There was only one major independent distribution firm left at this time, and that was British Lion. When Korda was advised to pack in, they [the NFFC] ran British Lion for about a year and a half, with David Kingsley, as [director and then] Managing Director. He referred to his records of films made, and it was discovered there were two film-making partnerships who had a pretty good financial record working at the studio. One group was Frank Launder and Sidney Gilliat, and the other was the Boulting Brothers.
>
> Kingsley said he was desperate to keep British Lion going for the independents, and asked us to join him. The idea of film-makers to run a distribution firm, that also owned Shepperton was very exciting. If only they'd had a circuit of cinemas, we'd have wiped the floor!

For a nominal salary, Launder and Gilliat and the Boutling Brothers were invited to join the Board of British Lion and Shepperton Studios and, in addition to their managerial commitments, would also be allowed to continue making films. Production fees would be very minimal, with deferments and share offerings taking their place.

Roy Boulting explains:

> David didn't want us just for the films we'd been making at Shepperton and contributing to the distribution arm. He needed people who could guide and advise the Board on filmmaking, the talent to be encouraged, the scripts that should be made into films. 'You chaps' he said 'have your own jargon, talk in terms a lot on our side of the business don't understand. You use the same language, will be able to talk to them and vice versa' he continued, his gaze unblinking. 'I'd better tell you right away that there won't be much money in this for any of us, certainly not at the start. The company is still in a loss situation. The tax payers' £600,000 gives it just one more chance. But it's the bank's line of credit that has made production possible. However, if you do take the job on, you'll get a stake in the Equity – you'll become part owners – and if, between us, we manage to pull the company around – and I believe we can – then that stake may be worth more than a bob or two – ultimately.'
>
> We were faced with a programme of films that had been made before we joined the board, which were pretty disastrous, and I think Kingsley realised this. In three years however, we turned the whole company around and were making a profit.

Although the NFFC said it did not intend to sell its shares in British Lion they did, a few months later, according to Roy Boulting, 'explore theoretical ways of making their shareholding available to the Board should, in the following year, they choose to exercise their theoretical right to sell their interest.' However, the Secretary of State for Trade decreed that the Government would not attempt to sell their shares in the company for the remainder of the Board's five year contract – and, in fact, suggested the contracts be extended to six year ones, expiring in 1964. Roy Boulting adds:

> We did not hesitate to focus the attention of Parliament and the media on the less attractive restraints the Combines attempted to impose. In the next few years, films were referred to the Monopolies Commission. This obliged both [combines, Rank and ABPC] to be on their best behaviour for quite a time. That and the popularity of so many of Lion's films at the box office safeguarded our ability to resist their desire to gobble us up! But it wasn't easy. As the saying goes, the price of liberty is eternal vigilance.

It seemed that the company was safe, for the time being at least. Douglas Collins was swiftly appointed chairman and managing director of British Lion Films and British Lion Studio Co Ltd.

The rejuvenation of Shepperton was spear-headed by the modernisation of the four stages, as Oscar Garry, the architect, explained the process:

> The studio company had felt for some time that the method of set rigging involved far too much wastage of manpower and that unnecessary studio space was lost by the use of tubular scaffolding for the erection of sets.

Demolition work got underway in 1957 for new stages at the studio. (Courtesy John Aldred)

The Directors felt that changes must be made and a brief was given to the architects to take down the roofs and modernise the four stages. The brief was rather indefinite … the question of what load is likely to be hoisted up on any truss member or grid is again a matter of opinion. It is also a matter for discussion as to what degree of soundproofing co-efficient for walls and roofs will give reasonably good practical working conditions inside the stage. On investigating, it was found that a practical and economical superimposed load would be about half a ton at any point on a 6 ft grid and that the sound reduction coefficient should be 45 and 55 decibels for roofs and walls respectively. A timber catwalk system was arranged on a 30 ft square grid between which the walking boards were fixed to ease handling the dead chains and securing them to the steel girders. It was decided to build a 6 ft wide gantry round the perimeter of each studio below catwalk level so that lighting and backing rails could be incorporated and the space used for storage of lighting gear.

From a production point of view the floor was also a problem, as it had to be free from squeaks and fairly firm. It was, of course, expected to be absolutely straight and level. In all four stages, new floors were laid and the tongue and groove softwood finish was oiled ready for use.

The ventilation system was entirely redesigned to give the maximum possible fresh air intake, and points were included to which flexible trunking may be attached for air to be taken to any point at floor level.

In covering the roofs, 12 ½ miles of felt were laid, 27 miles of glass quilt was used to soundproof the inside of walls and roofs. Half a million nails held down 40 miles of boarding, over which is suspended 525 tons of structural steel. The total time taken was just under nine months.

One of the new stages opens for business in 1958. (Courtesy John Aldred)

H Stage in the distance with new stages E, F and G and the new powerhouse in the foreground. (Gareth Owen Collection)

Harold Boxall, managing director of the studio company, wrote that:

> With the reconstruction of four major stages completed, Shepperton now stands as the largest single unit available for film production in Europe. By any standards it is efficient, economic; it is a studio with a great tradition of service and technical supremecy – it has a fine record of achievement in every branch of production – a reputation management, producers and technicians can share with pride.
>
> In 1952-53 we had to decide whether to replace the stages we had lost with the disposal of Isleworth Studios with three new stages at Shepperton – the block we now call E, F and G. My colleagues supported my belief that these new stages would play an important role in the history of Shepperton Studios, and so it proved. For last year, faced with the enormous task of reconstructing four main stages, it was the far sighted decision made five years previously to build the new studio block which kept Shepperton in production. Without these magnificently equipped stages, Shepperton might have closed down completely and only those in the production industry understand what that can mean to a studio.

Production did indeed continue. The Boultings lensed *Carlton Browne of the FO* which was their first film to feature Peter Sellers:

> John Redway, a great friend who also represented my brother John and I, said to us 'Do you ever listen to *The Goon Show?*' We hadn't. He said 'there's a chap there called Sellers and I think he's a brilliant comedian'. So John and I listened to the next episode, and saw what Redway meant. We met Peter. I was just about to start shooting *Carlton Browne* and thought, let's have a go with him, and in the meantime let's write him in for the much more solid and interesting part of the shop steward in *I'm All Right Jack*, a story we had recently acquired. So began our partnership with Sellers.

Val Guest next moved in with *Life is a Circus* starring Flanagan and Allen, along with the rest of the Crazy Gang. Camera Operator Ronnie Maasz says:

> The nice thing about working with Val is that he always did his homework, and every morning he would bring in a board and easel on set and on it would be the whole day's shooting – long shot here, close ups here and so on – he knew exactly how he'd shoot it and that was truly great for us crew. He knew what he wanted, and we knew what he expected. I must say though that Val had all the trappings of being a real flash lad – camel hair coat, collar turned up and a cigar with a band on. Great fun!

Jack the Ripper was a film that came from producer-director team Robert S. Baker and Monty Berman. Both produced, with Baker directing and Berman photographing. Baker notes:

> We actually wanted one of the small stages at Shepperton for the production; however they were all being used. The studio management therefore suggested that if they gave us a large stage, and we only used half of it, they would charge us the small stage rental!
>
> I don't think we ever actually 'crossed the halfway line' though it was tremendously helpful to us in having the extra space just to hold things like chairs and props, ready to be brought on to the set.
>
> *Jack The Ripper* was a co-feature, rather than a B feature, and so we kept an eye on the international market into which we could sell the film.

Production Manager Peter Manley adds:

> Oh yes, around that time there was a slight easing on censorship and what you could shoot, and to take advantage of this we filmed a number of scenes purely for the continental market.
>
> For instance, there was a theatre dressing-room scene and in the British version we shot the girls in their petticoats, making-up and getting changed. We

Robert Baker (third from left) and Monty Berman (second from right) produced and directed *Jack The Ripper*. Here they share a drink with their cast on their pub set at Shepperton. (Courtesy Robert S. Baker)

then shot the foreign version in which all the girls were nude. So after the first take, I'd call 'clothes off' and we'd go for take two. Of course this technique was only employed in a few scenes, but it certainly seemed to appeal to the more liberal European market!

I always found it amusing that when we were due to finish at 4pm one Friday, all of the electricians and stage hands who weren't needed, freely stayed on a little later whilst we did one of our 'continental' sequences. No overtime was requested!

'All of the East End alleyways were filmed at Shepperton,' concludes Baker, 'and we found some locations within the vicinity of the studio that passed for London streets. It all worked rather well.'

Director Ronald Neame next turned his attentions to *The Horse's Mouth*:

Some years before, Claude Rains had handed me a copy of *The Horse's Mouth* by Joyce Cary believing the character of Gulley was absolutely right for him. I remember struggling to read it and couldn't get more than halfway through. So when Alec Guinness later suggested it over the telephone, I groaned silently.

'Try again' said Alec 'maybe you'll think differently.'

'There is a film, I assure you' he said. 'Would you mind if I have a go at writing a screenplay?'

Within a few weeks we had a completed screenplay. Alec had shaped this complex story into a coherent screenplay.

Incidentally, John Bryan, our producer, loved the very foundations of Shepperton. In the cutting rooms he met his future wife Janie, and after his tragically early death in 1969 his funeral service was held at Littleton Church next to the studio, and he was buried in the graveyard there. And so he remains close to his beloved studio.

Needing someone to oversee the mechanics of the production, Albert Fennell became part of the executive team. Whilst he was busy making the necessary studio arrangements, John and I turned our attentions to finding an artist who could put down on canvas and walls the unconventional works of Gulley Jimson. We wanted a talented and outré contemporary painter.

Sir Kenneth Clark recommended John Bratby. In the 1950s he was one of the most important artists in Britain. He didn't paint with a brush. He squeezed large dollops of paint straight from the tube onto the canvas and used a palate knife to shape the thick oils.

John Bryan made initial contact with Bratby, visiting him at his East London home. He returned to our office. 'It's just awful Ronnie' he said. 'There are bedclothes strewn all over the floor and unwashed pans and dishes scattered everywhere but, he's our man!'

One of the toughest assignments for Bratby was for the finale of the film, where a great wall (which he had painted in his own unique style, and which had taken him ten weeks to complete) was to be torn down. John Bryan had been very clever in ensuring the art department had built this wall without any mortar in the central area. A few days before it was due to be pulled down, Bratby completed his work and said he couldn't bear to see us destroy it, so went home.

The pressure was on as I realised I only had one take on this – or risk another ten week delay to get another wall set up! A tractor was going to be used to smash the wall, and I decided to have four cameras running to capture every angle possible. I prayed!

All was set. I had my finger on the button, and gave it a press to 'go'. Mercifully it worked brilliantly and more so, the central piece of wall remained vertical for about three seconds whilst all around it crumbled, and then it too fell flat. It was quite dramatic.

After filming was complete, Ronnie Neame delivered a print to United Artists in New York.

> It couldn't have been received better. As we left the theatre, Arthur Krim said, 'I don't know how you made that film from that script.'
>
> 'That film was that script, Arthur' I replied.
>
> Alec Guinness received an Academy Award nomination for his writing. *The Horse's Mouth* was exactly what we had envisioned, and more. The picture was selected for a Royal Premiere on February 3, 1959, in the presence of Her Majesty Queen Elizabeth and the Queen Mother. In addition to our cast, an array of stars were in attendance: Sean Connery, Peter Sellers, Richard Attenborough, Maurice Chavalier, Peter Finch, Terry-Thomas and Lauren Bacall.

In a 1958 year-end report, Lion International Films Ltd stated that:

> Recent releases on the continent include *The Silent Enemy* which received a triple premiere in Paris and was seen by nearly 80,000 people in two weeks … its first release in the USA included *Private's Progress* and *Geordie* both of which proved widely popular and have brought back substantial dollar earnings for their producers. More recently *Blue Murder At St Trinian's* has played an excellent ten week season in New York and, in fact, at the end of August, Lion International had no fewer than four films playing simultaneously on first run New York, the others being *Law And Disorder*, *The Truth About Women* and *Lucky Jim*.

Plans were announced for Shepperton to extend to providing facilities and services for television production. Shepperton TV Productions Ltd was formed with directors Harold Boxall, Bernard Coote, Smedley-Aston and Lew Thornburn.

The question, of course, was asked – what had Shepperton to offer the television producer which he could not get elsewhere? An unrivalled plant in size, space and technical efficiency – a studio with the greatest variety of resources in Europe. Recently completed theatre and cutting rooms – bringing the total to thirty-six – with space for the editorial staff to work comfortably and with up-to-date equipment, was also deemed to be a great asset for the busy, fast-moving television producer.

Management stated that 'TV producers will get the same kind of service as feature production at Shepperton … Shepperton believes it has more to offer the TV producer than any other studio. In spirit and service it offers the best – at the most economical price.'

Eleven stages were now in full operation, along with a special effects stage, scoring stage and stills stage. Additionally, there were sixty acres of back-lot, with three lawns, a small forest, the River Ash and a ready-made set in the Old House. Shepperton was a formidable complex, and very much geared for the future.

Stage Dimensions

A	150 × 120ft (Tank 36 × 20 × 7ft)
B	120 × 100ft (Tank 16½ × 8 × 7ft)
C	150 × 120ft (Tank 36 × 20 × 7ft)
D	120 × 100ft (Tank 16½ × 8 × 7ft)
E	72 × 44ft
F	72 × 44ft
G	72 × 94ft
H	250 × 119ft
I	123 × 56ft (Tank 24 × 18 × 8ft)
J	80 × 36ft
K	36 × 35ft
Special Effects Stage	70 × 40ft
Scoring Stage	90 × 65ft
Stills Stage	45 × 22ft

1959 was a year which saw the company's fortunes turn, for it would move into a small profit again, of which more later. It was also the year that saw some great critical and commercial successes. Chief among them was the Boulting Brothers' production of *I'm All Right Jack* starring Ian Carmichael and Peter Sellers.

Peter Sellers is Fred Kite in *I'm All Right Jack*. (The Boulting Brothers Archive)

In a memo in 1997, Roy Boulting stated:

Peter, at first, didn't want to do the film, he couldn't see that it was funny. John and I talked and decided Peter should do a test, because he was so good but didn't really know why he was so good. We wanted him to see himself on screen playing a character role of this kind. Peter agreed. The costume and the little moustache helped him along the road but what clinched it was when one of the works committee, who happened to have entered at the start of a scene, started to laugh and then they all roared with laughter. Once Peter saw the test, he had no more doubts.

Kite was the part that established him as a screen character comedian.

Kenneth Griffith adds:

Those Boulting films were a special experience. All of it reflected from the unique character of the identical twins. They were very careful who they cast; everybody had to be a talented honest player and – I honestly believe – everyone had to be someone that they liked and respected. Every department reflected their professional and personal standards. In the cutting room: Max Benedict, one of the finest human beings that I have ever met, and Anthony Harvey. I enjoyed hanging around these two men in their workplace. Bob and Chuck, the property men at Shepperton, were essential on a Boulting film and if there was a hierarchy of importance poking through the roof of the essential democracy that prevailed, Bob and Chuck were very high up and never far behind the producer's throne. I must admit that a warm glow embraces me and tears prick my eyes at the very remembrance of those exclusive gatherings to make a Boulting film. And to add to my joy, Roy would usually drive me to Shepperton in his Rolls-Royce, and bring me home again.

Roy's son, Rupert, adds:

Bob and Chuck were famed for their wonderful sense of humour. One day whilst visiting the set, as a mere child, I was left in their charge whilst my father set up a shot. They said to me 'Rupert, do you know what "bristols" are?' Not knowing the slang [for breasts], I said no. They said 'Go and ask your father, but not now, wait until he shouts action then it's safe to ask'. I did just that, and my father cried out 'Bob and Chuck get off my set'. Though I think he was in hysterics at the time!

Actor Mark Eden recalls:

Chuck and Bobby were quite honestly the worst prop men you would want to meet, but they had such terrific personalities that you couldn't help but love them. Chuck was also probably the worst offender of swearing I've ever met.

It was f-ing this, f-ing that and he would often split words just to slip in an expletive. 'What a great i-fucking-dea' he once said to me. In the mid 1990s I co-wrote a radio play called *Props!* which was based on them. It was very well received, and we even drafted Roy Boulting in to play himself. In terms of Shepperton history, they deserve a book to themselves.

The Boultings admitted to writing the character of Fred Kite based on a man that actually existed and they knew – but he never recognised himself! Kenneth Griffith remembers:

> The film technician's union, the ACTT [now BECTU] got wind of *I'm All Right Jack*'s message and some of the brothers stopped working. Immediately the Boultings pretty well ordered us out onto the lawns at Shepperton to play cricket. But after a few days we went back to our work and the glorious film was completed!

The story followed naive Stanley Windrush returning from the war, with his mind set on a successful career in business. Much to his own dismay, he soon finds he has to start from the bottom and work his way up, and also that the management as well as the trade union use him as a tool in their fight for power. The trade union shop steward was Sellers' Fred Kite.

Ian Carmichael, who reprised his role of Windrush from *Private's Progress* alongside Richard Attenborough, who also reprised his role of Sidney Cox, confirms:

'Everybody out!' was a familiar cry amongst the union workers at Shepperton and was lampooned so brilliantly in The Boulting Brother's *I'm All Right Jack*. (The Boulting Brothers Archive)

This was the film that made him [Sellers], and I have to say I never had any trouble with him, he was very easy and very entertaining. I think it was only when he got bigger, as it were, more important, that he became more trouble.

Ian Carmichael next starred in political satire *Left, Right and Centre* for Launder and Gilliat, with Alastair Sim and Patricia Bredin. 'Sidney and Frank worked very much like Roy and John.' says Carmichael, 'in so much as they're a collaborative team, but with each taking turns in directing and producing. Sidney directed in this instance, and I found it a joyous film to work on with a terrific cast in support.'

In a different vein, Muriel Box directed crime thriller *Subway in the Sky*, which was based on the play by Iain Main. Starring Van Johnson, Hildegard Knef, Katherine Kath and Cec Linder, the film came in for criticism of heavy dialogue, and being based mainly on one set. It marked writer Jack Andrews' last credit. It was produced by a young John Temple-Smith, who comments:

I was engaged to produce a couple of B movies for the Rank Organisation with my partner Patrick Filmer-Sankey, the two bright young things as we were dubbed, and *Subway in the Sky* was the first. I didn't want to go to Pinewood and have the Rank production regime thrust upon me, and so I set up at Shepperton, where I knew I'd have more freedom – within reason, of course. I had a director in mind, and had discussed him with the people at Rank, and they readily agreed. However, I then received a call from Sydney Box, our co-producer, who said that his sister's film which she was setting up with Rank had fallen through, and he said 'I think Muriel would make a good director for your film, don't you think?' It wasn't so much a suggestion as an instruction!

A highly regarded film was next, from director Guy Green, entitled *The Angry Silence*. Green reveals:

It came about after Michael Craig – who I'd worked with on *House of Secrets* – came to lunch one Sunday, and told me that he and his brother had an idea for a screenplay. He gave me the outline, which I liked the sound of, and with that Michael said that if I was really interested he would go away and write a screenplay with his brother.

Six weeks later, he came for lunch again, and brought the script with him. I loved it and whilst realising it needed a few alterations, I felt it was terrifically strong and very well written. It was called *The Coventry Story*.

The reason, incidentally, Michael wrote it was because he felt he was being offered such awful parts that he would write himself a good one. He intended to play the part of Tom Curtis but in the event, and this shows how cruel this business can be, he was said not to have a big enough name for the distributors and sales people and Richard Attenborough was cast with Michael playing the second lead, Joe Wallace.

I nursed the project for a short time but then went off to direct a film with Richard Attenborough and Michael Craig called *Sea of Sand*. I told Dick about the script and thought there was a good part for him in it, as Joe Wallace (the second lead). Dick liked it very much, but thought perhaps some of the dialogue needed a polish and suggested Bryan Forbes would be the perfect one to do it.

Dick then suggested he could take the script, through his company Beaver Films, to the Boulting Brothers at British Lion. The Boultings were interested, but insisted the budget be reduced to £100,000 and the only way that could be achieved was by the principles deferring their fees and, hopefully, take a slice of the profits in return. The main leads, myself, Malcolm Arnold (the composer) … all deferred fees and that's how the film – then called *A Dangerous Game* – was made.

In a letter to Roy Boulting at British Lion, dated 6 April 1959, Richard Attenborough explained that:

After several exhaustive sessions by Andy Worker and Arthur Cleaver, we have, together, arrived at a budget figure of £97,866. This is based on a seven week schedule, made up of four weeks studio, two weeks daily location and one week away – plus an additional week for a second unit. We would like to stress that the final figure has only been arrived at after a most careful and detailed study of schedule and breakdown and while it must, perforce, contain an element of

Richard Attenborough starred in and produced *The Angry Silence*. (Courtesy Canal and Image UK Ltd)

guesswork – we have not, as yet, chosen our actual locations – both Andy and Arthur contend that it is a thoroughly realistic figure, and one on which the production could be brought in … all fees for Producer, Director, the two stars (Michael Craig and Richard Attenborough), the original story and the screenplay, have been omitted from the budget and will participate only in profits.

Bryan Forbes received an Oscar nomination for his screenplay, and as Lord Attenborough explained, the screenplay was given added impact with the casting of Pier Angeli:

> We'd acted together in *Sea Of Sand* and Bryan suggested she'd be perfect for the part of my wife in the film. He then explained his reasons. You see, in the script, there were various issues dealt with that might not have been too familiar with everyone watching, and particularly audiences outside Britain – but by casting Pier (a foreigner) that was the perfect excuse for my character to explain what terms like 'sent to Coventry' meant. It was a stroke of genius that effectively allowed us to explain things to the audience, but inside the story. Pier was a truly wonderful and very beautiful actress too, and it was a delight to work with her. I'm desperately sorry she cut her life short, as we were robbed of a wonderful actress and human being.

'It made all of our careers', concludes Guy Green. 'The reviews were quite, quite amazing. The film then went to the Berlin Film Festival and won the Berlin Bear. All credit really must go to Michael Craig because it was his idea, his story and his script. Yes, we all had our input, but Michael was the one who made it work.'

The first of Hammer's productions to pay a visit to Shepperton was Terence Fisher's *The Mummy*, to take advantage of the studio's lot and tank for the swamp sequences. Starring Christopher Lee as a notably human bandaged-encrusted Khari, the Shepperton scene required him to carry female lead Yvonne Furneaux through the swamp, during which Lee wrenched his neck muscles and was heard to mutter numerous cuss words from behind his inflexible make-up.

Carol Reed's next film was *Our Man in Havana*, in which Alec Guinness plays Jim Wormold, a vacuum cleaner salesman in Cuba, whose daughter Milly, aged seventeen, spends more money than he can afford, and so he accepts a job to work for the Intelligence Service. As he has nothing to report, he invents facts, pretends to recruit agents and to discover secret constructions.

'There was, of course, a lot of location work in Havana,' says the film's Director of Photography Ossie Morris, 'which took place shortly after Castro had taken power there. We had to be careful in what we did, and I suppose there were some restrictions, but nothing too major.'

John Mitchell, the film's sound recordist, adds, 'we were watched by a Castro-appointed censor, film script in hand, but unable to read much English. He and his wife soon got on Carol's nerves, often preventing him from filming things he had spent some time staging.'

'Castro himself,' continues Ossie Morris, 'did in fact come onto the set one evening, when we were filming a night sequence, and he seemed to thoroughly enjoy himself. The story, of course, was knocking the authorities and administration which Castro had so recently overturned, so I think he was quite amused actually.'

With the last day of location filming in the can, everyone made their way to the airport, all except Carol Reed and Alec Guinness that is. John Mitchell explains:

> They had been detained at immigration. The authorities refused to hand back their passports unless the film negative was handed over. It seemed like hours before they were allowed to leave. However, the exposed negative rolls had been transferred into unexposed film cans with only Kodak labels, whilst the original cans with their *Our Man in Havana* labels were handed over containing unused film!

Ossie Morris continues:

> When we returned to Shepperton for the interiors, I remember on one of the largest sets we filmed what was called 'The Blue Plate Luncheon Scene'. One

The Mummy was one of several Hammer films which lensed at Shepperton. (Courtesy Dave Worrall Collection)

afternoon, just as we were getting ready to shoot, we heard a voice call 'All out!' All the lights went out, we were plunged into darkness – the electricians walked out. It was a dispute over them wanting more money actually, but to do it in the middle of the afternoon just as we were about to film, was really quite callous. But that was the ETU for you.

It was all resolved that evening, and the following morning we could start work again.

Suddenly Last Summer saw the return of Producer Sam Spiegel to Shepperton. It was based on a short story by Tennessee Williams. Spiegel had called Williams and offered him a deal for the film rights over the telephone: $50,000 plus 20 per cent of the net profits, and a further $300,000 on completion of the film. Williams suggested that Gore Vidal be engaged to adapt his play for the screen, and Spiegel duly offered the young writer $35,000 for his services. Three weeks later, he delivered Spiegel the first draft screenplay.

Spiegel next secured Joseph Mankiewicz to direct the film – his career had recently fared disappointingly and Spiegel saw this as his opportunity to secure a brilliant director at a knock-down price.

The producer forged ahead with casting. He announced that Vivien Leigh and Elizabeth Taylor were his ideal choices for the leads ... but Vivien Leigh declined to be involved. It was then that Katherine Hepburn's name came up, and she readily agreed. However, Spiegel's lawyers forgot to erase 'Vivien Leigh' from the contract they sent her.

Taylor had only limited availability, which meant things had to be fast-tracked. She also insisted the film be shot in Britain, for tax reasons, and as well as securing a $125,000 fee for starring, she also secured a co-producer fee for her Swiss company Camp Films of $375,000 plus 10 per cent of the gross receipts in excess of $5 million.

Shepperton was transformed into New Orleans by Production Designer Oliver Messel, and location work was also set for the Costa Brava in Spain. Other casting was now confirmed: Montgomery Clift, Albert Dekker and Gary Raymond.

'Mankiewicz was a writer, director and producer and it really was a case with him that the writing came first,' says Script Supervisor Elaine Schreyeck. 'Katherine would often make suggestions about the script, which Mankiewicz would listen to and then say adamantly "but it's Tennessee Williams. I can't change it." Invariably he'd allow her to do it her way, and then they'd do it his way; and he would win out in the end. He was very strong and ruled the roost!'

Tony Searle, a (then) young visitor to the studio, explains further:

I gather there were tremendous tensions between all the complex personalities involved, and the director wanted to keep prying eyes out. Being a young whippersnapper, I wasn't going to let a closed set come between me and my idols. I wandered on to the set just before lunch and hovered in the background watching Elizabeth Taylor performing in the wonderful Southern States garden set. Suddenly she spotted me and her voiced boomed out: 'Who is that person?' Before I could react a voice came from one of the chairs by the set. It was Katherine Hepburn, who called out: 'He's a friend of mine', beckoning me over to the vacant seat beside her. She then proceeded to treat me as if I was a long lost friend and we chatted for about ten minutes. Elizabeth Taylor accepted the situation and went on working.

It obviously says a lot about Katherine Hepburn, who I continued to admire throughout her long and illustrious career.

The $2.5 million film went on to gross six-times its budget.

Rounding out 1959 at Shepperton was *Tarzan's Greatest Adventure* which was directed by John Guillermin. Starring Gordon Scott in the titular role, the cast was augmented by Anthony Quayle, Sara Shane, Niall McGinnis and a young Sean Connery. The plot focuses on a gang of murderous thugs, lead by Quayle, on an expedition to exploit a hidden diamond mine.

Production Designer Michael Stringer remembers:

We initially recee'd out in Uganda, but then switched to Kenya. On the last day of the trip, Ted Scaife [the cameraman] and I were asked to check out the river next to where we were thinking of building Tarzan's tree house. We took an inflated dinghy, but ran into fifty hippos in the river and decided we best abandon!

There was a lot of scope there, around the Fourteen Falls Hotel area, and we did in fact build a whole village (which was later set on fire), and Tarzan's tree house.

Back at Shepperton we recreated part of the jungle on a stage, and a piece of water with a canoe – we weren't risking hippos again!

CHAPTER 12

THE '60s BOOM

'Shepperton was bursting at the seams with so many productions,' states Sound Mixer John Aldred. 'In addition to the British Lion product, American finance supplied by Columbia, Universal and Paramount backed many of the productions. The sound department became overwhelmed and the management were thinking of building more facilities.'

1960 was the year in which Entertainment Duty was repealed in the UK, and twenty-nine films lensed at Shepperton. On 1 January, the year also saw the appointment of Adrian (Andy) Worker as managing director of the studio, following the death of Harold Boxall in August of the previous year. He was already very experienced in hands-on production, and his appointment was welcomed throughout the business, particularly when, a few months later, he and his fellow directors were able to report a small profit for the year 1959/60. The company was at last seeing its fortunes turned around.

The range of production was as broad as it was vast. Small films and blockbusters alike found their home at Shepperton. *The Flesh and the Fiends* was one of the smaller ones, albeit one to take over the whole of H stage, as producer Robert S. Baker recalls:

> It was the story of Burke and Hare, the infamous grave robbers.
>
> We had to build an entire Edinburgh square and so took over the giant silent stage to do it. The house and gardens were also used quite a lot, and you'll see the hallway with the black and white tiles if you watch carefully.
>
> To refresh my memory I dug out my files on the production, and came across the actual studio contract and I see that we had a deal for the silent stage of £1,000 per week!

The year also saw the return of the rebellious girl's school, with *Pure Hell at St Trinian's*. Leslie Gilliat remembers:

> When we were casting in the London office, Sidney was right in the far corner at a desk, working on another film. Frank and I were interviewing for the sixth

form girls whilst Sidney kept his head down. Then we had this really beautiful Burmese girl come in, so we thought we'll use her. She then left and Sidney looked up, and shouted out 'Now I know why they built that bridge over the River Kwai' and then went back to his work!

Much of the same was expected, and delivered. When the school burns to the ground it is clearly the work of an arsonist. The pupils are found guilty and the judge hands them into the care of a pretty dubious child psychiatrist. Much mirth and merriment ensues, although with a cast depleted of Alastair Sim; though George Cole as Flash Harry, and Joyce Grenfell as Ruby Gates steal the show.

Val Guest directed two films at Shepperton in 1960. The first was war drama *Yesterday's Enemy*. Cut off by the Japanese advance into Burma, Captain Langford (Stanley Baker) and his exhausted British troops take over an enemy-held jungle village. Guest explains:

I'd adapted it for Hammer from an exciting television play of the same name, and my only worry was how to shoot a complex, realistic jungle war film when your budget won't even allow a quick trip to the nearest jungle. The answer is you get a brilliant art director like Hammer's Bernard Robinson who not only fills an entire stage at Shepperton with Burmese jungle, but builds different sections of it on revolves so that without having to move the unit it can be turned around to look like entirely different locations. It was truly Academy Award art direction and garnished with Arthur Grant's incredible photography we even fooled Burma war supremo, Lord Louis Mountbatten. Our premiere at the Empire in Leicester Square was in aid of the Burma Star Association, of which he was president, and I had the honour of sitting next to him at the screening.

'I know that place … ' said Mountbatten at one point, stabbing his finger at the screen jungle. 'Know it well … Can't put a name to it … Where the hell was it?'

Not having the courage to tell him that it was the large stage at Shepperton, I lied diplomatically and said it was second unit stuff and I didn't know!

Val Guest then set about making *Expresso Bongo*, which was a London-set rock 'n' roll drama with Johnny Jackson (Laurence Harvey), a sleazy talent agent, discovering a teenager – Bongo – singing in a coffee house.

When Guest was financing the project, and before he had cast the role of young Bongo, he went to see Nat Cohen at Anglo Amalgamated. Guest recalls:

Nat listened attentively as I outlined the project, then his smile faded and he shook his head.

'Who cares about rock 'n' roll?' he asked.

'They care about Elvis Presley' I countered.

'When you get Presley, talk to me'.

In a way I could see his point. There were several good pop stars floating around – Tommy Steele, Marty Wilde, Adam Faith, Billy Fury – but by no stretch of the imagination could they be said to have internationally pulling power. In fact during my search to find the right one to play the young Bongo I had covered most of them … after my search had been reported in the London press, I received a telephone call from one Tom Littlewood, who owned the small 2 i's bar in Soho.

'Got a kid working here might be worth a look-see' he told me. I had my look-see that evening when, down in the tiny cellar of the 2 i's, I watched a small good-looking bundle of vitality with dark eyes, an angelic face, a good voice and a gyrating body that showed he was an Elvis fan. Tom said his name was Cliff Richard and the four lively lads backing him were the Drifters. And that, to tell it as it was, is how Sir Cliff landed his first starring role. At which time, being still under age, he brought his mother along to sign the contract for a heady £2,000 plus his one request, 'Can my mates be in it too?' And in it they were, but since there was an American group called the Drifters, Cliff's mates were launched as The Shadows.

John and Roy Boulting were then talked into giving us a British Lion distribution contract. Armed with this, my script, cast and fingers crossed I went to see John Terry of the National Film Finance Corporation, to ask for a loan. Two days later they called to say the board had approved my loan.

One of Shepperton's most endearing films was *Two-Way Stretch*, a prison-set comedy starring Peter Sellers, David Lodge, Bernard Cribbins, Lionel Jeffries and Maurice Denham. Dodger Lane (Sellers) has planned the perfect robbery while in prison. He intends – with his cellmates Jelly Knight (Lodge) and Lennie Price (Cribbins) – to break out of prison, steal a fortune in diamonds, then break back into prison before anyone notices. With only a few days' sentence left, and the perfect alibi – what could possibly go wrong? What indeed!

'We shot all the prison exteriors in Aldershot, including the quarry sequence where the prisoners are breaking rocks,' says Producer E.M. Smedley-Aston. 'And the rest at Shepperton. After all these years it's still being shown on television frequently and I recently got a cheque for £90 royalties!'

At the end of March, British Lion reported a profit of some £126,771. The company was turning around, and more good news was to come. Walt Disney arrived at Shepperton, with a film called *Greyfriar's Bobby*, as Disney Production Manager Peter Manley recalls:

Walt had made a few films in Britain by this time, and after a short break, Walt announced a new series of films to shoot, of which *Greyfriar's Bobby* was to be the first.

It was based on a true story of how a little dog, Bobby, slept on the grave of his departed master. The actual churchyard of Greyfriar's was recreated by art director Michael Stringer on the silent stage at Shepperton; it was enormous and took over the entire stage. Such was its enormity that communication across the stage with the electricians lighting could be tricky, and a new innovation had appeared on the sound scene where we could put an aerial wire around the stage, and equip certain gaffers up in the rafters with radio receivers. So when the cameraman, Paul Beeson, wanted a light moved he didn't have to shout, just merely speak into his handset.

The set required virtually every Brute [very large lights] that we could lay our hands on to light it. As such, they required a great deal of power, but with other pictures on the lot we realised that the powerhouse at Shepperton just wouldn't be able to supply the power we needed. That meant bringing in extra generators. Around that time, Walton on Thames studios had closed and we were able to purchase two generators from their powerhouse. Now, at the back of the silent stage was what was known as the old coach house, from days gone by. We cleared that building, and dug out the ground and placed a four foot thick piece of concrete to bed the generators on.

'On H stage,' adds Michael Stringer, 'I decided we needed some clouds in the sky over the Kirk yard. I arranged for a group of fibreglass clouds to be suspended by piano wire. It works terrifically well on screen. My other problem was in dressing the set with stones which looked like the Edinburgh stone we'd all seen on our reccee. I ended up going as far as Oxford to get an exact match.'

Bernard Cribbins, Peter Sellers and David Lodge in *Two Way Stretch*, with Lionel Jeffries as Officer Crout. (Courtesy Canal and Image UK Ltd)

Peter Manley continues:

> Disney had been planning this film for some time, and actually bred Bobby especially for the film – there was only one of him too, whereas on most films you'd always have a back-up dog. Bobby was truly magnificent and really carried the film. He became something of a celebrity afterwards and made a number of public appearances!
>
> The production turned out very well and so Walt immediately gave the green-light to the next, it was called *The Horsemasters* which was to be directed by Bill Fairchild. It was the story of when a 16-week course in horsemanship has a group of students learning the finer points of sportsmanship, jumping, horsecare, dressage and riding to hounds under stern and exacting teachers. Janet Munro, Tony Britton, Donald Pleasance and Millicent Martin starred.
>
> I was asked to join Hugh Attwooll (Disney's Associate Producer) on location, and direct a second unit with the horses – the shots took a bit of time to set up. I had Mary and Jimmy Chipperfield with me, looking after the horses, and we spent around three weeks on these shots.
>
> It was a hugely enjoyable production, but Shepperton was pretty packed with other films at this time too and so a decision was made by Disney to move the next film to Pinewood – where in fact we stayed for many years.

Amongst the other films occupying Shepperton's floor space were *Tarzan The Magnificent*, with Gordon Scott again reprising the titular role; Donovan Winter's crime drama *The Trunk*; *Nearly a Nasty Accident*, a comedy from director Don Chaffey (who also helmed *Greyfriar's Bobby*) starring Kenneth Connor, Shirley Eaton and Jimmy Edwards; *Spare The Rod*, a school-set drama came from director Leslie Norman and starred Max Bygraves and Donald Pleasance; *Surprise Package*, with Yul Bryner, Mitzi Gaynor and Noel Coward, was directed by Stanley Donen; as was *The Grass is Greener* with Cary Grant, Deborah Kerr, Robert Mitchum and Jean Simmons in a rather good comedy where Victor and Hillary (Grant and Kerr) are down on their luck to the point that they allow tourists to take guided tours of their castle. But Charles Delacro (Mitchum), a millionaire oil tycoon, visits, and takes a liking to more than the house. Soon, Hattie Durant (Simmons) gets involved and they have a good old-fashioned love triangle!

Sound recordist John Mitchell remembers:

> When I arrived during my usual pre-production visit to the set to sort out any sound problems beforehand, I found that, at a very late date, the film's backers had forced Stanley into filming in Cinemascope, the letter box shaped screen that had become all the rage. By the time they dropped this on him, all the sets had been built to the conventional format, much the same proportions as a traditional tv screen. This meant they were far higher than Cinemascope required. There wasn't time to make the set walls lower and this meant problems for all of us. Chris Challis' [the DoP] lights on the spot rails were much higher than necessary. As a result our microphones would cast shadows unless they were raised higher than the desired height.

Cary Grant could never be faulted. His style of acting, and timing was perfect. He always played Cary Grant of course. He was, however, an intensely selfish actor, making others wait before he was ready, and before each take he insisted that every hair of his immaculate hair style was in place.

I once heard him mutter – whilst tidying his hair on such an occasion, 'I like me'. On another occasion Jean Simmonds and Deborah Kerr came on set wearing beautiful model gowns complimented by some exquisite jewellery. Over the headphones I heard Cary call over to Stanley 'Get those jewels off them'. In reply to the query 'Why?' Stanley was told that the audience would be looking at the jewels and not Cary Grant!

With three directorial assignments under his belt, Tony Richardson turned his attentions to a stage play by John Osborne called *The Entertainer*. Archie Rice is a third-rate act, headlining a failing end-of-the-pier show in a run down seaside resort. Even as his life falls to pieces around him, Archie will do whatever it takes to keep the show going. Played on the stage to great acclaim, Laurence Olivier agreed to reprise the role for a big screen adaptation. 'The location,' says Director of Photography Ossie Morris, 'was to be Morecambe, a seaside town in Lancashire. I believe Tony Richardson's parents lived there, and he obviously knew of the surrounds very well as a result. In fact, the location was perfect – the theatres there were ideal, the pubs, and they had horse drawn buses on the prom, and the overall look and feel of the town suited our story of an entertainer who had really reached the bottom of his career.'

Olivier was at the time in *Coriolanus* at Stratford-upon-Avon, and so for a couple of months there was much to-ing and fro-ing from location and studio to Stratford. However, near disaster struck (for both productions) when at 7p.m. one day, just as the day's schedule of Archie Rice tap dancing had been completed, Tony Richardson asked if they could do one more take.

'I sighed and said ok', recalled Oliver in his autobiography:

and went right into it; I was feeling glad we were doing it once more, as it was going great guns, when – snap went my old cartilage. It hadn't happened for ten years and, God knows, my knee was warmed up; there was no accounting for it. It turned out to be a great nuisance. The next day I was to do two shows of *Coriolanus*, but I had to be confined to bed; so a promising baby of an understudy named Albert Finney went on for me.

The love affair that had started between Joan Plowright and Olivier during the stage version continued during filming. They were later married. Olivier received an Oscar nomination for his role. Ronnie Maasz was camera operator on the film, and recalls some fun sound recordist Peter Handford had:

At the beginning of every shot the number board, on which was written all the relevant information – the scene and take numbers etc – was presented in front of the camera and clapped. In large letters across the top was emblazoned the film's title *The Entertainer*. Through habit, it was seldom noticed as to what was precisely written on it. Peter, aware of this, had a special number board made up exactly the same except that the title had been changed to *The Undertaker*. It was a good two weeks before Tony Richardson asked 'How long has that been on there?' Even the editors had not noticed it.

Michael Powell next returned to Shepperton with *The Queen's Guards*, as yet untouched by scathing reviews for his last film, as his editor Noreen Ackland explains, 'Mickey was fresh from shooting *Peeping Tom* at Pinewood, which had yet to hit the headlines or be reviewed by the critics, with this semi-documentary film.'

The Brigade of Guards are the personal troops of the reigning monarch: the King's Guards or, in this case, the Queen's Guards. Tourists in London were drawn in great crowds to witness the Changing of the Guard at Buckingham Palace each day. The idea of a story centring on the Guards appealed to Powell who was a self-confessed 'sucker for stories about the services'.

'It started with Micky going off on a trip with a cameraman to the desert to film the Guards on manoeuvres,' adds Noreen Ackland, 'and I remember lots of footage of wonderful coloured parachutes descending from the skies. That was the beginning, from where he engaged Roger Milner.'

Initially, the story developed as a documentary, but was rapidly expanded into a feature for 20th Century Fox. Roger Milner was the man charged with penning a script. Things moved so quickly that the project moved into production without a completed script, and furthermore Powell was starting to have trouble with censors and critics for *Peeping Tom*.

'Milner was literally writing the next day's shooting as we went along, and it was very difficult working like that,' adds Noreen Ackland, who also edited *Peeping Tom*, for which Powell was vilified by the press during the production of *The Queen's Guards*. 'The film was running over budget, and Mickey was pushed-off.'

Martin Cahill was appointed Fox's representative on the production.

It dragged on and on and on. We were shooting desert sequences down on Camber Sands (at the castle) in October/November and it was pouring with rain. After four weeks the editor told me she had enough to make a battle of it and so I told the Associate Producer that the picture had over run too much in both time and certainly money. It was my intention (and I had the authority to do so) to call a halt and shut the movie down. He told me that it was MICKEY POWELL and I would not dare. But I did. I walked over to the generator, told the operator to switch it off for a couple of minutes and then announced the wrap.

Michael Powell retreated to a hotel in the south of France and Noreen Ackland was charged with completing the edit, though she remained in contact via the telephone from Shepperton with Powell. The film – as it stood – was screened at Fox in Soho

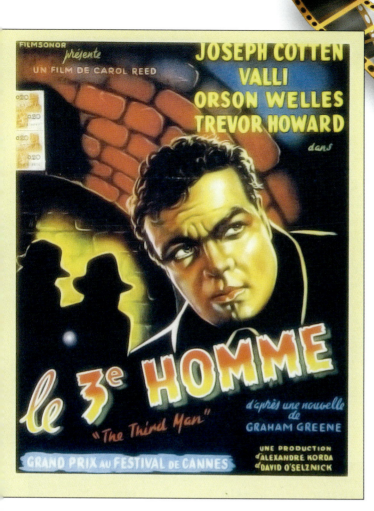

Left: 1 *The Third Man*, French poster. (Gareth Owen Collection)

Below: 2 The grave of Britain's greatest movie mogul is a simple one, at Stoke Poges Memorial Garden in Buckinghamshire. (Photograph by Tony Harwood)

3 Humphrey Bogart in *The African Queen*, as filmed on the tank in Worton's large sound stage.

4 Poster artwork for *The Ringer*, Guy Hamilton's first feature film and one of several modest budget films green-lit by Alex Korda. (Gareth Owen Collection)

5 John Huston's *Moulin Rouge* pioneered a new look for colour film. (Gareth Owen Collection)

6 *The Guns of Navarone* gathered an all-star cast together, including Stanley Baker, David Niven, Gregory Peck, Anthony Quinn and Anthony Quayle. (Courtesy Dave Worrall Collection)

Left: 7 The German poster artwork for *Dr Terror's House of Horrors*. (Gareth Owen Collection)

Below: 8 Peter Cushing played Dr Who in two feature films for Amicus, and is seen here with the legendary Daleks. (Courtesy Canal and Image UK Ltd)

Opposite top: 9 *The Land That Time Forgot* was one of Doug McClure's Amicus adventures – often cited as a forerunner of the Indiana Jones films. (Courtesy Canal and Image UK Ltd)

Opposite bottom: 10 David Niven, John Huston and William Holden – just a few stars in the confusion that was *Casino Royale*. (Courtesy Dave Worrall Collection)

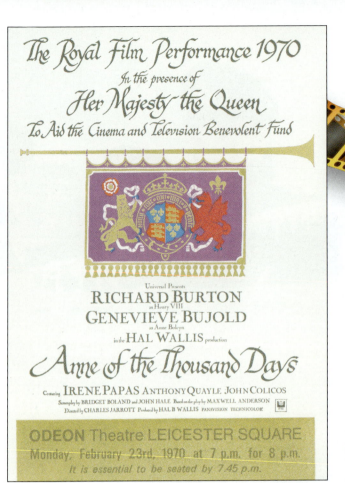

11 A ticket for the Royal Premiere of *Anne of a Thousand Days*. (Courtesy John Aldred)

12 Robin Hardy's *Wicker Man* has become a cult film, yet was originally made and released as a supporting feature as part of EMI's production programme. (Courtesy Canal and Image UK Ltd)

13 James Cagney (right) made one last trip to the UK to film *Ragtime* at Shepperton. (Gareth Owen Collection)

14 Laurence Olivier and Gregory Peck in a tension-filled, fight-to-the-death sequence from *The Boys From Brazil*. (Gareth Owen Collection)

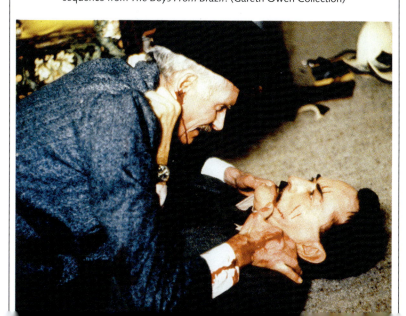

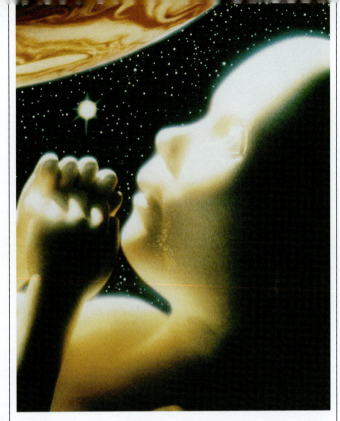

15 *2010*, the follow-up to Kubrick's *2001: A Space Odyssey*. (Gareth Owen Collection)

16 Kenneth Branagh as Henry V. (Gareth Owen Collection)

17 Mel Gibson as Hamlet in Zeffirelli's production. (Gareth Owen Collection)

18 One of the sets at Shepperton for *Robin Hood: Prince of Thieves*. (Roy Pembrooke)

19 A chalet for *Mary Shelley's Frankenstein* built next to the River Ash. (Roy Pembrooke)

20 A night sequence on *Mary Shelley's Frankenstein*. The crane is being used to spray water over the set to simulate rain. (Roy Pembrooke)

21 The exterior set for *Judge Dredd* was built on the lot's car park, where J and K stages now stand. (Roy Pembrooke)

22 Sir Ridley Scott, brother of Tony, assumed control of the studio in the 1990s. (Gareth Owen Collection)

Above: 23 Shepperton's favourite son, Kenneth Branagh, was the next actor to take on *Hamlet*. (Gareth Owen Collection)

Left: 24 Glenn Close as the wonderful Cruella de Vil in *101 Dalmatians*. (Gareth Owen Collection)

Right: 25 Brendan Fraser in *The Mummy*. (Courtesy Geoff Freeman)

Below: 26 The Korda Theatre was one of three buildings re-christened to reflect the studio's historic past. (Roy Pembrooke)

27 Heath Ledger starring in the re-make of *The Four Feathers* – the second version of the story made at Shepperton. (Gareth Owen Collection)

28 Renée Zellweger in the first of two *Bridget Jones* adventures filmed at Shepperton. (Gareth Owen Collection)

Right: 29 Daniel Craig in *The Golden Compass*. (Gareth Owen Collection)

Below: 30 Kirsten Dunst starred with Paul Bettany in the tennis-set romantic drama, *Wimbledon*. (Gareth Owen Collection)

Left: 31 Daniel Radcliffe as Harry Potter. (Gareth Owen Collection)

Below: 32 Littleton Park House as it stands today. (Roy Pembrooke)

Square, and the executives did not quite know what to make of it, as Noreen Ackland relates:

> Spyros Skouras, the big cheese at Fox, was in the theatre and said 'I see the editor is scratching her head.' And he then turned to me and asked, 'what do you think we should do?'
>
> I told him to bring back Mickey as it was he who had conceived the idea and he was the one who should have the final say on the film. They sent for Mickey, he came back and we completed the picture. It wasn't a happy experience, at the end, sadly and the film didn't turn out as Mickey had initially intended.

Small crime thriller *Offbeat*, on the other hand, hit the jackpot. It was directed by Cliff Owen and starred William Sylvester, Mai Zetterling and Anthony Dawson. The producer was E.M. Smedley-Aston, who said, 'That was a real turn up for the book. It was a second feature made for £27,000 and has grossed over £56,000. It was actually Cliff's first film as director and set him on a path to great success.'

It was about time for another big hit for Shepperton and that came with *The Guns of Navarone*, a blockbuster in every sense of the word. Gregory Peck, David Niven, Anthony Quinn, Stanley Baker, Anthony Quayle and Richard Harris headlined the action adventure, based on Alistair MacLean's story of the two powerful German guns that control the seas around the Greek island of Navarone, making the evacuation of endangered British troops on a neighbouring island impossible. Air attack proves useless, so a team of six Allied and Greek soldiers is put ashore to meet up with partisans to try and blow up the guns. Carl Forman adapted the screenplay and produced.

Director of Photography Ossie Morris recalls:

> Alexander (Sandy) MacKendrick was signed to direct the film. I went out on a recce with Sandy to Athens and Rhodes. Sandy was one for taking Polaroids and he had a secretary with him – who incidentally became my wife – and her job was to take these photos and pin them up on boards so as we could have a discussion about them all later on.
>
> We returned to Shepperton, where the script was completed after we delivered our verdicts on locations we felt would work well, and the schedule was drawn up. Eight weeks were to be spent in Rhodes with a little on the mainland. A terrific deal was struck with the Greek army to double as Germans, and they painted all of their vehicles for us; it really was looking terrific.
>
> But on location, we just sat around discussing these Polaroids and ideas for filming, and did not shoot a single frame. Carl Foreman [the producer] arrived about two days later and was horrified. He asked why Sandy hadn't started. I said I didn't know, but I was trying. Carl asked I try a bit harder!
>
> The next day we went out, and I said to Sandy that the pressure was on us – meaning him and I – to shoot some film. He told me not to worry as we would start soon. Another day went by, no film. Carl was furious. He asked me

what on earth was going on. I simply didn't know! He said 'Right I'll give you one more day, and that's it'.

The following day we went out to what was the most inaccessible location you can imagine to the very top of a cliff, looking down at the ocean. Sandy said 'We'll shoot here'.

After spending much time setting up, I just had to ask – 'Why?'

His reply was 'Vertigo.' That's all he said.

When we returned to the hotel, someone told me that Sandy's wife had arrived. I thought it very ominous. Within an hour the news came down that Sandy was off the picture and would be leaving. Carl Foreman said he would take over until another director was agreed with Columbia. Carl in fact took charge for about three weeks, just doing second unit work with the Greek army. The actors meanwhile, being such high-rollers, weren't scheduled to join the payroll just yet – thankfully!

Word then reached us that, on the Thursday, a new director would be arriving with the principal actors from America, ready to start on the following Monday. He was J. Lee Thompson. I knew him from my days at ABPC in Borehamwood actually. He stepped off the plane with Greg Peck, David Niven, Tony Quayle, Tony Quinn, Stanley Baker … that was a cast to die for.

Lee was very nice, very gentle and a bit nervous. Whilst I think he may have shot a bit more coverage than was needed, it did all work terrifically well and gave the editor plenty to work with.

We then returned to Shepperton for interiors, and exteriors – as we built the enormous gun cave out on the studio back-lot, with the two huge guns. All of the night shooting was scheduled for this set, but disaster struck after the first night when it poured with rain. The opening of the gun cave was a mass of plaster supported by tubular steel you see. We walked in the following day to see the whole load of plaster that bridged the top of the cave had collapsed and landed on top of the guns. The studio went into overdrive to try and repair the set, with advice from structural engineers, but meanwhile all of the actors were hanging around so we literally shot anything we could with them until the set was ready. It was certain a tension filled film – on screen, and on set!

The film broke box-office records, and spawned a sequel – *Force Ten from Navarone* in 1977, also filmed at Shepperton.

It was proving a notable year for great films at Shepperton, and *Tunes of Glory* was no exception. Directed by Ronnie Neame, it starred John Mills and Alec Guinness. Ronnie Neame comments:

This is most definitely my favourite film. Colin Lesslie was an independent producer at ABPC in Elstree, and he handed me this superb script by James Kennaway.

I felt it a perfect vehicle for Alec Guinness, and sent him a copy and asked him to consider the part of commissioned officer Colonel Basil Barrow.

A few days later, Alec called me to say 'no'. He felt he had just played that type of character in *Bridge on the River Kwai*. However, he suggested if I would allow him to take the other role, the red-haired boozer Jock Sinclair, then he was my man. I knew Alec well enough to realise if he said he could play a part, then he could.

Between us, Alec and I decided that the part of Barrow would be perfect for Johnny Mills. They had worked together many years earlier on *Great Expectations* and it was quite exciting to bring them back together again.

Sir John Mills adds:

When people, who knew the script, heard that Alec and I were to star, they did indeed all think that I was playing Sinclair, and Alec playing Barrow. I relish new challenges, and directors who cast me against type. Working with Alec again was truly delightful and Ronnie Neame was, and is, one of my dearest friends. We all got on like a house on fire!

'A nineteen year old Susannah York was suggested for Jock's daughter Morag,' adds Ronnie Neame. 'It was her first ever film audition, and to give her every advantage Alec agreed to make a test with her at Shepperton, a most unusual and generous offer.'

'After it was done,' recalls Susannah York, 'I was on the train going home, and suddenly realised "My God I've just done a screen test with Alec Guinness". It was a difficult scene and he was very helpful.'

But who would take top-billing?

'Mary [John's wife] phoned me,' recalls Ronnie Neame, 'insisting he wouldn't do the film without top billing. I assured her it would be sorted. In the event Johnny and Alec tossed a coin for it. Alec won.'

A boom in production in 1961 saw the Shepperton management undertake a small expansion plan: new post sync, music and dubbing theatres, the North Office Block was reopened with new rooms and rooms in the Old House, previously used for storage, were adapted into offices.

With the closure of Walton-on-Thames studios, Shepperton acquired some of their staff and also the complete RCA re-recording installation – in addition to generators for Disney's *Greyfriar's Bobby*.

I Stage was also bought and rebuilt on the Shepperton lot. Meanwhile, the Shepperton restaurant received a make-over and a new pub was opened, The British Lion, by stars Bob Hope, Bing Crosby and Joan Collins, who were filming *The Road to Hong Kong* – the last of the 'Road' movies.

Sound mixer John Aldred explains:

Shepperton was not really equipped for a full scale Hollywood type musical. We were working under difficulties. The music stage did not have a vocal room, so it was impossible to completely isolate vocals from the music being recorded at the same time. So the Westrex theatre was used for vocals, with Bob Farnon's orchestra on the scoring stage being relayed through headphones. Both Bob and Bing were extremely keen golfers, and Bob was heard to quip 'Bing plays a mean game for a man still using wooden shafts!' Their portable dressing rooms on the set were equipped with television so that they could watch golf tournaments, and it was quite a problem asking them to keep the sound down so that it did not interfere with production!

Another Hollywood blockbuster came to Shepperton with *The War Lover*, starring Steve McQueen as Buzz Rickson, a dare-devil Second World War bomber pilot with a death wish; before *Only Two Can Play*, a delightful slice-of-life comedy based on a novel by Kingsley Amis, moved in. Peter Sellers played John Lewis, an assistant librarian who has a chance for a promotion (and a much-needed rise in wages) if he has an affair with Liz Gruffydds-Williams (played by Mai Zetterling), the wife of the local council chairman. Producer Leslie Gilliat reveals:

> It was filmed in South Wales, with stage work back at Shepperton. Peter Sellers, who I wanted for the lead, was under contract to the Boultings at that time. He had one more film left, under the agreement, but the Boultings didn't have any projects, and so let us take Peter on for this film. It was all agreed on the Monday, and John Boulting asked me on the Tuesday if I'd got his contract signed. I said we were just drawing it up.
>
> 'What you must realise, Leslie' he said 'is that you're dealing with a monster. Get it signed or you'll lose him!'
>
> There was a very funny incident with Graham Stark. He played a bit of scruffy, furtive character wearing a dirty mac, who took dirty books out from the library you see. We set up a scene where he had to walk from around a corner, in his mac, looking very shifty whilst carrying a bundle of books. We called action, but Graham was nowhere to be seen. I then walked around the corner only to find a policeman in the middle of arresting him for loitering!

Upon seeing the final film, Peter Sellers – according to Roy Boulting – 'had no faith in it, in fact he really hated it'. Sellers decided to sell his share of profits, and the Boultings paid him £17,500. Had he kept them, he would have seen them valued at some £120,000!

Shepperton had proven itself with *The Third Man* television series as being willing and able to service television productions. Lew Grade's ITC was achieving considerable success with the first series of *Danger Man* starring Patrick McGoohan.

Series one was produced at MGM Studios in Borehamwood, but after a few episodes at MGM, series two found its home transferring to Shepperton when producer Aida Young left to start work on a film and was replaced by Sidney Cole. Editor and Second Unit Director John Glen recalls:

Patrick McGoohan was Dangerman. (Courtesy Jaz Wiseman – www.itc-classics.com)

The final day at MGM was incredible. We had to be out by Friday night, but still had three episodes simultaneously shooting. We didn't want to have to carry the sets over to Shepperton, so I was on the floor shooting one unit and Pat was changing costumes and rushing from one stage to another. At the end of the day, all inserts were completed and we started shooting new episodes at Shepperton the following Monday morning. It was quite an achievement.

A couple more ITC shows were produced at Shepperton that year too: *Man of the World* with Craig Douglas, and *Sentimental Agent* starring Carlos Thompson who, according to Editor John Glen, 'went AWOL towards the end of filming. We had to shoot the last episode without him.' Neither show made it to a second series.

The Innocents was a curious offering from Jack Clayton – curious in its content. It is said that modern-day films *The Others* with Nicole Kidman and *The Sixth Sense* both owe more than a passing nod to this chiller, based on Henry James's *Turn Of The Screw*. Spooky sound effects, weird music and a general sense of tension-lead uncertainty all culminate in an ending which has been called awesome as many times as it has been labelled ambiguous – but that depends on just what you see in the film!

In late nineteenth-century England, an inexperienced young woman (Deborah Kerr) becomes governess to a small orphan girl living in a lonely stately home with a housekeeper and a small complement of servants. Then, eerie apparitions and inexplicable behaviour on the children's part cause her to wonder about the house's history, especially about the fate of the previous governess and the former valet, Peter Quint (Peter Wyngarde), and to fear for the children's souls and for her own sanity. Eventually convinced that there is an unnatural force at work, perverting the innocence of her charges, she sets out to secure the children's salvation by wresting them from its power.

'*The Innocents* is one of my favourite films,' says Cameraman Ronnie Maasz:

It was beautifully photographed by Freddie Francis, and we shot in Cinemascope. Jack [Clayton] had this thing about doing six or seven minute takes, and it was really a two-hander between Deborah Kerr and Meg Jenkins. We did all sorts of things, wandering through this house on set, going up stairs, down stairs, going through doorways – they were all constructed especially wide so as to allow the dolly through – and we shot on the floor with every aperture available to us, as Jack was very keen to get a great depth of focus. It also necessitated a tremendous amount of light, and in some sequences, for close up, with a narrow aperture, Deborah would have a couple of Brutes right in front of her. The light (and heat) would have been very uncomfortable, but such was her professionalism, she never complained. Then we'd go the other way, when say she was walking holding a candle, and shoot it absolutely wide open. It was a very challenging film to photograph.

Norman Wisdom was one of Rank's biggest stars in the 1950s, and following this success he branched out to make a few films for Producer John Bryan and United Artists. Sadly, none were as successful as his Rank films, least so *The Girl on the Boat* from a novel by P.G. Wodehouse. Millicent Martin, Richard Briers, Sheila Hancock, Athene Seyler and a host of other British stars lent support, but failed to lift this period tale to above average.

'Henry Kaplan was a Canadian,' recalls Editor Noreen Ackland, 'and I guess they were trying to transform Norman Wisdom into an America star following his great success in his films for Rank. I have to say it was a pleasant film to work on, but I'm afraid the story really didn't have the comedic elements the public had associated with Norman.'

Norman Wisdom says of Producer John Bryan:

He was a bit strict, though not over money – I leave that all to my agent – but I remember one incident where I left the set for a short while. I had a terrible headache or something so went to the dressing room to rest. I was away for longer than the few minutes I said I'd be and John came in and gave me a real telling off. I just said I was sorry and went back on the set. He was very efficient as a producer but not so jovial as Hugh Stewart [his Rank producer].

Val Guest next returned to Shepperton with an apocalyptic sci-fi drama called *The Day the Earth Caught Fire*.

'Every writer, every director has had some pet project they've struggled over the years to get made,' recalls Guest:

I had one I'd been bashing against the walls of Wardour Street to no avail for the best part of seven years. It was a story I'd dreamed up called *The Day The Earth Caught Fire* – my vision of the future where mankind had done so many things to the atmosphere, then topped everything by inadvertently testing two atomic bombs at opposite ends of the globe at the same moment. All of which had altered the earth's orbit by one millionth of a degree, and set us spinning slowly but surely towards the sun with disastrous climatic changes. Where upon the government puts a security clamp on the whole incident which is eventually ferreted out by a relentless Fleet Street reporter.

At that time I had no idea how near I was to predicting global warming. I had even less idea that the finished picture would win me a British Academy Film

Val Guest's *The Day the Earth Caught Fire* with Leo McKern, Janet Munro and Edward Judd. (Courtesy Canal and Image UK Ltd)

Award, or that Eleanor Roosevelt would ask for her own personal copy and that President Kennedy would screen a print in Washington for a meeting of foreign correspondents.

Having struggled to realise the project for seven years, Guest found himself in a 'green-light' position with Michael Balcon and Maxwell Setton setting up PAX Films in order to co-present with British Lion.

In retrospect, *The Day The Earth Caught Fire* was probably the toughest film assignment I'd ever set myself. For instance, one line in the screenplay reads: 'They cross a debris strewn Fleet street, derelict and almost deserted ... ' How easy it is to write. Now try and shoot it.

Fortunately, the City Police co-operated fully, as did the *Daily Express*. Meanwhile, production commenced in Battersea Park:

It was a sequence in which climatic change brings a mysterious fog swirling up the Thames, engulfing South London and Battersea Park. Armed with all the necessary permits our machines were happily belching out clouds of grey fog when a gentle breeze began wafting it across to Chelsea Embankment. Within minutes a squad of police cars had raced to our location, ordering us to shut down. It seemed our fog was swirling over the Royal Chelsea Flower Show which Her Majesty The Queen was, at that moment, trying to declare it open in rapidly worsening visibility. Somehow we managed to finish filming by employing delay tactics with the police, explaining it took a long time to turn these machines off etc.

The Fleet Street scenes had to be filmed early on a Sunday morning, and with military precision and in very short time, between bursts of London traffic. Exteriors completed, it was back to Shepperton for all the interiors and pick-up shots. Within eight weeks the film was in the can. Sixteen weeks later it premiered at the Odeon Marble Arch. Social realism was becoming more popular in British cinema. John Schlesinger's *A Kind of Loving* was perhaps Shepperton's first film in the genre. It presented the censor with a few dilemmas too.

In a 1993 interview, John Schlesinger said:

I suppose, that once the Royal Court had started their famous period with *Look Back in Anger*, and films like that, and Tony Richardson and John Osborne had formed the *Woodfall* films, and insisted that they made the film of *Look Back in Anger*, and that kind of thing; they really paved the way for us that followed, into making a certain kind of gritty realistic film. And *Saturday Night and Sunday Morning* had preceded *A Kind of Loving*, but that was newish territory, and it was territory that became, and was, quite popular at the time.

I remember the censor being very hard on us, because there was a scene in which to get his girlfriend aroused, Alan Bates, who played the part of Vic, was looking at a sort of semi-pornographic magazine and the censor was rather against this. Also the idea that they would go into a shop, a chemist shop and buy condoms – now a common practice, alas – was absolutely taboo in a way. I mean it was, had never been seen.

Alan Bates (a draughtsman) and his co-worker June Ritchie live a dreary northern English town, and must marry when she becomes pregnant. Together they persevere to enjoy 'a kind of loving.' Thora Hird turns in a truly wonderful performance as Bates' mother. A beautiful piece of film making, which won the Golden Bear at the Berlin Film Festival.

1962 was equally busy at the studio, with twenty-six films moving before cameras. Following the success of *A Kind of Loving*, John Schlesinger set his sights on his next project: *Billy Liar*. Producer Jo Janni employed much of Loving's production team, including Cinematographer Denys Coop, Art Director Ray Simm, and, of course, Schlesinger. (Janni and Schlesinger would go on to produce a string of hits together, including *Darling, Far from the Madding Crowd* and *Sunday Bloody Sunday*.) The screenwriting partnership of Waterhouse and Hall – now officially in business together with their Waterhall Productions – were naturally paired again for the Billy Liar screenplay.

Schlesinger chose the introverted actor Tom Courtenay to play Billy, after his success with the character on stage. Two other actors were cast directly from the play: Mona Washbourne as Billy's long-suffering mum; and, as Billy's senile grandmother, Ethel Griffies, who, two years later, would repeat her stage and screen role in the Broadway production – at the age of eighty-eight. Wilfred Pickles stepped in as Billy's sourpuss dad. Helen Fraser, who had a brief comic role in *A Kind of Loving*, was cast as the prim, virginal Barbara, while Gwendolyn Watts became the foul-mouthed Rita.

But it was the part of the free-spirited Liz – who offers Billy both marriage and the chance to escape to London – that posed the greatest casting problem. The part was originally to be played by an actress with the unlikely name of Topsy Jane, who had played Courtenay's girlfriend in *Loneliness of the Long Distance Runner*. A month into the twelve-week-shoot, she suffered a nervous breakdown and was replaced by an unknown actress who had already been tested and rejected by Schlesinger: Julie Christie, who previously had only small parts in two 'Quota Quickies'.

The introduction of Liz/Christie in the film became the film's most famous sequence. John Goldstone was the film's producer and remembers how 'we made great use of the whole lot at Shepperton and for a funeral sequence, we covered it all in fake snow. It was ideal. We'd have had difficulty doing it anywhere else.'

In his biography of David Lean, Kevin Brownlow relates how that one scene influenced Lean in the casting of *Doctor Zhivago*, as he immediately offered Julie Christie the role of Lara, ending a long search on the spot. *Billy Liar* was a triumph for Schlesinger, Waterhouse and Hall and for twenty-six-year-old Courtenay. Nominated for six British Academy Awards, it was also included in the British Film Institute's poll of The 100 Greatest British Films of All Time.

The Boulting Brother's next production was *Heavens Above!* with Peter Sellers – possibly in one of his finest roles as Revd Smallwood, a socialist priest mistakenly

The many faces of Billy Liar. (Courtesy Canal and Image UK Ltd)

sent to an upper-crust English village. The film is a perfect satire on British society as well as religion's role in it. Support came from Cecil Parker, Eric Sykes, Irene Handl, Mark Eden and Ian Carmichael as the 'other Revd Smallwood'.

'It was a little favour actually,' said Ian Carmichael. 'The Boultings rang up my agent and said that they were sorry but there just wasn't anything for me in the picture, but asked if I might be interested in a little two-day-filming part of the other Smallwood. Would consider it? I was delighted to, as I loved working with them. It was a favour from them to me, and me to them.'

Mark Eden played Sir Geoffrey Despard:

I was doing a play at the time, earning £20 a week, and received the call to go and see Roy and John. They offered me the part, and a fee of £3,000 – which was a fortune back then. I remember we were on location at the gypsy site one day, standing around, waiting – as is the norm – and suddenly Roy appeared and said 'do you play cricket Eden?' I said I hadn't since school. With that he opened the boot of his Bentley, and produced two cricket bats, two sets of wickets, and we had a scratch game.

Locations included Guildford, St Alban's, Feltham and, of course, Shepperton, where *The Smith's House* (Eric Sykes' family) was built on the back-lot.

'I think *Heavens Above!* was a brilliant piece of comedy acting,' noted Roy Boulting in a 1997 letter on Peter Sellers and the film:

Peter's performance was so well controlled, with simplicity and beauty. Peter was a natural. All that he had to learn from John and myself was that you don't have to 'act' if you're thinking right, you don't have to project if you're thinking the part and therefore living the part because it's going to come out on screen.

No matter what is said which may appear to be detrimental to Sellers, the fact is that all over the world there are millions of people who receive pleasure from the work he did. I can think of no other comedian actor who has created such a variety of characters. His ability to produce characters of such diversity and with such assurance, which inform millions of people who recognise themselves, makes him the greatest talent this country has produced since Charlie Chaplin.

'It was, in my opinion,' concludes Mark Eden, 'Peter Sellers' best film. I only had one major scene with him, but found him a total delight to work with. I also remember all of the gypsy children … they were getting a bit restless between takes, and so Peter produced a ukulele and entertained them with a George Formby act. He was a unique.'

It was a particularly busy time for Shepperton, which prompted Roy Boulting to pen a memo entitled '*Heaven's Above!* Or How I Learned to Stop Worrying And Live With A Dozen Other Producers In The Same Studio At The Same Time.'

He stated that 'there are never less than six films including those being edited and in post production, at the studio.'

He went on to explain that:

Rumbles of protest are heard from different quarters which called for an opportunity for studio management to re-evaluate the economic basis of its relationship with the renter. Too much of craft labour is of poor quality. The proportion of able, reliable craftsmen available to each production becomes smaller when a greater number of films have to be serviced. Sets therefore take longer to construct and finish. A greater amount of overtime has to be worked. As a result the producer has to pay more for less in quantity and quality.

Heaven's Above! – the Smith house on the Shepperton back-lot. (The Boulting Brothers Archive)

Strong words indeed. One of a new breed of directors making his mark in the business was Michael Winner. Having made coffee-bar set *Play It Cool* with Billy Fury over at Pinewood, he turned his attentions to *The Cool Mikado*, which was loosely based on the Gilbert & Sullivan operetta.

Camera Operator Ronnie Maasz confides:

Michael was at his best on this; that is, he was generally unpleasant all round. He fired people at random and could be incredibly rude. The only way to deal with him was to give back as good as he gave. I managed to survive by employing this technique.

When shooting the musical numbers we would always cover it with two cameras. For reasons known only to himself, Michael took a dislike to second camera operators, no matter how efficient they were, and would not have the same one twice. On the final day, we had one last musical number to shoot on the stage, so I called a friend and colleague, one Neil (Ginger) Gemmell. I warned him to be wary of Michael.

At lunchtime, we were just leaving the stage when, sure enough, Michael called him over. I went with him.

Michael (very pompously): 'Now Ginger, I always ask the second camera operator whether he has done anything wrong this morning. Have you?'

Ginger (very slowly): 'Yes, yes, I have.'

Michael (triumphantly): 'And what was it?'

Ginger: 'It was coming here and working with you in the first place!'

Winner roared with laughter and Ginger could do no wrong from then on in.

Roy Baker, after leaving the bosom of the Rank Organisation and his great successes therein, directed his second Shepperton film after the misfiring *Valiant*, entitled *Two Left Feet* starring Michael Crawford, David Hemmings, Julia Foster and Nyree Dawn Porter.

Says Baker of the film:

It was a simple comedy of teenaged boys having trouble with girls, and vice versa. The setting was bang up to date London 1962. I took it to British Lion: David Kingsley, John and Roy Boulting, Frank Launder and Sidney Gilliat. What a pleasure it was to be with people all talking the same language. They were cautious, but after long discussions they liked it and agreed to set it up. Leslie Gilliat agreed to produce. The script needed some work, so I roped in John Hopkins, who straightened out the construction, shortened it and gave it a fine polish.

Just when we were all set to start serious preparation, casting and so on, there was a hitch. I can't remember what the problem was, probably studio space, but we had to postpone shooting for six months. The picture would now not be shown until the next year and I was afraid that by that time it would no longer be topical. Also I knew that there were other people in the field with pictures about young people in the sixties. If I had been really brave I would have suggested abandoning the project, but I wasn't and we waited.

Producer Leslie Gilliat adds:

I don't really remember a six month delay as such. I know we had to do a re-write, and I remember Roy taking me to one of the West End theatres to see a young Michael Crawford in *Come Blow Your Horn*. I seem to recall we had to wait for Michael to become available, as we were quite set on having him. Perhaps it was a combination of this, script and maybe studio availability?

Roy Baker notes:

When at last it came to casting, we laid down one qualification: everyone must be under twenty-one. The cast turned out to be one of the best I've ever had. They were all terrific and the picture turned out well. At least, I thought so, especially at a sneak preview one evening at a cinema in King's Cross. The audience laughed their heads off. However, the circuit bookers who had been present throughout took no notice of the audience reaction. They turned us down – no general, or even limited, release. After a lot of pleading and bargaining by Frank and Sidney, and the Boultings, we were given a limited release in a double bill shared with another film none of us had ever heard of.

Modest fare helped keep the production at full capacity. Lance Comfort directed *The Break*, a crime-thriller, while editor-turned director Charles Saunders ended his career by directing *Danger By My Side*, another crime thriller. Meanwhile, John Paddy Carstairs completed his film career by directing a Germany-UK-US co-production called *The Devil's Agent*, starring Peter van Eyck and Christopher Lee, which filmed primarily in Ireland and Vienna!

Lee points out that the 'production moved from crisis to crisis as it was never certain whether the money would be coming for the next reel.'

Bryan Forbes recalls how his next project came into being:

I was in the Beverly Hills Hotel, and passing through the dimly lit Polo Room a hand came out of the gloom and thrust a book at me. 'Read that, and if you like it write a screenplay for me.' It was producer James Woolf. I looked at the title of the book. It was Lynn Reid Banks' *The L Shaped Room*. 'Take it away and let me know', he continued. That was always how he did deals, on a hunch, on a handshake, and his handshake was good.

The *L Shaped Room* had originally been earmarked for Jack Clayton to direct, but Jack was ever so slow to come to a decision and after six months or so Jimmy got tired of waiting and gave the direction to me. The film starred Leslie Caron and Tom Bell.

Bryan Forbes directs Nanette
Newman in *The L-Shaped Room*.
(Courtesy Dave Worrall Collection)

Actor Mark Eden describes:

I was a friend of Tom's, and went
along with him to the studio
one day to meet Forbes and
Attenborough, in the hope of
getting a little part. 'You look like
Tom Bell' they said to me. I guess
I did a little. They went away for
a minute or two, and then came back. Leslie Caron's character had to fall for
another man, and fall pregnant. If she was attracted to Tom Bell, they thought it
would make good sense to have me as 'the other man', Terry. And so I got the
job.

Leslie asked me if I'd ever worked for the Royal Shakespeare Company. I
said no. She seemed surprised, but I explained that I'd never been asked. A few
weeks later, having thought no more about it, I got a call from her husband
Peter Hall, asking if I'd be interested in starring with Judi Dench in a play. He
didn't need to ask twice!

Forbes adds:

When the film was finished, we ran into difficulties with the censor, who sent
us four closely typed pages of items that were unacceptable. He was not happy
with any references to contraceptives, breast and thigh rubbing and copulatory
dancing were totally ruled out, as were all erotic visuals. I remember that Leslie
Caron had to have her nipples covered with Elastoplast for the love scene, and
the sequence where she visited the Harley Street abortionist, played with sinister
charm by Emlyn Williams, was tortuously oblique.

Cy Endfield returned to Shepperton with a film called *Hide and Seek*, as star Ian
Carmichael recalls:

Producer Hal Chester, who made *School for Scoundrels* in which I appeared, had
what I thought was an absolutely marvellous script. He offered me the lead,
and quite honestly I was thrilled as it was a super Cary Grant-style thriller with
romance.

Hal was a very volatile man, and far too much of a hands on producer.
There were constant battles between him and Cy all the way through and a

consequence of this was that we got to practically the end of our ten-week schedule, with a lot still left to shoot. Universal, who were behind it, granted us an extra week, but still it wasn't completed. In, I dare say, total frustration, Universal then said they were pulling the plug and we had until Friday to finish. In a hurry, a lot of bits of sets were constructed in one stage in Shepperton, and we raced around doing pick-up shots all over the place. By the time Friday came around, the film was not finished, but we all went our separate ways.

A few weeks later Janet Munro and I were called back to do a day's location shoot, somewhere near Torquay, and the footage was slung together. It was a great, great heartbreak to me as it was a wonderful story and we had a terrific cast: Curt Jurgens, Hugh Griffith, Kieron Moore and the delightful Esma Cannon. I think it had a showing, but was more or less 'lost'. I don't know what happened to it.

I do remember, however, that mid-way through shooting the Cuban Missile Crisis broke, and we all left to go home on the Friday not quite knowing if we'd be around to return to work on Monday. We were of course, but it was quite nail biting.

Wendy Toye made a welcome return to Shepperton, after her happy association with Alex Korda some years earlier, with a short film called *The King's Breakfast*. She recalls:

We had the most incredible cast for a short: Maurice Denham, Michael Pearson, Larry Bowers and David Warner in his first film; he was one of the four trumpeters. It was based on a three minute poem: ... 'The king asked the queen, and the queen asked the dairy-maid, can we have some butter for the royal slice of bread' ... and I made it into a twenty-two minute film!

'It was, in fact,' adds camera operator Ronnie Maasz, 'a gigantic butter commercial for a Danish company!'

A film being developed by United Artists, for Judy Garland, was entitled *The Lonely Stage*. Whilst he was completing filming in the USA on another project, Ronnie Neame was sent the script. He readily agreed to direct:

Judy was a woman with immense energy, yet with a vulnerability coming through her eyes. I was absolutely elated to have the opportunity of making a film with someone of her talent. The film was to be shot entirely at Shepperton and on various locations in that area, including two important sequences at the London Palladium.

Dirk Bogarde was cast opposite Garland, and worked on polishing the script with Mayo Simon – but refused on taking a screen credit for his work.

'By late spring 1962, the script was ready,' continues Ronnie Neame. 'I was ready, and Judy arrived in London with her three children – Liza, Lorna and Joey. After the first day of filming, she bestowed upon me the nickname "Pussycat". From then on, when I was in favour, she would say "We're all right Pussycat aren't we?" Giving her a hug I would reply "We're all right Judy."'

Garland did have a reputation of being a difficult actress to work with, but Ronnie Neame was confident these stories were exaggerated as he found her a total delight. However, things started to change a week or two into the shoot. Neame's assistant, Colin Brewer, would receive an early morning phone call from one of Garland's entourage saying, 'Miss Garland won't be in today'. No excuse was offered. Her mood swings were significant. On good days, no one could come close to her magical presence; and on bad days, everyone avoided her.

'I learned a lot from working with her,' confides Neame, 'particularly about helping actors who are insecure. One must build their confidence, and so I would praise Judy before moving to the next setup. I knew little about her early history and how she'd been given drugs by the studios to keep her going. This led to her lifetime usage and eventual death.'

The final song in the film was *I Could Go on Singing*, and was one of the last sequences to be filmed with Garland. Relations between the director and star in the final week had deteriorated. Garland insisted Neame be removed from the film at one point, but Arthur Krim at backers United Artists gave Neame his full support and asked him to finish the film, and threatened Garland's agent with a lawsuit unless she cooperated, as the picture would have to be closed down. The song was to be staged at the Palladium. Thousands of extras were recruited to fill the theatre, many from Garland's fan club.

However, there was no Garland. With time ticking by, Ronnie Neame played *Judy*, miming the song to playback. The enthusiastic and noisy audience reactions were shot. Suddenly, 'She's in!' was whispered across the stage.

I managed a cordial 'Hello Judy' when she came on, and she asked 'What do you want me to do?' I showed her. 'That's okay, Pussycat', she replied as though the last week had never happened. Judy completed the scene as brilliantly as anything she'd ever done. The very last shot of the film was on a lovely sunny day on the lawn at Shepperton. The entire unit was there. It was a simple exterior close shot. Once done I said quietly 'That's it Judy darling, it's finished, it's really finished.' She repeated 'It's really finished.'

She looked at me, then the whole unit and said 'You'll miss me when I'm gone!'

As she left the set for the last time, many of us were in tears. It had certainly been an emotional roller-coaster ride. The song, *I Could Go on Singing*, became the title of the film. And all these years later, she was right. We do miss her.

Whilst not filmed at the studio, Producer Sam Spiegel and Director David Lean chose Shepperton for the post production of *Lawrence of Arabia*. The film won an Oscar for best sound in 1963, a tribute to John Cox who was the chief re-recording mixer.

The Victors was a film from Carl Foreman and is most certainly a 'spot the star' movie, with a top-notch cast and even smaller roles filled by substantial named actors,

Carl Foreman and Rosanna Schiaffino on the set of *The Victors*. (Courtesy Geoffrey Helman)

Vince Edwards, George Hamilton, Albert Finney, Peter Fonda, Eli Wallach and George Peppard amongst them – Carl Foreman spared no expense, it seemed.

The film's location manager, Geoffrey Helman, reveals:

Well actually, Carl was one of the most cost conscious producers I've worked with. He was never mean, but kept a tight rein. In fact, when I was invited to meet with him for the film, I was under contract to the Danzeiger brothers out at Elstree making very low budget television shows such as *Interpol* and *Richard The Lionheart*. Our schedules were so tight that I couldn't get away from the set to meet Carl, and so I asked if it could be a Saturday morning. His secretary, Eve (whom he later married), confirmed that Saturday morning was fine. When I met him he asked what I was currently working on. Slightly embarrassed (as the Danzeiger brothers had a reputation for being cheap) I told him. He told me that on no account should I be embarrassed as I was learning at one of the best film schools around – that of the no-budget production. You had neither time nor money to go for take two, so everything had to be right first time. I could see he admired that.

Needless to say, Helman got the job and was soon dispatched to the main location in Naples. He continues:

Vince Edwards was very famous on television at the time as Ben Casey, a top doctor/surgeon. One day, out on location, I received a call to say Vince had slipped whilst climbing and grazed his knuckles very badly, and needed a tetanus jab. I 'phoned to the town, and alerted the local doctor. When Vince arrived back at base, I put him in my car and drove him to the surgery. He point blankly refused to have the jab on account of the doctor's surgery not being clean enough. I asked what we could do, and he suggested I drive him to the US Naval Base some two hours away. I had no option. Into the car we got, and drove. Once at the Naval base, he again refused to have the injection, making various excuses. The Naval doctor was growing impatient and said as we'd driven all that way, he may as well have the jab. Just then Vince fainted. Apparently he was terrified of injections! An actor famous for playing a surgeon … terrified!

CHAPTER 13

AMICUS

Shepperton could never really claim it had a 'series' of films – like the *Bonds* and *Carry Ons* at Pinewood – based at the complex. That changed with the arrival of two Americans: Milton Subotsky and Max J. Rosenberg.

Amicus (which is Latin for 'friend') – Subotsky and Rosenberg's company – was to make thirty films in twenty years and employ the likes of Freddie Francis, Roy Ward Baker and Kevin Connor behind the camera, with talent such as Peter Cushing, Donald Sutherland, Donald Pleasance, Britt Ekland, Joan Collins, Christopher Lee and Vincent Price in front of cameras.

Already familiar with the studio, having made *City of the Dead* there in 1960, and *It's Trad Dad* the following year, Subotsky and Rosenberg were to embark upon an extremely successful and popular franchise of horror films, starting in 1964 with *Dr Terror's House of Horrors*. In themselves, they were quite intriguing characters. They sought no personal publicity, unlike Hammer's James Carreras, and Rosenberg was primarily US based, leaving the UK side of operations to his partner.

Milton Subotsky was born in New York in 1921, and entered the film industry at the age of seventeen as a general gopher, and there he learnt the business – from studying scriptwriting and editing, to camerawork and in the evenings, to appease his parents, he studied chemical engineering at night school. He then turned his hand to acting in a few films and television programmes until 1954, when he met Max Rosenberg, who at the time was enjoying considerable success as a film distributor. A friendship was formed, and Rosenberg backed a television series written by Subotsky called *Junior Science*.

Rosenberg, born seven years earlier than Subotsky in New York, graduated from law school in 1938, and moved into the low-budget film distribution business. Often he would take on foreign films for distribution through North America.

Having made a couple of rock 'n' roll films, *Rock, Rock, Rock* and *Disc Jockey Jamboree*, turning a good profit for the duo, they next decided to turn to horror. Subotsky wrote a screenplay entitled *Frankenstein and the Monster* and submitted it to Warner Brothers, who in turn presented it to Hammer. The Hammer executives passed on the project. Shortly afterwards, Hammer moved into production with their own *The Curse of Frankenstein*, written by Jimmy Sangster, but after threatened legal action agreed to pay Rosenberg and Subotsky a $6,000 fee and a cut of box-office returns, which were sizeable. Needless to say, it clearly sowed the seed in Subotsky and Rosenberg's minds that there was much money to be made in horror films.

'I thought it would be advantageous to have a British production company,' says Rosenberg on the setting up of Amicus, 'to take advantage of the Eady Plan. Milton, who was unmarried, and unhappy living in New York, went to London to do just that.'

However, having sent Subotsky to the UK to set up their new venture, it is curious to note that he never ever met with the financiers of their films. He was totally disinterested in that side of the business and left the negotiations and deal-making to Rosenberg.

'Never once in all the years we were together did Milton ever meet an executive. He never met anyone who featured in the financing or distribution of our films,' claimed Rosenberg after the company's winding-up some years later.

Rosenberg made a co-financing deal for their first UK-based production, *City of the Dead*, and both he and Subotsky served as executive producers on the film – a very atmospheric witchcraft chiller. The film benefited from all the fog Shepperton could produce too. 'It was American Gothic,' says Christopher Lee, one of its stars. 'It really was a very good picture in many ways, insofar as it did combine ancient superstition and ritual with modern university life.'

The final budget came in at £45,000 – some £5,000 over the initial costing.

Christopher Lee thought his greatest achievement in the production was his American accent: 'It is a very difficult thing for a British actor to do. They usually exaggerate it beyond belief.'

The black and white film had difficulty in finding an American release, however, competing with the lavish colour Vincent Price/Edgar Allan Poe productions of the time. Rosenberg renamed the film *Hotel Horror* and sold it to a minor distribution outfit.

The film made a healthy return on its investment from British and European screens, and it confirmed to Rosenberg and Subotsky that it had made financial sense to bring their production base to Britain. However, they decided to go back to their musical film roots for their next two productions, the first of which, *It's Trad Dad*, was made at Shepperton.

The mayor of a town (Felix Felton) and his council try to banish the music that young people are all listening to, so the kids try to get major disk jockeys and musical artists to come to town for a liberating concert. Cue guest appearances from Helen Shapiro, Craig Douglas, Acker Bilk, Gene Vincent, Chubby Checker and others!

It was actually Richard Lester's collaboration with Peter Sellers and The Goons, and their eleven-minute short, *The Running, Jumping, Standing Still Film* – which cost £70 to make – that led to him being offered *It's Trad Dad*, as he explains:

They showed it [*Running, Jumping*] at the Edinburgh Festival and there was this man from San Francisco who said 'I'll show it at my festival'. And then it got an Academy Award nomination so the film that we had made for ourselves for no money – we only had the one copy – was an Academy Award-nominated film and I thought, 'I've got a future now. I'm a contender.' What happens is everybody said 'We love the film, if we ever want a long version of that' – well, it was a silent film for God's sake – 'we'll let you know.'

But nobody spoke to me for two years. Until a producer called Milton Subotsky sent me a 24-page script and I said 'I think I can do something with it' – it was with pop-stars Gene Vincent and Helen Shapiro and a lot of trad bands, so I said 'I've been around this kind of music all my life. I think I know how to deal with it. As soon as you get a first draft screenplay I'd be delighted to read it'. He said 'That's the shooting script and you start in three weeks'. I said, 'But it's only 24 pages long', and he said 'You'll find a way to pad it out'.

So we gathered these poor pop people with this feast of moveable sets behind them and shot them three a day. At the end of the last week of shooting, the Twist started – Chubby Checker and his first big twist success. So I said to Milton 'I think it would be a great idea, we could be the first film in history to have the twist in it. He's in New York I could go over and shoot him'. And he said 'If you pay your own way over you can go.' So I did and we got him in the film, and that was one of the contributing factors to getting *A Hard Day's Night*.

Their next film, *Just For Fun* (1963), featured popular music groups The Crickets and The Tornados, and DJs Jimmy Saville and Alan Freeman. However, it failed to make much impact and refocused the partners on the more profitable horror genre.

A year later, in 1964, *Dr Terror's House of Horrors* commenced production. Five men, all strangers, board the evening train from London to Bradley, and just before it departs they are joined by a sixth man, Dr Schreck.

The portmanteau film incorporated a vampire, werewolf, creeping vine, voodoo and a disembodied hand. A budget of around £100,000 was raised and the title for the collective stories was suggested by Rosenberg.

Freddie Francis, the acclaimed cinematographer, had made his directing debut with *Two and Two Make Six*, closely followed by some co-direction on *Day of the Triffids*, followed by a few Hammer productions, of which Subotsky was a fan. He was approached, and readily agreed to direct.

It was next decided to recruit two of the biggest names in (Hammer) horror, Peter Cushing and Christopher Lee, and as their parts were ones that could be contained within a modest schedule, their respective fees were in line with Rosenberg's budget.

Michael Gough, Bernard Lee and Alan Freeman were also cast – DJ Freeman playing the lead in the 'creeping plant' segment. He remembers:

Going back before the film, my phone rang one day, and a voice asked 'Is that Alan Freeman?' I said 'Yes'. 'Oh I'd like to discuss you taking the lead in a stage production of Noel Coward's *Private Lives*'. I laughed and said 'Sorry you have the wrong Alan Freeman'. He then hummed my radio theme – *At the Sign of the Swinging Cymbal* – and said 'Yes, Alan Freeman the DJ'. Cutting a long story short, I was cast in the production and had the time of my life working opposite Shirley Anne Field. It was all quite mad!

I had done a couple of little things for Milton Subotsky, and maybe it was from him hearing about me – or seeing the reviews of me (which weren't terribly brilliant!) – in the play, that he put me in mind for *Dr Terror*. I was asked to go along and meet Freddie Francis, but when I heard who else had been cast, I said 'Look, I'll be honest with you, I'm terrified of letting the others down. I'm not an actor, I have trouble with lines' – but they were adamant that they wanted me. I was thrilled.

Can you imagine the feeling of going on to a set with Peter Cushing, Roy Castle, Christopher Lee and Donald Sutherland? In fact I phoned my dear old mum in Australia.

'Hello darl, what you up to?' she asked.

'Oh I'm just starting a film with Peter Cushing mum.'

'Yes love, and what are you really up to?'

It was a tremendously happy experience, and despite a hectic schedule, it went like clockwork. I'm very proud of being a part of it.

A few years ago I had a little group of friends around to my apartment, and Donald Sutherland popped up on the television. 'Ah dear Donald' I said. They all looked at me. 'I did a film with him you know.' Everyone laughed and said to pull the other one!

The late Roy Castle also made his first straight acting debut with the film. He was, in fact, a last minute replacement for Acker Bilk, who had suffered a heart attack.

The production was not without its problems, however, when soon into the shooting a large chunk of promised finance failed to materialise. Subotsky suggested scrapping the film, but Rosenberg meanwhile set about persuading Joe Vegoda, a businessman, to invest, and additionally he borrowed money from a friend in the UK and set about pulling a two-picture deal together with Paramount, to encompass this film and their next project.

The film opened to positive notices and did terrifically at the box office.

It is no surprise, therefore, that much of the same team was kept on for the next Amicus production, *The Skull*, which was based on Robert Bloch's short story *The Skull of the Marquis de Sade*. Freddie Francis again helmed, whilst Peter Cushing and Christopher Lee starred. Francis had much more of an involvement in the pre-production and casting than on *Dr Terror* and it soon became apparent to him that Subotsky's script was underwritten and knew that it would need beefing up.

Again, the budget and schedule (at five weeks) was tight, and virtually all contained within one composite set at the studio.

Joe Vegoda, now installed as Amicus' resident associate producer, next brought a project to Rosenberg and Subotsky that was based on a BBC series called *Dr Who*. At the end of 1963, the long-running series made its debut on British television screens with William Hartnell in the titular role. The 'Time Lord', travelling in his blue police box, aka the TARDIS (Time And Relative Dimensions In Space), became an instant hit – more so when the strange armour-plated villainous blobs called Daleks were introduced.

Amicus saw the potential in a film version, and did a deal with the show's creator, Terry Nation, for the film rights to story *The Dead Planet* and two projected sequels. They paid just £500.

Whilst William Hartnell was a familiar and popular face in British films, the producers knew he was little know in the USA, and therefore opted to cast Peter Cushing in the role of The Doctor.

Subotsky and Rosenberg approached British Lion with their package, and immediately received the financial backing they were seeking. As the project was seen as a family feature it was decided not to release the film as an Amicus production, which was now becoming renowned for horror films, and as such AARU Productions was formed. The company also produced the sequel, the following year.

The Daleks themselves proved an interesting assignment for Pinewood-based special effects engineer Bert Luxford:

> In the BBC series, the Daleks were made by Bill Shawcraft, who had workshops near Uxbridge. There were only ever four Daleks made for the television series, but here we needed at least twenty. Bill was now really retired, and didn't have his large premises, and so I was approached. I think I made eighteen in the end.
>
> I didn't have any drawings, only pictures. They didn't have to move around much, which simplified things, but when it came to the 'bubbles' on the outside of their bodies, we were a bit stuck as to what we should use.
>
> 'Hang on', I thought, 'I'll go to Suter's [a department store] in Uxbridge to see what I could buy roughly four inches in diameter'. I eventually ended up in the toy department. I spotted these plastic balls which were about the right size.
>
> 'How many of these have you got?' I asked.
>
> 'About twenty, I suppose', the young lady said.
>
> 'Can you make it about fifty?'
>
> 'Pardon?'
>
> 'Well, I need about fifty so as when I cut them in half ... '
>
> She gave me a strange look and said she'd have a word with the manager. I eventually came out of there with a giant bag, full of balls! I had to walk the length of the High Street to my van. I won't repeat the comments I got.
>
> Back at the studio, I took the hollow balls, drilled a small hole and injected them with PVC foam, as it's not always easy to cut plastic balls in half. This way I had a solid ball that I could take to my lathe, where I spun them and cut a perfect circle with a blade lined up exactly in the centre. We rubbed them down, stuck them onto the hardboard bodies and sprayed them, before sticking on the sink plungers (and they were sink plungers) and lights, which I bought from car spares shops.

The 'weaponry' of the Daleks fell to another special effects engineer, Allan Bryce, and after flame throwers were briefly considered and then dropped when the chief censor expressed concern, the idea of using a gaseous type of weapon struck. Fire extinguishers were employed to create just that effect!

Principle photography commenced in April 1965, with a six-week schedule. A massive publicity campaign ensued, even seeing the Daleks travelling to the Cannes Film Festival!

Reviews were not overly kind, but the box-office returns were quite sensational, at least in Britain – the film flopped in America, as the television series was completely unknown. But with profits in the bank, the team rolled on. A second *Doctor Who* film was swiftly put into production for British Lion.

Daleks – Invasion Earth 2150 AD had many of the same key personnel, including Director Gordon Flemyng and Peter Cushing as The Doctor, and production cranked up in March 1966. Roy Castle and Jennie Linden were, however, both committed to other projects, and in their place Bernard Cribbins and Jill Curzon were engaged.

Again with its British release, in July of the same year, critical response was not positive. In America it fared even worse, with a minimal distribution and advertising campaign. Plans for any further outings for the TARDIS were duly shelved, though occasional rumours surfaced throughout the 1970s and '80s, with Subotsky behind them. Alas, nothing came of them.

The producers decided to go back to their earlier horror success with the next project, *The Psychopath*. It is the story of four men who were involved in the investigation of a German millionaire at the end of the Second World War, and are now found murdered with tiny dolls left next to their corpses. Part suspense thriller, part horror, *The Psychopath* was the type of film Subotsky loved.

'I like to keep an audience guessing – keep them puzzled right up to the very end,' he said.

Freddie Francis returned to the fold, and delivered one of his very best pictures as director, with an intelligent and powerful story. Patrick Wymark was cast in the lead role of Detective Inspector Holloway, with support from John Standing, Margaret Johnson, Alexander Knox and Thorley Walters. Filming started at Shepperton in September 1965 for approximately six weeks.

Early the following year, the film was released to positive reviews in both Britain and America. The company was back on course.

'Hives of horror!' – 'Excited by the smell of fear, they inflict their fatal stings!' So read the tagline for Amicus' next offering, *The Deadly Bees*. It was the first of the 'killer bee' films, and by no means the best – which is saying something when Michael Caine's *The Swarm* is universally considered to be an awful movie.

Disappointed with the finished film, Rosenberg commented, 'the result was, in my opinion, a hybrid affair with no inner consistency or logical storyline. The bees were menacing but the characters were not.'

The original screenplay was by Robert Bloch, but then received a re-write by Anthony Marriott and an almost daily re-write by Director Freddie Francis.

'I thought the original screenplay was better than the finished film,' commented Subotsky at the time. 'Freddie Francis re-wrote the entire script and then changed it almost daily whilst shooting … the re-written script made absolutely no sense at all. It was full of unnecessary dialogue and almost had no discernable storyline.'

Two million Australian bees were imported, and were temporarily housed in one of the dressing rooms at Shepperton.

Meanwhile, production got underway at neighbouring Twickenham Studios, where a room was adapted near the small stage, painted blue to look like the sky and lit with the brightest (and warmest) lights available, until the bee keeper received the nod to gather them up and release them on set.

Francis' delivered cut came in at over two hours. Subotsky then took his usual role in the cutting, and re-edited. He delivered a film of just seventy minutes and was forced to add in a dream and flashback sequence to give eighty minutes.

With so much uncertainty about the film, it must have come as a great relief when one of the US television networks bought it, paying more than the production cost, and a modestly successful theatrical release buoyed up the bottom line return. Critical response was, however, decidedly savage.

After the disappointment of the second *Dr Who* film, it came as a bit of a surprise when the producers announced two more sci-fi productions: *The Terrornauts* and *They Came From Beyond Space*. They were shot back-to-back at Twickenham in two months by Freddie Francis, and are widely regarded as the two worst films to come out of the Amicus fold. Undeterred, the producers moved straight into pre-production with their next offering, a return to the portmanteaux genre, with *Torture Garden*.

Having also made the return to Shepperton, Rosenberg and Subotsky went some way to restoring faith in Amicus' box-office potential with this film. Freddie Francis was back, and a headlining cast included Jack Palance, Burgess Meredith (these two American stars were cast at the insistence of the backers, Columbia), Peter Cushing, Michael Ripper and Ursula Howells. Robert Bloch penned the screenplay adapted from four of his own short magazine stories. The writer, however, was not overly happy with the finished films, claiming that less than 70 per cent of what he had written had been used.

Freddie Francis, now having served his contractual commitments, decided it would be his last film for Amicus for the time being (five years in fact), as he was growing tired of working with scripts he didn't particularly rate, and the ensuing constant battles with Subotsky over them and the films' editing.

Torture Garden was closely followed by Director Seth Holt's *Danger Route* with Richard Johnson, Barbara Bouchet, Sylvia Syms and Diana Dors; though alas with an intractable plot about cross-Channel espionage it was not destined for great things. No doubt it was trying to cash in on the success of the early *Bond* films, and the thirst for espionage thrillers, though compared with the lavish 007 productions it really didn't come close. A more respectable film, at least in its attempts at story and critical success, was *The Birthday Party* in 1968. Based on a Harold Pinter play and directed by William Friedkin (pre-*The Exorcist*), it starred Robert Shaw, Patrick Magee and Dandy Nicholls. It was a story of a down-at-heel lodger (Shaw) in a seaside boarding house being menaced by two mysterious strangers, who eventually take him away. However, an overly pretentious plot (perhaps something was lost in the stage-to-film adaptation?) saw it appeal only to Pinter purists.

1969's *A Touch of Love*, on the other hand, was a more successful venture. Directed by first-time feature director Waris Hussein, and starring Sandy Dennis and Ian McKellen, it was adapted from 'kitchen sink' story *The Millstone*. Rosenberg was so fascinated by the story that he paid a £1,000 option fee. It was quite a brave film for the time, about a young girl (Dennis) deciding to have a baby without a husband for support – the single parent was a bit of a taboo subject and frowned upon. She is told to give the baby up for adoption, but refuses, and as the bond between her and her baby strengthens, her initiative and instinct prevail and she learns how to be a mother – a good mother.

Critical and box-office success came with this film. Was Amicus now a 'serious drama' production house? Certainly Rosenberg would have liked to think so, but their next dramatic project failed miserably. That project was, in fact, *The Mind of Mr Soames*. Since his birth, thirty years ago, John Soames (Terence Stamp) had been in a coma. Now he has been operated on and brought to life in a neurological clinic. The plan is to oversee him develop from a 'thirty years old baby' to a man, but there's no time for the love and care a normal baby would receive.

A very ambitious project, with twice the budget of their last film, backed by Columbia, headlining artistes were secured in the shape of Robert Vaughan and Nigel Davenport. As Subotsky suggests:

> This could have been one of the great science-fantasy films of all time. The trouble was that we never knew what to do with the basic idea – a thirty year old man in a coma since birth, made conscious. How does one bring up a baby that has the strength and desires of a man? The film floundered in the last half hour and despite a great performance by Terence Stamp did not perform well at the box office.

Realising that most of their attempts to break into the sci-fi and drama market had failed, Rosenberg and Subotsky turned their attentions to another horror film, *Scream and Scream Again*. The heavies of film horror were drafted in too – Vincent Price, Peter Cushing and Christopher Lee, under the direction of German-born Gordon Hessler. It was perhaps the most unusual film they had made to date, with a mixture of science fiction, vampires and a police thriller. Subotsky penned a screenplay from the novel *The Disorientated Man*, and subsequently American International Pictures agreed to back the production, with a budget of $350,000. AIP already had Vincent Price under contract and suggested him for the lead. Everything dovetailed. The first historical teaming of the cast was something of a let down though. Cushing's role as Benedek was little more than a cameo, and was in fact an afterthought, once Lee had been cast. Knowing Cushing would accept any role, big or small, it would be publicised as 'the first teaming of the three horror heavyweights'. It was well-meaning, but ill-thought out, as it really was a wasted opportunity.

Like Freddie Francis before him, Gordon Hessler was less than impressed with Subotsky's script, declaring it 'just awful'. He then brought in Christopher Wickling to rewrite it. With a totally fresh approach, Wickling removed all mention of aliens (as were featured in the original story) and instead turned Price's mad doctor character into the one responsible for creating 'superhuman creatures'. From there, genetic experimentation became involved as the main story thrust – a much more dramatic horror style: because it was actually science fact, though ever so slightly exaggerated.

Subotsky was not happy with the new screenplay. He continually raised the matter with Hessler, who refused to be drawn into a discussion. Hessler had the ear of Louis Heyward, AIP's Head of European Production, and asked he stop Subotsky interfering, the result being that both Rosenberg and Subotsky were barred from the set. Hessler claims that:

> They were difficult to work with. They tried to take control. We engaged a freelance editor, and kept Milton away from the cutting rooms. Milton would have loved to cut it, but we knew he would argue for frame upon frame.

The completed film was released without further alteration, in January 1970, to mixed reviews ranging from 'nonsense' to 'first rate'. The cinema-going public loved it though, and it became one of AIP's most successful productions.

Sticking with the episodic theme, Rosenberg and Subotsky turned their attentions to *The House That Dripped Blood*. Comprising four stories – *Method for Murder*, *Waxworks*, *Sweets to the Sweet* and *The Cloak*. With finance dependent upon the casting of Cushing and Lee, the producers secured them early in the planning stages and augmented the cast with Ingrid Pitt, Jon Pertwee, Nyree Dawn Porter, Denholm Elliott and Joss Ackland. Peter Duffell was signed to direct and Robert Bloch to pen the screenplay. Duffell liked Subotsky immensely, and would often bring ideas to the table to be discussed and incorporated into the script. Rosenberg was a different beast, however, and from an initial dispute over the title (Duffell wanted it to be called *Death and the Maiden*) the relationship was at best prickly.

An eight-week schedule in and around Shepperton ensued, but organised so that the principles (the costly actors!) worked only for only around six days on their respective episodes. Vincent Price was offered the part that was eventually played by Jon Pertwee, but was committed elsewhere.

Milton Subotsky was now keen to shoot a film using a 3-D process. He was also keen to film Robert Louis Stevenson's *Dr Jekyll and Mr Hyde*. He convinced the backers, the NFFC and British Lion, that now was the time to combine these two desires in a film, and *I, Monster* was born.

Having adapted the screenplay himself, though carefully omitting to use the names Jekyll or Hyde, Subotsky offered directorial duties to Peter Duffell. Duffell declined due to unease with the 3-D process. Freddie Francis was next approached, but declined for the same reason.

Christopher Lee and Peter Cushing had already agreed to star, and the clock was ticking without a director being secured. Lee suggested a twenty-two-year-old named Stephen Weeks, who had impressed the actor with a show reel he had compiled. A few days before principle photography was due to commence, Weeks was signed.

Problems soon arose, however, when the young director became uncomfortable with the 3-D ideas Subotsky was hailing. Added to this, Subotsky had recently married a psychologist, and incorporated pages of Freud into the script. The director argued that the dialogue was 'static' and subsequently chopped pages out. The 3-D scheme required the camera to move from left to right, and so the director was faced with static dialogue, movement that had to flow from left to right and sets built the other way, after production designer Tony Curtis decided it would work better right to left. The actors were equally mystified as to what Subotsky was trying to achieve. After just one day's shooting, Christopher Lee pleaded with Subotsky to abandon the 3-D experiment, and re-shoot. The producer refused point-blank. He had convinced himself, and his partner, that the process worked brilliantly, though everyone else disagreed.

A virtual mish-mash of footage, that proved almost impossible to edit, was blamed on the inexperienced director, by Subotsky. He claimed Weeks didn't understand and that he never liked him in the first place. After weeks in the cutting room, an eighty-minute film was delivered – nearly half an hour of scripted tracking shots were dumped, and the 3-D process abandoned. The film was an unmitigated flop.

After an ill-fated attempt with non-Shepperton-based *What Became of Jack and Jill?*, involving two psychopathic lovers in a murder plot, to get back on track, Subotsky and Rosenberg once again turned to their old faithful – anthology horror, with *Tales From The Crypt*. Keen to have a successful and proven director on board, Subotsky approached Freddie Francis. He readily agreed, after himself experiencing a run of poor quality films. An impressive cast was assembled: Ralph Richardson, Joan Collins, Peter Cushing, Richard Greene, Ian Hendry, Nigel Patrick and Patrick Magee. The film opened to massive business in the US, and was 1972's second highest-grossing movie!

Asylum was next on the roster. A young psychiatrist interviews four inmates in a mental asylum to satisfy a requirement for his employment. He hears four stories: about a man's revenge for his murdered wife; a tailor who makes a suit with some highly unusual qualities; a woman who questions her sanity when it appears that her brother is conspiring against her; and a man who builds tiny toy robots with lifelike human heads. Roy Ward Baker, who had recently been making horror films for Hammer, was approached by Subotsky to direct *Asylum*:

All the characters in the stories are lunatics, except one and it was vital that their obsessions and fantasies should be absolutely genuine, not people putting on an act. Milton assembled a marvellous cast which was simply a list of first class actors who all responded beautifully. I was in my element and thankful to have such a group around me.

Baker asked Arthur Grant to photograph the film. Grant accepted but only a few days before filming was set to start, he explained to the director that he was ill and he felt it was irresponsible to continue with the project. A few months later, he died.

The cast assembled included Peter Cushing, Britt Ekland, Herbert Lom, Patrick Magee, Robert Powell, Richard Todd, Barbara Parkins and Charlotte Rampling. Baker recalls:

Milton and I had now established a solid working relationship, and I directed two more pictures for him. The first was from a modern novel called *Fengriffin*, a serviceable ghost story set in 1785. The centre of the piece was the leading lady, and Stephanie Beacham fitted the bill perfectly. It is true that *Fengriffin* is not much of a title for a film, so Milton's partner, Max Rosenberg, barged in. The title he chose was, *And Now The Screaming Starts*.

Released in 1973, Peter Cushing, Herbert Lom and Patrick Magee – who were together becoming something of an Amicus rep company – co-starred. The budget was some $500,000 – more than other recent Amicus offerings. It was greeted enthusiastically upon its release. Baker continues:

> The third picture was *The Vault Of Horror* (1973), another of Milton's magazine [anthology] scripts, based on an American comic. It had another star studded cast – Terry-Thomas, Dan Massey, Tom Baker, Denholm Elliott, Anna Massey and Curt Jurgens. I had never met Curt before; the charm just poured out of him and the suavity of manner was incredible. But the stories were not strong enough and the result was not up to the standard of the previous ones. It is difficult to capture the style of strip cartoons in moving pictures.

Originally prepped at Shepperton, production was moved to nearby Twickenham Studios. Baker concludes:

> Milton was one of the nicest people I ever worked with. Shy, honest, modest – not the popular image of a film producer! An admirable man. He loved the stories, and he loved film; to him, it wasn't just a business.

The film's failure, best summed up by Baker, wasn't helped by the lack of one star 'horror name'. Subotsky was heard to lament the fact that Christopher Lee was now too expensive as his agent kept increasing the asking price.

The old faithful anthology films were kept going with *Tales That Witness Madness*, a four-story asylum set drama starring Jack Hawkins, Donald Pleasance, Joan Collins and Kim Novak, all ably directed by Freddie Francis.

Realising this type of film was both popular and profitable, Rosenberg and Subotsky were immediately interested when Editor Kevin Connor – who had achieved considerable success in cutting *Oh! What A Lovely War* and *Young Winston* for Richard Attenborough – approached them with an idea. As Connor remembers:

> I spotted the short stories of Chetwynd Hayes [*The Unbidden*] at London airport whilst on my way for a holiday. They were all modern 'supernatural stories' which took place in everyday places of work. I thought this might be a cheaper way to make horror genre films. I optioned twelve of the stories with the idea of making a television series. Having secured the options, I set about with two other writers – Robin Clarke and Raymond Christodoulou – to turn

them into half hour series. Together we created the series but was turned down by every television outlet. Quote: 'there is no market for horror films on tv!!' Fortunately the screenplays found their way onto Milton Subotsky's desk via my agent John Redway. Milton had already made several 'compilation' films before and liked the idea of some of the stories. He took four of them and linked them with the old junk shop theme. I had always envisioned producing the scripts but Milton offered me the directing assignment. His theory was that editors can make good directors. So *Beyond the Grave* was born. I have Milton and Max to thank for giving me my first directing break.

John Dark, a production manager and subsequent associate producer on films such as *Casino Royale* and *Ferry to Hong Kong*, was appointed Executive in Charge Of Amicus Productions. He would later go on to produce all of Kevin Connor's UK-based features.

As Connor mentions:

It was a quiet time in the business, and assembling the cast was relatively easy at that time. The movie business was in the doldrums – Shepperton virtually empty – but everyone wanted to work for whatever money was available. Peter Cushing, Donald Pleasance, Ian Bannen, David Warner, Nyree Dawn Porter, Diana Dors, Jack Watson and Margaret Leighton – all agreed to be in the film. Also the fact that the wonderful actors I had could be in and out in a few days was a major consideration too.

It was Milton's idea to have Peter Cushing as the intermediary character; and he also wrote the links. Milton also 'advised' on the screenplay, but I think it was pretty well left intact.

Connor adds that Subotsky – unusually – did not insist on re-cutting the finished film: 'His comments on my cut where actually quite minimal and we only had one disagreement over the removal of one scene.'

The film went on to great box-office success, and even made *Variety* magazine's top fifty films of the year.

Kevin Connor (looking through the camera viewfinder) was one of a number of talented young British directors employed by Amicus. He is pictured with his director of photography, Alan Hume. (Gareth Owen Collection)

Amicus' next, the 1973 horror *Madhouse* – as it eventually became known – was to bring together Vincent Price and Peter Cushing again. Price, who was under contract to AIP, was then based in London and readily accepted. Young Editor Jim Clark, who had just directed *Rentadick*, was signed to direct the project – his last before he turned back to editing full time. Filmed at Twickenham, and on location and at Wembley Studios, the film fared poorly at the box office. It was a great disappointment to all involved. Were Amicus losing their touch? With the exception of Kevin Connor's anthology, recent films had, at best, faired only reasonably. The low-budget horror film had had its day it would seem.

Desperate for a hit, they decided to have one more crack at the horror genre with a werewolf story, *The Beast Must Die!* Peter Cushing was engaged – this time as a Nordic werewolf expert – with Anton Diffring, Charles Gray, Calvin Lockhart and Michael Gambon lending support. Television director Paul Annett was offered the directorial reigns and all seemed set for a terrific horror film, even distribution through British Lion. Much of Shepperton itself is in evidence in the film, and the 'old house' is dressed and used brilliantly.

However, a major problem ensued when, with a low budget and under-developed script, the film makers had to portray the beast on screen convincingly. They turned to a large Alsatian wolfhound named Sultan. The terrifying dog was, however, tremendously friendly and affectionate – as can be seen when he attacks in the film: he is in fact wagging his tail madly. This, the script and awful performances all meant the film could not help but flop. And it did.

Milton Subotsky claimed that 'they' never got the script right, and 'the director didn't do a very good job'. Annett – who actually did a pretty good job with what he was given – hit back, claiming that, with the exception of Kevin Connor, Subotsky hated all directors and was a terrible editor who thought he could improve any film he touched. Connor confirms:

> I had only the best experience with Milton, even though he backed off the later productions for whatever reasons. Milton asked me to re-shoot one scene in *The Land That Time Forgot*, which I duly did – because I hadn't shot it very well first time. He never came on the floor or interfered with my day to day shooting.

The Beast Must Die! was to be the last-ever horror film produced by Amicus. The company had certainly had a good run for its money in the genre, but it was time to move on and look elsewhere – that elsewhere was with Kevin Connor and Edgar Rice Burroughs.

The aforementioned *The Land That Time Forgot* was a story Subotsky had wanted to film for some years. A script was developed and Rosenberg persuaded Samuel Z. Arkoff to stump up a massive $1 million against US distribution rights. It was the biggest-budgeted Amicus film to date. Kevin Connor was signed to direct, and whilst supporting cast was secured in the shape of Susan Penhaligon, John McEnery, Keith Barron and Anthony Ainley, the main lead was still not cast with only a couple of weeks before shooting commenced. Originally Stuart Whitman was signed, but Arkoff declared him unbankable to open a picture. He was paid off and Doug McClure was brought in. McClure, though bankable, was in fact going through a marriage break up and was drinking heavily, which lead to some tension on set, though nothing Kevin Connor couldn't handle.

The family fantasy film is set in the prehistoric world of Caprona, where dinosaurs and beasts rule, stumbled upon by Doug McClure and a First World War German submarine crew, who had sunk McClure's ship and taken him and other survivors prisoner.

Some of the creatures, as created by Derek Meddings, were little more than string puppets and very basic versions of Ray Harryhausen's work, but their creaky charm added much to the film. Combined with lush production design by Maurice Carter, and wonderful photography by Alan Hume, the film rises well above its $1 million budget.

The working relationship between Subotsky and Rosenberg was, by now, waning. Subotsky was spending less and less time at the studio, claiming that he had had enough and just wanted to get away. 'We signed an agreement in June 1975,' he said, 'and I withdrew from the company.'

Kevin Connor observes:

I can't say I noticed any tensions surfacing between Milton and Max, though I never met them on a social level – only at the studio from time to time. Max was usually in America. I really don't know the reason for Max and Milton splitting. Through it though, John and I became partners and we made several films for EMI. I'm not sure if the parting of Amicus was amicable or not – probably not.

The success of *The Land That Time Forgot* saw AIP request a follow up. Another Burroughs story was chosen, *At The Earth's Core*, and was filmed over at Pinewood Studios due to Shepperton going four-wall, meaning all productions would have to take all of their own crew. John Dark and Kevin Connor were left to run the show, which Rosenberg seemed happy with.

At The Earth's Core starred McClure again, with Peter Cushing and Caroline Munro. It was a great success. Naturally another film of the same ilk followed swiftly on its heels: *The People That Time Forgot*. It was more of the same hokum and prehistoric monsters.

Before the film was released, however, Rosenberg reportedly overheard John Dark on the telephone asking, 'Why do we need the old man?'. Rosenberg decided to quit and Amicus was folded, leaving AIP to take the production credit for the film upon its release. He returned to America and re-entered the distribution arena, as well as producing occasionally.

Meanwhile, Subotsky set about a return to production with a new company. He made one of his post-Amicus films at Shepperton in 1977, *Dominique*.

It was sad day when Amicus closed down. Arguments over scripts and editing aside, Subotsky and Rosenberg brought some terrific films to the screen.

Milton Subotsky died in 1991, whilst Max Rosenberg continued financing and producing films into the late 1990s. He died in 2004.

CHAPTER 14

THE TALENTED
MR KUBRICK

1963 remained busy for the studio, with some nineteen productions cranking up. Amongst them was *Ring of Spies* starring Bernard Lee, David Kossoff and William Sylvester.

'The film is based on the actual events of the Portland Spy Ring trial,' says Producer Leslie Gilliat, 'when Iron Curtain spy Gordon Lonsdale operated a sophisticated information network centred on the leafy London suburb of Ruislip, where his contacts Helen and Peter Kroger lived – and ran a second hand bookshop.'

In November 1960, MI5 picked up the trail of the Krogers in London, identifying them with the Soviet network operated by Lonsdale. Lonsdale delivered secret information he had obtained by British traitor Harry Houghton, who, in turn, had been getting top-secret data from his girlfriend, Ethel Gee, an employee at the Admiralty Underwater Weapons Establishment in Portland. MI5 agents kept the Krogers under surveillance until Lonsdale, Houghton and Gee were arrested in early January 1961. Agents then went to the Kroger home and confronted the pair, arresting them. A search of the Kroger home yielded a mother-load of espionage equipment, including cipher pads on quick-burning flash paper, ciphers, code books, sophisticated photo equipment, a device for reading microdots, a specially-built Ronson lighter containing a coded message inside, and numerous other items. After a week of searching, agents found a powerful transmitter capable of sending in rapid bursts. There could be no doubt that the Kroger home was the communications centre for sending information to Moscow. Twenty years later, the new occupants of the Kroger home dug up a second high-speed Soviet radio transmitter in the backyard.

No one suspected anything like this could ever have happened in a sleepy London suburb. In fact, former Worton Hall Studio Assistant Doris Spriggs, whose parents lived a couple of miles north of Ruislip, recalls her father – who was a radio ham – once saying, 'Someone in this area is operating a powerful short-wave radio'. Little did they know!

'We actually filmed in the bungalow where the Krogers lived', says Gilliat, 'and it was quite something to see the many hiding places where they secreted micro

Bernard Lee headed the cast of *Ring of Spies*, a superior British thriller based on the true Kroger-spy scandal. (Courtesy Leslie Gilliat)

film, documents and other sensitive material. It was a terrific story and one that received wonderful reviews!'

So good was the story, in fact, that even before the film's mainstream release, television mogul Lew Grade approached British Lion with a view to setting up a television series based on the film – much like the BBC had many years earlier with *The Third Man* – with producers Bob Baker and Monty Berman to follow hot on the heels of the film's release. However, in an internal memo dated 5 November 1962, British Lion's David Kingsley turned down the idea:

> Frank and Sidney [Launder and Gilliat – the film makers who instigated the feature] could not give time to it. They do not feel it could be put into production as a quality series in the time required. I also told him [Lew Grade] we might be interested in reconsidering if the whole thing were made with a view to a release in September 1964 [a year later]. Meanwhile we would be willing to consider selling him the title and first script, and we would be interested in making our studios available.

Lew Grade was keen to make one hour episodes for £22,000 (the budget of his *Saint* series which Baker and Berman produced) but Kingsley was minded otherwise. He argued that the reason *The Saint* was £22,000 was because there was no location work – it was all filmed at Elstree. He felt *Ring of Spies* should be a more elaborate production. Also, he was keen to push for episodes to be eighty minutes in duration in order to get some possible cinematic mileage from a release. It was obvious that both men were thinking in different directions. The series was never made.

Peter Glenville's production of *Becket* was a Shepperton film noted for remarkable sets. The film, starring Richard Burton, Peter O'Toole, Donald Wolfit and John Gielgud, had its look created by production designer John Bryan. The set of the interior of Canterbury Cathedral (built on the silent H stage) was remarkably accurate down to the last detail, and showed off the craftsmanship of the Shepperton construction staff. Richard Burton and Peter O'Toole both received Oscar nominations as Best Actor. *Becket* did win for Best Screenplay and nothing for Art Direction or acting.

Interestingly, the director had fired Burton, some years before, from *Adventure Story*. Burton accepted the part of Becket saying 'providing I don't get fired again.' Burton later said, referring to himself and O'Toole:

We had the reputation for terrible wildness. So our colleagues were quite surprised to see us holding nothing but tea cups for ten days. When it became clear that the two of us had a common rapport I put on my best Irish accent and said 'Peter, me boy, I think we deserve a little snifter.' Then we drank for two nights and one day. We appeared quite blasted for the scene wherein the King puts the ring on Becket's finger making him Chancellor of England. There was no dialogue, so that was no problem. But O'Toole had a dreadful time putting that ring on me. It was rather like trying to thread a needle wearing boxing gloves.

Another film in 1963 was to star Peter O'Toole – *Lord Jim*, directed by American Richard Brooks.
Sound Mixer John Aldred describes how:

Brooks had dictated that nobody other than certain members of the unit could see the rushes. He even went up into the projection room to black out the viewing ports, but the projectionists explained that they had to see the screen. All through the production a separate crew was making a 16mm film of the day-to-day activities, which was finally called *Do it on the Whistle!* This was in reference to Brooks using whistles to direct the crowd scenes. The end of picture party was a lavish affair in the studio grounds, to which I was invited, and *Do it on the Whistle!* was screened for the entire unit and proved to be hilarious. Richard Brooks took it all in good humour.

Perhaps the most important film of the year came with *Dr Strangelove: Or How I Learned to Stop Worrying and Love the Bomb*. In it, an insane general starts a process to nuclear holocaust that a war room of politicians and generals frantically try to stop.
    This was the height of the Cold War, the Cuban Missile Crisis and so on, and Director Stanley Kubrick had become fascinated by the threat of nuclear Armageddon. He felt there was a very powerful story to be told. Initially he set about reading dozens of books on the subject and formulated all of the elements of a tense thriller in his mind. He then realised, however, that perhaps the best way of telling his story would be from a satirical angle: a nightmare comedy. The absurdities would, though, be placed within a realistic framework. Kubrick turned to writer Terry Southern, whose novel *Candy* had caused a sensation with its satirical look at modern sexuality.
    'He was an incredible character,' says Production Designer Sir Ken Adam, 'with a quirky sense of humour, and he contributed greatly to the satire that Stanley was looking to achieve.'
    In a 1990s interview, Screenwriter Terry Southern explained a little about the background of the film:

When Kubrick and [Peter] George first began to do the script, they were trying to stick to the melodrama in Peter George's book, *Red Alert* [for which Kubrick paid $3,500 for the option]. There was an outline. They didn't go into a treatment,

Stanley Kubrick, the reclusive director, made the journey from America to film *Dr Strangelove*. He subsequently settled in the UK. (Gareth Owen Collection)

but went straight into a script. They had a few pages. Kubrick realized that this was not going to work. You can't do the end of the world in a conventionally dramatic way or Boy Meets Girl way. You have to do it in some way that reflects your awareness that it is important and serious. It has to be a totally different treatment and black humour is the way to go. That was Kubrick's decision.

Following the success of Kubrick's *Lolita*, and particularly the casting of Peter Sellers, Columbia Pictures – who were committed to backing Strangelove – insisted Sellers be cast, not in one, but in multiple roles.

Kubrick contacted the Boulting Brothers to arrange contracting Sellers. In a letter to John Boulting dated 7 September 1962, Kubrick wrote, 'As Pete may have told you, I am trying to decide between England and America, there being absolutely no exterior problems with either place.'

He went on to ask – in a typed, though ink-corrected letter – a series of questions about the problems posed in requiring a break-away mock-up of the interior of a large jet bomber, for background shooting: 'Might there be any stock units (say of a Boeing 707 or a Comet) which might be altered and added to? If not, what would your guess be to build something like that from a clean start?'

He went on to explain that:

I have about forty shots of an eight foot model of a jet bomber and actual flying backgrounds, to be matted together. I have so many questions about this, I wonder if you could ask whoever is the top colour (model and matte) man to call me collect in New York … I trust there would be no great problem in having a marvellously detailed, eight foot model of a jet bomber – no?

Taking an approximate guess, how much more would you say it would add to below the line costs to shoot in colour instead of black and white, assuming an ideal crew?

Do you have the new high-speed Eastman colour stock in Britain? Is it operational?

Can one do really good back projection in colour in Britain? That may sound like a silly question but I can't remember anything recent I've seen in colour.

He concluded with:

> If there are no overwhelming problems, I should love to work at Shepperton under the benevolent eyes of you and John [meaning Roy] and I appreciate your offer to get me a hard-hitting, split-second, fabulously talented, steadfastly loyal crew.
>
>   Best Stan
>
>   PS Do you have electricity at Shepperton?

Roy Boulting telephoned Kubrick and reassured him of everything on 12 September.

Peter Sellers now refused to leave England. It was suggested the reason was 'romantic', but Kubrick (who was still undecided between shooting in Britain or America) knew he needed Sellers for the film, and so offered the star a deal – $1 million and the promise to film out of a British studio. Sellers agreed.

A letter dated 4 October 1962 from Mo Rothman at Columbia Pictures in New York, to John Boulting, indicated that they too had suggested shooting in Shepperton to Kubrick:

> Dear John
>
> We have been having several meetings here in New York with Stan Kubrick who tells me he knows you and Roy quite well.
>
> I am sure you will be pleased to hear that we have signed a two picture deal with Kubrick, the first of which will be *Dr Strangelove*.
>
> Kubrick is proceeding to London very shortly and is looking for suitable studio space to shoot his picture. This naturally gave Mike Frankovich the opportunity to explain our close relationship with British Lion and that we would prefer to see him make the picture at the Shepperton Studios. Kubrick was most receptive to the idea and has promised to contact you immediately upon his arrival so that he can carry this idea further forward to what we all here hope will be a fruitful conclusion.

Further correspondence ensued between Kubrick and the Boultings. Kubrick was booked to sail on 4 October, just prior to which the Boultings had asked him for an idea as to his studio requirements – he still had no final budget nor schedule, and so could not answer, instead requesting, 'Can you wait until I get there for a definite answer … I am too much in the dark on all the details (every detail).'

He did add, tongue-in-cheek, however, 'I have heard nothing but praise about Shepperton, and I would like to work there, assuming there are no importantly unfavourable comparisons with other studios on terms, facilities, toilets etc.'

In the event, Kubrick was hugely happy with Shepperton, and pre-production commenced. Sir Ken Adam, who Kubrick engaged as his production designer, notes that:

He was fascinated by my war-time record as a fighter pilot, and we immediately hit it off. I would in fact drive Stanley to and from Shepperton in my E type Jaguar which was the fastest sports car around, but Stanley insisted I did not drive above 30mph.

Southern added:

The financing of the film was based almost 100 per cent on the notion that Sellers would play multiple roles [it was suggested five at one point]. About a week before shooting, he sent us a telegram saying he could not play a Texan, because he said it was one accent he was never able to do. Kubrick asked me to make a tape of a typical Texan accent. When Sellers arrived on the set, he plugged into this Swiss tape recorder with huge, monster earphones and listened to the tape I made. He looked ridiculous, but he mastered the accent in about ten minutes.

Principle photography started in January 1963.

Soon into shooting Peter Sellers – who was not happy about playing the Texan – (conveniently) sprained his ankle leaving a restaurant, and when he returned to set Kubrick told him to climb down two separate ladders into the belly of the plane (as Kong, the Texan character). He negotiated the first ladder, but slipped on the second and fell. Sellers saw the company doctor who ordered him to rest his ankle. Just to be sure, Sellers also let the completion bond people know, who immediately threatened to pull out if Kubrick forced him to continue. Thus Sellers got his way.

'It was a question of replacing him,' added Southern:

Stanley had set such store by his acting that he felt he couldn't just replace him with just another actor. He wanted an authentic John Wayne. The part had been written with Wayne as model – Wayne was approached and dismissed it immediately. I said there was this very authentic big guy who played in *Bonanza* named Dan Blocker. Without seeing him, Kubrick sent off a script to his agent. Kubrick got an immediate reply: 'It is too pinko for Mr. Blocker.' Stanley then remembered Slim Pickens from *One Eyed Jacks*, which he almost directed for Marlon Brando, until Brando acted in such a weird way that he forced Stanley out.

Peter Sellers in one of his many guises as Merkin Muffley, the American President. (Gareth Owen Collection)

Kubrick allowed Sellers to improvise, though despite some accounts to the contrary, Sellers did not create any scenes that did not already exist in the script – he merely embroidered it, and changed the odd line of dialogue slightly. One thing he did add to great effect, though, was after Kubrick suggested he wear a black glove in the wheelchair – intimating something quite sinister. Sellers remembers:

> I put on the black glove, and looked at the arm and I suddenly thought that is a storm trooper's arm. So instead of leaving it there looking malignant I gave the arm a life of its own. That arm hated the rest of the body for having made a compromise. That arm was a Nazi.

Sellers, without warning, shot his arm up into the air and shouted 'Heil Hitler!'

The most famous set of the film was, of course, the war room. Production Designer Ken Adam, fresh from success with the first *James Bond* film, was charged with the look of the film. He recalls:

> He loved it. He said it was exactly right. I had designed it on two levels … a few weeks later, on our drive into Shepperton, Stanley said he had been thinking about my designs and was worried about it being on these two levels, as he didn't know what he would do with the extras who would be on the upper level. He asked I rethink it. I was really thrown. I took a walk in the gardens, calmed down a little, and started doodling again.

B stage was transformed into an amazing room, comprising some 1,200sq.m of polished black flooring; a massive black circular table some 22ft in diameter; a chandelier suspended above it; and a looming map of the world, with small lights representing centres of human population. The actors were all dressed in dark woollen suits too, to further compliment Adam's set. To protect the floor, everyone had to wear felt overshoes, which, of course, are never seen in shot. During its construction, Sir Ken employed over 150 tradesmen. The set was 130ft long by 100ft by 35ft. Over ten miles of cable was employed in lighting the giant board, which keeps track of US nuclear bombers.

The room has banqueting tables piled high with food, including masses of custard pies. This is how Kubrick saw the world end – in pure slapstick. He did script and shoot a two-week sequence involving hurling thousands of pies, in a chaotic, comedic, climax to the story, but later decided against using it as he felt it killed the satire that had preceded it – though the footage still exists in the BFI vaults.

Ken Adam's war room has gone down in both American film and political history, for when Ronald Reagan took office, on being shown around the White House one of his first questions to his Chief Of Staff was, 'Where is the war room?'

'They explained that there was no such room', says Sir Ken Adam, 'and Reagan said "but I saw it in that film *Dr Strangelove*". It's one of the best sets I've ever designed. It still stands up. It's big, powerful and very simple. It creates the right sort of atmosphere of claustrophobia.'

More difficult to accommodate was Kubrick's insistence that the thirty-six actors in the scene be lighted solely from a light ring suspended above their heads. After much trial and error, the effect was accomplished.

John Aldred explains:

The film was re-recorded in the relatively new RCA Theatre, which was equipped with all the gear brought from Walton Upon Thames Studios. During re-recording Kubrick paid great attention to every sound, and the balancing between music, dialogue and effects. The film's release had to be postponed from late 1963 until early 1964, due to the assassination of President Kennedy. In fact we had to change a line of Slim Pickins dialogue from 'a good week-end in Dallas' to 'a good week-end in Texas' and Columbia added a disclaimer ahead of the main titles.

Kubrick was noted for his generosity in remembering people he had worked with, and after the re-recording was finished I received a message that there was a bottle of whisky for me in the Production office. I was truly amazed to find that in fact there was a whole gallon of malt whisky in a wood case, with the label saying 'Specially blended for John Aldred'.

Production designer Ken Adam, on his infamous 'war room' set. (Gareth Owen Collection)

In *Dr Strangelove* Sellers delivers three of his best career performances, and Kubrick's first film in Britain was an assured masterpiece.

A little later in the year, Director Jack Clayton made his first Shepperton film, *The Pumpkin Eater*. Ossie Morris was the director of photography, and recalls:

This, I believe was Jack Clayton's first feature as director. He had made *The Bespoke Overcoat* which was a short, and which in fact won an Oscar, and of course had worked with John Huston on a number of films. Now Jack was very much set on the road of being a great director.

Anne Bancroft headed the cast, along with Peter Finch and James Mason. Anne was nominated for an Oscar, playing the part of Penelope Mortimer – which was an autobiographical part – and a few eyebrows were raised at the idea of casting an American actress in such a British role. Anne came into Britain to see Jack, at no charge, and I remember I went along with him to meet her at a hotel. She was so upbeat and excited and promised she could play the part and wanted to screen test, which she did and Jack there and then gave her the role as he was so impressed, and indeed her name was of great use in securing finance.

We had a major scene with Anne at Harrods department store where her character suffered a nervous breakdown. Now, it was absolutely unheard of for a film to use the grand store and so it really was quite a coup for us to be granted permission. They opened up one Sunday especially for us.

Jack wanted a shot, looking at her feet as she walked along. We gave her the camera, with a rig hooked over her shoulder and it sat on her chest just below her chin. We switched on and Jack directed her like that. It was the only time I have ever known an actress to take over the camera and it's tremendously effective.

CHAPTER 15

THE FILM CRISIS

'Whilst they are doing well, let's sell it off', was how Roy Boulting summed up Government intentions to sell its interests in British Lion. 'But by that time', continued Boulting, 'British Lion had become a kind of flagship for the independent film-makers and they rallied around to help us resist such a sale.'

In a letter to Sidney Gilliat dated 5 March 1988, Roy Boulting recounted the period surrounding the Government's announcement:

You will, I hope, recall those weeks just before and immediately after Christmas of 1963. We, the Board of British Lion, had been told that the Government intended to exercise its option, pay us out, and then go on to a disposal of the company, lock, stock and barrel. At some moment in time, Michael Balcon was persuaded (with the greatest of ease) to throw his cap into the ring and proclaim himself as the head of yet another consortium seeking to acquire British Lion. An important meeting took place early in the New Year. It was attended by you and Frank, and Arnold Goodman in his various capacities of lawyer, adviser and friend. By this time various and significant independent film makers had indicated their fear that the company might fall into other hands, such as the washing machine tycoon, John Bloom – or Sydney Box, or Herbert Wilcox. As a result, at this time Attenborough and Forbes, Osborne and Richardson, Janni and Schlesinger, together with that rather doubtful figure-juggler, James Isherwood (what the hell was he doing there?), had assembled, as I seem to remember being given to understand, for the purpose of working out a future modus operandi agreeable to all.

Am I right in believing that the meeting was intended, after a free exchange of views, to establish a framework for a British Lion in which all the groups might contribute to the purchase and financing of the company, as well as outlining the basics of a working constitution under the titular leadership of Michael Balcon?

Incidentally, Sidney, I seem to remember that following the meeting there was more than a hint given from Michael Balcon's camp to the effect that the members of the existing Board of British Lion would not be welcome as members of the new consortium. Just one further, incidentally; we, the members of the Board, were given what was virtually an ultimatum; we were going to be allowed to purchase the company ourselves and, as I recall it, were given a derisory time in which to acquire the finance, should we wish to do so. It was shortly before Christmas, and the holiday period made the time limit even more derisory than otherwise.

In fact, the Government option was exercised on 9 December 1963. Four days later, the directors were notified, and formally offered the company at valuation price. Their acceptance had to be given by 31 December, and full payment made by 8 January. Everything was classified as secret, and the Government were keen it be kept that way. According to Lord Goodman's autobiography:

> The NFFC made an effort summarily to buy them out, sending round cheques by hand to the office with a request for their resignations. Not unnaturally an interview was demanded with Sir Nutcombe Hume [chairman of the NFFC]. With minimum grace he declared that the NFFC had found another purchaser for British Lion and therefore had bought them out … the new purchaser was Sydney Box, whereupon all five directors walked out of the office straight to Fleet Street to make the loudest clamour possible and thence to the House of Commons. It was no doubt the hope of the Board of Trade that British Lion's sale would be conducted quickly and silently during the Christmas Parliamentary recess, but the determined efforts of the five directors managed to get the matter raised on the adjournment debate.

On 28 December, it was made public that negotiations were underway with Sydney Box, who was backed by the Standard Industrial Trust. Box had formerly been managing director of Rank subsidiary, Gainsborough, and since 1951 had been in charge of London Independent Films. The Government saw such an injection of private finance as having 'a stimulating effect'. Box had made assurances that he would continue to operate British Lion as an independent, outside of the combines that were Rank and ABC.

Meanwhile, Sir Michael Balcon, as chairman of Bryanston, Bryanston Seven Arts and Pax, was 'greatly concerned' because his groups had supplied more films for distribution through British Lion than any other group of independents. Sir Michael wrote in his autobiography:

> Just before Christmas, I was a guest at a luncheon with Sir Colin Coote who, as editor of the *Daily Telegraph*, was interested in the contemporary film scene – the clash with the circuits was at this time at fever pitch. Roy and John Boulting were present and, on arrival, Roy came to me and said 'I bet you can't guess the name of the person to whom the NFFC are selling.' Without hesitation, I said 'Sydney Box' and, from that moment, don't ask me why, I became hooked. I was genuinely concerned at the high handed attitude of the NFFC. It seemed to me

a very unusual procedure for a para-Government institution to sell Government property other than by competitive tender, and as justice had to be seen to be done, I decided to take action. I was confident that I could raise the funds to enable me to make a competitive bid, and this information was given to the press.

On 7 January, John Terry, the managing director of the NFFC, announced 31 January as the closing date for applications to purchase British Lion. By that date, five others were in the field: a consortium of John Woolf, Sam Spiegel and the Grade Organisation, headed by Leslie Grade; the Federation of Film Unions; John Bloom; Edward Martell's Freedom Group, which owned the New Daily; and an unidentified group negotiating through theatrical agent Stanley Durbens. Other potential suitors courted the press (briefly) with an interest in bidding, British comedians Morecambe and Wise being two. Said Ernie Wise, upon writing to Edward Heath for full details of the sale:

> We are considering approaching people like Ken Dodd, Tommy Steele, Harry Worth, Max Bygraves, Harry Secombe and others. If our offer is accepted we would hire a production unit to make musical and comedy films for export. I believe we could do a good job for British films.

No formal bid was made, but audiences at their Bristol pantomime increased thanks to the press coverage. Carl Foreman announced he was also interested, but on 1 February announced he was pulling out of the race. The whole period is referred to as simply 'the Film Crisis' in Roy Boulting's diaries. At risk was the only major independent voice in British Film.

On 16 January, Trade Secretary Edward Heath made a statement to the Commons in which he said:

> I have agreed with the corporation [NFFC] that, subject to my final approval, it will negotiate the sale of the whole of the business at valuation price [some £1.6 million] to a purchaser able to give assurance satisfactory to the corporation and the Government that the company will remain independent and that the facilities it provides for independent production will continue to be available …

Sir Michael Balcon. (Gareth Owen Collection)

Mrs Eirene White, Labour's spokesperson for the cinema, asked about the monopolistic situation, to which Mr Heath replied, 'I am awaiting the recommendations of the Films Council, which I hope to receive very shortly.' Four days later that reply came – the council decided to oppose the sale, and committed itself to establishing a third circuit, alongside Rank and ABC.

In early February, discussions continued in the Commons, and the NFFC then announced its revised timetable: 11 March would be the date by when all offers had to be considered. The ensuing business was acrimonious, angry and bitter. Three groups dropped out of the race: John Woolf's consortium, the Union bidders and the Grade Organisation. It was now a three-horse race between Balcon, Bloom and Box.

On 31 March, a press release confirmed that contracts had been signed between the NFFC and the consortium headed by Sir Michael Balcon, the successful bidders, for £1.6 million. Sir Michael became chairman of the Board, and in a press statement said:

> British Lion belongs to the people who are making so many of the best British films. Shepperton studios are fully occupied until June, mostly with *Lord Jim*, which began interior shooting there this week. For the rest of the summer, the studios expect to be continuously busy with pictures being made for British Lion and they are awaiting the announcement of plans before the end of the month. We hope to produce 16 films a year. Good films.

'*Lord Jim*,' chips in Prop Master Roy Pembrooke, 'shot extensively on H stage, and I recall vividly we recreated a Cambodian river scene, and were working with 4 foot of water around us. The nice thing was that we received an extra £2 per day for "unusual working circumstances".'

Balcon later wrote in his autobiography: 'My conviction was that the best people to run British Lion were the people who had been running it before.'

The five original directors – Launder and Gilliat, the Boultings and David Kingsley – had invested £1,800 each into the company back in 1957. They now realised a profit of £157,000 each thanks to the sale. The Government, meanwhile, was to retain a veto on future change of ownership of British Lion or Shepperton.

Balcon's team consisted of Roy and John Boulting; Frank Launder and Sidney Gilliat; American distributor Walter Reade; John Osborne, Tony Richardson, Oscar Lewenstein; Border Television Ltd (in which company Balcon was a substantial shareholder); James Isherwood; Brian Epstein (and his clients, The Beatles) and Karel Reisz; Joe Janni and John Schlesinger; David Kingsley; and, also on the Board, Baroness Wootton of Abinger and Sir Lionel Head, MP.

'I saw in this group,' Balcon wrote, 'a strong force of creative talent.'

On 25 April, it was reported that Sidney Gilliat – who was chair of Shepperton – had appointed his new Board following Roy Boulting and David Kingsley announcing their resignations. Replacing them were Producer Jo Janni and Hal Mason, formerly of Ealing Studios. Andy Worker remained as managing director.

Roy Boulting and Frank Launder, two of the
ownership team then running British Lion.
(The Boulting Brothers Archive)

Following his success with *Billy
Liar*, and now with a vested interest in
the studio, John Schlesinger shot his
next film at Shepperton, *Darling*. Julie
Christie, Dirk Bogarde and Laurence
Harvey starred, and Christie won
an Oscar for her performance. It is
essentially a character study of model
Diana Scott (Christie) and her search for
love and happiness. The film touches on
taboo subjects for the time, like adultery,
abortion and homosexuality. People
asked if Schlesinger, himself openly gay,
was trying to make a statement about
homosexuality?

Schlesinger later said:

I don't think it arose when we were
doing *Darling* in 1964, and there was
a character in it that was openly homosexual and very sympathetically played
by Roland Curham. In my first film I remember going round Manchester
and seeing sort of strange pubs which had drag shows and that kind of thing,
and I thought maybe we should include one of these. Jo Janni, my wonderful
producer of many films, said I don't think it's wise to have such a sequence in
the film. But it wasn't 'til later when the original idea of *Darling* came up that
we invented this gay character of the photographer who was very sympathetic.
And from then on, quite often I've included characters that are gay in my films
– notably of course in *Sunday Bloody Sunday*, which was all about the subject
really.

Costume Designer Julie Harris mentions:

I came into the production about ten days before it started shooting, because
John had a friend working on it who knew a lot about stage design and not
much about film, and I then received a phone call from Joe Janni asking me to
help. It was rather a rush to get the clothes ready!

Nobody thought the film would cause the stir it did, nor did I expect to
win an Oscar. Back then the Academy had two categories – black & white, and
colour. The winner of the colour category was *Dr Zhivago*, so I'm ever so glad
we shot in black and white!

The Boultings, meanwhile, continued with their own production programme, and next offered *Rotten to the Core*, which was a semi-follow up to another Shepperton production, *Two-Way Stretch*. Devoid of the cast of *Stretch*, a few of the character names were kept – Lennie The Dip, Jelly Knight, Anxious O'Toole – and Anton Rodgers, Charlotte Rampling, Eric Sykes, Ian Bannen and Kenneth Griffith were recruited. It was an amusing double-crosser crime caper, but lacked the gloss that Sellers lent *Stretch*.

With the adverse press and uncertainty over the company's future, profits understandably slipped, but an upbeat start to the first half of the year prompted the Board's confidence that the studio's future was rosy. However, in May 1965 (with a slight rise in profits), Michael Balcon retired. Lord Goodman took his place as chairman. Roy Boulting recalls, in a private memo, the circumstances leading to Balcon's resignation, and the fragmentation of the new Board:

> It should have been a sort of British United Artists. It should have worked, but didn't. There were a number of reasons for this. For something like two years, for example, Osborne, Richardson and Schlesinger now had commitments to Hollywood; they were unable to make films themselves for British Lion. As well, there were, perhaps, just too many differing creative minds at work to achieve rapid decisions at Board level. Not all the disparate elements, either, had the same commitment to the 'ideal' of independence and a 'third force'. This was understandable. How could they when their interests straddled the Atlantic? But what emerged eventually, was a situation in which Launder, Gilliat and ourselves [the Boulting Brothers] were the only film makers willing or able to devote all our time and efforts to the making of product for Lion to distribute.
>
> Yet another complication was Walter Reade, an American art theatre exhibitor, who had been brought into the consortium by Michael Balcon. We later came to feel that his principal purpose and belief, was, that by doing so, he would secure for himself the distribution of British Lion's films throughout the States and Canada. This was not acceptable, could never happen. So, all in all, one way or another, a deal of bitterness was engendered, a certain unhappiness, generated. This couldn't go on. When Michael Balcon decided to retire on reaching his seventieth year, Lord Goodman – the distinguished lawyer, who had been a good friend to British Lion since 1958 – brought in Sir Max Rayne (now Lord) to take over the disgruntled Walter Reade's interests in the company. He also took over the shares of other groups who either didn't wish to, or couldn't continue.
>
> With Goodman taking over the Chair from Balcon; with Rayne now an active participant; and the Board slimmed down to fighting fitness; decisions became easier: war, war, for a change, proved better than jaw, jaw!

Balcon remembered things somewhat differently, and wrote:

> I had regarded my taking the chair of British Lion as a relatively short term job; I visualised that in about three years the new organisation would be running

smoothly and I would then retire. My usefulness was obviously in the negotiations for the acquisition of the company, but the honeymoon was soon over.

He complained that there was not any office accommodation available for him at the British Lion headquarters for nearly nine months; when he wanted to see any of his colleagues outside of Board meetings, he claimed he usually had to wait in the entrance hall or in the passage if the man he wanted to see happened to be engaged.

When an office eventually became vacant, he had little contact with the resident colleagues, except for an occasional gossip with Roy Boulting. Balcon continues:

> They [his partners] were falling back on the old belief that we would not be able to get our films into the circuits and that therefore the risks inherent in producing as many films as we had envisaged were too great. This was totally opposed to my view of supporting independent producers, and if this policy was not to be carried out I saw no point in my continued presence as Chairman or in any other capacity. I bowed out. In doing so, I fixed a date to coincide with my seventieth birthday, but I did say I would be prepared to go at any time when they had found a suitable successor.

Not long afterwards, Lord Goodman made a statement that the company's policy was to be one of 'increasingly limited involvement'. Balcon claimed that had he known that the British Lion adventure would turn out this way; there would have been no justification, except on principle, for him interfering over Sydney Box's deal for control of the company. 'I have no reason to believe that Mr Box would not have done just as much by way of actual film-making as was now the official policy of British Lion,' he concluded.

Casino Royale is mentioned in the history of every major British studio – because it shot in every major British studio! Columbia Pictures had bankrolled the one 007 property that got away from Broccoli and Saltzman's cash cow series. Producer Charles K. Feldman had hoped to better anything that Eon could produce and trotted in a dozen stars and their star friends for the occasion. Before long it would be claimed that the film was a runaway mini-Cleopatra at a then outrageous $12 million budget.

Peter Sellers was cast, along with Woody Allen, David Niven, Orson Welles, Ursula Andress, Deborah Kerr ... the list went on and on. Sellers, with his career riding high, was no doubt the clinching factor in Columbia agreeing to back the film, and Feldman courted the actor for several months, eventually signing him after offering $750,000 plus expenses. Sellers insisted that his friend, Joe McGrath, direct. It would be his first feature film. The star was also keen that Sophia Loren be cast opposite him, but alas she declined Feldman's offer. The first few drafts of the script had been written by Ben Hecht, but he died before pre-production commenced. Sellers suggested Terry Southern, fresh from their collaboration on *Dr Strangelove*. He was engaged purely to work on Seller's dialogue.

Wolf Mankowitz was then drafted in by the producer to work on the rest of the script. A January 1965 start date was set at Shepperton, but in November 1964 Sellers stated he was not happy with the script – and Feldman didn't have a supporting cast either. Shirley MacLaine and Trevor Howard were courted, to no avail, but then came Orson Welles, Woody Allen, Ursula Andress, George Raft, William Holden, David Niven, Jacqueline Bisset et al.

It was a troubled shoot from the outset. Sellers was unpredictable and suffering problems in his romance with Britt Ekland, which saw him disappear for days on end. The relationship between Sellers and his other co-star, Orson Welles, was stretched even before they met. Sellers was terrified of having to work with Welles, and turned it into a resentment of the actor. This was brought to a head when Princess Margaret was invited to Shepperton by Peter Sellers. Welles, unbeknown to Sellers, had become a friend of the Princess some years earlier. When the Princess arrived on 18 February, she passed right by Sellers and went over to Orson Welles: 'Hello Orson', she said, 'I haven't seen you for days!' Sellers reportedly went as white as a sheet. He had planned to introduce Welles. This turn of events infuriated him beyond belief. As a consequence, Sellers insisted that all of his scenes with Welles be shot in such a way so as neither actor had to appear together. They were shooting in widescreen however, and Joe McGrath contested it would look 'stupid' to employ a single-cut shooting technique. He then went further, addressing Sellers' poor timekeeping and general unprofessional attitude to the film and his co-stars. The actor seemed to listen, take it in and then retired with McGrath to his trailer to discuss a scene.

There, Sellers said, 'I've had enough of this,' and swung at McGrath.

'He hit me on the side of the jaw,' the director said, 'and it sort of bounced off me, you know – it was half hearted – but I thought, what the hell?' With that, McGrath swung back.

The pair were separated by Stunt Man Jerry Crampton. Sellers, totally embarrassed, disappeared again. The cast and crew were furious. When Sellers therefore said, 'I'll come back if I don't play any scenes with Orson,' McGrath said, 'Get lost', and with it, he left the picture.

'It was all very unfortunate,' says Art Director Michael Stringer, 'as Joe had brought some terrific ideas to the production. His leaving created havoc. Nobody knew it at the time, but Feldman's plan all along was to have six directors! We saw very little of him on set, but he'd have several assistants running around and keeping him informed.'

Feldman asked Blake Edwards to take over, but could not meet the director's financial demands, and so turned to Clive Donner – Sellers rejected him. The producer then hired Val Guest … and Robert Parrish … and Richard Talmadge … and John Huston … and Ken Hughes.

Val Guest remembers:

When I arrived on the scene, I was handed a gaggle of scripts, none of which had much to do with the Ian Fleming book, but from which – I was told – I might get some ideas. Somehow we managed to start shooting on the scheduled date with each of us directors managing to pull our re-written segments together. Added to the chaos, we had telephone calls from Charlie [Feldman] with overnight inspiration as well as calls telling us who was in town, and how we had to write them in. 'Bill Holden is in town, change such and such for him, he'll do it' he would say.

Production expanded across to Pinewood and MGM Borehamwood studios. 'I would wake up,' says Guest, 'and ask what studio I was at that day. It was that mad.'

'Jerry Bresler walked onto the set one day,' adds Michael Stringer, 'and announced himself as the new producer – new producer, new ideas: consequence of which saw us scrap £1 million worth of sets. He ordered we move the *Casino* set from A stage, to the giant H stage and include a big staircase in the set. It was crazy.'

Re-writes were a daily occurrence. It is said that some eleven writers in all had a hand in the script, including Val Guest, John Law, Michael Sayers, Wolf Mankowitz, Ben Hecht, Peter Sellers and Woody Allen.

'Oh yes, one of the rewrites called for the Elgin Marbles to be used,' reveals Stringer, 'and I had to get casts from the British museum. What with this, and flying saucers appearing it was becoming sheer madness.'

Over-budget and over-schedule production continued through the spring. At the end of May, Peter Sellers decided he'd had enough and left the production. Terence Cooper was drafted in as yet another 007 to replace him. It had become a mess. In April 1967, the film premiered in London in the presence of Her Majesty Queen Elizabeth. The film was a box-office disaster, and the scenes with Welles and Sellers – in which they actually only appear together in one set up – look like they were shot separately.

Staying with comedy, the next in the *St Trinian's* series, the first to be shot in colour, was *The Great St Trinian's Train Robbery*, and saw George Cole return as Flash Harry, and Dora Bryan and Frankie Howerd cast as the other 'grown-up' leads. Leslie Gilliat produced:

> When we were talking to Frankie Howerd, who was to play a hairdresser in the film, I said to him that it would be rather nice if he would wear a toupee. He said he didn't like that idea. But I thought it would be very funny, so suggested it could just be a very small one. He agreed … and then I found out that he was wearing a toupee in real life!

Dora Bryan laughs:

> Oh I remember it being such wonderful, wonderful fun. The girls were terrific to work with though people ask me if Frankie was too. Well, no, he wasn't. He wasn't a funny man. He never made me laugh once, and you never had a giggle with him – though he was always very nice. He invited me out to dinner a few times, though never my husband!

Gilliat adds:

> This was the last *St Trinian's* film, though Frank Launder did ill-advisedly make another in 1980, which was called *Wildcats*. It was a mistake, and a total disaster.

But rumours abound of a re-make were proved true in 2007 when Ealing Studios started production on *St Trinian's*. It looks promising. I was invited to the set, and read the script. Very funny!

Producers Jack Parsons and Robert Lippert, who had both worked at Shepperton independently making B pictures, formed a partnership and between 1964–65 produced a half dozen films together. In 1951, *TIME* magazine dubbed Lippert 'The Quickie King', in reference to the speed with which Lippert could make a movie. He was also credited for first bringing a popcorn machine into a movie theatre. His teaming with British producer Jack Parsons, who had an equal reputation for making inexpensive films quickly, seemed a comfortable fit.

Former Fox Executive Martin Cahill speaks:

> They were made under my sole control as Fox did not have a TV arm in Europe at the time. They were the very first 'Made for TV Only movies' Fox made. They were basically designed to use up final months of stock players Contract artistes such as Pat Boone, Lon Chaney, Conrad Phillips etc. which Fox (après *Cleopatra*) were dumping. The tax 'dodge' for which I had to appear before the Inland Revenue Commissioners, was 'How could Fox charge the Production something like £40k for Boone when his contract rate (which somehow they knew about) per picture was $1.5M?'
>
> I had to stand up and explain that they were 'pay or play contracts' and that to get $40k back plus a TV movie with a star in it was worthwhile to Fox rather than to just pay 1.5m bucks and get nothing.

Their output saw some top directors like Terence Fisher and Don Sharp direct films including *Witchcraft*, starring Lon Chaney Jr, Jack Hedley and Jill Dixon; *The Earth Dies Screaming* with Willard Parker and Dennis Price; *The Return Of Mr Moto* with Henry Silva; *Spaceflight IC-1* with Bill Williams; *The Murder Game* with Ken Scott and Conrad Phillips; and *The Curse of the Fly* with Brian Donlevy, Carole Gray and George Baker – Lippert was one of the producers of the original *The Fly* movie in 1958, and this film was a poor sequel in both story and budget. After *The Curse of the Fly*, Lippert stepped back from the business. Parsons went on to make just one more film before committing suicide.

1966 was a much quieter time at the studio with just ten productions cranking up, most notably of which was Fred Zinnemann's *A Man for All Seasons*. Zinnemann later wrote:

> In London I had been in the doldrums for a few weeks, when Mike Frankovich phoned: 'Have you seen the new play *A Man For All Seasons*?' he asked. 'Yes' I replied. 'Would you like to direct the picture?' 'Yes'.
>
> It was a strong play written by Robert Bolt. It dealt with the sixteenth century English statesman Thomas More, beheaded on the orders of King Henry VIII for refusing to sanction his marriage to Anne Boleyn.

As far as Columbia was concerned this was a very modest and, in a box office sense, totally unpromising project. It was a costume movie, with very little action, let alone violence; no sex; no overt love story and, most importantly, no stars. In fact hardly any actors that the US public had heard of – Venessa Redgrave, Wendy Hiller, Robert Shaw, Paul Scofield.

Because of the tiny budget, we had to be enormously careful about building sets and making costumes. Fortunately one of the great production designers, John Box, was with us. Using three enormous flats raised in perspective, he built a replica of the Palace at Hampton Court for £5,000. When comparing photographs of the movie set and the real thing, no one could tell the difference.

The following year fared quieter still, with just nine films on stage floors. Among them, *Hostile Witness* saw actor Ray Milland direct his last picture, in which he also starred with Sylvia Syms, whilst after his sojourn on *Casino Royale* Director Robert Parrish took on superior London comedy caper *Duffy* with James Coburn, James Fox, James Mason and Susannah York. Meanwhile, Peter O'Toole, Jean Moreau, Zero Mostel and Akim Tamiroff headed the cast in Gordon Flemyng's *Great Catherine*.

Cinematographer Ossie Morris recalls:

Understandably Gordon was nervous working with such a cast, and on top of that he spoke to everyone in a thick Scots accent – which wasn't tremendously helpful for the foreign artists!

The sets, designed by John Bryan, were truly wonderful. However I discovered that the stages were never quite big enough for John! He was designing a wonderful Russian palace with enormous columns which were to be cast in plaster, about 30 feet high, but John wanted thirty of these made. That was a heck of a job for the carpenters shop, but they delivered – however, so big were these things that we couldn't get them into the stages in one piece! They had to make them in three sections, and they were reassembled on the stages. The sets looked truly magnificent, but boy was it an effort.

You could always expect excitement from Peter O'Toole! One Saturday we were at the studio, and Peter came on set for a rehearsal and we said that we'd call him in an hour or so when we were ready to go for a take. By around noon we were ready and a runner was sent to collect Peter. He knocked on the door but there was no answer. He could, however, hear voices. So, he opened the dressing room door to see the television was on, and it was Kempton Park Races – which are about 10 miles from Shepperton. Then he heard the commentator say 'we're glad to welcome Peter O'Toole who is with us here today' and the camera closed in on Peter O'Toole and Peter Perkins!

The runner had to report that our star was at the races. He duly bombed off to Kempton Park to collect them, and that afternoon O'Toole walked onto the set, roaring with laughter. He really thought it was hilarious!

Ossie Morris remained busy at the studio, as no sooner had he wrapped on *Great Catherine* than *Oliver!* moved before the cameras. He remembers:

> Lewis Gilbert was originally going to direct before I came on board, but I think he was contracted to another film and couldn't do both. Carol Reed was then engaged, by producer John Woolf.
>
> Johnny Green was the musical orchestrator and conductor – he was a doyen of film music from MGM; and John Sloan was production manager though I remember he wanted to be called 'producer' and John Woolf said no, that wasn't possible. In the end he asked for his name not to be credited at all.
>
> Johnny Green was such a lovely man, but before he arrived he sent a list of requirements. One of them being that he wanted a piano in his office, not just any piano but a grand piano! Now, anyone who knows Shepperton will realise that production offices are modest in size, and a grand piano would fill one of them without room for anything else. They managed to find an office big enough, and somehow got the piano in. Then they needed a dozen pencils sharpened to a very fine point and always available.

The cast of *Oliver!* (Gareth Owen Collection)

Ossie Morris lights one of the stages in use for *Oliver!* (Courtesy Ossie Morris BSC)

Well, we really expected him to be a real pain, but he was the complete opposite: very, very helpful and tremendously likeable. I learned so much from him. Unfortunately however, Carol began to hate him. Carol wanted complete command of the entire film [as we saw on *The Third Man*], and he fell out with Honor White the choreographer too. Carol didn't like Honor and Johnny working whilst he wasn't around you see, and became very resentful. He became very unkind in fact, though in non-musical sections he was quite different. It was apparent that he really didn't like the musical numbers and we just couldn't work out why he'd accepted a film like this. It turned out that it was because he just adored working with children, and that went back to *The Fallen Idol*.

Staying with a musical theme, *Half a Sixpence* was a lavish musical from Paramount. It starred Tommy Steele, Julia Foster and Jean Anderson. It was Director George Sidney's last film – he had made many musicals from the *Ziegfeld Follies* to Elvis' *Viva Las Vegas*. John Aldred reveals:

It was the biggest re-recording task I was given in 1967. It was released in 70mm with stereophonic sound, before the days of Dolby. Based on the 1905 novel *Kipps* by H.G. Wells, the story concerns a young drapery clerk who inherits a fortune, only to lose it and his girlfriend in spectacular fashion.

The success of any musical film depends largely on three people, the musical director, the choreographer, and the music editor. For this film Paramount sent over Oscar winning Irwin Kostal as musical director, who had recently received Academy Awards for *Sound of Music* and *Mary Poppins*, and Charles Knudson a senior music editor. British ballerina Gillian Lynne was the choreographer. As the production progressed it became more and more behind schedule, and there was tension between producer and director. Eventually it became clear that the production would run out of time and its allotted studio space, so Paramount relieved producer Charles Schneer of his responsibilities and engaged John Dark as the new producer to sort out the mess. John Dark reserved space at ABPC Elstree in order to finish the picture, and the entire unit moved away from Shepperton for 2 or 3 weeks to shoot the 'What a Picture!' wedding sequence.

1968 saw production almost double with fifteen productions, and optimism was raised. So much so, Lord Goodman put forward a proposal that British Lion should go public 'in order to secure fresh capital for production, together with suggesting that Shepperton Studios be mortgaged with the same end of increasing funds available.'
Roy Boulting takes up the story:

> With the benefit of hindsight, one can see now that the capital sum suggested for the Issue, was totally inadequate and served only to eliminate the existing debenture on Shepperton Studios, whilst providing little for future production. In the event, the Issue was over subscribed 29 ½ times over and seen as a considerable success. It was, in fact, a grave error. For Peter Walker was already tramping the City of London streets and would shortly become its white haired boy. We were into the 'takeover' era, the 'asset strippers' moment in Paradise.

The Issue was for over one million shares at 16s 6d. Interestingly, the Boultings and Lord Goodman owned the lion's share of them.
   A slight overspill from Pinewood with *Battle Of Britain* and MGM Borehamwood with Stanley Kubrick's *2001: A Space Odyssey* (the film later blamed for bringing about the

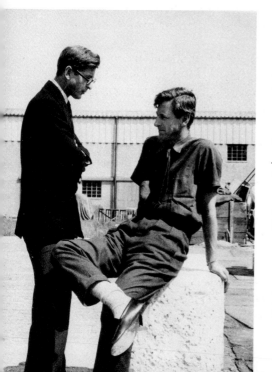

closure of MGM) came Shepperton's way; the latter's giant moon-base set was build at the studio, due to all nine stages at the MGM Borehamwood and the Elstree studios being fully occupied with Kubrick's other sets – the production, incidentally, had a three-year schedule.

   Acclaimed comedy writer Dick Clement made his feature directorial debut with a *James Bond*-esque comedy, *Otley*, starring Tom Courtenay. He explains:

As well as writing with Ian [La Frenais] I had also directed episodes of *The Likely Lads*,

The Boulting Brothers on the Shepperton lot. (The Boulting Brothers Archive)

Not Only But Also with Peter Cook and Dudley Moore, and a few commercials. Ian and I were engaged by Bruce Cohn Curtis (the nephew of Columbia's Harry Cohn) to adapt Martin Waddell's book. About half way through I said to Bruce that I'd rather like to direct the film. Columbia, keen to support a young upcoming director (maybe) – or realising I would be cheap (probably) – said ok. I got the gig. We started on 4 March 1968.

It was a marvellous cast, I really couldn't have asked for better. About a week into shooting Ian came on set and asked how it was all going. I said 'I'm having the time of my life'.

This was Bruce Cohn Curtis' first feature too, and Columbia appointed Carl Foreman our Executive Producer – it gave them a feeling of comfort. Carl only ever made one observation to me. It was on the script. He said 'This is a good script. It is a very good script. But it needs a chariot race. What do I mean by that? I mean that sequence when people walk out of the cinema and say "what about that … "That is what I mean.'

And so we wrote in a sequence with *Otley* taking his driving test – and a chase that followed. It was the best bit of the film!

We had some terrific sets, but one I wish we had built was a houseboat. I don't know why, but we decided to use a real boat, out on the river. It was a disaster – terribly cramped, we couldn't light it as we wanted and there wasn't any room to move the camera. So, with hindsight, I'd change that – but otherwise everything went very smoothly and I felt very comfortable working at Shepperton.

As the year came to a close, it was announced that BBC Television had bought the rights to British Lion's feature film library. Meanwhile, over at Elstree, EMI bought a stake in Associated British Picture Corporation by acquiring the remaining Warner Bros shares and launched a bid for full control. EMI would soon move to take over British Lion too, as we shall see.

1969 saw a slight downturn in the number of films at the studio. Amicus were keeping the facility busy with their low-budget pot boilers. Perhaps one of the most lavish films of this year, and indeed of the recent few years, was *Anne of the Thousand Days*, directed by Canadian Charles Jarrott. As Sound Mixer John Aldred recalls:

I returned to Shepperton in the summer to work on the film for Universal Pictures and Producer Hal Wallis. It starred Richard Burton as Henry VIII, and French Canadian actress Genevieve Bujold as Anne Boleyn, who was Queen for just 1000 days before she was beheaded.

Shooting began in June 1969, and was completed by the end of August – just over two months. Many of the scenes in the film recreate history in the places where it actually happened.

Indeed, the first location was Hever Castle in Kent, once the home of Anne Boleyn and where she was courted by Henry VIII. Other locations were Penshurst Place, once owned by King Henry, and the Plantagenet Manor House at Lingfield in Surrey, whilst remaining sets were constructed, such as the main hall in Greenwich Palace that was the scene for two balls, the first being where Henry meets Anne, and the second where he meets Jane Seymour, and Anne's fate is sealed. Elizabeth Taylor, wife of Richard Burton at the time, made a clandestine appearance as a masked courtesan. The main hall took 150 men three months to build. Other sets included the Banqueting Halls at Greenwich and Hever Castle, and the Royal Apartments at Greenwich. On the studio lot was the exterior of Tower Green and the Tower of London.

Anne of the Thousand Days was selected for the Royal Film Performance in 1970, held at the Odeon Leicester Square in the presence of The Queen and Prince Philip. The film also garnered ten Academy Award Nominations.

Val Guest returned to Shepperton with a Hammer production called *When Dinosaurs Ruled the Earth*. When he was approached in the summer of the previous year to direct, by producer Aida Young, Guest said, 'Could be interesting. How soon can I see a script?' Aida Young replied, 'As soon as you finish writing it!'

'I find it almost unbelievable,' admits Guest, 'that we commenced shooting at Shepperton on 14 October and less than three weeks later, on 4 November, I was filming in the Canaries for 12 concentrated days before flying back to Shepperton, filming through Christmas and New Year to wrap up the whole production, excepting effects, by 8 January!'

Dick Clement followed his success of *Otley* with another film for Columbia, *A Severed Head*, which starred Lee Remick and Richard Attenborough in a high comedy of sexual desire, based on a novel by Iris Murdoch.

'Ah now, Richard McDonald was our production designer,' says Clement, 'and I said to him re the banqueting scene, that what I really envisaged was lunch at the Connaught. He virtually built me the Connaught – but better, as he gave me lots of space to achieve a terrific tracking shot.'

British Lion found itself overstretched in its investments. With the duopoly of Rank and ABC still strong in exhibition, Lion found itself in the middle of higher-risk production with, relatively, fewer avenues of recoupment. Many films flopped and coupled with, as Lord Goodman puts it, 'a fall-off in American-sponsored production', Shepperton's turnover had been much reduced. He adds:

> It was about that time, with the consent of the board, I began discussions with the heads of the other two studios as to whether there might be some form of studio rationalisation which would, in effect, result in the three majors (Pinewood, Elstree and Shepperton) being reduced to only two. In the event, a limited agreement was drafted which would pool Shepperton with Pinewood and eventually lead to the closure of Shepperton. These proposals needed the approval of the NFFC, which in our view was refused for insufficient reason.

At the end of 1969, EMI bought out the total interests of ABPC, including its studios in Borehamwood and its ABC cinema chain. The following year, 1970, MGM closed its Borehamwood Studios and, in partnership with EMI, formed EMI-MGM Elstree Studios at the former ABPC studios. MGM guaranteed an annual subsidy of

£175,000. The two British major combines, Rank and (now) EMI, were growing in strength with their stranglehold on production and exhibition.

Production at Shepperton broke into double figures again – just.

In the comedy strand was the popular BBC series *Dad's Army* receiving a big screen outing. Norman Cohen, who had directed *Till Death Us Do Part* a couple of years earlier, took the reigns. During production he commented:

> There's a lot of visual humour which arises naturally out of the gags in Jimmy Perry's script, and we aim to expand those wonderful opportunities. It's clean, harmless fun. I'm all for family entertainment. *Dad's Army* may be regarded as old-fashioned by some because it doesn't call for gimmicks or tricksy camera work. The natural humour is in the playing, and it's in my job as director to bring it out and make it work on the big screen.

Exteriors were filmed at Seaford in Sussex (the seafront scenes), and Chalfont St Giles in Buckinghamshire (the village and church). The late James Beck spoke about the small to big screen transition:

Don't panic! Clive Dunn, Ian Lavender and Arthur Lowe were three of the mainstays of *Dad's Army*. (Gareth Owen Collection)

None of us had ever worked together as a team before [the TV series], yet we all hit it off right from the start. I think this is part of the success of the TV series, as well as this film. We've been working together for three years now, and we know each other's ways, mannerisms and are able to respond accordingly. For myself, I didn't find there were many difficulties transferring the television characters to the cinema. It's like asking an experienced tennis player to adapt from hard courts to grass. If he's good he should be able to play on both.

Director Ronnie Neame returned to Shepperton, and returned to his earlier success with Dickens.

I was asked if I would fly to New York and meet with Leslie Bricusse and producer Bob Solo. Leslie had written a script, music and lyrics for a musical version of Dickens' *A Christmas Carol* and they wanted to talk to me about it. Dickens was right up my street. The great author was stepping into my life again and the timing was perfect.

There had been several screen adaptations of the story; however, this was to be the first in colour and the first as a musical. It was to be called *Scrooge*.

In turning their attentions to casting, the lead role was initially offered to Albert Finney. He turned it down flat, without reading a single word of the script. Richard Harris was briefly attached but commitments to another film saw him fall out of the project. Other roles were cast and regulars such as Gordon Jackson, Kay Walsh, Dame Edith Evans and Alec Guinness were signed.

The director continues:

With less than a month to go, we still never had our Scrooge. Then the financiers hit upon the idea of Rex Harrison. He was committed to a play in the West End at the time, but we decided we could buy-out the last two weeks of his contract. Meanwhile, Michael Medwin had accepted the role of Scrooge's nephew. Medwin shared an office with Albert Finney. The plot thickens. One day Albie casually picked up the script and started reading. I received a phone call: 'I've changed my mind. I've just read your script and, if the part is still available, I'd like to play Scrooge.'

I explained we'd just signed Rex Harrison. But everyone agreed Albie was the best choice. I'm afraid we behaved rather badly and made the excuse to Rex that we couldn't put up the money to buy out his contract and had to start the picture.

All of the musical numbers were pre-recorded for lip-synching to playback and production was underway. The main set was created on the huge H Stage.

Art Director Terence Marsh recalls:

The set at Shepperton was on the biggest stage in use in England at the time. In order for it not to look like a set, I wanted to slope the street so the houses would have some steps up to them, railings – all different levels. This is much more expensive to do because there was so much rostruming. As it was Christmas, the ground had to be covered in snow and for that we used fire-fighters foam and mostly Epsom salts because it has such a nice sparkle. The actors and dancers walked on it, sending up 'dust' which is hardly visible. After inhaling this, everyone seemed to be running to the toilet more than usual!

Scrooge received five Oscar nominations. Another benefit of returning to Shepperton, which Neame was looking forward to, was taking a pint at the bar:

Having worked in both Britain and Hollywood, I have to say that one of the things I really missed in the USA was the studio bars – their studios don't have booze! Not that I'm a drunk, you understand, but there's something quite special about getting together after shooting in the bar; and over a drink discuss any problems or plans for the next day. That was something I very much enjoyed at Shepperton, in The Lion pub. It had a terrific atmosphere.

Rounding out the year was Roman Polanski's gore-fest, *Macbeth*. Continuity Supervisor Angela Allen says:

Oh I think I was on that film for seven months in all. We were always running out of money, going over schedule, taking re-take after re-take. It was something else. But that said, Roman Polanski – whilst he could be very difficult and hard to work with – is an extraordinarily talented man with a wonderful, wonderful personality. Everyone loved him.

Double figures were just about achieved again in 1971's output. Don Sharp directed what is described as a 'hippie, horror, zombie' film with *Psychomania*. Editor Richard Best takes up the story:

We filmed a lot around Walton on Thames, and curiously at a block of flats which had replaced the old Nettlefold Film Studios! We also filmed on part of the uncompleted M3 motorway, with lots of exciting motorcycle action.

It was one of George Sanders' last films, as soon afterwards he committed suicide in Spain. He left a note saying: 'Dear World, I am leaving because I am bored. I feel I have lived long enough. I am leaving you with your worries in this sweet cesspool. Good luck.' It was very sad. He was a charming man, and I remember he often wore his slippers on set if his feet weren't in shot. And another thing I remember was that he asked for a piano on set, so he could play between set ups; he was quite marvellous.

You'll see the old house at Shepperton quite a lot too, and the black and white tiled hallway several times.

The other notable production of the year came from Charles Jarrott, *Mary Queen of Scots*. Sound Mixer John Aldred confirms:

This was a relatively poor year for film production, and represented a general slump in the industry with free-lance work hard to find. *Mary Queen of Scots* was another Hal Wallis Production with Vanessa Redgrave in the leading role.

The film was nominated for five Oscars: Best Actress (Vanessa Redgrave), Best Art Direction (Maurice Carter), Best Costume (Margaret Furse), Best Musical Score (John Barry) and Best Sound (John Aldred and Bob Jones).

Set against the background of these and other productions was the fear that British Lion was in great trouble. Roy Boulting notes:

Now, apart from our vast film library built up since the middle thirties, and, faced with the rapidly increasing requirements of television, daily becoming more valuable, there was also the eight stages of our studio at Shepperton, set down in 66 ½ acres of green countryside – a setting invaluable for exterior shooting, but doubly attractive to the property developers involved in a booming building industry. As a public company, British Lion was speedily recognised as a plum ripe for the picking. The predators gathered and circled. We were able to resist a number of bids. Still short of money to finance the Company's production programme, when a most substantial offer was thrown on the table, our bankers advised that, as a public company, we had an obligation to let our shareholders know about it. We did – and that was that. The Company changed hands.

CHAPTER 16

THE ASSET STRIPPERS

A former stockbroker's messenger named John Bentley was soon to change the course of British Lion and Shepperton Studios' fate. Bentley was a protégé of James Slater – whom Roy Boulting described as 'the city's white haired boy' – of Slater Walker. In the space of eight years, Slater had turned a mere £2,000 of savings into an investment banking complex which, in 1972, was valued at over £220 million and was one of the largest 100 companies in the UK. Bentley worked closely with Slater in the late 1960s, in a spree of takeovers.

'As you may know, in some countries the words "Slater Walker" are synonymous with the word "takeover". Now I would like to make it quite clear at the beginning that we have never taken over another company! We always merge with them,' said Slater on company policy.

Bentley's success with the company in this period saw him rewarded with pharmaceutical company Barclay & Sons, which he renamed Barclay Securities. In 1972, *Business Week* described John Bentley and his activities thus:

> At thirty-two, Barclays Securities' John Bentley is one of the youngest company chairmen in Britain. He is also probably one of the most unpopular. And he is nowhere more unpopular than Parliament. During the recent debate on company mergers and takeovers, one MP described Barclay as the 'fastest buck multiplier in town.' As a result there will very likely be some new legislation on monopolies and mergers, and it is almost certain to be a 'block Bentley bill'.
>
> Bentley has aroused Parliamentary ire because of his reputation as an 'asset stripper'. The technique is familiar to Americans. Bentley buys up what he considers badly managed or moribund family owned companies in laggard industries, merges several in a single industry into a viable group, and spins off the group at a handsome profit. What has roused critics about these operations are the casualties they incur in the form of plants closed and jobs lost. Most recently, Bentley shut down a toy factory in South London six months after he bought it from a liquidator. Some 1,200 workers were discharged in the move.
>
> What has really focused Parliamentary criticism, however, is Bentley's plans for one of Britain's two major film studios, owned by British Lion Ltd. He

intends to slim down the studio and sell forty-five acres of its sixty acre back-lot for home and office development.

When Secretary Of State for Trade and Industry, Edward Heath MP, said – at the time of the Government sell off – that 'no purchaser of British Lion shares can strip it of its assets or do anything but continue to operate it as a going concern,' the studio management and workers felt a level of comfort and security. Bentley was unconcerned, and firmly set his sights on the studio – or rather, the land on which it sat.

British Lion posted a net loss for 1971-72 of over £1 million (largely due to a write-off of some £800,000 on British Lion productions in the period). The Lion was now at its most vulnerable. Bentley was poised, but then found a fly in the ointment. Star Associated Holdings, Britain's biggest bingo company, was also interested in taking over British Lion. Lord Goodman wrote:

> With the approval of our merchant bank we had entertained a proposal to do a reverse takeover operation, with an important cinema group in the north of England. When we announced this intention, we also asked that the British Lion Stock Exchange quotation should be suspended pending the production of sets of accounts. We had assets of considerable value [in the library], and the cinema company owned a circuit which produced good profits. Added to our assets this seemed a favourable agreement for a fresh floatation. Unfortunately, the cinema owners ran into Revenue trouble, of which until almost the moment of signature we had no idea.

Negotiations were suspended, while Lord Goodman met with the chairman of the Inland Revenue who, after a swift series of enquiries, advised Goodman to 'not become involved.'

With dealings suspended, the company was now exposed. Bentley saw his chance. British Lion and Shepperton could not afford to continue operating as things stood. The past few years had been lean in terms of renters, and 1972 would only pick up slightly on the previous year.

'We were short of money to finance the company's production programme,' wrote Roy Boulting in a memo, 'when a most substantial offer was thrown on the table.'

Lord Goodman recalled that Bentley said simply, 'I would like to buy British Lion'. Goodman told Bentley that he would not be able to make the purchase cheaply, and bearing in mind shares, when suspended, were at 40p – he threw down a generous figure of 100p.

'I did not accept it,' continued Goodman, 'since it was clear to me that Mr Bentley had a special use for the company. In the end we settled at 135p per share on the basis that Bentley would buy out all the shareholders who were willing to sell. In fact he bought them all out.'

That offer came from Bentley, and was cash of 137p (not 135p) per share, and was accepted by the Board on 25 April. Barclay securities acquired British Lion (Holdings) Ltd, and Shepperton Studios for £5.5 million. Shepperton Studios, or rather the land it sat on, itself was valued at some £3.5 million. 'Mr Bentley was a pleasure to do business with,' concluded Goodman. Bentley went on record to say that there was a programme of films through to September 1972, with John Boulting in charge, and that there would not be any changes until then. However, he also indicated that he felt the studio could occupy less land than it did, and also suggested another idea would be to merge Shepperton with Pinewood. That deal, though without Bentley, would have to wait a further thirty years. Furthermore, he suggested that the various divisions of British Lion – production, distribution, library, property etc – held assets worth £20 million.

When Edward Heath gave his undertakings about the future of the studio, in the light of a takeover, he appointed the NFFC guardian. It was somewhat alarming, therefore, to hear NFFC Managing Director John Terry saying, 'it [the NFCC] cannot prevent Barclay selling or redeveloping all or part of the land if Shepperton is bleeding British Lion to death with its losses or if the film industry has spare studio space available.' He was offering up a noose with which Bentley would hang Shepperton – all he needed to do was show the studio was unprofitable, then he would be unchallenged in his plans to sell off land for development.

Meanwhile, the one thing which Bentley hated – publicity – was swinging against him. His takeover was a 'pernicious and deadly wrong', claimed Maurice Edelman MP in a Commons debate. He continued, saying, 'property speculation is the sickness of our age. Asset stripping in this form is very grave and a potentially deadly blow, where you have an industry closed down in part, or in whole, and the assets diverted simply for cumulative reasons.'

A few months after Bentley's acquisition of British Lion, with mounting concern for the studio, the Shepperton Studios Action Committee was established by Derek Threadgall, a former employee. The initial action was that of holding up any plans Bentley was formulating for the development of the site; this was achieved by the committee applying for a preservation order on trees in the studio grounds, particularly the giant, old oak tree in the gardens. The local media were the first to take up the committee's cause, and once the support of Sir Alec Guinness and Spike Milligan had been secured, the national press picked up on the looming crisis.

Studio employees were recruited by the action committee to report, secretly, any areas of management running down the site. All of the major UK studios were suffering from a downturn in production activity, and Trade Under Secretary Eric Deakins, in a Parliamentary debate on the problems facing UK studios and possible rationalising of the industry, stated that, 'the company [Lion] has been making substantial losses over the past few months, and this cannot continue'. Tory MP for Spelthorne, Humphrey Atkins, said 'Shepperton is the only independent studio left and it should not be allowed to go out of existence. It would be deplorable if Shepperton had to close.' Lion International claimed that the studio was losing some £12,000 a week. Ideally, they wanted the site trimmed or closed.

Two deals were suggested. One would have seen Shepperton closed, all of the equipment moved to Pinewood, and a Rank-Lion holding company formed which, in turn, would lease Pinewood from the Rank Organisation and operate the studios.

Plan two would see four (of the eight) stages closed, and the giant H stage – the largest in Europe – dismantled. This would offer up two-thirds of the lot to Bentley to sell as he wished, and the NFFC would be happy with the resulting studio space. Both plans were regarded as 'reasonable' for negotiation by the Government. Bentley was keen to see a resolution, as he was waiting to float a slightly reorganised Lion, now including Barclay Securities' profitable poster advertising arm, Mills & Allen. Lion's Chief Executive was reportedly also looking to diversify the group into record production companies, managing pop artists, and commercial radio advertising companies. For the company to move forward, re-quotation was necessary, and that all hinged around Shepperton. Barclay Securities won 65 per cent of the shares in the takeover, but by folding in his Mills & Allen company, Bentley saw that increase to beyond 80 per cent.

In the summer, at a meeting with the NFFC, Bentley's Lion International proposed that it be allowed to sell off 55 acres of the studio, and develop the land for whatever property planning permission could be granted for, whilst maintaining the remainder on a 'care and maintenance basis' with production activities continued elsewhere. This was rejected. However, a revised plan was then set out by Bentley: forty acres of the lot would be sold off, with the remainder continuing to operate as a film studio.

Roy Boulting wrote in the *London Evening Standard* on 9 November that, 'the Shepperton saga may yet, once again, prove the sterile nature of the Luddite mentality in alliance with the bureaucratic and political huckster working in a scene of which they have little knowledge and for which they have even less feeling.'

The studio management claimed that the studio was operating at a loss, yet was hosting more productions than in recent years. Among them were the fantastic *Alice's Adventures in Wonderland* which, according to Production Designer Michael Stringer, 'was virtually entirely studio based'. Moreover, the film employed all of the studio's effects departments in achieving many of the shots. 'Lots was filmed on the huge H stage', added Stringer, emphasising the importance of the building which would fall foul of Bentley's redevelopment plans.

The year saw Michael Powell and Emeric Pressburger make a welcome return to the studio with *The Boy Who Turned Yellow* for the Children's Film Foundation. It was their last collaboration. Meanwhile, Fred Zinnemann completed studio interiors for his brilliant *The Day of the Jackal*. Carol Reed also made a return to the studio for his final film, an adaptation of Anthony Shaffer's play *Follow Me* – great people were at work again. Sir Alec Guinness was chosen to play the lead in *Hitler: The Last Ten Days*, which was the story of end of the Third Reich, as seen in Hitler's bunker. Editor Richard Best remembers his engagement:

I had a call to ask if I would go and see Wolfgang Reinhardt, the producer, at his London flat about *The Last Ten Days*. I knew it was in post-production by now, and the editor was Kevin Connor. So my next step was to call Kevin. I think they'd had a difference of opinion or a falling out, and Kevin just said if I wanted the money then I should do it.

It was the kind of film that you could do anything with. There was no narrative as such, it was episodic and consisted of scenes of Hitler in his bunker intercut with newsreel of the time of Berlin being captured. There were a few rooms in the Bunker, which were all recreated on stages at Shepperton: one where he met the Generals, another where he had a model of a rebuilt city which he had designed, then the 'suicide room' and so on. It was quite intense.

I took the film on and started work. I guess I was on it for about a month.

In the room next to me was Kevin's dubbing editor, and he kept coming into my room to do different things; and I discovered he was making whispered phone calls to London! I later found out that Kevin had a dupe copy, and he had gone into London with it.

After a month we ran the film for producer John Heyman, who requested he see it alone in the theatre. Soon afterwards he called an end to our recutting.

However, this thought of a dupe copy being cut niggled away, as I didn't know which copy – mine or Kevin's – was going to be used, or a mixture of both? But I do know that one of my cuts ended up in the final film, it was a shot of a hallway and a telephone. Joss Ackland had a frantic phone call before putting the phone back onto the hook, and running off up the corridor. When I looked at this scene I felt it lacked a little something, so looked at the original trim and there I found that the phone actually missed the hook, dropping and swinging. I felt it was more dramatic, so I added this little bit in. I know it was in the final print.

Perhaps more notable still was Robin Hardy's film of *The Wicker Man* (written by Anthony Shaffer). It was a British Lion production, and Peter Snell served as producer. Filming started on 16 October and Christopher Lee, for whom the script was written readily agreed to star, later stating that it was 'the best scripted film I ever took part in'.

Director Guy Green made a welcome return to the studio with Luther, as he recalls:

It was an experimental attempt to try and change a stage play to film without any changes. I had the idea of using a church or a cathedral as a basic background and dress each area with props and costumes appropriate to the scene. For example, one of the chapels in the church became Luther's living room, and the main congregation area became a market place. It worked very well and reduced production costs considerably. Once the idea was expanded, the play fitted perfectly into these surroundings. I did in fact adapt the stage script into a screen script which we needed for the various departments to work with – in setting the scene, lighting, camera movements etc. though I never got a credit as the Writer's Guild wouldn't allow me to share a credit with Edward Anholt, as he claimed as soon as he shared his credit he'd lose his 2% of the box office returns.

Peter Mullins created the sets and Freddie Young photographed the film, and it wasn't any more difficult to make than any other film except it was a heavy burden for the actors to handle such heavy dialogue. Though Stacy Keach was very hard working and collaborative, and I was happy – and fortunate – to be able to call upon people like Judi Dench, Maurice Denham and Hugh Griffith for supporting roles.

Yet against this backdrop of production, Lion International claimed the studio was fast going bust. Mis-management, perhaps? Then came Bentley's next offer. With the great opposition against redevelopment of Shepperton – and thus his inability to offer up for floatation his Lion International – Bentley knew he was at risk of losing millions of pounds. He called a meeting with the studio workforce on B stage. Bentley offered the 381 employees a 50 per cent share in Shepperton, providing they dropped their opposition to his development plans for forty acres of the lot. He warned them that 'the alternative could be very unsatisfactory.' He explained that he would form a new company, Shepperton Studios (1973) Ltd, and half of it would be put in trust, free of charge, to be administered by the film unions. Furthermore, Lion would undertake to maintain at least 275 employees for a minimum of one year.

This plan was overtaken, however, as what unknown at this time was that John Bentley was more desperate than ever to move forward with his plans, as he himself was fighting a takeover attempt by Vavasseur. He was effectively in limbo, just as British Lion was when he had swooped the previous year.

Negotiations with Bentley continued through to early March. At last a compromise was achieved, and an agreement for the future of a twenty-acre working studio site was close to being signed. But then the hammer blow hit – David Stark's J.H. Vavasseur group had made a bid for Barclay Securities, and planned on taking control of the company. He said that 'no one will be thrown out of work if the offer is accepted – no one except John Bentley that is. But he is a rich man, he can afford to retire.'

'Mr Who?' asked Bentley when he heard of Stark's bid, 'of what?' when he was told Vavasseur. Vavasseur offered £18.5 million for Barclay Securities, and left Bentley with no option but to recommend formally to the shareholders, in March 1973, that they accept the bid. On the news, a spokesman for Vavasseur said, 'We are going to talk to everybody who is interested [in Shepperton] and then we will formulate a policy'. Everybody, of course, included the Government, the NFFC, workers, unions and the Studios Action Committee which itself had formulated a £2 million bid for the studio.

Bentley resigned from the Board and pursued other business interests. He declined the opportunity to be interviewed for this book. It seemed that the immediate danger of losing the studio to Bentley's development plans had been overcome, but then new owners Vavasseur reinstated Jeremy Arnold (who had, two months earlier, resigned from Bentley's Lion International) and he immediately re-opened negotiations with the NFFC on the future of the studio.

Under a new development proposal, it was suggested that of the eleven film stages, eight would remain, including the giant H stage. The rest of the lot, including I, J and K stages, would be sold for housing development. To compensate for the loss of the lot, Lion agreed with the Metropolitan Water Board to lease 5 acres of open land adjacent to the studio. It was certainly better than Bentley's proposals, which would have seen seven stages demolished. Now there would be twenty-two acres of studios – studios that could still compete with Pinewood.

On 2 November 1973, an agreement was reached between Lion International, the NFFC and the unions for the plan, and assurances were made that there would be no redundancies. Planning permission was sought to dismantle H stage and rebuild it elsewhere in the studio, but the move did not materialise. H stage was to remain on the site where Sir Alexander Korda put it in 1948.

Production during 1973 was considerably quieter than the previous year, with just seven films shooting. It was not much better at other studios and, over at Borehamwood, following MGM's withdrawal from film distribution in the USA, the company withdrew from MGM-EMI Studios, which reverted to full EMI control and introduced extensive cost cutting.

The Boulting Brothers announced their next production, *Soft Beds Hard Battles*. Their return to Shepperton caused workers to threaten an embargo when talk of them taking another production elsewhere was made known. Unless the Boultings – who the workers felt somewhat aggrieved by for sanctioning the sale to Bentley – guaranteed all of their future films would be made at Shepperton, the workers said they would not service this one. The Boultings threatened, in return, to move this film elsewhere and 'possibly take legal action to recover £100,000 lost production money'. The unions stepped in and thankfully the embargo was lifted after the brothers gave a pledge to give Shepperton 'prior consideration' in future projects.

1974 started as a year of great uncertainty, though with a slight upturn in production. Vavasseur, having paid cash for Barclay Securities, were struggling. The studio itself posted losses of over £100,000 in the six months to April. Jeremy Arnold announced that Shepperton Studios would close in June, and a basic maintenance staff was kept on in the hope the (twenty-acre) studio site would be in a position to reopen in the years ahead.

At a mass meeting at the studio, workers demanded to know why producers, who had expressed an interest in filming at Shepperton, were not materialising. Alan Sapper, the general secretary of the ACCT union, said 'Certain films are not coming to the studios as promised. This is to be absolutely investigated.' The workers rejected proposals to close the studio totally.

Meanwhile, Vavasseur was seeing 90 per cent of its share value wiped. A massive restructuring operation took place. Shepperton went 'four wall' – that is to say, it became a production facility 'for hire', to which productions brought their own staff. Only a skeleton administration and maintenance staff would be employed directly by the studio. By losing the workforce, the significant weekly payroll would also be lost, and the company – it was hoped – would become more competitive and profitable in the longer term.

As part of going 'four wall', the management decided to sell off as many assets as it could: costumes, props, equipment, furniture etc. A great sale took place over five days in late September. 'One of the sale items,' recalls former studios' resident Malcolm Burgess, 'was the cup used in *Oliver!* It was described as being "unique". I witnessed the sale of a least a dozen of these over the five days!'

Andy Worker left his post of managing director, though not willingly it has to be said, and Lion International's Charles Gregson took over. His job was to turn the studio around from loss-making to profit, whilst refurbishing the complex, which was now looking quite shabby. John Aldred explains:

> When Shepperton Studios Ltd. ceased to exist in November and the Shepperton Studio Centre was born, the Studios were an industrial complex, but mainly film orientated. Most of the moveable items of equipment were sold at the public auction. The Westrex re-recording theatre itself was stripped and became a review theatre, and two sound mixers formed Delta Films to take over the RCA re-recording theatre as a going concern. They installed a new mixing console, Dolby equipment, and a large screen.

Eight films found their home at the complex during the year, including John Wayne's *Brannigan* – which saw one of the best car chases in London ever staged, before or since – and Nic Roeg's *The Man Who Fell to Earth*. Meanwhile, Blake Edwards, who was now living in London with his wife Julie Andrews, had been approached by Sir Lew Grade about the idea of bringing back the *Pink Panther* series, and Peter Sellers as Clouseau, some ten years after the last film. Edwards was convinced that Peter Sellers would never work with him again, but Grade spoke to the actor and found him 'surprisingly willing to do the film'.

David Niven was invited to reprise his role of Sir Charles Litton, but was committed to another movie. Douglas Fairbanks Jr was approached, but dropped out ahead of filming, when Christopher Plummer was cast. Other familiar characters returned: Chief Inspector Dreyfuss (Herbert Lom), Andre Maranne (Francois) and Cato (Burt Kwouk). As well as Shepperton and France, there was further location work in Gstaad, Switzerland. Victor Spinetti remembers:

> Ah yes, that was my big part – the Concierge at the Gstaad hotel. In fact it was Shepperton, but Gstaad sounds more exotic. I had some terrific sequences with Peter and Mike Grady, and – don't ask me why – but they ended up being cut. I don't mind, I was paid. Why should I mind? My sole line in the film is now when Peter comes into the hotel and says he wants 'A reum'.
>
> I say, 'A reum?'

John Wayne is Brannigan. (Courtesy Dave Worrall Collection)

'Yes, a reum', he says. That's it!

When the film premiered, Lew Grade decided to do it in style in Gstaad. He threw the most enormous party, and no expense – and I mean no expense – was spared … and I was invited. I was rather nervous in fact, because here was I in front of the world's press, on the premiere of one of the most anticipated films of recent years. What if a journalist stopped me? What if I was asked 'Mr Spinetti, how did you prepare for your role in the film?' My god, how would I say 'A reum?' took some preparing for?

The tremendous success of the film saw Sellers and Edwards team up again the next year for *The Pink Panther Strikes Again*.

In a different vein, an American ambassador learns to his horror that his son is the antichrist – that was the plot for Richard Donner's brilliant *The Omen*. A superb cast was headed by Gregory Peck and Lee Remick. Continuity Supervisor Elaine Schreyeck says:

That was the best script I have ever read. When I read it, I really felt it could all be real. It was chilling. Richard Donner was one of the 'new' American directors coming in, and was wonderful – so focused, and so good with the little boy.

Greg Peck had retired briefly form acting in the early 1970s and produced a couple of films which weren't very successful, before then taking this part that was a comeback role really. Several other actors had turned it down can you believe? Lucky for Greg though.

In the middle of the year, an announcement was made that troubled Lion International was to sell all of its film interests (minus Shepperton) to a group headed by new Shepperton Chairman Barry Spikings and Lion Managing Director Michael Deeley (the Oscar-winning producer). Deeley explains:

It came about because Barry and I controlled a significant number of shares in Lion International, and when the company made it known that they weren't really interested in film production and distribution, Barry and I arranged to exchange our shares in Lion International, for the British Lion company and catalogue.

It was their intention to run the company as an independent power house. Meanwhile, Lion International (renamed Mills & Allen) maintained ownership of the studio lot, and their housing estate proposal had now received outline planning permission for 250 houses.

Producer and subsequent head of British Lion and EMI Films, Michael Deeley. (Courtesy Michael Deeley)

CHAPTER 17

ENTER EMI

Shepperton would continue – it was said – operating as a film studio, and an extra assurance was granted to the NFFC that, should the studio be deemed bankrupt or run at a sizeable loss, then the NFFC would be able to purchase the freehold of the site at market value for future film production, or subject to planning permission, for other purposes.

1976 was perhaps the worst year in Shepperton's production history. Only three films were made: Terry Gilliam's weak comedy *Jabberwocky*, a German production of *The Marriage of Figaro* and a women's lib take on King Kong, *Queen Kong* – quite a dismal start to the new Shepperton's future. However, there was a visiting production, which made use exclusively of H stage that has previously been unaccredited with the studio and it is one of the biggest films of all time – *Star Wars*. George Lucas had taken over most of Elstree's stages, but when he could not find one big enough for some of the sequences, he looked to Shepperton. It led to the Hertfordshire studio building a new stage specifically for its sequel, *The Empire Strikes Back* – stage 6; also known as 'The Star Wars Stage'. The stage would eventually transfer to Shepperton, as we shall read later.

Meanwhile, there was some surprise when the new owners of British Lion, Spikings and Deeley, entered into conversations with EMI. Or was it, as some cynics believe, all part of their plan to acquire British Lion and then sell out to EMI at the first opportunity. But sell out they did in August 1976. Deeley elaborates:

> That's not quite the whole story. When we took over British Lion, we realised – as others had before us – that the weakness lay in exhibition. We had only a modest amount of money to make films, and always tried to pre-sell at least 50 per cent against the American market, but if we didn't get a good release in Britain … we needed our own circuit. With the help of Harold Wilson, we approached Rank. They had their Odeon cinema chain, valued in their books at £39 million, which was losing money hand over fist and had a sizeable debt. Their London cinemas were turning a respectable profit, but the others were floundering. We suggested a deal to John Davis at Rank whereby we would pay £7 million for a ninety-nine year lease on their cinemas – the money was coming from entrepreneur Jimmy

Goldsmith, whom Wilson had introduced us to. Should any of the cinemas have closed, and the buildings and land sold for other purposes, the deal was structured so as Rank would get the majority of any profit.

Everything was agreed. But a short time later, John Davis changed his mind. He said 'I've thought about it and don't want Rank's interests in film terminated – I don't want to be known as the man who destroyed the British film industry'.

Along with talking with Rank, we had started a discussion with EMI regarding their chain of cinemas. Whilst the Rank deal fell through, the EMI one progressed and it was suggested we fold British Lion into their company and form a partnership. After clearing all debt, selling them the British Lion library netted us just £168,000 [the library was valued at £1.2 million at the time of its acquisition from Lion International].

Spikings and Deeley were duly appointed joint managing directors of EMI Distribution Ltd, with former Anglo Amalgamated chief Nat Cohen serving as chairman and Chief Executive. Roy Boulting commented:

The new owners resold British Lion to EMI who had only recently acquired the film interests of The Associated British Picture Corporation (ABPC). Thus, did Monopoly – or Duopoly – win the last unequal battle.

In June of that year, former *Bond* producer Harry Saltzman put in a bid to Mills & Allen for Shepperton. He wanted the whole studio – all 60 acres – and offered £8 million. Saltzman had recently dissolved his partnership with 'Cubby' Broccoli, who went on to continue producing *Bond* films on his own. Saltzman had now moved from Pinewood out to Shepperton with a new planned production programme. Saltzman was adamant – it had to be the whole 60 acres, but a deal had now been signed by the Studio Board with Spelthorne Council, to build housing. Saltzman's bid – which would have saved the studio from being cut up and sold off – was flatly rejected.

'He was very surprised they did not want to sell to him,' says his son Steven Saltzman. 'He felt that along with the Labour Government's high taxes [causing many film makers to refuse to work in the UK], nobody wanted to do concrete things to help the UK movie industry.'

Towards the end of the year, the decision was made to close the studio restaurant in the Old House and relocate it near the workers canteen, the reasoning being that it then freed up the house should a company wish to hire it.

Further fury was felt by tenants in January 1977 when the main studio entrance was sold off for the land to be incorporated into the housing development. The studio was fast falling into disrepair. Mills & Allen were reluctant to spend any money on repairs or renovations. Their short-sightedness lost them one of the biggest movies of the year (and its sequels), as Production Executive Geoffrey Helman recounts:

Superman was originally set-up in Rome. This proved problematic on a number of counts, and not least because after starring in *Last Tango In Paris*, Marlon

Brando was persona non grata in Italy. Brando was deemed an essential part of the production – hence his massive $1 million fee – and to accommodate him, the producer Alexander Salkind has arranged to hire studio space in the South of France, and transport all the sets by road from Rome.

I thought it was crazy. The sheer logistics alone would be a nightmare, and as all of the effects work – of which there was much – was to be completed in the UK, it really did make sense to shoot in the UK. I persuaded Alexander Salkind that it would save money in the long run, and make the whole production run more smoothly.

I made enquiries, and Shepperton was the only facility with the space we needed. Meanwhile, the film's director Guy Hamilton, announced that he couldn't work in Britain – for tax reasons – and left the project. He did however leave with his full salary. It was something he always thanked me for later!

We began setting up at Shepperton, and on the giant H stage constructed the wonderful Ice Palace set. As you may know, the few years prior to our arrival were pretty lean ones as far as film production went. Shepperton itself had a rocky few years with ownership changes and asset striping, and the place had really not been looked after tremendously well and was in fact rather shabby.

This horrified Alexander Salkind. He was very much a showman, and liked to invite distributors and financiers to the studio to show off his production. He told me that he couldn't possibly bring such important people to such a badly maintained studio. He then asked that I find another studio to relocate the whole shoot!

A number of secret meetings then took place between myself and Cyril Howard, the Managing Director of Pinewood, and timings proved just right in so much as the *Bond* film was wrapping, and space was becoming available. We moved the rest of the shoot – and the subsequent three sequels – to Pinewood.

Guy Hamilton did complete a tiny amount of work on *Force Ten From Navarone*, though 'nothing of any great significance' at the studio, before American Director Franklin Schaffner and his producer, Robert Fryer, who were very keen on turning Ira Levin's novel of *The Boys From Brazil* into a film, moved in.

Schaffner knew the real challenge of the film would be in the casting. Centring around two aging men – a former Nazi 'death doctor', and a Jewish Nazi hunter, Josef Mengele and Ezra Lieberman – Director Schaffner said 'I would like to say rather fondly that I was faced with casting a geriatric movie.'

Laurence Olivier was suggested for the role of Mengele. However, having only recently played a similar part in *The Marathon Man*, the part lacked fresh challenge. Gregory Peck had expressed an interest in the Lieberman role. It was then that Schaffner had a brilliant idea. Cast against type and reverse the roles: Olivier as the Jewish Nazi hunter, and Peck as the Nazi doctor. Olivier was agreeable, as was Peck. Both were signed.

Olivier's health was the cause of great concern for the production. In recent years he had suffered prostate cancer, myositis, a kidney operation and thrombosis. During filming he was recuperating from cancer, nerve tissue disease and pneumonia. Fyer recalled:

> We started our meetings with Greg [Peck], and Greg started his voice lessons, the accent lessons, and worked very hard. Olivier meanwhile was in a nursing home in Brighton and his doctors said he was not able to travel.

Schedules were re-arranged to accommodate Olivier's later start. Other casting continued, and James Mason was persuaded to play – and in doing so lent considerable style and effectiveness to – the icy Nazi Colonel Eduard Seibert.

The doctors vouched for Olivier's health and his first scenes at Shepperton were filmed with Anne Meary as Mrs Curry (mother of one of the children Lieberman was investigating), and Uta Hagen as Freida Maloney, the Nazi who was in charge of a mass adoption programme in the USA. The story centred on a group of seven notorious Nazi officers gathering in Paraguay for meetings. The chilling combination of their coming together proved to be in preparation for the Fourth Reich. Through a section of skin, and some blood taken from the Führer before his death, Mengele hatched a plan to clone ninety-four boys in the mould of Hitler, and all aspects of Hitler's background (including the death of his father) must follow in the lives of the ninety-four boys. But Lieberman is on his trail.

Olivier's weight was a painful 140lb; however, not one day of filming was lost to his ill health. Schaffner recalled:

> He was sickly, he was in pain, but yet he was there for every call through every working day involved; never requested any release. And you could tell when he was having a good day physically and when he wasn't. You could read in his eyes. On a bad day, he would just train his mind to what we were doing. On a good day, he'd feel so great – such relief – that he would blow lines all over the place.

Peck and Olivier worked together for the first time towards the end of the schedule. The long time character adversaries meet just once in a showdown from which only one man will survive. The fight scene was shot in short sequences to accommodate Olivier, yet its violence, which including biting, scratching and gouging, was not affected one iota.

The film was released in October 1978. Its performances received excellent reviews, and Laurence Olivier was nominated for an Academy Award. Producer Milton Subotsky, now independent of Amicus, made his last Shepperton film in 1977, *Dominique*. Editor Richard Best recalls:

> I must admit it was a horrid experience, in every way. The cutting rooms were dreadful, the equipment was horrible and the newly installed racks were too small to take the cans – that was just typical of the whole experience. I was in a room next to the building that belonged to The Who, the pop group. All I could hear all day long was the thud-thud-thud of music.

It wasn't a bad film itself, but the producer – Milton Subotsky – wanted every single line of dialogue that wasn't deemed necessary to drive the story, cut. He sat with me at the moviola and almost filled a notebook with tiny little cuts he wanted made. But the director – Michael Anderson – wanted everything tension-full; so I had opposing forces. I had to go along with the producer, and when I screened the work print to the line-producer and director they declared it dreadful, and then Michael said if it was going out like that, he wanted his name removed.

They phoned Milton Subotsky and reported, and he said 'oh well put all the cuts back then'.

I took nearly a week putting back all the little cuts I'd made, and that was ten times harder than taking them out! I completed the edit, and the schedule was getting tighter with Christmas looming and so it didn't receive the attention it deserved in the fine cut process. Time was a luxury we just didn't have.

The Who, as Richard Best refers to above, were indeed resident at the studio. In July 1977, Ramport Enterprises took a 999-year lease on the Old House for £350,000, over half of which was to be spent on the much-needed repair and upgrade of the studio. The Who were the major shareholders in Ramport, and took control of J and K stages along with the house. For four years they controlled the area and it was very much 'off limits' to Shepperton personnel and crews.

Around this time British Lion announced that it had 'ceased to trade'. The film library was swallowed by that of EMI, and the company name and trademark was later bought by Producer Peter Snell, who produced films and television under the banner.

Just seven films lensed in 1978. 'In space, no one can hear you scream' – declared the posters. *Alien* was a benchmark in science-fiction movies. It also brought a much-needed lifeline to Shepperton, where Ridley Scott had previously worked filming commercials. A couple of decades later, he would own the studio, as we shall read later.

Winning the Academy Award for visual effects, it was the sci-fi thriller that started all sci-fi thrillers. 'Jaws in space' was how it was sold by Scott:

I think the film works very hard to introduce you to a world that's very, very real. It's exotic beyond your possible experience, but it's also very real – that's why I took so much time with the opening waking-up scene. I have them having breakfast, and so on. Then the question comes up of why they were awoken. I take you by the hand and into the texture of their environment. That's as important as the script and the acting.

I had enjoyed sci-fi before, films like *The Day the Earth Stood Still*, but *2001* really was a turning point. I was just out of college and was working at the BBC when I went to see it by myself. I thought, 'My God, this world can exist, it could be real.' It was like NASA in about twenty years time. When Kubrick was making it, the space program was in full swing. They spent a lot of time figuring out precisely how the technology would be designed and how it would look, so it had this incredible authenticity. I worked to make *Alien* feel that real too.

I'm very proud of the sets. They were very good. Even now, they're not dated. That's why I don't think I've touched science fiction again, because I did it so well with *Alien* and *Blade Runner*.

Director John Badham next came into the studio and injected new blood into Bram Stoker's classic story, as Costume Designer Julie Harris explains:

This particular production of *Dracula* had been a play on Broadway, with Frank Langella starring. He was very much a big matinee idol there, and they queued up to see him after each performance! The Mirisch brothers bought the rights, and engaged director John Badham – after his recent success with *Saturday Night Fever* – and Frank Langella reprised the role on the big screen. A terrific supporting cast included Laurence Olivier, Donald Pleasance, Kate Nelligan and Trevor Eve. Sadly Laurence Olivier wasn't at his best, and was saddled with an awful Dutch accent that was very over the top.

The following year, two television movies – television had begun playing a more significant role in Shepperton's output now – moved in to the studio: *All Quiet On the Western Front*, and *SOS Titanic*. Only one feature film lensed, Mike Hodge's *Flash Gordon*.

Initially, another director had been attached to direct the comic strip's big screen outing, but bowed out, allowing Hodges to take up the reigns. He says:

I have no idea why Dino hired me, except that Nicolas Roeg was going to do it and they parted company. It was a very light-hearted experience. I couldn't do anything else but make it up as I went along, because I had this massive Italian art department that couldn't speak English. I'd come in every day, see what they'd made and try to figure out what to do with it.

'I've done about 2,000 storyboards for *Flash* over the past two-and-a-half years, along with a number of 20 x 40" detailed set studies for the construction department,' said illustrious Production Illustrator Mentor Huebner shortly after the film's release:

The script was rewritten four or five times along the way. Much of the drawing was very detailed because Dino [DeLaurentis] wanted the technicians to see everybody and everything in every panel. When you have over $25 million invested you want to know what's happening to all of it. We were on six stages at Shepperton, all the *Star Wars* facilities at EMI, and in a six-million-cubic-foot complex at Brooklands. I had to do a lot of drawing to fill all that space.

During the year, EMI (and the British Lion library) merged with British electrical giant Thorn to become Thorn-EMI. A few months later, in 1980, Rank announced that it was withdrawing from film production. The British Film industry was again in one of its many crises. The Eady Levy and NFFC were granted a life extension in July 1980 in a Government attempt to help the business recover.

Production picked up slightly at Shepperton and saw directors such as David Lynch, Richard Marquand, Milos Foreman and Mel Brooks take up residence. Brooks was behind the rather weak comedy *The History of the World Part One* as writer, actor, producer and director, but his company also produced the excellent story of John Merrick, *The Elephant Man*, directed by Lynch. It is the story of how a Victorian doctor comes to care for Merrick who was catastrophically deformed with Proteous Syndrome, and displayed as a freak at public shows. Anthony Hopkins played the doctor, Sir Frederick Treves, from whose memoirs the story was partly based on.

The film had its share of problems. Just ten days before production was due to start, David Lynch revealed his ideas for Merrick's horrific make-up. However, the assembled crew were unimpressed, describing it as unimaginative and amateurish. Consequently, it was back to square one, and the design project was handed over to expert Chris Tucker. Production, meanwhile, had to start, and the scheduling changed so as to film the scenes with Merrick (played by John Hurt) wearing the sack cloth over his head. The re-arranged schedule resulted in a 25 per cent hike in the budget.

Anthony Hopkins decided to grow a beard, which he felt was in keeping with his Victorian character. It immediately caused a rift between him and Lynch, who demanded he remove it. Hopkins refused.

'Lynch wore this big brown trilby,' said Hopkins, 'a long black coat and tennis shoes and I had the feeling that most of his performance as director was going into his hat.'

Mel Brooks said to Hopkins, 'The guy's a genius. Even I don't know what he's talking about.'

Hopkins described Lynch as displaying 'an arrogant lack of communication'. Consequently, Hopkins knew he would receive very little direction for his character, and decided to play it 'very muted, as if the camera wasn't there at all'. He believed his performance to be 'as simple – sparing – as possible'. Hopkins was keen not to play the doctor as an overly sympathetic character, as though he has rescued Merrick from the circus freak show; he in turn has now put Merrick on show to his colleagues

Anthony Hopkins and, in full make-up, John Hurt in *The Elephant Man*. (Courtesy Canal and Image UK Ltd)

and students. The doctor eventually realises he has (unwittingly) set Merrick up in a sideshow of his own, and is ashamed of himself. Hopkins struck just the correct balance to make both facets of the doctor believable.

Chris Tucker's brilliant prosthetic make up – some 38in in diameter and taking five hours to apply – was inspired. It certainly helped the film secure its eight Oscar nominations, though alas it did not win in any of the categories.

Legendary American star James Cagney travelled to the UK to star in what was to be his last film, *Ragtime*, set in 1910s New York.

Property Maser Roy Pembrooke admits:

It wasn't a great film, and Cagney was frail and ill at the time. But there was a great excitement and anticipation associated with it. Cagney had tremendous difficulty in walking, yet on his first day at the studio, his car was driven round to the stage where we were all waiting to greet him – including the producer and director – he got out and walked (with difficulty) across to my colleagues and I – the behind the scenes boys – and shook our hands saying 'I'm pleased to be back'. That's a real star!

We had a double for Cagney, who was used in all the 'walking shots'. If Cagney was sat in a chair for example, he'd stand up, then we'd cut, bring in his double (filming him from behind). Once the 'walking shot' was in the can, we'd get Cagney over to where the double stopped, and cut to him sitting down. It's the only way we could do it.

There was a big set constructed on the land near the reservoir. I remember the script called for a big explosion in New York and the production designers, of which there were five, recreated a bit of Manhattan for us to destroy!

The 1980s marked something of an upturn from the uncertain production of the 1970s. Whilst 1981 was a rather lean year for production in Britain, and in particular at Shepperton, it was a year that would mark a renaissance of sorts in the industry. Richard Attenborough produced and directed his long-cherished *Gandhi*, completing some studio and its post-production work at Shepperton, and Producer David Puttnam's *Chariots of Fire* was released in cinemas. Both films went on to garner a clutch of Oscar statuettes. In fact, at the 1982 Oscar ceremony, the writer of *Chariots of Fire*, Colin Welland, optimistically announced that 'the British are coming'.

Brit Tony Scott made his first film at Shepperton in 1981. 'Shepperton had been my home over hundreds of commercials,' he says, of the bread and butter supplement to film and television work at the studio from the 1970s, 'so when I shot *The Hunger* at the studio, it had a lot of nostalgic value.'

Little did he realise that in the next decade he would co-own the studio.

In February 1982, trade paper *Screen International* headlined a '£20 million Holmes series'. The story reported how American producer Sy Weintraub had 'acquired the rights to the 56 short stories and four novels … he is planning to turn between twenty and thirty of them into feature length films'. The first shoot at the studio was *The Hound of the Baskervilles*, directed by Douglas Hickox over five weeks and on location around the Thames. Much of Dartmoor was build at Shepperton as Hickox was fearful of the British winter, saying, 'We'd have ended up lost in a bog, or weeks behind because of the weather'. The second film was Sherlock Holmes' *Sign of Four*, directed by Desmond Davies, and again starred Ian Richardson as the famous sleuth. Weintraub's proposed series then hit a major problem – a rival television series from Granada, starring Jeremy Brett, was in production. A law suit was immediately launched by Weintraub, but fought by Granada on the grounds that the author had died in 1907 and as such the stories and characters were in the public domain. Weintraub reportedly settled out of court with Granada for a figure which matched the budget of the two films produced. His series came to an end, with the two films going straight to television.

Of the other six films produced, only the *Jigsaw Man* really merits a mention, for its teaming of Michael Caine and Laurence Olivier for the last time.

1983 saw just four films at Shepperton, the first being *Bullshot* from Director Dick Clement. He explains:

> It was made for Handmade [the company founded by ex-Beatle George Harrison] and was an enormously enjoyable film to make – it was George Harrison's favourite.
>
> We were all convinced that we had made a good film. We had certainly made the film we set out to shoot. However, it just didn't find an audience. I remain exceptionally fond of it though, and one of the most elaborate sets I've ever worked on was the 'Dungeon' built on one of the stages at Shepperton– which we flooded. In it we had an octopus but as the budget was rather tight, ours only had five tentacles. I don't think you notice on the screen though!

The Company of Wolves was the other notable film of the year, from Director Neil Jordan and Producer Stephen Woolley. 'The forest set in the film,' says Woolley, 'was built on the two stages that link together [A and B] and we opened the doors between them to create a sense of vast size and scale.'

The next year at Shepperton stepped up a gear. It marked the return of David Lean. It also saw a change of ownership at the studio which had, in recent years, limped along as best as it could. The year was, of course, 1984. George Orwell, in his book, predicted the future of the modern political system and 'Big Brother' watching everywhere we go. Now at Shepperton, Richard Burton delivered a performance that wowed the critics in Director Michael Radford's film version. Sadly, it was to be his last performance. He died in Switzerland later in the year.

Dick Clement also returned to Shepperton to direct his next feature, again for Handmade – a comedy called *Water* – about a tiny and impoverished Caribbean island that has been completely forgotten by its British colonial masters … that is, until an oil drilling team (who haven't found a drop of oil there) strikes a mineral water well. Clement comments:

> I have to admit that I probably had less pleasure directing this film than any of my others – and that all stemmed really from the fact that Ian [LaFrenais] and I

were not happy with the script. We had written it, but felt the ending was weak, and as I began shooting, it began preying on my mind.

We did, though, have some terrific location shooting out on St Lucia and then – doubling for the far side of the island – we moved to Devon!

Michael Caine, Leonard Rossiter, Fulton Mackay and Billy Connolly starred.

Dylan Thomas' *Doctor and the Devils* – the story of infamous grave robbers Burke and Hare – was given the big screen treatment by Director Freddie Francis and Producer Geoffrey Helman. Timothy Dalton, Jonathan Pryce, Twiggy and Patrick Stewart were among the star cast.

'We never intended to film at Shepperton,' says Helman, 'as the film was all set up out of the smaller Wembley Studios which, at the time, were owned by John and Benny Lee. However, when the brothers took over Shepperton, it was suggested we might like to move and take advantage of the better facilities.'

John and Benny Lee played a very important part in Shepperton Studio's history. They were the next in the line of brothers who had done so – first there had been the Kordas, then the Boultings and later, as we shall see, the Scotts.

The Lee brothers were film electricians, and very good ones. John Lee confirms:

Benny and I started our company Lee Lighting in around 1960 at Goldhawk Studios, Shepherds Bush. It came about after a group paid about £8,000 to buy these buildings, and we were recommended to them for the electrical

The cast and crew of *Doctor And the Devils* including Mel Brooks and Shepperton owners John and Benny Lee. (Courtesy Geoffrey Helman)

installation. It was really just a one stage facility, with dressing rooms etc. We did the installation, but they ran out of money and couldn't pay us! They knew Benny and I had worked at MGM, and knew all about lights, and so they suggested we buy in our own lights and operate the studios … that's how the company started.

A few years later, the studio was sold, and we weren't wanted by the new owners so moved to new premises. Some years (and a few more premises) later, in 1968, we found ourselves filming up in Kensal Rise at the old biscuit factory. The owner of the building told us he was interested in selling the site; he wanted £60,000 or £65,000. We went to see the bank manager, raised the money and bought the three acre site.

We converted the buildings into a three-stage facility, and operated on a 'four wall' basis. We were the first four wall studio in fact, as all the others were fully serviced. Along with commercials and television work, we attracted films such as *Ten Rillington Place*, *The Virgin And The Gypsy*, *Tommy*, *A Touch Of Class*, *Under Milk Wood*, *Spring And Port Wine*. Our lighting company operated from there too, and so we also did a lot of location work on films.

In 1977, the Lee brothers bought Wembley Studios. Wembley Film Studios was established in the late 1920s and soon became busy with 'Quota Quickie' films and, in 1934, 20th Century Fox bought the site. During the Second World War, film production virtually ceased and the site was used by the Army Kinematograph Service and then the Royal Air Force Film Unit. Following the war, the one-stage studio was rented out and, in the mid-1950s, sold to Associated Rediffusion for television work. 'We sold Kensal Rise and bought Wembley, which we completely refitted and used for television and film productions, along with it being a base for our Lee Group companies.'

By 1984, Shepperton's owners, Mills & Allen, had made it known that they wanted to get out of the film business. The Lee brothers weren't strangers to the studio, as they had serviced many films based there over recent years and decided to make a bid for the complex, which was duly accepted. John Lee elaborates:

We bought eighteen acres for just under three and a half million pounds. The rest of the lot with the Old House and J & K stages, owned by The Who, and H stage, owned by Spelthorne Council [as part of a housing development deal struck, but never built on] on which a split on rental from it of 70:30 was set in the council's favour, were not part of our initial deal.

However, we then set about doing a deal with Ramport [The Who] and bought them out for £550,000; then paid a further £1 million to buy H stage and its land back from the council. The Government then assigned us the NFFC special share, as we were firmly committed to running the studio as a going concern.

The studio was re-named Lee International Studios, Shepperton. 'We always liked to put our names in front of our companies,' explains John Lee. 'The next year, we decided to float the combined company [which carried their name in every subsidiary], for $180 million [£100 million].'

Denis Carrigan, who had been an electrician at the Kensal Rise studio and took on the role of studio manager of the site when Ross MacKenzie gave up the post, later moved to Wembley as studio manager and, when the Lee brothers took over Shepperton, they appointed him managing director, with Paul Olliver remaining as studio manager. A £15 million programme of studio investment and renovation began. Lee explains:

We couldn't do too much at once as many of the facilities were leased out: E, F & G stages for instance were leased to the BBRK Group for commercial production. We had to wait for their lease to expire before we could do anything to upgrade 'their' stages – and there was a conflict of interests with BBRK actually, as they were operating a studio within a studio. They went off and bought Ealing (which we were looking at doing) and carried on from there [until going bust in 1994].

Meanwhile, former scoring and effects stages L and M were refurbished and used as fully functioning sound stages; new workshops were built and generally the studio's appearance improved, as did the power supply, with a complete electrical re-wiring.

2010 was always going to be a difficult job for Director Peter Hyams. Even with big budgets, lavish special effects and high production values, Hyams was following in the footsteps of Stanley Kubrick (who turned down the idea of directing this sequel) and his masterpiece, *2001*.

Hyams explains how he was approached to direct the film at Shepperton:

The chairman of MGM asked me to do it. 'Here's this book [by Arthur Clark] and it's got to be in the theatres 17 months from now.' I was petrified and reluctant and intrigued. When I read the book, I said, 'It's a fascinating book but there are things about it that I really don't agree with. If you want me to do this film, two things have to happen. One, Stanley Kubrick has to say that it is ok with him. He's God and I will not displease God. Two, I want to change the film from the book. The book was written without politics. This was 1984 and Ronald Reagan. I'd like to make this a movie about Americans and Russians not getting along whereas in the book they got along. I want to add something about brinkmanship.' And he said fine.

They arranged a first phone call between us [Kubrick and Hyams]. I was in the office when the first phone call came through and I stood up. I picked up the phone and stood up. Kubrick didn't even say hello. He said, 'In *Outland*, you've got a shot that went through … How did you do that?' He talked about all the crap he'd gone through with the cinematographer's union and how they wouldn't let him in. He was asking me about shot after shot after shot. I was on the phone with him for almost three hours. I told him everything and he told me nothing.

A couple of months later, I was sitting around at a club and talking to someone. I asked him what it was like when he first met Stanley Kubrick. And he said, 'We sat on a park bench and we spoke for about three hours. And I told him everything and he told me nothing.'

The only thing to do with *2010* was to make a film so unlike *2001* that people could not compare it. I met Jim Cameron because I'd seen *Aliens*. I got his number and I called him up. I said, 'You did exactly what I tried to do. You made a film so unlike the first movie that you can't compare them'.

The film wasn't received positively by the press, and the cast (Roy Scheider, John Lithgow and Helen Mirren) were criticised for performing only 'competently whilst obviously mindful of walking in the ghostly footsteps of the *2001* cast.'

After David Lean had completed *Ryan's Daughter* he was all but destroyed by the terrible reviews. The worst, 'This is a real turkey, take it away', resulted in Lean saying, 'I didn't want to do another film. I thought I'll do something else.'

It was fourteen years before Lean started filming his next project, *A Passage to India*. He had, however, been attached since 1981 when Producer Lord Brabourne approached him. He also wrote the screenplay 'in a room at the Maura Sheraton Hotel in New Delhi,' he later said.

In 1984 production commenced on location in India, and then a little work at Shepperton along with post-production. Sadly, it was Lean's last film. He had plans to realise another, *Nostromo*, and even started full-scale artist tests at Shepperton, but alas he died before filming could start.

Shepperton had, for many years, been linked or controlled by the Government. The Government of the 1980s, under Prime Minister Margaret Thatcher, undeniably changed the state of the British film industry. Thatcher, who never exhibited more than a dislike for film, made major cuts in support for arts institutions. The Tory government wanted the film industry treated like any other business, and hence be accountable to market forces. A Films Bill in 1985 abolished the Eady Levy, the law that had channelled a percentage of box-office takings in Britain back into British production. Also, the 25 per cent tax break for investors in film was abolished,

The great David Lean, who completed his last feature at Shepperton. (Gareth Owen Collection)

making film investment more risky for businesses. The NFFC, the only direct source of government film financing, was privatised. No new measures were introduced to replace the lost revenue.

In one foul swoop, the Prime Minister caused irreparable harm to the British film industry. Yet the 1980s saw the first upturn in cinema attendance since the 1950s, when television became the medium of mass popular entertainment. In 1945 there were 1,585 million cinema visits per year; this fell to an all-time low of 54 million in 1984 but has steadily been increasing since, attributed, some say, to the rise of the multiplex, the first having opened in Britain in 1985.

Unfortunately, the growing audiences were not championing British film, with the box office being consistently dominated 85-90 per cent by Hollywood. This may have been good news for the exhibitors and distributors but, with the Eady Levy abolished, it did not benefit the producers in any way.

Most ironically of all, 1985 was declared British Film Year, coming at a time when production was at an all-time low, the cinemas were 90 per cent Hollywood dominated and there was a huge exodus of British talent to America.

Shepperton hosted just five productions, including the disastrous *Absolute Beginners* from ex-video director Julien Temple and Producers Steve Woolley and Nik Powell. A former Goldcrest executive, who wishes to remain anonymous, comments:

It was over budget before the first day of shooting. Goldcrest Management (then Brent Walker & Co) did not have a clue what was going on, they either did not know or were in too deep to care. Virgin were only in it for the music rights so they did not care either. Warners, as distributors, were not investors so they were quite happy for it to go millions over budget (they thought at a higher cost they would be getting a better movie – wrong!). When Goldcrest eventually said no more shooting on a particular set or sequence Nik Powell put up his company, Palace's, money and carried on shooting the sequences anyway. Meanwhile Chris Brown, his co-producer, thought his job was to borrow the stars' wardrobe and wear it around the studio whilst the Wardrobe department, Joyce Stoneman and her team, were doing their crust looking for it. The Associate Producer David Wimbury and the completion guarantor Garth Thomas had a five minute discussion once a week and then adjourned to the bar. Steve Woolley tried but failed against all odds. They were re-writing to the very end (and even had Alan Parker in to try and sort out the mess). When it came to the editing period they had the best of the British editing gurus (all with one reel each) trying to make a movie out of a lot of Pop promos. In the book *The Egos Have Landed* Powell implies that they were victims of 'hide it in the drawer accounting'. This was very wrong and had he lived, David Saggs the production accountant, would have carried on filing a lawsuit against them and the writer.

In spite of the big Pop cast, and the ultimate in hype, a star studded premiere – covering over Leicester Square for the reception and ball – the movie was almost the bomb of the century and to my knowledge has not even made 10 per cent of its true cost (though God alone knows what that was) back.

Richard Attenborough's South African set for *Cry Freedom* was completed at Shepperton. Attenborough comments:

> President Mugabe used to come on location with his wife, Sally. We showed him the film and afterwards he clambered onto the platform and said that the future of Zimbabwe was in this film, that the whole concept of a dual relationship between black and white was an absolute prerequisite. Then Sally died, and for some reason, the compassion and understanding which flowed from their relationship … I can't believe it's the same man. Sheila [Lady Attenborough] thinks he's [twirls his finger by his head].

Experienced Stage Director David Jones brought a delightful movie, *84 Charing Cross Road*, to Shepperton, produced by Mel Brooks' company. It is based on the true story of a transatlantic business correspondence about used books that developed into a close friendship, and stars Anthony Hopkins and Anne Bancroft. Seventy-five per cent of the story is told off-screen, and the two stars don't share one scene together. Yet it is a tremendously powerful movie. Jones wanted Anthony Hopkins to play the role of London bookshop owner Frank Doel, and upon sending him the script received a reply from the actor, thanking him for 'the most intelligent, literate script I've been offered in ten years. When do we start working?'

Producer Geoffrey Helman takes up the story:

> Mel Brooks' production company was financing the project, it was an inexpensive film – at $4.3 million – but Mel seemed to think that we would be able to close down Charing Cross Road in London for real, and recreate the 1950s period. I explained that it just wouldn't be possible.
>
> I have a background in design, and I called upon my days at art school to think of a way of achieving a location shoot, in a controlled environment. It was then I had the brainwave.
>
> The bookshop, which stood at number 84, could be built on a stage at Shepperton I thought. And here's the twist … build it so as the glass frontage and door stands at the mouth of the stage. In effect we had an interior set (on stage) and an exterior (just outside the stage). Opposite the stage I could construct a façade of other shops and in between run traffic and buses along the road in the studio. That's just what we did. It lent the whole set a tremendous authenticity.

Over at EMI Elstree, there was a change of ownership – and consequently with the British Lion catalogue too – when Cannon acquired the studio, cinema chain and film library. Thorn-EMI withdrew from production and distribution, thus ending the duopoly they shared with Rank over several decades.

The Lee Group continued to expand in associated support services, including acquiring a small Manchester studio and setting up subsidiaries for their companies throughout the world: London, New York, California, South Africa, Canada, Paris, the south of France, Madrid, Barcelona, Vienna, Israel, Malta; employing around 2,000 people. The group was now operating twenty-one stages – more than their main competitors joined together.

In the mid-1970s, the Lee brothers joined forces with former video engineer Joe Dunton (who created 'video assist' for film cameras) to establish Joe Dunton Cameras. The camera, lens and grip rental company was the perfect compliment to Lee Lighting, Lee Filters, Lee Electric, Lee Lifting and Lee Scaffolding. They next set their sights on their main competitors, Panavision. It was to be both ambitious and risky. Two stars of the music world, meanwhile, made Shepperton their home for a few weeks: Bob Dylan, who starred in *Hearts of Fire*, and Madonna, who, with then-husband Sean Penn, took the lead in Jim Goddard's *Shanghai Surprise* for Handmade Films.

The film was envisaged as a romance similar to the one that developed between Humphrey Bogart and Katherine Hepburn in *The African Queen* and was due to be filmed totally on location in Macau. However, the off-camera action attracted more attention than the movie in-production, thanks to the various tussles between the stars and the press, causing George Harrison to fly out to try and make the peace, and as a result the rest of the film was transferred to Shepperton.

Harrison's intervention prompted Madonna to say, 'He's great, very understanding and sympathetic. He's given me more advice on how to deal with the press, though, than how to make movies'.

Prop master Roy Pembrooke confirms:

The 'stars' were subjects of much gossip for being difficult. Much of it was actually warranted. I remember when Madonna heard that access to the restaurant was through the bar, she refused point blank to go in there. They ended up creating a new doorway on the side (which is the entrance today) and built her own private toilet too!

Bob Dylan was quite the opposite in *Hearts of Fire*, as Cinematographer Alan Hume recalls:

He played a reclusive pop star; and I found Bob to be very reclusive in real life – quite withdrawn. I remember when we were shooting (other) artist tests at Shepperton, he came along to watch but stood in the far corner of the stage. Perhaps he was deep in thought and contemplating his own performance, but he showed little interest or enthusiasm and I found that a bit strange to be honest.

In 1987, Lee International, the holding company for the Lee Group's many companies, announced that the purchase of Panavision was going ahead, with backing from American group Citicorp, after the City of London stated that the 'enlarged' Lee Group with Panavision would not be suitable for listing due to Panavision's short trading record. John Lee explains:

Citicorp syndicated eighteen banks, and through them we raised $350 million. We bought out the Lee Group's shareholders (becoming a private company again), paid $100 million for Panavision and had some working capital left to play with. With hindsight, which is a terrific thing, I know we overpaid to buy the company back, but our hands were tied. The banks, who owned the majority of the shares, determined how much we paid out to the shareholders and, of course, continually pressed for as much as they could. We effectively paid out twice the price we floated at, eighteen months earlier, because of them.

Alas the new private company's fortunes took a turn for the worse when Financial Director David Mindell plunged the brothers into financial difficulties.

'He was dipping into the company,' reveals John Lee, 'and my brother and I, personally, lost £10 million through him. We called in the Serious Fraud Squad. It ended up in court, and we won the case, but the damage had been done.'

Coupled with these internal problems, the stock market crash of 1988 and a general slump in production, particularly American, hit both Panavision and Shepperton hard. The studio's future was, once again, uncertain.

In late 1988, American bankers Warburg-Pincus Capital Company stepped in to buy Lee International. 'They were GE [General Electric] pension fund, and others,' recalls John Lee, 'and we were rather pleased as not only did they save the company, and jobs within, it took the question mark from over Shepperton.'

The Lee brothers stepped back from the empire they had built, and saw the company immediately restructured, leaving Panavision with all of the camera interests, and the lighting and studio interests under Lee International.

John and Benny Lee continued working in the film industry on innovative projects, including mobile lighting units. Sadly, Benny Lee died in 1994 and John Lee in 2008.

Meanwhile, in 1988 the troubled Cannon Group decided to get out of the British market. They sold the film catalogue – including British Lion – to Weintraub, and announced plans to close their Elstree studio. The complex was bought by Brent Walker Entertainment Group, who agreed with the planning authorities to retain fifteen and a half acres of the site as a film studio whilst being allowed to sell off the other twelve acres to a supermarket. Brent Walker would continue running the studio as a going concern under the aegis of Goldcrest (which they owned).

The most important film of the year, and the first of many the director would make at the studio, was *Henry V* with Kenneth Branagh. From being the youngest actor to play Henry V on stage with the Royal Shakespeare Company, he next set his sights on the big screen version:

Even before I played it at Stratford, I had a strong feeling about this particular piece. I feel it has been unjustly treated as a jingoistic hymn to England. Olivier's film, because it was made in 1943, inevitably became a propaganda vehicle and cut out the less amiable aspects of Henry's character. There was no mention of his threat to the Governor of Harfleur to show 'your naked infants pitted upon spikes'.

The film was made under the banner of Renaissance Films on a $10 million budget largely assembled by its executive producer, Stephen Evans. The financing came from a variety of sources, including a government-sponsored business expansion plan, BBC TV and a small army of private investors. With financing coming together, Branagh requested an audience with Prince Charles, so he could better prepare to play Henry V.

Just ahead of production commencing, Branagh – in an interview with *The New York Times* – pointed out that:

> 60 per cent of the film will be shot on two sound stages and that Agincourt will be re-created in the surrounding fields [Olivier spent a quarter of his $600,000 budget shooting the battle scenes in Ireland]. He points to a vast wall on the back lot that will serve for Harfleur and for a night-shoot of 'Once more unto the breach' with the King desperately trying to stem the retreating tide of soldiers. He also points to slit trenches being dug in the ground and providing an instant visual reminder of World War I. 'I want,' he says, 'to make a popular film that will both satisfy the Shakespearean scholar and the punter who likes *Crocodile Dundee*.'

For Branagh, the film was the culmination of the work his company Renaissance had done over the previous eighteen months. He took great pride in announcing that 90 per cent of his then current theatre company would be in the film (including Judi Dench and Geraldine McEwan); the few newcomers included Paul Scofield as the King of France, Ian Holm as Fluellen and Alex McCowen as Ely.

The fact remained, however, that directing a film on this scale must have been a huge and daunting undertaking. Branagh described himself as 'A man who has done a crash course in film history. Orson Welles said that when you make a film you should either know everything or very little. I'm not saying which I know!'

At just twenty-nine, Kenneth Branagh went on to receive Best Actor and Best Director Oscar nominations.

As the 1980s came to a close, George Harrison's Handmade Films made Shepperton their home once again with 'a tale of the immaculate deception', *Nuns on the Run*. Director Jonathan Lynn recalls:

> Shepperton in 1989 was a ghost studio. It was virtually deserted. We had our production offices at Shepperton, but we only shot there ourselves for about ten days. The restaurant/commissary (whatever it was called) had to be specially opened for us.
>
> As I recall it, *Nuns On The Run* was the only film shooting there. In fact, according to Screen International, I think we were the only cinema film being made in the UK at the time. Branagh had made *Henry V* the year before, and one or two others were scheduled for later, but nothing else for the movies was being made at the time. The British film industry was on its knees.
>
> There were one or two commercials shot there, and a couple of TV shows such as BBC's *The Choice* and CBS' *The Secret Life of Ian Fleming*.

Director Jonathan Lynn shares a joke with his *Nuns On the Run* – Eric Idle and Robbie Coltrane. (Courtesy Jonathan Lynn)

Furthermore, it seemed to us, that the idea of making something simply because it was funny was rather out of style. Only 'important' films were being made. Handmade Films was the exception to the rule: Eric Idle took the script to George Harrison, who liked it and wrote the cheque, for just over £3 million.

We edited at Shepperton too. I don't think it got much busier during that time either.

CHAPTER 18

THE '90s: GREAT SCOTT

In 1989-90, there was a significant upsurge in television produced at Shepperton. Whilst the American blockbusters and occasional British film helped fill the sound stages, a more embracing attitude was adopted towards television, lucrative commercial and pop promo productions. The schedules were often short, enabling the studio management to fit them around the American blockbusters that were coming in taking stage space, and with the uncertain, up-and-down film production environment; a vital 'bread and butter' income. Television shows such as *Red Dwarf*, *Smith & Jones* and *You Bet!* made their home at Shepperton, alongside dramas *Gawain and the Green Knight* and HBO's *Manhattan Project*.

Large budget features were still the staple diet of the studio, however, with Franco Zeffirelli's *Hamlet*. The film's continuity supervisor was Angela Allen and she explains how the film came about:

I rather like Shakespeare, and this really had a wonderful cast – headed by Mel Gibson – and Franco is a real anglophile at heart and lover of Shakespeare too. It really came about through Mel who wanted to play Hamlet, I guess to prove he wasn't just an action-film actor. He had, of course, started in the theatre as a young man in Australia, and he worked very hard with his accent and is a very conscientious worker. He and Franco had a falling out during the production, and I think Mel is someone who does bear a grudge. Even though the film looked wonderful, and he gave a wonderful performance, I don't think they ever spoke afterwards.

Glenn Close, again, was tremendously professional and such a hard worker. She would come into the studio every day, whether she was working or not, and she would always insist on speaking off-screen lines herself to 'feed' the other actors.

Franco, being an art director himself, was very meticulous and he knew exactly how to light his wonderful, luscious studio sets. I found it a hugely enjoyable experience!

Robin Hood – Prince of Thieves was one of two films with the Nottinghamshire outlaw
to shoot in the UK during 1990. The other, starring Patrick Bergin, was at Pinewood.
Shepperton played host to one of Hollywood's hottest stars, Kevin Costner, in the
role of Robin. Support came from Morgan Freeman, Mary Elizabeth Mastrantonio,
Christian Slater and Alan Rickman, many of whose scenes were later cut when
Costner felt overshadowed by Rickman's wonderful performance.

A fifteen-week schedule was fixed; however, during pre-production period it
was announced that two weeks was being shaved off. Kevin Costner complained
that valuable rehearsal time had been sacrificed in the shortened schedule and the
production was 'too loosely planned'. Furthermore, with daily script changes and
six producers on the project, frustrations at the endless indecisiveness were at a high.
Initially, Robin Wright was cast as Maid Marian, but announced her pregnancy a few
weeks ahead of shooting commencing. A last-minute replacement was secured with
Mastrantonio.

Filming was set for the UK and France, and out of Shepperton, but throughout the
shoot the elements were unkind – grey mist and drizzling rain floated over much of
the exterior shoot, leading to further 'rushing' of the shoot, which Costner felt was
'sacrificing the quality of the performances'. Costner, who had considerable clout in
Hollywood following his Oscar-winning success with *Dances with Wolves*, considered
using his influence to call a halt in the production until production matters were
ironed out to his satisfaction. He was also concerned about his trying to master an
English accent was becoming ever more conscious in his mind, and affecting the
naturalness of his performance. He thought better of calling a hiatus, and continued
with the idea of correcting his accent in dubbing during post-production. Ultimately,
the film over-ran its schedule by three weeks. However, the end result is a polished,
tension-filled, gritty romp through the *Robin Hood* legend. Whilst some geographical
issues remain – such as Robin landing in Dover and then, by foot, arriving in
Nottingham by nightfall – it did not prevent the film grossing a terrific $150 million
in cinemas.

Throughout the film, many references were made to the 'return of King Richard
from the crusades'. He did, of course, return at the film's end in the shape of Sean
Connery. It was dubbed 'Hollywood's worst kept secret of the year'. The canny Scot
contributed one day to the shoot at Shepperton, resulting in thirty seconds of screen
time, for a fee of $500,000 – which he donated to charity. His arrival was kept a secret
from the crew, but provided a much-needed break in tension. On set he recalled his
earlier film, *Robin and Marian*: 'We filmed it for $5 million in five weeks,' he told a
disbelieving Kevin Reynolds, 'with three days of re-shoots.'

When Mark Herman graduated from the National Film and Television School,
he wrote a script which soon received the backing of British Screen Finance (the
follow-up to the NFFC) and Channel Four films, as Producer Steve Abbot recalls:

> Simon Perry of British Screen called me up and told me about Mark, and how
> he'd won an award for his graduation film, and that Channel 4 thought he was
> a talent to be watched.

Simon knew I had connections in Hollywood, and was also from Yorkshire – Mark was born in Bridlington – and wanted to introduce us both.

My partner, Jennie Howarth, and I met Mark and got on famously. The script *Blame It on the Bellboy* was budgeted at around $10 million which, then, was outside the capabilities of the two companies, and so they thought I might be able to help move it forward. I made a few phone calls, set up some meetings and within six months we were in the enviable position of talking to three studios, two of which started a bidding round! Hollywood Pictures (a division of Disney) won.

Our main location was Venice, and the rest studio. We did approach one London studio who seemed totally indifferent as to whether we went there or not, which was rather bizarre as here were we with a $10 million budget film at a time when there were maybe only twelve films being made each year! So, I put a call through to Shepperton. The studio manager, Paul Olliver, couldn't have been more helpful. He offered us an incredible deal and really looked after us.

One of Dudley Moore's contractual stipulations was that he have a piano in his dressing room. I remember, with great fondness, sitting in my office at Shepperton (which was below his dressing room) and hearing him play the most elaborate pieces when not required on set.

We previewed the film to get audience reaction, and it actually went rather well in the UK, but some of the British in-jokes went over the heads of the American audiences, so we made a few cuts. Then the studio asked we make a few more cuts and tighten bits here and there – improving our scores at previews. But we were cutting the running time back. It reached a point where we were down to seventy-six minutes! We daren't have cut any more. But we thought we had a tight, sharp comedy at the end of it.

Although the identity-confusion comedy, starring Moore, Bryan Brown, Richard Griffiths and Penelope Wilton, previewed well, it failed to find an audience upon its release.

Meanwhile, Richard Attenborough was busy readying his next project, a biopic of Charlie Chaplin:

When I was ten or eleven my father brought me up to London, as he had meetings, and said 'I know somebody who you'll like very much. Let's walk along to the London Pavilion'. Which is what we did and saw *The Gold Rush*. And I was totally shattered by this man who seemed to me to have not only genius but to have a unique genius – perhaps genius is unique, because it applies to a particular person – but he was able to grasp my attention, either emotionally or cerebrally, however he chose. He was able to make you laugh and cry, etc. I thought he was just incredible. And so right from that age, I was fascinated by him.

I had the great joy of meeting Chaplin towards the end of his life, and indeed Oona, who died, bless her, just before we started to shoot. The picture was not as good as it should have been. And, I think, partly it was not as good because I didn't have the degree of autonomy that I would have wished, because the budget was very high and the result was that the company that was financing it made certain requirements as far as the script was concerned.

Attenborough believed that having three contributing screenwriters, William Boyd, Bryan Forbes and William Goldman, working from three base stories (Chaplin's autobiography, David Robinson's biography and Diana Hawkins' story) proved detrimental.

Forbes elaborates on his involvement:

It proved to be a tragedy of good intentions. Immediately after I had delivered my second draft, the dead hand of a young script executive, fronting for the chief executive, fell upon it. He delivered a lengthy screed listing all his objections, but, since I was barred from meeting him and since most of his comments bore little or no relation to the craft of screenwriting, the exercise did not advance my cause. I was to write no less than a further three drafts and worked many months in the false belief that I was satisfying everybody's requirements. Sadly, this was not the case. I later found out that I had been on a loser from day one, Dickie confessing that Universal had always been unwilling to employ me and had only been reluctantly persuaded at his insistence. He finally revealed that their first choice had been an American writer, though when my contract was terminated they employed William Boyd and then Tom Stoppard. At which point Universal top brass disagreed with the casting Dickie preferred and put the project into 'turnaround', a euphemism for we-don't-want-it-so-take-it-elsewhere-but-make-sure-we-get-our-money-back-plus-interest. It was eventually made for another company, and a fourth, American, writer was brought in to rehash yet again my original screenplay.

In the event, an American actor, Robert Downey Jr, was cast as Chaplin and actually won many plaudits, including an Oscar nomination, as did Stuart Craig, the film's production designer, for his authentic recreations of London's musical halls and the Keystone studios in LA. Attenborough concludes:

I tried stupidly to put too much into the movie, and the result was that if it hadn't been for a bewildering performance by Robert Downey, I mean a just staggering performance by Robert Downey, I think the picture would have been a real failure. But his performance was such that, and indeed so was Geraldine's and a number of others, that it was OK, but it was not as good as I ought to have made it and I'm sad about that because I admired him so much.

Britain's most successful feature film (to date) was Neil Jordan's IRA thriller *The Crying Game*, which won him an Oscar for Best Original Screenplay. The film's release in the UK wasn't anything spectacular, but when Miramax got hold of it in the US they crafted an ingenious marketing campaign hinging around the film's surprise twist. It became the 'must see' movie. People were desperate to see what the twist was. As a result it grossed some $62.5 million in the US and Canada.

Television production outweighed features in 1992. Top dramas *The Borrowers*, *Inspector Morse*, *Covington Cross* and *Jeeves & Wooster* nestled alongside *Red Dwarf VI* and *You Bet!* (series 6), whilst just four features lensed, one being from former Monty Python Eric Idle, who announced that his screenplay *Splitting Heirs* would move into production with backing from Universal Pictures. His fellow Python, John Cleese, would appear in support along with Rick Moranis, Catherine Zeta-Jones and Barbara Hershey.

'I wrote *Splitting Heirs*, and I produced it,' says Idle. 'I went to Hollywood and got the money for it, and went back to England and made it. That wasn't an easy thing to do, and they treated it with the correct amount of disdain that they should when you do such a thing for them!'

Things were starting to look up for the industry when, in his budget speech, the Chancellor of the Exchequer, Norman Lamont, announced tax concessions for the British film industry: immediate 100 per cent write-off of pre-production investment and writing down of production costs over three years after completion. The measures were valued at £5 million in the first year, and £15 million in 1993-94.

The Muppet Christmas Carol was the first project featuring the characters following creator Jim Henson's death. His son, Brian, took the helm. The only 'live' actor to participate was Michael Caine.

Said Henson: 'Despite it starring Muppets, the film brought a faithful adaptation of Dickens to the big screen and introduced children to the literary world by ending on the line "You've seen the film, now read the book".'

1993 was a year when one of the studio's former main competitors, Elstree Film Studios, was closed by owners Brent Walker, with much of its back-lot already given over to a Tesco supermarket and petrol filling station, and its giant 'Star Wars Stage' was dismantled. A source involved with the 'Save Our Studio' campaign at Elstree says:

> Shepperton were very keen to buy the stage, but owners Brent Walker were extremely reluctant to let anything be recycled from the site. They just wanted it closed and forgotten. The stage should have been re-assembled on the remainder of the back-lot, as part of the council's agreement to give planning consent to the supermarket, but it wasn't. Shepperton, surreptitiously, bought an off the shelf company, and approached Brent Walker again, with an offer to buy the stage for scrap. A deal was agreed and, before anyone knew what was happening, Shepperton then announced the stage was to be re-assembled on their lot [as R and S stages]!

Undoubtedly, *Four Weddings and a Funeral* remains one of the most successful and popular of British films. Directed by Mike Newell and produced by Duncan Kenworthy, it shot on location and at Shepperton.

'I went through a whole decade when I went to so many weddings – either seventy-two or sixty-eight, I forget, but an enormous number of Saturdays – gone! Never to be reclaimed', says writer Richard Curtis on the idea behind his script. 'Always with that frantic trying to get there on time, which I never, never managed.'

The film cast a relatively unknown Hugh Grant alongside American beauty Andie MacDowell, and surpassed all expectations across the world. Richard Curtis wrote the script with Grant in mind, but Grant explained the one reservation people had upon his casting:

> I swear this is true. When we sat down to make that film, everyone was concerned that it might look as if it were easy for me to get Andie MacDowell, and the whole idea was to make me look shitty. So I sat down with the hairdresser to make the worst haircut we possibly could for it. It was meant to be like Jim Carrey's in *Dumb and Dumber*.

His foppish hair soon endeared him to millions of female admirers, and no doubt considerably helped the film's box-office success!

Mary Shelley's Frankenstein was Kenneth Branagh's first major Hollywood movie, shot on a series of vast sets at Shepperton Studios on a budget of $45 million, and starring Robert De Niro as the Creature.

The film was not Branagh's original inspiration. Columbia Tri-Star had a *Frankenstein* script going the rounds and sent it to him. His response was to accept the central role and direct it, to re-work the screenplay, insist it be made at Shepperton – starting the new wave of big-budget, dollar-financed movies that arrived on these shores – and wooing Robert De Niro into co-starring as the monster.

He said, 'Having been around Hollywood and looking at a subject as familiar as this, I was a bit leery at first. But I read the novel and it has everything you could want, a tragedy of Shakespearian proportions with a bit of Faust thrown in.'

One of the ironies of *Frankenstein* is that usually nobody remembers very much about the title character and many cinema-goers think the Creature is Frankenstein. Branagh decided to make an attempt to broaden the focus of the story.

> We did a lot of a work on the Shelleys themselves, their crazed, incestuous, rather brilliant, extraordinary lives. The sort of incredible passion which existed between those people we try to give to the relationship between Victor and Elizabeth (Helena Bonham Carter), who, in the book, is rendered as a sort of idealised object of her time. It's a challenging thing, in that Elizabeth is no longer downstairs going 'What's in that funny old lab, honey?' We also had to see what Victor Frankenstein is risking.

Robert De Niro is famously able to physically transform himself for the requirements of a given role, as *Raging Bull* demonstrated so strongly, but this was the first time he had submitted himself to major prosthetic make-up to alter his appearance. Yet how did he persuade Robert De Niro to take on the role?

I knew I needed a great actor. I needed someone who was going to be brave enough to take on a role which has become a modern icon. We're used to Boris Karloff and all the versions since then of THAT make-up. Bob and I met and, thank God, we seemed to get on. He relaxed a lot when he knew I was Irish rather than English. He does have a strong sense of humour, more than I expected. I think he was glad to do it, as part of his interest is in being different from part to part, and in stretching himself. He didn't want to be confined by some kind of big suit, and it took us about nine months to get the make-up right, so that he could continue to act as simply and beautifully as he's capable of. The triumph of the make-up is that you don't really notice it. It's certainly not Boris Karloff. I thought Karloff was wonderful, especially in the first picture; it was a beautiful piece of acting, but quite different. I think De Niro will make his own significant mark on the role.

The birth of the Creature – the word 'monster' was banned on set by Branagh – was quite a significant scene for the director, and De Niro was adamant it should be 'just right'.

Instead of real amniotic fluid [in the tank] we had this ton of KY Jelly, plus a lot of rubber eels, which tended to slap around us at the wrong time. Bob had these simple but effective tricks to make it more real. Before we shot, he'd revolve in circles for three or four minutes so he was completely dizzy and didn't know what he was doing … he was almost sick. And for me, it was like picking up a dead weight.

Having spent two years on the film, from development through shooting, editing and promotion, Branagh declared himself 'exhausted'. He had given his all. He had done his best, and now could sit back and finally be free of the darkened editing room that had dominated much of the year leading up to the film's release. Sadly, the film received very mixed reviews from the critics upon its release, and took only $22 million at the US box office. A great disappointment for all involved.

It's a film I wouldn't have made any other way, and I'm very proud of it, but it clearly didn't strike the right chord with lots of people. But the fact is … it's done $100 million theatrically worldwide. I wish more people had liked it, but it'll make its money back. That's not much of a disaster.

'I loved the property immediately,' says Sylvester Stallone, on starring in the 1994 blockbuster *Judge Dredd*:

because it takes a genre that I love, quote, 'the action morality film,' and makes it a bit more sophisticated. It has political overtones. It shows how if we don't curb the way we run our judicial system, the police may end up running our lives, because nothing else seems to work. I love the movie, because it deals with unemployment, it deals with archaic governments, it deals with cloning and all kinds of things that could happen in the future. It's also bigger than any film I've ever done in its physical stature and the way it was designed. It shows how all people are dwarfed by the system and by architecture, and how insignificant human beings will be in the future. There's a lot of action in the movie and some great moments of acting, too. It isn't just balls to the wall.

The comic book hero's big screen outing was guided by British director Danny Cannon, who, a couple of years earlier, had scored a big hit with *The Young Americans*. The entire shoot was housed at Shepperton including a large exterior set which took over one of the car parks.

Another big-budget American film which considered basing itself at Shepperton was Mel Gibson's *Braveheart*. Destined to film on location in Scotland before moving down to the studio, the producers appealed to the British Government to loan some of its troops for the battle sequences. The request was politely turned down whilst, over the Irish Sea, the Government there had introduced a major tax incentive and freely offered its army to the production. Gibson and company shipped out.

With troubles still ongoing at the closed Elstree Studios, and a campaign launched by the council to save them, Ealing Studios' management, the BBRK Group, announced in early 1994 that they were now in receivership. The studio was to remain open, but a great cloud hung over it – would the property developers move in?

Meanwhile, at Shepperton, *The Madness of King George III* was a film that had to be re-titled *The Madness Of King George*, because research demonstrated that American audiences might wonder what had happened to parts I and II in the series and not bother to see 'part III'. Just prior to the film's release, Sir Nigel Hawthorne explained:

> King George III wasn't really mad at all. He kept telling people he was nervous, that was all, that he wasn't insane. But he was diagnosed with porphyria, something not medically understood at the time. He was treated for insanity, but it's subsequently been proved that he was ill, not insane.

'It started,' recalls Production Designer Sir Ken Adam, 'when Nick Hytner, the director, visited me in New York. He just had a plastic bag in his hands. He'd never made a film before, but in the plastic bag there was this unbelievable screenplay of Alan Bennett'.

Hytner had already directed the stage version of *King George* very successfully, and his vision for the film was firmly set, but Ken Adam was fearful that the studio bosses would force him into making compromises: 'I told him if the producers want to have more close shots, give it to them, it doesn't cost you anything. But if they want to talk down your concept, then send them to hell.'

Ken Adam went on to win his second Oscar for the film. 'The sets are a good example of reducing to the basic,' he says. 'One has to feel, what one wants to say, to emphasize the drama of a scene. A chair, two pictures, one room, that's enough. One mustn't over fill a room and draw attention away from what the director wants us to see'.

In the castle, where George receives his 'curative treatment', Ken Adam deliberately had pictures taken off the walls, the faded areas around where they once hung were to 'remind of faded memories'. The spiral staircase, which the king runs up, creating a giddiness effect, he saw as a metaphor for a staircase to madness: 'I love this scene. The King starts to run in the studio set, up the original staircase of St Paul's Cathedral and finally reaches the roof of Arundel Castle. That is production design!

Ken Adam included additional chimneys on the Arundel rooftop to achieve 'a cold forest of dead chimneys, like a set made for a Greek tragedy.'

The film grossed a very respectable $15 million in the USA for its troubled production company, Samuel Goldwyn Films, and garnered a clutch of other Oscar nominations, including Best Supporting Actress for Helen Mirren and Best Screenplay for Alan Bennett.

Staying with the royal theme, the Court of King Charles II was recreated for *Restoration*, a film that would be the 'premiere of the century' in 1995's centenary of cinema's celebrations. Sadly, its mainly American cast and poor script did little to help the wonderful design by Argentinian Eugenio Zanetti and Oliver Stapleton's luscious photography.

The early 1990s were years of great uncertainty for Shepperton, with its modest production activity. Following financial troubles with Bank-owned Lee International, in late 1994 and early 1995 there was some doubt – yet again – as to its future. Many sceptics didn't give the studio a chance. With the future of Elstree and Ealing in doubt, it seemed all too easy to think the Middlesex Dream Factory would go the same way. However, following much media speculation the summer before, in January 1995 a consortium headed by film makers Tony and Ridley Scott, and Candover Partners, assumed control of the studio in a deal worth £28.5 million. Again, it was brothers who came to the rescue, as with the Kordas, the Boultings and the Lees. It was very much business as usual, with the Scott Brothers maintaining the same team employed by Lee – Denis Carrigan as managing director and Paul Olliver as studio manager.

'We recognised that,' stated Candover in a press release, 'with the right investment, the team had the broad experience, excellent world-wide contacts and a proven track record needed to grow revenues and attract a greater volume of higher added value business.'

'We are delighted to have been able to structured this sale,' commented William Scott, president of Lee International, 'to a group headed by two of the UK's most successful film makers. Their ambitious plans will be of significant help in further developing Shepperton as an important element of the UK film industry.'

Ridley Scott said, 'I have made films there for the last twenty years so there is a historical attachment. But we are also finding that American and European film makers are coming over to make movies and we hope Shepperton can share in that influx of new business.'

The news was greeted positively throughout the film business. The then director of the British Film Institute, Wilf Stevenson, aware of the brothers' success in making

American movies, added that he felt it 'extremely good news if the end result is that they intend to come back and work here'.

The brothers were certainly intent on investing in the facility – updating existing facilities, as well as giving a much-needed facelift to many of the studio buildings, and in the process naming them. The Korda Building and The David Lean Building were the first two names to appear on Shepperton's many buildings in recognition of the two cinematic greats and their contribution to the studio. It was a positive, upbeat time.

The year saw Shepperton's tenant Kenneth Branagh extremely busy with not one, but three films. Before Branagh took on two Shakespeare projects himself, another cranked up under the direction of Oliver Parker, who enlisted Branagh as one of his leads.

Parker a former stand-up comic, next turned to acting. 'I was just trying things out', he says. In the theatre, as well as acting, he tried his hand at stage management and direction. After playing the part of Iago in a stage version of *Othello*, he became impassioned: 'I was obsessed with the play and realized how exciting it was and how it should really capture an audience in a more physical, visceral way'. So he began developing his own version of the play for the big screen. It got bigger and bigger, and he eventually gave up the idea of playing Iago.

> A lot of people were getting interested in the project – sizable personalities. I couldn't afford to be thinking about myself. I thought, 'I've got to give all my attention to these people.' More importantly, when I wake up at 6:30, I don't want to worry about whether or not I look like shit or not.

Othello turned out to be an excellent film starring Laurence Fishburne in the title role, Kenneth Branagh as Iago and Irene Jacob as Desdemona. Parker earned both praise and boos from Shakespeare purists for cutting the text down for the movie.

> You're always gonna bump up against the purists. I don't give a damn. Part of the reason I do the thing is to make sure I'm stirring it a little bit. I've acted in Wilde and Shakespeare myself, and so I don't feel like an outsider coming to the material. I feel like an insider who has a passion to deliver what feels to be the essence of these pieces, which tend to be much more vibrant than they often seem. And if you do them without making any alteration for the new medium you're working in then I think you're going to do the piece a disservice. It's sort of obvious to me. You have to do something or *Othello* would be four hours long!

Four hours was something Kenneth Branagh was proposing for his adaptation of *Hamlet*. However, before he got stuck in to that project, he had his own, personal film he wanted to make. *In the Bleak Midwinter* is a black-and-white tale of a bunch of resting actors putting on a production of *Hamlet* in a village called Hope, in order to save the local church. Said Branagh at the Venice Film Festival that year:

The film is partly autobiographical, although not because the central character is necessarily me, but because most of the characters in fact live situations that I have lived myself at the time when I was working in the theatre. Many of the roles were also written for people with whom I had worked and shared these experiences and many of their experiences are part of this story. Most of the crazy element comes from the life that we all shared.

Following the lavishness (and expense) of *Frankenstein*, Branagh was keen to return to smaller, intimate film making. 'It's a very small film. Less than a million quid.' He put up the money for the film himself. 'People were calling to say don't spend your own money, let us do it. But this was how I wanted it.'

With a tiny budget, Branagh was determined to move away from high-priced studio fare to return to the terrain of his 1992 film, *Peter's Friends*, a modest, contemporary ensemble comedy about issues close to the director's heart and life. Branagh said doing a film about a play appealed to him because the stage offered 'an image of something romantic and, alas, disappearing, that is very powerful as a symbol for what drew many artists to our profession.'

His next, and bigger, project took the central piece of Midwinter – *Hamlet*. The $18 million, 70mm production (funded by Caste Rock) was quite the opposite to his previous, small, low-budget black-and-white film. *Hamlet* was to employ Shakespeare's entire text for the first time on film. Branagh said he envisaged his film being on a similar scale to a David Lean film, with a cast mixture of British and American actors. Certainly its use of 70mm film was the first time the format had been used in Britain since Sir David Lean's grand *Ryan's Daughter*.

A state hall with balconies around its edge, a gantry spanning its entire width, two imposing thrones on a dais and a vast expanse of chessboard floor. The long walls of this cavernous room were lined with mirrored doors, behind which were smaller chambers – studies, bedrooms and salons for clandestine intrigues and conspiracies. This was one of the sets Branagh ordered the creation of at Shepperton Studios. Production Designer Tim Harvey also created a romantic Danish court with a tangible sense of corruption, an excess of sex, food and alcohol, and a militaristic culture. For two weeks of outdoor scenes he 'dressed' Blenheim Palace, at one point covering its grounds with fake snow. To stress the court's grandeur Harvey joined two adjacent soundstages. The full effect can be seen in an eight-minute tracking shot starting in Gertrude's bedroom and advancing down a long corridor to the resplendent state hall.

Branagh commandeered a stellar cast of sterling British stage actors in key roles and international celebrities in cameos. Thus came Julie Christie as Gertrude, Hamlet's mother; Derek Jacobi is Claudius; and young star Kate Winslet playing Ophelia; while Branagh's frequent cohort Richard Briers tackles the scheming Polonius. Two veteran knights round out the UK contingent: John Gielgud, then ninety-two, is Priam in the play-within-a-play, and John Mills, a mere eighty-eight, the ailing Norway.

Hollywood's finest: Charlton Heston (the Player King), Jack Lemmon (Marcellus), Robin Williams (Osric) and Billy Crystal (First Gravedigger) added further clout. Gérard Depardieu also appears as a servant.

'I just went for the best actors, people I liked,' Branagh said. 'I wanted to work with Depardieu for some time. I always admired Jack Lemmon. I enjoyed working with Robin on *Dead Again*. I also wanted the parts played in an original way with people who weren't bringing the baggage of having played a role before or seen this play a thousand times.'

The three-and-a-half-hour film – with intermission – must have been a tough sell on Branagh's part to the Hollywood executives. His methods were unveiled with the publication of the film's screenplay, which included his notes on the text, aimed at clarifying the play to Castle Rock executives. At one point, he described the King of Denmark as 'going into Norman Schwarzkopf mode'. After a gravedigger's speech, Branagh added the phrase: 'Says Judge Ito' – a reference to the judge in the O.J. Simpson trial. And when, in the script, the king and his courtiers are seen marching down a corridor, Branagh observes: 'It feels like a team of spin-doctors, media advisers and security experts briefing the President on the way to a White House press conference.'

> It was wonderful having so many stars involved. All actors in the end are as star-struck as their audience and they loved meeting one another – Billy Crystal was in love with Julie Christie forever, and in the middle of the night we'd be sitting in an overcrowded trailer listening to Jack Lemmon talk about being fired from his first acting job.

The production overlapped with Ang Lee's *Sense and Sensibility* on neighbouring stages, which was written by – and starred – Emma Thompson: with whom Branagh had recently separated after six years of marriage. Kate Winslet starred in both productions. Was there an ill feeling or rivalry at the studio? She said of working with each of the separated couple:

> I've never really given it a second thought, because I'd never really known them when they were Ken and Em; I'd only met them as two totally separate people. I just consider myself lucky to work with two such fantastic actors. Emma's a great writer and Ken's an amazing director. They are two people who are so prominent in the British film industry and essentially make it what it is. They certainly put it on the map.

Producer Lindsay Doran had met actress Emma Thompson on the set of the thriller *Dead Again*, which Doran produced. During the first weeks of the shoot of that film, a Los Angeles public television station aired a British television comedy series consisting of short skits written by Thompson. Doran was impressed: 'The writing was funny and sweet and romantic and real.' When Doran decided to produce *Sense and Sensibility* she asked Thompson to write the script.

It took Thompson almost five years to finish the script. Doran then searched for a director who could handle both romance and satire, which led her to Ang Lee. An unlikely choice to direct, the Taiwanese Lee hoped to give the English novel a new perspective: 'What I wanted most to do with this film is to make people cry after they've laughed … I think it takes an outsider to do this. It is good for this project that I am not English.'

Thompson herself had initially considered directing the film: 'I thought about it for thirty seconds, and I had to lie down. How can you direct in a corset? You simply can't.'

Everything gelled – the cast, the direction, the script, the locations. The film was a terrific hit both critically and commercially and won Emma Thompson an Oscar for Best Adapted Screenplay.

The big-budget films were certainly back with a vengeance at Shepperton. Aside from the above, The Muppets returned with their *Treasure Island*; Terry Jones breathed new life into *Wind in the Willows*; Ridley Scott brought post-production of *White Squall* to be completed and Disney chose the studio to bring the much-loved animated feature *101 Dalmatians* to life in a blockbuster that went on to gross $135 million in the USA alone.

'She's an iconic character,' said Glenn Close on being cast as dog-napper Cruella De Vil. 'She's like the Wicked Witch in the great Disney animated classics. I'm incredibly lucky to play her. The key is her sense of glee. You feel she's playing this game in which she's the only one who knows the rules.'

Director Steven Herek tossed aside the industry golden rule 'never to work with children and animals' and embraced both – including scores and scores of Dalmatian puppies. Second Unit Production Manager Terry Bamber, who worked extensively with the four-legged animals, states:

I would suggest that we must have used over 1,000 puppies in the production. We scoured the country for Dalmatian kennels, because whilst there were only 'a hundred and one' in the film, the puppies grew at such a rate that we could only ever use them for two weeks. We then had to replace them with younger ones to maintain the continuity.

Our main concern was the puppies' well being and as most of them were too young to have completed their course of inoculations, we had to make sure that the set and their living quarters were regularly disinfected.

The lead dogs had their own make-up artists too, as Bamber reveals:

There were several dogs used for the 'lead characters' and of course, their spots wouldn't necessarily be the same, so we had a team of 'spotters' to apply extra ones as needed.

Oscar-winning British costume designer Anthony Powell was largely responsible for Glenn Close's 'De Vil look'. He put the star into corsets that pinched her waist down to 23in. 'The shoes alone help me get into character. Just marching through the costume workshop in them inspires me,' said Close in an on-set interview. 'The artistry that goes into making those costumes is incredible. Once I'm decked out in them, Cruella comes to life.'

The costumes and make-up are so effective that the dogs need no other motivation to be frightened of their screen nemesis, as Bamber recalls:

> One of the little dogs was called Whizzer, as when he was scared or nervous, the gag was he'd do a little pee. The prop department made up this little plastic puddle, and it was my job to make sure it was 'inserted' on set at the appropriate moment!

Was having so many animals on set noisy?

> Definitely. In one sequence we had the various dogs answering the call – rallying for battle – and off camera, all of the trainers were calling their animals and shouting directions. The noise!
>
> We also had our temperamental ones. Not so much the dogs, but I do remember with great fondness a pig called Lily. I'd also schedule her scenes first thing in the morning, as her trainer said she was at her best then. However, if Lily didn't feel like it, when brought on set, she'd attack her trainer in the groin and make her position quite clear. So we'd move on to another set up. She was a brilliant character, but more temperamental than most actresses I've worked with!

Along with dogs and pigs, there was also a lovely sequence featuring racoons (who are not, of course, native to Britain) sabotaging the car of Cruella's henchmen, Hugh Laurie and Mark Williams. It was filmed on H stage, as Terry Bamber reveals:

> We had to lock off the whole stage, because the trainers were worried that if the racoons smelled food – and all of the animals are trained by offering them food treats as rewards – then they'd be off from the set! The sequence involved a racoon placing a large nut in the exhaust pipe of the car, and I was assured that the little chaps were fully trained and ready to go. I was a little dubious – I've learned nothing is ever certain in this business. However, in they came, action was called and the sequence was done in one take. Whilst we were all congratulating ourselves, the lead racoon shot off. Someone had left a half eaten sandwich on the far side of the stage. We lost him for two hours!

Along with the real racoons, there were also animatronic ones engaged for the sequence where Cruella is trapped, and plunged into a vat of excrement. The racoons then 'high five' each other.

The success of the film saw a sequel put straight into development – *102 Dalmatians*. It was also shot at Shepperton. Glenn Close reprised her role for director Kevin Lima, who admitted:

> The puppies in particular were afraid of Glenn when she was in costume, so I capitalized on the fact. When Glenn was not in costume, I kept her away from the dogs as much as possible so they'd have as natural a reaction as possible to Cruella.

'I think it's safe to say unless I get another exceptional character in my career, people are going to remember me for *Fatal Attraction* and as Cruella,' quipped Glenn Close. 'Those two characters have had the biggest impact of anything I've done.'

The popular children's books *The Borrowers*, by Mary Norton, have been filmed before, and in the early 1990s became a popular BBC television series produced by Working Title (at Shepperton in fact). In 1995 writer Gavin Scott was engaged to write a feature film script for the company, which was to start production the next year at Shepperton.

The production utilised the most complicated and believable miniature people in the modern age of film. With lots of composites of actors shot against blue screen and straight, clean shots of actors performing on oversized sets, but the use of computer-generated characters as humans, both for massive wide shots and relatively tight, hero shots, sets *The Borrowers* apart previous miniature-people efforts.

Another interesting use of special effects was with *Fairytale – A True Story*. When Sir Arthur Conan Doyle (the creator of Sherlock Holmes) declared that pictures taken by twelve-year-old Elsie and eight-year-old Frances of fairies in flight are authentic, the photographs astounded the world and forever changed Elsie and Frances' lives. The First World War period drama is based on actual events.

Near disaster struck during pre-production, however, when part of the finance collapsed. The film's future looked decidedly rocky, along with the jobs of the cast and crew lined up for it, and indeed Shepperton. Thankfully Mel Gibson's company, Icon Films, stepped in at the eleventh hour and covered the funding shortfall. Gibson then took an uncredited cameo part as Frances' father returning from the Great War.

Alan Parker, somewhat relieved to be home from Argentina where the cast and crew were greeted with signs reading 'Go home, Madonna', or 'Go home, Alan Parker and your film crew', headed to the studio to finish off his big budget version of *Evita*, which starred Madonna and Antonio Banderas. On leaving South America, Parker said: 'We've had an extraordinary time here in Argentina, which is very gratifying, because it's my job to capture Argentina and put it on film. What we'll do in other places is just the illusion and magic of film.'

Illusion and magic is certainly Shepperton's byline. Richard Attenborough next returned with his World War I-set love story, *In Love and War*, starring Sandra Bullock and Chris O'Donnell. Sadly, it failed to find an audience, as the director laments:

In Love and War, which had a wonderful performance by Sandy, Sandra Bullock, who the authorities and, the supposed authorities, in cinema didn't want to know about. They wanted her to play the sort of kooky girl next door which was her box office label, as it were, and perhaps they were right and I was wrong. I thought she gave the most wonderful performance in *In Love and War*. It was a picture that didn't come off, in large measure, again, because of that terrible thing, there were six, seven writers. It was not my own picture and it didn't work. It didn't work. And it's a pity because there was some terrific stuff in it.

The television epic returned to Shepperton in 1996 when producer Duncan Kenworthy, on behalf of the Jim Henson Company, Channel 4 and Robert Halmi, mounted 'a big mini-series with lots of British and American stars'. It was *Gulliver's Travels*. The cast included Ted Danson, Mary Steenburgen, Peter O'Toole, Omar Sharif, Kristin Scott Thomas and John Gielgud amongst many others. The studio's owners also made good use of the studio in 1996, with Ridley Scott editing *G.I. Jane*.

When it was announced that the long gestating feature version of *The Avengers* was finally to go before the cameras, there was great excitement and interest. When Ralph Fiennes, Uma Thurman and Sean Connery were announced at the principle players, there was even greater excitement. The film, large in scope and size, would be housed between both Pinewood and Shepperton Studios, as both were busy with other productions and neither studio could offer enough stage space – and so they co-operated. Sir Sean Connery says:

> Well, from the beginning, I always tried to have humour in any film I do. I've always felt that to find it is the most important and sometimes the most difficult thing. I thought there was quite a bit of humour in *The Avengers*, and I had a bit of fun – until they put the film together. And if ever there was a licence to kill, I would have used it to kill the director and the producer. But eventually they'll be found out.

Sadly, the film was an unmitigated flop. The company refused to organize any press screenings and instead released the film globally on the same day – obviously hoping that by the time bad word of mouth got around, they'd have made a decent return on their budget. Alas not.

Indian director Shekhar Kapur was an inspired choice to direct the lavish biopic of Queen Elizabeth I. At a Toronto Film Festival press conference, he commented:

> It was a great advantage for me to approach the project as an outsider. Since Elizabeth's story isn't part of my culture, I wasn't saddled with that automatic reverence for royalty which still keeps the English from being able to see her as a real person. Even now, they're obsessed with the idea of her being a literal virgin – it's like the way they treat the existing Royal Family. As long as they're looking at her, they never have to look at themselves.
>
> But the facts of the case are always so different from the way that 'approved' history makes them appear. I mean, let's face it: no one wore underwear, they all stank and Elizabeth had wooden teeth. So anything we say about her can't be too insulting – especially since it's true.

Lost in Space was the next in a line of television to big screen adaptations. An all-star cast was recruited: William Hurt, Mimi Rogers, Gary Oldman, Matt LeBlanc, Jared Harris and Edward Fox. The pressure of updating and transferring a show with millions of fans on the small screen to the big was not lost on director Stephen Hopkins. In an interview with *Starburst* magazine he said:

I wanted to have reverence for it because some people remember it with great sincerity and nostalgia. I didn't want to betray that. Obviously, you couldn't make a 'camp' two-and-a-quarter-hour epic science fiction movie. At the same time, we didn't have all the money in the world, like *Godzilla* or *Titanic*, so we wanted to approach it in some kind of stylistic, wacky way. I had to start from somewhere, and I didn't have a lot of time to think, so I just flew into it and tried to be a kid again. I tried to remember in the '60s and '70s how they saw the future.

Certain elements were to be kept from the television series, including the robot: 'I wanted to put the robot in, but I didn't want to put it in like it was in the script, so I had the idea that Will [the ten-year-old son of Professor Robinson] would rebuild it and that's why it looked as funky as it does.'

There were reportedly 750 special effects used in the film. Second Unit Continuity Supervisor Angela Allen says:

I must admit, at times it was incredibly boring as there was so much special-effects work! That was the nature of the project though; but it wasn't helped by the robot continually breaking down – I used to say to the director 'do you think she'll be well enough to come out today?'

The main unit was supposed to film during the day, and we on the second unit would come in at night to film on the same sets. It never worked out however, as invariably the main unit would work late. We'd then come in, move things around, and of course we then had to put everything back for the first unit ... so much so that if we achieved two shots in one night we were doing well. It really wasn't the best idea of planning I've ever seen.

Reaping the benefits of the American influx, Shepperton realised greater use was being made of special computer effects in post production, for which many went into central London to specialist houses or back to the US.

'In 1997 we invested further funds,' reported the Scotts' backers, Candover, 'to enable the team to acquire a 40 per cent stake in The Mill [post-production effects company, based at the studio], and to expand into feature film special effects. The Mill subsequently acquired the Magic Camera Company.'

These further funds enabled the studio to build the new J and K stages (on the old car park area, a few years earlier home to the *Judge Dredd* sets) and the old J and K stages (latterly owned by The Who) were converted into offices and cutting rooms, and dubbed 'The David Lean Building'. In reflection of other great names, during refurbishment of facilities, The Korda Building and Orson Welles Buildings were also christened. Devoid of any back-lot to speak of, the studio struck a deal to buy an adjacent twenty-acre piece of land on the other side of the River Ash for £1 million. Planning permission was granted only for 'temporary structures' to be built on the land: ideal for a new back-lot. The studio also has a deal with the Metropolitan Water Company to use the land lying between Studios Road and the Queen Mary Reservoir for further temporary buildings.

With an increase in Lottery Funding, through the Arts Council and three newly created lottery funded film franchises, in 1998 the British film industry was brimming over with production. Sadly, only a small percentage of the films made would, however, secure a theatrical distribution deal. Nevertheless, production created employment and Shepperton hosted fourteen feature and television movies – its greatest number since in the early 1970s. Amongst them was the romantic romp *Elephant Juice*, so titled because if you mouth the title in a mirror it looks like 'I Love You'. Hallmark Entertainment spared no expense with their all-star television adaptations of *Alice in Wonderland* and *Cleopatra*, while Kenneth Branagh turned his attentions to *Love's Labour's Lost*.

One set on A Stage at Shepperton was built to resemble an Oxbridge college. From the door of the School of Social Philosophy appears a tap-dancing Kenneth Branagh, in top hat, white tie and tails, and singing Fred Astaire's *Dancing Cheek To Cheek*. *Love's Labour's Lost* had been moved from its late Elizabethan setting to Europe in the 1930s and turned into a musical, with a bouquet of familiar songs by such twentieth-century greats as Cole Porter, Irving Berlin, George Gershwin and Jerome Kern.

'These particular twentieth-century geniuses can stand next to Shakespeare if you give the story a '30s setting,' Branagh says. 'It's amazing to take Shakespeare's text and the words of these songs and put them together and see how well they work.'

It was the first musical made at Shepperton since the disastrous *Absolute Beginners*, and thankfully much more successful.

Loosely based on Karl Freund's 1932 classic horror film *The Mummy* with Boris Karloff, Director Stephen Sommers took a very different approach with his 1998 version. Unit publicist Geoff Freeman says:

> On the day before shooting, I sat down with producer James Jacks, on a sand dune out in the desert if you please, and he explained that it wasn't going to be a film in the style of the Boris Karloff version, with him walking out of a crypt, fully bandaged and arms outstretched. It was in fact more like a *Boy's Own* adventure, a *Raiders Of The Lost Ark* ... and he wanted to make sure I would, in my writing of the production notes, get across the fact that the essence of the film was adventure in the desert with a little bit of 'the supernatural' going on.

Brendan Fraser, Rachel Weisz and John Hannah led the cast on location in the Sahara and back at Shepperton, where the lavish interiors of the Egyptian pyramids were recreated. Freeman adds:

> When we got back to Shepperton, we realised that a lot of people at Universal really didn't know what the film was about. They were thinking, as we originally did, 'Boris Karloff and his bandages'. And so they brought over a load of Universal executives across from Hollywood to Shepperton, filled a huge empty stage with a lots of monitors and ran footage of what Stephen had shot

out in the desert, along with Electronic Press Kit material, to let them see the sort of film they had. They left that stage very excited, and then went on a walk-about of Allan Cameron's sets. I've been on many sets in my hundred and odd films, but these sets were tremendous – especially the ones built on H stage which, incidentally, was the reason Stephen chose Shepperton.

The $80 million film became the surprise blockbuster hit of the summer, knocking *Star Wars: Episode One* off the box-office top spot, and grossing $413 million worldwide. It was no surprise, then, that Universal Pictures hired Sommers to write and direct a sequel.

'It was Stephen's unique vision for *The Mummy* that was the driving force behind its success, and we're both very pleased that he will be bringing his talent, imagination and enthusiasm on board for a sequel', Universal's co-chairmen Stacey Snider and Brian Mulligan told *The Hollywood Reporter*.

Sommers, keen to repeat the first film's success, recruited the original cast again and insisted it be shot at Shepperton, starting on the same day as the first film and with a similar release date. He also requested that all office-based crew have the same offices at the studio as they did on the first film, and the same dressing rooms for the stars. He wasn't taking any chances! He said about the sequel:

> It had to be better. We knew we could make a bigger movie. That's not the hard part. The hard part is making it better. We had to come up with a better story. And to get the actors back. Because after *Mummy I*, all of our careers really took off, and we didn't have to do a sequel. But we all had so much fun, we all thought, 'Oh, wouldn't it be great? But let's not screw it up. Let's not do a lame sequel. Let's not damage our careers or the legacy of the first movie.' So the key was, for me, to come up with a better script, a better story, evolve all the characters. Make them all more interesting, more intertwined, and just make it better.

The sequel is set in 1935, ten years after the events of the first film. Rick O'Connell (Fraser) is now married to Evelyn (Rachel Weisz), and the couple have settled in London, where they are raising their nine-year-old son Alex (played by screen newcomer Freddie Boath).

It was certainly bigger than the first film, with one scene alone featuring an army of 32,000 computer-generated warriors. Fraser himself cited a fun sequence set on a London bus, during which he is fighting an ancient Egyptian who is not actually there:

> There was a lot to react to and also a lot to play with, which turned out in the final edit. When I saw that scene put in via the computer, it was extraordinary. It allows one to really use one's imagination, a powerful actor's tool in a film like this. The continued technology has evolved since the first *Mummy*, and that's pretty cool.

H stage again played an important part in the film, as Geoff Freeman reveals:

> There were three huge sets that Steve [Sommers] wanted to build. One was on a
> boat, with people and animals, and when a fight breaks out they go into the water,
> so he wanted to use the flooding facility. The final scene with 'The Rock' inside
> the vast pyramid, and the big fight with Brendan Fraser, was all shot on H stage. I
> know he cited the technicians as his reason for wanting to come back to Britain,
> but H stage really lured him to Shepperton. It was very important to the picture.

The sequel budgeted $18 million higher than the first *Mummy*, and grossed a
staggering $418 million worldwide. Needless to say, there was continuing speculation
about a third outing for the characters (which came in 2008).

Working Title films' golden touch was yet again proven with *Notting Hill*. Producer
Duncan Kenworthy was keen to replicate his success with Hugh Grant in *Four
Weddings and a Funeral* and cast the actor alongside American co-star Julia Roberts.

'I wanted it to feel like London meets Florence,' says Director Roger Michell on
the look of the film:

> I wanted it always to be sunny with pastal colours – it was in fact the most awful
> weather ever, but in the movie it looks like a lovely summer holiday.
> We built Hugh Grant's bookshop on the lot at the studio, and his house
> – which he shared with Rhys Ifans – on a stage which looked so real and
> effective that my twelve year old niece said to me 'that part where Hugh and
> Julia kissed, in the hallway, were you there?' That was the greatest compliment
> to the production designer I could hope for. I was there though – along with
> about 400 other people scratching their bollocks!

Actor Hugh Bonneville recalled a restaurant scene during the film:

> We needed the perspective of being in the restaurant and seeing out across the
> street outside. But there was no stage big enough to do that, and so the exterior
> was painted in perspective and all the crowd who walked by were 'perspective
> artistes' – all under 5ft tall. In reality what would have been 40ft across the street
> was now just 10ft.

Julia Roberts had been attached to *Shakespeare in Love* a little earlier in its history,
in 1992, over at Pinewood, and when Daniel Day-Lewis declined the part of Will
Shakespeare, she pulled out and the financing collapsed. Now, a few years on, new
backers had been secured and Gwyneth Paltrow was cast alongside Joseph Fiennes.
Paltrow secured herself a Best Actress Oscar for her part. Further Oscars were
bestowed for Best Film, Best Screenplay, Best Supporting Actress (Judi Dench) and
to Martin Childs for his set design, and Sandy Powell for costumes. Producer David
Parfitt reveals:

We built two Globe/Rose theatres, the exteriors of which were on the back-lot, along with part of a town and an intricate maze of streets which we used for the majority of the London scenes. The interiors meanwhile were built, in real oak, to take a real crowd of 700 or 800 people, on a stage. There was a wonderful atmosphere in building a working theatre to the right proportions and seeing how it all would have worked back then.

Director Tim Burton chose to film his next project between Leavesden and Shepperton Studios. *Sleepy Hollow* was described as being an 'exhilarating Gothic fantasia', reviving the legend of the Headless Horseman, last seen in British cinemas in the late 1930s in Will Hay's *Ask a Policeman*. Burton is famous for his moody, dark and gothic looks, yet he actually requested more lighting than could easily be supplied. Great use was indeed made of lighting, though curiously it is still a rather dark picture.

Johnny Depp, Christina Ricci and Christopher Walken headed the cast, so to speak, which featured a great many British stalwarts in support, not least Michael Gambon, Miranda Richardson, Richard Griffiths and Christopher Lee who, the following year, spent several months at the studio working on the epic BBC production of *Gormenghast*, for which Production Designer Christopher Hobbs created 120 sets.

1999 was just as busy as the previous year with an excellent mixture of film (of all sizes), television and commercials. The surprise hit of the year came with 1980s, miners' strike-based film *Billy Elliot*, which filmed on location in the north of England and completed photography at Shepperton.

Writer Lee Hall said on the film's release:

Stephen Daldry, the director, is a friend of mine. We got together, wrote the thing, and after many years got the money to do it. The BBC funded the script, but it didn't want to talk about the miners' strike at all. It was absolutely resistant to the whole idea. In the beginning there were five or six different companies that reluctantly put money in because no single place would take it on. The ludicrous thing is that it's made a fortune for the companies, yet they couldn't see that it might, so the amounts of money we received were quite tiny. In fact, it was the lottery that saved us because it gave us about £1 million.

Billy Elliot was the first film to be made by Working Title's 'independent' arm, WT2. Everyone was pleasantly surprised by the staggeringly positive reception that greeted Daldry's debut: sobbing reviews, roaring audiences and a £1.54 million opening weekend box-office take, outdoing *Four Weddings and a Funeral*.

Next, as part of the (then) forthcoming Millennium celebrations, a special thirty-minute, 70mm film was commissioned by the New Millennium Experience Company called *Blackadder: Back & Forth*, to be shown in the Millennium Dome. *Blackadder* was a popular BBC comedy program in the 1980s and starred Rowan Atkinson, star of the *Mr Bean* series. It had been ten years since the last Blackadder was filmed, and Working Title Productions, the company behind the series, chose to film the special at Shepperton. The production was filmed on Super 35mm and then transferred at Technicolor labs in London on to 70mm.

A lavish television production of *Don Quixote* with John Lithgow, Bob Hoskins and Isabella Rossellini, joined a television remake of *Jason and the Argonauts* and fanciful Irish fairytale *Leprechauns* – all from Hallmark Entertainment – whilst Ben Elton made his directorial debut with *Maybe Baby* in August.

What prompted Elton to think he could translate his novel *Inconceivable* to the big screen himself?

> An excessive overconfidence on my part, and the fact that I don't really watch films, so I didn't know the mistakes I could make. Also this film had a subject matter that I knew a great deal about. I didn't want to direct a film about car crashes or spaceships, but when it comes to people interacting, and the problems with their little vanities and hopes and dreams, that's what I write about. I thought that I was well-equipped to work with the actors and that's why I wanted to direct it.

The year was drawing to a close, and the Scott brothers took executive producer credits on *RKO 281* – a television movie based around the making of Orson Welles' *Citizen Kane*.

As the century was came to an end, it was comforting to think that the studio, having gone through its many crises, was busier now than it had been in decades. It had two film makers for owners, and with *RKO* was paying homage to one of Shepperton's most enigmatic stars who, fifty years earlier, made arguably the most famous film to come out of the studio, *The Third Man*.

CHAPTER 19

2000 AND BEYOND: A NEW MILLENIUM

Helen Fielding's best-selling *Bridget Jones' Diary* was the next project to receive the 'Working Title touch'. The film follows a year in the life of 'singleton' Bridget Jones, a woman in her thirties living in the West End of London with a career as a researcher in the television industry. She smokes 5,277 cigarettes within the year, thinks she's hideously overweight and she can't seem to find a stable boyfriend, but she is determined that all that will change.

Renée Zellweger was cast as Jones, and piled on the pounds to play the plump, cuddly character. Hugh Grant – the favourite of the romantic comedy movie – was cast, somewhat against type, as the shallow, selfish and untrustworthy Daniel Cleaver.

There was some concern when it was announced the most British of British characters, Bridget Jones, was to be played by Zellweger though. Producer Jonathan Cavendish explains:

> We all had a clear idea of what we were looking for – director Sharon Maguire and l even had a word for it: 'Bridgetness'. When Renée walked through the door, we were half thrilled and half appalled; we'd found Bridget, but she was a Texan!

'Bridgetness' comprises 'enthusiasm and vulnerability, intelligence mixed with lack of confidence, a sympathetic, good-natured quality – and wildness'. To which he adds the rider, 'and of course Bridget fans know she is not perfectly slim – and here was this perfectly slim actress standing in front of us'.

On the first day of shooting, on a set full of people, Zellweger described her scene at Shepperton in *Time Out* magazine as having her 'ass essentially landing on the camera operator's face twenty times'. This is in reference to a scene where Bridget, having just got a job as a television reporter, must slide down a fireman's pole in a mini-skirt straight onto the camera. No stunt bum was used.

> Yes, I'm ashamed to say the Brazilian-sized bum was mine; and I don't mean Brazilian in reference to the people, I mean in reference to the country. That

was scary for me because I'm a fairly modest person. Not any more … before, with other shoots I'd be covering myself and going, 'Boys out' and now I'm like 'Whatever.' I didn't feel familiar or recognize my own body. It was strange to feel so uncomfortable and to be running around half naked with the crew full of men. That was a real challenge for me but it became fun.

The movie, which cost $25 million, grossed a staggering $280 million worldwide. It's no wonder, therefore, that in 2003 a sequel moved before the cameras in London.

Director Lasse Hallstrom, fresh from his success with *The Cider House Rules*, next chose to make *Chocolat*, an enchanting film with Juliet Binoche playing a single mother who opens a chocolate shop in a small French village, with Sunday opening – and located right opposite the church and at the start of Lent. The French locations were actually all filmed around Bath in south-west England, and then back to Shepperton for studio and post-production work.

Tony Scott visited the studio to complete *Spy Game*, his Robert Redford/Brad Pitt film, but bigger still was *The Mummy Returns*. But there were also smaller films making an impact such as Neil Jordan's fourteen-minute Samuel Beckett adaptation of *Not I* with Julianne Moore; tense gangster film *Dog Eat Dog*; *Possession*, starring Gwyneth Paltrow; and HBO and the BBC's big budget *Conspiracy*, a dramatic recreation of the ninety-four minute Nazi Wannsee Conference where the Final Solution phase of the Holocaust was devised. It starred Stanley Tucci, Colin Firth and Kenneth Branagh, who won an Emmy for his role. Branagh states:

> It was a practical meeting in which these bureaucrats wished to facilitate the physical process of exterminating a race. It seems incredible, yet they were pressing the button that started the Holocaust. This is an important story to be told, but its very grimness meant that the creative challenge was quite difficult. The idea was to keep it normal and naturalistic, not melodramatic. It didn't want showy acting. It's nothing to do with having a bunch of stars in the room.

Director Frank Pierson primarily cast British character actors, and they rehearsed for two and a half weeks. Once filming started, the actors spent every day sitting around a conference table on a Shepperton stage, delivering or listening to inhuman dialogue. The set was built with its four walls to the exact dimensions of the original room, while exterior scenes at the beginning and end were shot at Wannsee. With several extended scenes and long tracking shots, it feels like a play being filmed. The eye-level camera angles underline the feeling for viewers of being present in that room. It was shot in twenty-one days.

2001 was a slightly less hectic year for the studio production-wise, though its output rated as the best in British production in many decades. A string of British films such as *Anita and Me*, *About a Boy*, *Bend It Like Beckham*, *Dirty Pretty Things*, *Gosford Park* and award-winning television drama *The Gathering Storm* were all brought to life at Shepperton. Between them, the features grossed almost $270 million worldwide, on combined budgets of $50 million. A pretty good return on investment!

2001 was also the year in which the studio merged with Pinewood. It had been suggested in the past, even by asset stripper John Bentley, but in early February it was officially announced that Pinewood Studios – which itself had been bought out from parent Rank in 2000 by a consortium headed by Michael Grade for £62 million – was buying rival Shepperton, thus creating a firm valued at more than £100 million. The move brought together two of Europe's biggest studios, enabling the joint company to attract big-budget film makers. Michael Grade, executive chairman of the enlarged group, said: 'The two studios have been competing for years against each other. In an increasingly global market, this makes no sense. Together, we can enhance Britain's share of the international movie making business.'

The Scott brothers were to remain as active shareholders in the enlarged group and continue as co-chairmen. Ridley Scott added that the UK was a 'great place to make movies. This consolidation of our leading film assets is long overdue. Tony and I are committed to the growth and continued success of these historic studios.

The merger was part-financed by the venture capital firm 3i. Chris Graham, a director of 3i London, said they were 'delighted' to be working with Ridley and Tony Scott. 'These studios are unique assets supported by a world class management team and 3i is proud to be associated with such an innovative deal. The addition of film directors Ridley and Tony Scott makes this Board one of the most powerful in the industry,' he added.

The two studios will continue to retain their individual trading identities, although they will be under common ownership and management. The Pinewood Shepperton Studios boasted to having thirty-six varied stages, western Europe's largest water tank and the largest permanent stage in the world, the famous 007 stage, all set within over 200 acres of magnificent grounds.

Since acquiring Shepperton in January 1995, the Scott brothers and Candover invested more than £17.9 million in the facility. 3i reported that:

> The structure and timing of the merger – which included the simultaneous management buy-out of an associated business [The Mill] – required all of 3i's considerable finesse, as well as the knowledge of their specialist media sector team and their experience in the management of large, complex transactions.
>
> The merged studios offer unmatched facilities for the production of feature films and television. Both operate as 'four wall' film studios and provide the highest quality stages and support facilities for all sizes of production. Together, their 'credits' include a galaxy of blockbuster movies from *James Bond* to *102 Dalmations*.

Meanwhile Robert Altman, the American director of *Gosford Park*, saw himself in the financial headlines too, when a little controversy was caused at the Film Council's announcement that they were backing the project with £2 million ($3.2 million) – its largest single grant. 'An American director getting British lottery money!' went the cry. It was, however, a truly British film, with a cast of primarily British actors. It was awarded the Alexander Korda award at the 2002 BAFTA ceremony, as 'Outstanding British Film'.

Ron Webster was cast as Constable Dexter, to Stephen Fry's Inspector Thompson.

'Wotham House, north of London, has been devoted to film making for the past twenty years,' he says of the film's main location. 'The other part of the film sets were built in Shepperton, it was unbelievable as soon as you walked onto the set, you would forget you were in a studio.'

Altman described the below stairs whodunit as 'Agatha Christie's *Ten Little Indians* meets Jean Renoir's *The Rules of the Game*.' An all-star cast: Dame Maggie Smith, Sir Michael Gambon, Kristin Scott Thomas, Charles Dance, Jeremy Northam, Bob Balaban, James Wilby, Ryan Phillippe and Clive Owen were gathered together by the director. Owen notes:

> I don't think there's a director alive that could put that kind of a cast together for a film, and keep everyone so happy. It was a genuine ensemble. We were all pre-warned: There would be no getting in to do your bits and getting out. Everyone needed to be there because they might be needed for someone else's scene.

Actor-turned-screenwriter Julian Fellowes, who went on to win an Oscar for his screenplay, explained:

> My lucky break was that Robert Altman wanted to have a look at the English class system. He'd never made a British picture in that way. He wanted to play with the genre of a murder mystery, but not make a murder mystery. He said right at the beginning, 'This isn't a whodunit. It's a who cares whodunit.' And he wanted an examination of class. He is interested in very desperate people who are brought together by circumstance rather than desire, all with a different agenda. And he felt that the extraordinary proximity of the servants and the masters in this great house was a very good opportunity for this. Basically, it was a satirical, hopefully amusing, social commentary pretending to be a murder mystery. The murder's nothing, as you know.

Some sixty years after Zoltan Korda directed *The Four Feathers*, Shekhar Kapur took charge of a less than successful Hollywood re-make with Heath Ledger. It was a troubled shoot, and the film was much delayed to a 2002 release, where it was critically panned. Location work started in the African desert.

'It was tough; it was really, really tough,' said Kapur at a press conference upon the film's release, 'but in that toughness lies the adventure. And in the adventure lies creativity. And in creativity lies art. And in art lies life. I can go on but I better shut up.'

Television production was still a big part of the studios output, and in 2001 comedian Steve Coogan starred in a six x thirty-minute-episode series called *Dr Terrible's House of Horrible* – a send up of the horror genre and, of course, based lovingly on the *Amicus* film that filmed at Shepperton.

Kenneth Branagh breathed life into another historical figure for Channel 4's two-part, £10 million epic *Shackleton*, based on adventurer Sir Ernest Shackleton's 1914 expedition to the South Pole.

Writer and Director Charles Sturridge had immersed himself in research, knowing he had a transmission deadline just over a year away and had to deliver a four-hour film. There was talk of other film versions too: a lavish Hollywood studio project to be directed by Wolfgang Petersen (with Russell Crowe signed up for Shackleton); Working Title apparently had a script; and the BBC, which had previously done its own four-hour version in 1983, was also keen to reprise the story. More recently, there has been the release of a spectacular Imax version of the expedition. Sturridge admits:

> From the beginning I said to the financiers that they should expect a film to come out. And did they mind? Because I certainly didn't. It just meant we had to concentrate on making ours better than anyone else's. The competition was, if you like, a sign of interest in the story. It should, I added, be taken as a positive, as something definitely not to frighten us off.

Sturridge wanted Kenneth Branagh to play the explorer, even before he had a script as, like Shackleton, he is Irish-born and was aged forty at the time of the expedition.

> I didn't know Ken at all when I rang him up to take him to lunch. I didn't tell him properly beforehand what it was all about. When we met, at a Chinese restaurant, I told him that although I hadn't started writing yet, he was the person I wanted to play Shackleton. Now if it had been me, I would probably have said, 'Very interesting, let me know how you get on with the script and, of course, I'd like to read it'. With terrific grace, he said straightaway: 'What a great idea, I'd like to do it'.

With a script completed, and finance in place, and armed with some practical tips about filming in the cold gleaned from Sir John Mills – who'd played Scott of the Antarctic more than fifty years earlier – Branagh, Sturridge and the rest of the cast and crew set off to spend five weeks on a Norwegian icebreaker.

2002 was a busier year still, with eighteen features and almost as many television productions taking space at the studio. *Black Ball* was a comedy from director Mel Smith. With location work on the Isle of Man, Shepperton became the studio base for completion and post production. It was probably the first comedy film about bowls – and a player being suspended from it – to ever be made. But why? Mel Smith reveals:

> I was very intrigued and amused by the notion of somebody who can get banned for ten years [referring to a true story he read in a newspaper], for playing bowls in a fashion that annoys people. It was a case of, 'Let's see if this can be as extraordinary and as odd as it sounds'.

Another true story lent itself to film when, a few years ago, two members of Rylstone and District Women's Institute became determined to raise a serious amount of money to benefit hospitals and leukaemia research. They hit upon the idea of a calendar showing the members of the WI engaging in the activities traditionally associated with the group, like baking and flower arranging, but without clothes on. 3,000 copies of the calendar were sold on the very first day. That became 88,000 nationwide with startling rapidity. And the product was very successfully exported to America, moving 250,000 copies.

Director Nigel Cole says he 'immediately knew it would be a great film, but did nothing about it.' That is, until the women who lived the story in real life chose producers Nick Barton and Suzanne Mackie to tell their tale on film. Cole was approached, joined the project and thus *Calendar Girls* was born. An all-star cast was recruited including Dame Helen Mirren and Julie Walters.

'Women in their 50s are almost invisible [in movies] in terms of sexuality', says Julie Walters. 'My daughter thought I was joking when I told her I was doing the film.'

But what about the nudity?

'We were all apprehensive of the nudity up to a point. We were glad when it was over; it was a terrible thing hanging over us', she reveals.

'Myself and the crew offered to go naked during the shoot,' adds Nigel Cole, 'to put them at ease, but they actually begged us to keep our clothes on! They had enough to worry about without having to look at us!' The film went on to gross almost $90 million (£55 million).

A slightly inept 'spy' in the rogue *James Bond* film, *Never Say Never Again*, was played by Rowan Atkinson, and duly lead to an acclaimed advertising campaign for Barclaycard. The next step? A blockbuster film, of course. And so came Atkinson as Johnny English: an accident-prone MI-7 agent on a mission to rescue Britain's crown jewels and save the country – and the monarchy – from a Machiavellian French business magnate, after Number One Agent is wiped out in a dastardly bombing.

He knows no fear.
He knows no danger.
He knows nothing.

Said the posters.

Peter Howitt directed the successful Bond-esque comedy *Johnny English* with Rowan Atkinson in the title role. (Courtesy Peter Howitt)

Natalie Imbruglia plays English's sassy sidekick, and John Malkovich the evil Pascal Savage, with a terrible French accent. Ben Miller says:

> John was such fun. He does actually live in France. The amazing thing about him is that he's a force of nature. I don't think I ever saw him do the same line twice. It's that American thing, he's not in character; he is the character. To begin with, when they told me he'd be playing the villain, I was like 'Who? John Malkovich?' But when I thought about it after reading the script, I realised it was actually a brilliant idea.

The script was written by Neal Purvis and Robert Wade who had penned two Bond movies. In fact, *Johnny English* and the then Bond film, *Die Another Day*, were filming simultaneously at different studios.

'That was quite something,' says Neal Purvis. 'We were shooting the *Bond* at Pinewood and would say, "we're just popping over to Shepperton for a while to see our other film".'

'It was quite a feeling,' adds Wade, who explains that, 'William Davies was also involved in the writing, and really took over during production when we had to depart and work on the Bond.'

Johnny English had originally been scheduled to film at Pinewood in the autumn of 2001; however, the events of 9/11 saw the film postponed whilst 'sensitive scenes' were re-written. Peter Howitt, who also directed *Sliding Doors* at the studio, explained that whilst he had great fun filming around London, he much prefers a studio environment:

> There is so much concentration required with Rowan, with lots of tweaking going on, and what a studio gives you is a very concealed compartment with no outside noise or interference. For instance, the parachuting sequence ... we filmed around Canary Wharf but recreated much of the scene at Shepperton where we had much better control over it all.

After Producer Duncan Kenworthy teamed up with Writer Richard Curtis on successes *Four Weddings and a Funeral* and *Notting Hill*, the duo's next collaboration saw Curtis trying his hand at directing. His script, an ensemble piece set in London just before Christmas, following the lives of eight very different couples, was christened *Love Actually*. It boasted one of the most glitzy casts ever: Hugh Grant, Emma Thompson, Liam Neeson, Colin Firth, Alan Rickman, Bill Nighy, Keira Knightley, Laura Linney, Rowan Atkinson, Andrew Lincoln, Martine McCutcheon, Thomas Sangster, Olivia Olson, Rodrigo Santoro, Lucia Moniz, Martin Freeman, Joanna Page, Billy Bob Thornton, Denise Richards and Claudia Schiffer.

The film was split between Shepperton and Pinewood. Curtis handled the chores of screenwriter and director with great aplomb. Colin Firth observes of Richard Curtis:

He really does have this fantastically intelligent and self-deprecating wit that you associate with the films that he writes. He is doing something, which however mainstream it is, is quite different from what other people do and I think that it is actually only mainstream because he single-handedly made it so. It is quite hard to write about middle-class professional people, which is usually the stuff of sitcoms, but he actually manages to get some drama out of it.

Hugh Grant played a Tony Blair-esque Prime Minister. Producer Duncan Kenworthy explains:

We built the whole of Downing Street in a parking lot, outside one stage, so that we could actually have Hugh Grant, as Prime Minister, drive along Downing Street and go to the door of number 10.

When asked if he'd be inviting the premier to the premiere, the producer quipped, 'We'll ask him but he'll probably have other things on his plate.'

Stealing the show, however, was actor Bill Nighy as washed-up pop star Billy Mack. His character's single, *Christmas Is All Around*, was released in the UK as a charity song, peaking at number 12 in the charts. Nighy went on to win a Best Supporting Actor BAFTA at the British Academy Awards. The film went on to be one of the highest grossing British films of the year, completing a trio of huge Shepperton hits for Producer Duncan Kenworthy; with *Four Weddings* and *Notting Hill* before.

Television projects through the year included the now regular visitor, *Last of the Summer Wine*, reality television show *Fame Academy* and dazzling BBC documentary *Walking With Cavemen*.

Whilst some effects and a little stage work for *Harry Potter and the Chamber of Secrets* was completed during 2002, the following year the third instalment in the franchise, *Harry Potter and the Prisoner of Azkaban*, split more of its shoot with Shepperton from its home base of Leavesden.

'The trees are massive, the trunks several metres thick and stretching far towards the fake sky. The woods are dark, of course, with a menacing air, and like a couple of tiny shadows Harry and Hermione are standing under a tree', said Swedish newspaper *Aftonbladet*, reporting on its set visit at Shepperton.

Alfonso Cuaron, the Mexican-born director who had taken over the reigns from Chris Columbus, endeared himself to the cast and crew with his easygoing style.

'The difference between him and Chris Columbus,' said star Daniel Radcliffe when asked about the new director, 'is that Chris got an energetic way of working which suited the first films. Alfonso's got a mild intensity that works better with this material.'

The movie is certainly darker and more menacing than the first two, and Cuaron's style has seen him employ mostly wide-angles in the shooting, and also insisting that the lead characters wear modern clothes … jeans, tracksuit jackets and even trainers! Sadly, one 'regular' cast member, Richard Harris, who played Professor Dumbledore, passed away after the second film. Sir Michael Gambon was recruited in his place.

The Harry Potter team were in distinguished company as, following a gruelling shoot in Malta and Mexico, Wolfgang Peterson's epic re-enactment of the siege of Troy moved in. Brad Pitt headed an all-star cast including Orlando Bloom, Eric Bana, Sean Bean, Peter O'Toole and Julie Christie. Orlando Bloom explained to *Sugar* magazine:

> It's an epic style film but it's more acting-based that action-based. It's more of a performing piece and a progression for me, despite being part of an ensemble. I play Paris, an anti-hero. I'm more a lover than a fighter, which is kind of cool for me because I haven't had many kissing scenes in the past!

Despite the starry cast, the film fared poorly at the box office, and reviews were very mixed.

No sooner had shooting commenced, than Peter Sellers' son appealed to audiences to stay away from a new movie starring Geoffrey Rush as the famous comedian, called *The Life and Death of Peter Sellers*, based on the book of the same name by Roger Lewis.

'This film is based on 800 pages of unintelligible rubbish,' Sellers told British newspaper *The Times*. Roger Lewis, in his book, concluded that Sellers was certifiably insane. Director Stephen Hopkins made matters worse – when asked why he had pursued the Australian actor Geoffrey Rush to play the part, he said: 'Geoffrey is very good at playing loonies.'

'Geoffrey Rush, in my opinion,' says Sellers' ex-wife Britt Ekland, 'is terrific in the part. But if he has a failing it is that he is a nice man. Sellers was a monster. His redeeming features were few and far between.'

At the 2003 Cannes Film Festival, Hopkins said:

> I have read both of Michael Sellers's books [about his father] and all the others by people who were great fans of his, as I am. I think you will find the film will not attack Sellers on any level. It is very compassionate. You will feel sorry for him.

The film recreated many of Sellers' famous roles, including from *I'm All Right Jack* and *Dr Strangelove* – and by virtue of filming at Shepperton, recreated them on the same stages and lot where Sellers had originally worked. Hopkins explains:

> We re-built the War Room set from the original designs on B-Stage. That was quite an awesome experience – to walk on that set. Much of the studio exterior hadn't changed, and the famous sequence from *I'm All Right Jack* of Kite walking through the company works was re-created exactly.

Britt Ekland did criticise the film's accuracy:

> They were very 'creative' with my part of the story – perhaps because they knew I had written my autobiography and registered a screen treatment based

on it with the Writer's Guild. I first met Sellers in a freezing cold January. They portrayed us as having a long love affair with picnics in the park. Untrue. We were married within a week, after he proposed to me in a cleaner's cupboard at Heathrow airport!

Without doubt, the world's most famous tennis championship takes place in South-West London for two weeks every June. It is, of course, Wimbledon. A film of the same name moved into production at Shepperton during the summer of 2003, with Working Title producing. Paul Bettany and Kirsten Dunst headed the story of a hopeless British tennis star (Bettany) who manages to score a wild card, allowing him to play in the prestigious tournament. There, he meets and falls in love with American tennis star Dunst.

'Kirsten had agreed to do the film before *Spiderman* (2002)', says Casting Director Irene Lamb, 'but we didn't then have a male lead. Then when we talked to Paul and he agreed to star, we had to wait for him to finish the Peter Weir film [*Master and Commander*]. And so it was summer 2003 before the film could start.'

Centre court was recreated on the Shepperton back-lot by Brian Morris, but during the Wimbledon fortnight, play on the real centre court was delayed for thirty minutes after lunch so the actors could take to the famous green to film a sequence. With film cameras dressed as television cameras covering the event, the crowd became enthusiastic extras and cheered on the actors as they played.

Australian Wimbledon champion Pat Cash served as tennis advisor on the film, and put the actors through their paces during several weeks of training. Richard Loncraine directed, following happy associations with Shepperton the previous two years with *The Gathering Storm* and *My House in Umbria*. The top cast, appealing story and that 'Working Title touch' all combined to make the film a hit. But did the actors really play tennis? Loncraine reveals:

Yes and no. Yes the serves and some of the returns were filmed 'for real' but much was created later, digitally. The actors had to make it look like they were hitting all sorts of weird and wonderful shots – and did train for that – but we put the ball in later!

As 2003 came to a close, a Warner Bros film with the working title *Intimidation Games* moved into pre-production. Brit Christopher Nolan was announced as director, followed by the casting of Christian Bale, Morgan Freeman, Liam Neeson and Michael Caine. The title was soon changed, though, to *Batman Begins* – the caped crusader returns! As *Variety* magazine reported:

This time around, it's about the genesis of Batman: How billionaire Bruce Wayne makes a series of decisions that turn him into the Caped Crusader. Batman will be more realistic and less cartoonish. There are no campy villains. Wayne – younger, more vulnerable, more human – will be getting as much attention as his masked alter-ego.

Shepperton also played host to films that were primarily based at other studios, but needed a little extra room: zombie-hit *Shaun of the Dead* and comedy sequel *Bridget Jones II* from Ealing; and Oscar-nominated *Closer*, along with the big-screen outing of Douglas Adams' *The Hitchhiker's Guide to the Galaxy* popped over from Elstree Studios. It was all welcome work.

One of the bigger films of 2004 was perhaps also one of the most troubled – *Sahara*. The 'Indiana Jones style' adventure commenced principal photography in 2003, with Matthew McConaughey, Steve Zahn and Penélope Cruz; though it was troubled from the very beginning. The author of the book, Clive Cussler, was paid an 'extremely handsome price – even by Hollywood standards', but was deeply unhappy with the commissioned scripts. He said, in an interview with the *Denver Post*, 'they sent me seven scripts and I've inserted each one in the trash can.' In 2001 he approved a script, but the producers then made substantial changes without consulting him. He then called for the film's release to be blocked as they made it based on a script he had not approved. Re-shoots and court action delayed its first screening until early 2005, where reviews were mixed.

CHAPTER 20

THE FUTURE

2003 was, according to the UK Film Council, a record year for film production spend in the UK, with a total expenditure of £1.17 billion – in indigenous, co-productions and inward productions. The UK was involved with some 177 features, which saw production spend more than double from £550 million in 2002, and indigenous production increase by 21 per cent in the same period.

British Film Commissioner Steve Norris said: 'The UK continues to be recognised by international filmmakers as one of the best places in the world to make a film.'

That was certainly true of Shepperton. With optimism and vigour, Shepperton moves full-throttle into the twenty-first century with an impressive list of big-budget British and American films under its belt, from the first few years of the new millennium and many more bookings in the diary. The future looks rosy.

Continuing improvements to the studio include transferring the old Special Effects Department into a new state of the art reception and administration block, and moving the canteen around into the old British Lion pub – the sign from which, featuring Winston Churchill, has been donated to Shepperton Museum Committee member Roy Pembrooke plans to restore it to its former glory for its pride-of-place position in the museum. The conservatory, which featured significantly in the studio's early activities, had fallen victim to previous owners' lack of upkeep, and has recently been replaced by The Orangery, a wonderful, light and airy room ideal for functions, parties and even filming!

In personnel changes, Managing Director Denis Carrigan retired at the end of 2002 and handed over to Pinewood's MD, Steve Jaggs, who became Group Managing Director; whilst Paul Olliver was replaced by his former assistant David Godfrey as studio manager. Godfrey was subsequently promoted to oversee Pinewood, Shepperton and Teddington Studios' operations (when the latter was also taken over by the group) and Jaggs' son Kristian became studio manager.

Owners, the Pinewood Shepperton Group, under the chairmanship of Michael Grade, announced a ten-year plan for future improvement and development of the site, which includes refurbishing existing stages and buildings along with constructing new offices, stages, underground car parks and support facilities. Phase One will see

The British Lion Pub
(and sign) at Shepperton
– now the studio canteen
and restaurant. (Roy
Pembrooke)

the existing H stage, brought to the studio by Sir Alexander Korda, demolished, the land sold off for housing so as to 'blend the studio in better with the existing housing estate', and a new H stage built in the centre of the complex. The plans will no doubt bring many emotive issues to the fore, but they also secure Shepperton a future as a leading production facility for the next hundred years – and beyond.

To finance the ambitious proposals, the Group announced it was to float on the stock exchange. The company said the 'main purpose of the flotation was to refinance its debt, which would allow it to pursue expansion plans'. Details of its debt were not given, but it is said to be 'less than 50 per cent of the enterprise value of the company, which is between £130m and £140m.' Group Chairman Michael Grade said:

> The demand for both film and television content continues to grow, offering us many opportunities to increase our business. Pinewood–Shepperton plays a major part in the international film production industry, hosting movies from the major Hollywood studios and the independents at our facilities.

Group turnover for the year to 31 December 2003 was £37.9 million with an operating profit of £10.9 million. On 7 May 2004 Pinewood–Shepperton plc floated with an opening price of 180p per share. By the end of the day's trading shares were 200p, and it was reported that Michael Grade picked up £250,000 from the flotation of just under 139,000 of his shares, whilst maintaining a 1.35 per cent stake in the studio – worth some £1.24 million. More than £46 million of new money was raised for the company.

In an announcement of six month results to 30 June 2004, the company said turnover for the half-year from continuing operations was up 10.3 per cent at £20.4 million (2003 – £18.5 million). Operating profit from continuing operations, before exceptional IPO (initial public offering, floatation)-related costs, was up

15.8 per cent at £6.7 million (2003 – £5.8 million). The successful IPO raised £46.9 million through institutional placing. A new £60 million revolving credit facility was arranged.

Michael Grade said of the interim results:

> This performance demonstrates the continuing strength of the television and film markets in which we operate. The capital structure put in place following the IPO will allow the Board to further the Company's growth opportunities.

Ivan Dunleavy, Chief Executive of Pinewood-Shepperton plc, said:

> I am pleased to announce these maiden results. Pinewood-Shepperton performed slightly ahead of expectations for the first half of 2004 reflecting strong sales of studio facilities. In the second half to date the Company is performing in line with expectations across all business lines and the Directors view the Company's prospects for the current financial year with confidence.

Alas, the following year was a different picture. Due to uncertainty in the Government's tax allowances to the film industry, a great many American producers stayed away from UK shores. Pinewood-Shepperton later said that operating profits were down 70 per cent in 2005, from £6.4 million in 2004 to £571,000. Profits fell from £11.3 million to £3.7 million. Chief Executive Ivan Dunleavy said the 2005 performance was 'in line with market expectations.'

'Trading conditions, particularly for the first half of 2005, were challenging, resulting principally from our film customers' uncertainty, now resolved, over the outcome of the Government's review of UK film fiscal policy,' said Chairman Michael Grade.

With the new UK tax laws further clarified by the government, Pinewood said that it expects its business to rebound. Dunleavy said, 'We and the rest of the industry can now look forward with greater confidence and clarity.'

Things did pick up towards the end of 2005, when Shepperton regular Kenneth Branagh filmed *As You Like It*, and other visiting features, including *The Da Vinci Code*, brought much-needed optimism to the studio.

2006 witnessed the company announce plans to enter into a joint venture with Morley Fund Management to form a partnership to 'further develop Shepperton Studios'. Morley, a division of Aviva, paid $19.8 million (£10 million) in cash for its 50 per cent stake in the Shepperton partnership, which Pinewood's equity contribution matched. Also, Morley will fund a long-term loan of $37.8 million (£20 million) to the partnership. 'This is a highly attractive structure for both the Company and its shareholders,' said Pinewood CEO Ivan Dunleavy. 'It provides us with significant new development funding for the Shepperton Studio and reduces development risk and our gearing from the outset. This new partnership will accelerate the pace of the development process at the Group.'

A year on from a pretty gloomy period, the studio's future seemed more secure than ever, and with development funds in the bank too.

2006 played host to film shoots including Kenneth Branagh's *The Magic Flute*, where the director was engaged to 'take the opera out of opera' and bring it to a wider screen audience. It was a commission from the Peter Moore Foundation. Branagh says:

> *The Magic Flute* was conceived for a popular theatre audience. The challenge appealed to me. And the project arrived like a surprise present. I said I needed to listen, listen, listen, and they were patient. It's a real luxury to work that way.

In thinking how he might tell the story, Branagh decided to set it during the First World War.

> It came to me while I was thinking about how to tell the story in such a way that the audience would be gripped by real suspense. I have always been passionately interested in the First World War. And I am particularly fascinated by the moment that preceded it, the atmosphere on the eve of the taking up of arms. I remember a book, *Bird Song*, written by one of those poet soldiers who were in the Great War. The sense of the beauty of the world and its imminent destruction is an infinitely poignant vision for me. I wanted to recapture that in the overture: nature, calm and splendid, and then the deflagration. With the presence of the four elements: air, earth, water, fire, which were very important to Mozart. And I wanted Tamino to have something of those soldier poets, at once sensitive and courageous. That seemed to me to correspond to the spirit of *The Magic Flute*, written by Mozart when he knew he was ill. A sort of meditation on life and death, serious beneath its light and sparkling surface, carried forward by a profound desire for peace, or in musical terms, harmony.

At the film's world premiere on 7 September, held at Venice's opera house La Fenice, Branagh was given a warm reception. One critic described his production as 'that rarest of beasts – an opera you can eat popcorn to.'

'It's not a recording of a great performance,' says Branagh. 'It's trying to use cinema to get people in and give them a taste of opera, not as a bit of cultural medicine.'

New Line's *The Golden Compass*, starring new 007 actor Daniel Craig and Nicole Kidman, also moved on to Shepperton's stages. It became one of the mostly highly anticipated films of the year, and the hot topic of conversation at the 2007 Cannes Film Festival. H stage was transformed to perhaps the biggest-ever green screen stage, where child star Dakota Blue Richards filmed scenes with her animated co-star Iorek, a warrior bear that has travelled the Arctic with her to end the diabolic plot to kidnap children. Alas, upon release it wasn't quite as successful as backers New Line Cinema had hoped, though took a respectable $372 million worldwide, based on a $180 million budget. Rumours of further adaptations in the series of books by Phillip Pullman was soon thrown in to doubt, however, when New Line was folded by parent company Warner Bros. The decision was partly due, it was reported, to disappointing returns on *The Golden Compass* – the studio's most expensive single production – which had also had a troubled production history, involving re-shoots, several directors and a replaced editor.

2007 saw a marked downturn in production at Shepperton, not helped by a threatened writers' strike and a weak dollar. Along with television productions including *Last Of The Summer Wine* and acclaimed BBC drama *Cranford* utilising stages, along with a few commercials, Shepperton kept ticking over with post-production work, primarily zombie sequel *28 Weeks Later* and *Love in the Time of Cholera*.

The writers' strike did hit, at the beginning of 2008, though many productions were purposely green-lit at the tail end of 2007 and into the new year in order to continue supplying the distributors and cinemas in the uncertain times ahead – with deadlock between studios and the Writer's Guild there seemed to be no light in the tunnel ahead. Consequently, in 2008, Shepperton's post-production theatres bustled with activity on big-budget movies such as *10,000*, *Doomsday*, *Hellboy II*, *How to Lose Friends and Alienate People*, *The Chronicles of Narnia*, *Prince Caspian* and *Vantage Point*. The anticipated return of Richard Curtis to the director's chair followed with pirate radio station drama *The Boat That Rocked*.

The Boat That Rocks contains 'very few humanitarian interests, apart from the rights of all mankind to enjoy rock and roll,' said Curtis. The film tells the tale of disc jockeys living on ships in British waters and committing pirate radio in the mid-1960s. Picture 'eight of the most extreme disc jockeys you've ever imagined having to live in a corridor, and a corridor that moved,' he says. 'And with no girls.'

Variety reported the movie is being released through Working Title Films and Universal Pictures, and is described as the first 'non-rom-com' by Curtis (who made his directorial debut with *Love Actually* and wrote *Four Weddings and a Funeral* and *Bridget Jones's Diary*). The cast includes Philip Seymour Hoffman, Bill Nighy, Rhys Ifans, Nick Frost, and Kenneth Branagh.

Everyone's favourite wizard was back too. *Harry Potter and the Half-Blood Prince* used L, R and C stages whilst over from its main base at Leavesden Studios. Star Daniel Radcliffe said, 'It's a complex story, it isn't a simple romance because Harry is such a close friend of Ron's, and Ginny is his sister, and Harry feels as if he's walking on eggshells.'

According to Director David Yates, 'the fifth [film] was pretty intense, but this one has more comedy in it … There are many subtleties in the relationship, and a lot of sexual and emotional tension.' The movie also promises a lot of action and magic galore, and it will count at least one scene that is not in the book. However, controversy surrounded its premiere when, soon after announcing it as the Royal Film Performance for November 2008, Warner Bros. decided to delay the release by eight months to July 2009, citing lack of 'tent pole product' for that summer after the writers' strike delayed many planned productions.

Royalty, albeit a fictionalised account, played a part in Shepperton's busy year too, when *The Young Victoria* moved on to G stage. The film chronicles the early and often turbulent years of a young girl who became queen of Great Britain. Victoria was a girl of barely eighteen when she was crowned – vivacious, fond of parties, and prone to flirting with the gentlemen of the court, and even her ministers. The film focuses on her romance and marriage to Prince Albert. Martin Scorsese and Graham King teamed-up again after *The Departed*, *The Aviator* and *Gangs of New York* to retell the story of the famous queen with a little help – as producer – from the outspoken Duchess of York, Sarah Ferguson. Graham King told *Variety* magazine:

> We all think we know Queen Victoria from the latter part of her life, but in fact she was an amazing, dynamic, romantic personality from a very early age that is largely unknown. I had been searching for a British project for many years so I am just thrilled to bring her story to life.

Emily Blunt was cast as Victoria whilst Rupert Friend was cast opposite her as Prince Albert, and they were supported by an all-star cast including Paul Bettany, Miranda Richardson and Jim Broadbent.

Despite the actors' strike, 2008 proved a much stronger year than 2007, not only for Shepperton but for the other studios in the group too. Pinewood Shepperton told markets that its pre-tax profits rose to £3.8 million ($7 million) for the six months ending 30 June 2008, up from £2.9 million from the same period in 2007.

Revenue at the group hit £21.7 million ($39.8 million) in the first half, up from £18.3 million in 2007. Shareholders enjoyed a 5 per cent increase in the group's interim dividend and could rest easy knowing that the board secured a five-year banking facility of £70 million ($128 million) in August to fuel its expansion ambitions. Operating profits hit £4.8 million ($8.8 million) in the first half, up from £3.6 million at the same time in 2007.

'The past six months have continued to demonstrate Pinewood Shepperton's ability to diversify and deliver consistent revenue streams even in times of wider economic uncertainty,' Pinewood-Shepperton Chief Executive Ivan Dunleavy said.

Revenue from film making reached £13 million ($23.8 million), up from £10.8 million in 2007.

Norman Loudon's vision in the early 1930s was to build a world-class production complex. Despite the many ups and downs, Shepperton Studios has survived and thrived. Long may it be part of British film-making history.

SHEPPERTON STUDIOS' FILMOGRAPHY

Year relates to year of production, not release.

Through extensive research, particularly through the Department of Trade and Industry records – where all British Films qualifying under the Quota Act had to be registered – a number of films previously unaccredited to the studio have been found to have been based, in full or part, at the facility. This filmography represents the definitive production (excluding post-production) listing for Shepperton.

D = Director
W = Writer
P = Producer
LP = Leading Players

W.H. = a Worton Hall Studios production*

* Post-1946, when Alexander Korda took control of both Shepperton in addition to his Worton Hall Studio, many films crossed between the two facilities, and they became inextricably linked. Only Worton Hall productions between 1946 and its closure in 1952 are listed here (except in the case of *Sanders of the River*). Korda also produced several films at Worton Hall in the 1930s.

1932

Reunion
D: Ivar Campbell; W: Herbert Ayres, Reginald Hargreaves; P: Norman Loudon; LP: Robert Newton, George Bishop, Robert Dudley.

Watch Beverley
D: Arthur Maude; W: N.W. Baring-Pemberton, Cyril Campion (play), John Cousins; P: Ivar Campbell; LP: Francis X. Bushman, Dorothy Bartlam, Frederic de Lara.

Five shorts
Aerobatics (no information)
Capture (no information)
Pursuit of Priscilla (no information)
Reward (no information)
The Safe W: W.P. Lipscombe; LP: Angela Baddeley, Michael Hogan.

1933

Colonel Blood
D/W: W.P. Lipscomb; P: Norman Loudon; LP: Frank Cellier, Anne Grey, Arthur Chesney.

Doss House
D: John Baxter; W: Herbert Ayres; P: Ivar Campbell; LP: Arnold Bell, Hubert Leslie, Wilson Coleman.

Drake of England (Part)
D: Arthur Woods; W: Marjorie Deans, Clifford Grey, Louis N. Parker (play), Ákos Tolnan, Norman Watson; LP: Matheson Lang, Athene Seyler, Donald Wolfit, Moore Marriott.

Eyes of Fate
D: Ivar Campbell; W: Holloway Horn; P: Norman Loudon; LP: Faith Bennett, Valerie Hobson, O.B. Clarence.

Golden Cage, The
D: Ivar Campbell; W: Pamela Frankau, Lady Trowbridge (play), D.B. Wyndham-Lewis; P: Norman Loudon; LP: Anne Grey, Anthony Kimmins, Frank Cellier.

Moorland Tragedy, A
D: M.A. Wetherell; W: Allen Francis, Baroness Emmuska Orczy (story); P: Hayford Hobbs; LP: Haddon Mason, Barbara Coombes, Moore Marriott.

Paris Plane
D/W: John Paddy Carstairs; P: Ivar Campbell; LP: Edwin Ellis, James Harcourt, John Loder.

She Was Only a Village Maiden
D: Arthur Maude; W: N.W. Baring-Pemberton, Fanny Bowker (play – *Priscilla the Rake*), John Cousins; P: Ivar Campbell; LP: Anne Grey, Lester Matthews.

Side Streets
D: Ivar Campbell; W: Philip Godfrey; P: Norman Loudon; LP: Jane Wood, Paul Neville, Diana Beaumont.

Song of the Plough
D: John Baxter; W: Reginald Pound; P: Ivar Campbell; LP: Stuart Rome, Rosalinde Fuller, James Harcourt.

Taking Ways
D: John Baxter (no other information)
Wishbone, The
D: Arthur Maude; W: N. W. Baring-Pemberton, William Townend (story); P: Ivar Campbell;
LP: Nelly Wallace, Davy Burnaby.

1934

Breakers Ahead
D/W: Anthony Gilkinson; P: Fraser Foulsham; LP: Barry Livesey, April Vivien, Billy
Holland.
By-Pass to Happiness
D/W: Anthony Kimmins; P: Ivar Campbell; LP: Tamara Desni, Maurice Evans, Kay
Hammond.
Designing Women
D: Ivar Campbell; W: N. W. Baring-Pemberton; P: Norman Loudon; LP: D.A. Clarke-
Smith, Tyrell Davis, Edgar Driver, Kathleen Kelly.
The Dictator (part)
D: Al Santell/Victor Saville; W: Benn W. Levy, H.G. Lustig, Hans Wilhelm; P: Ludovico
Toeplitz; LP: Clive Brook, Emlyn Williams, Hilda Campbell-Russell.
Falling in Love (also known as 'Trouble Ahead') (part)
D: Monty Banks; W: E. Bard (story), John Paddy Carstairs, Alan Hyman (story), Lee Loeb
(story), Miles Malleson, Fred Thompson; P: Howard Welsch; LP: Charles Farrell, Mary
Lawson, Gregory Ratoff.
How's Chances?
D: Ivar Campbell, Anthony Kimmins; W: Curt J. Braun (play – *Der Frauendiplomat*), Ivar
Campbell, Harry Graham, E.B. Leuthege (play – *Der Frauendiplomat*); P: Norman Loudon;
LP: Harold French, Tamara Desni, Davy Burnaby.
The Iron Duke (part)
D: Victor Saville; W: H.M. Harwood (story), Bess Meredyth; P: Michael Balcon; LP:
George Arliss, Gladys Cooper, A.E. Matthews.
Lady in Danger (part)
D: Tom Walls; W: Marjorie Gaffney (scenario), Ben Travers; P: Michael Balcon; LP: Tom
Walls, Yvonne Arnaud, Anne Grey.
Lest We Forget
D: John Baxter; W: Herbert Ayres; P: Norman Loudon; LP: George Carney, Wilson
Coleman, Esmond Knight.
Lily of Killarney (part)
D: Maurice Elvey; W: Dion Boucicault (play – *The Colleen Bawn*), H. Fowler Mear; P:
Julius Hagen; LP: John Garrick, Gina Malo, Stanley Holloway.
Mister Cinders
D: Frederic Zelnick; W: Jack Davies, Clifford Grey, George Western, Kenneth Western; P:
Walter C. Mycroft; LP: Edward Chapman, Finlay Currie, Esme Church, Renee Houston.
Once in a New Moon
D: Anthony Kimmins; W: Anthony Kimmins, Owen Rutter (novel – *Lucky Star*); LP:
Gerald Barry, John Clements, Mary Hinton, Wally Patch.

Rolling Home
D: Ralph Ince; W: Frank Launder; P: Norman Loudon; LP: Will Fyfe, Ralph Ince, Molly Lamont.

Sabotage (also known as 'Menace')
D: Adrian Brunel; W: Heinrich Fraenkel, A.R. Rawlinson, Victor Varconi (story); P: Norman Loudon; LP: Victor Varconi, Joan Maud.

Sanders of the River (part) (W.H./Shepperton)
D: Zoltan Korda; W: Lajos Biró, Jeffrey Dell, Edgar Wallace (story); P: Alexander Korda; LP: Paul Robeson, Leslie Banks.

White Ensign
D/W: John L.F. Hunt; P: Ivar Campbell; LP: Anthony Kimmins, Molly Lamont.

Youthful Folly
D: Miles Mander; W: Heinrich Fraenkel, Josephine Tey (play); P: Norman Loudon; LP: Irene Vanbrugh, Grey Blake.

1935

Birds of a Feather
D: John Baxter; W: Gerald Elliott, George Foster (play – *A Rift in the Loot*), Con West; P: John Barter; LP: George Robey, Horace Hodges, Eve Lister.

Emil and the Detectives
D: Milton Rosmer; W: Cyrus Brooks (adaptation), Margaret Carter (dialogue), Erich Kästner (book – *Emil und die Detektive*), Frank Launder (scenario), Billy Wilder (uncredited); P: Richard Wainwright; LP: Derek Blomfield, Marion Forster, Mary Glynne.

Father O'Flynn
D: Wilfred Noy/Walter Tennyson; W: Frank Miller; P: Wilfred Noy; LP: Thomas F. Burke, Jean Adrienne, Henry Oscar.

Maria Marten (aka 'The Murder in the Red Barn')
D: Milton Rosmer; W: Randall Faye; P: George King; LP: Tod Slaughter, Sophie Stewart, Eric Portman.

Radio Pirates
D: Ivar Campbell; W: Donovan Pedelty; P: Norman Loudon; LP: Leslie French, Mary Lawson.

Two Hearts in Harmony
D: William Beaudine; W: Samuel Gibson Brown (story), Robert Edmunds, A.R. Rawlinson; P: John Clein; LP: Bernice Claire, George Curzon.

1936

Captain's Table, The
D: Percy Marmont; W: John Paddy Carstairs; P: James A. FitzPatrick; LP: Percy Marmont, Marian Spencer, Louis Goodrich.

Crimes of Stephen Hawke, The
D/P: George King; W: Jack Celestin, H.F. Maltby, Tod Slaughter (opening – unaccredited), Paul White; LP: Tod Slaughter, Majorie Taylor, Eric Portman.

Crimson Circle, The
D: Reginald Denham; W: Edgar Wallace (novel), Howard Irving Young; P: Richard Wainwright; LP: Hugh Wakefield, Alfred Drayton, Niall McGinnis.

David Livingstone
D/P: James A. Fitzpatrick; W: W.K. Williamson; LP: James Carew, Percy Marmont, Hugh McDermott.

Grand Finale
D: Ivar Campbell; W: Vera Allinson, Paul Hervey Fox (story); P: Anthony Havelock-Allan; LP: Mary Glynne, Guy Newall, Eric Cowley.

Happy Days are Here Again (aka 'Happy Days Revue')
D: Norman Lee; W: F.H. Bickerton, Daniel Birt, Renee Houston (story), Alan Rennie; P: John Argyle; LP: Renee Houston, Billy Houston, Shirley Houston.

Hearts of Humanity
D/P: John Baxter; W: Herbert Ayres; LP: Bransby Williams, Wilfred Walter, Eric Portman, Pamela Randall.

King of the Castle
D: Redd Davis; W: Frank Atkinson (story), George Dewhurst; P: Basil Humphrys; LP: June Clyde, Claude Dampier, Wally Patch.

Make-Up
D: Alfred Zeisler; W: Jeffrey Dell, Reginald Long; P: K.C. Alexander, C.M. Origo; LP: Lawrence Anderson, Nils Asther, June Clyde.

Men of Yesterday
D/P: John Baxter; W: Gerald Elliott, Jack Francis; LP: Ian Colin, Frederick Culley, Barbara Everest.

Mill on the Floss
D: Tim Whelan; W: John Drinkwater, George Eliot (novel), Austin Melford, Garnett Weston, Tim Whelan; P: John Clein; LP: Frank Lawton, Fay Compton, Geraldine Fitzgerald, James Mason.

Murder by Rope
D: George Pearson; W: Ralph Neale; P: Anthony Havelock-Allan; LP: Guy Belmore, Daphne Courtney, Wilfrid Hyde-Whyte.

On Top of the World (aka 'Everything Okay')
D: Redd Davis; W: Evelyn Barrie; P: Basil Humphrys; LP: Leslie Bradley, Ben Field, Betty Fields.

Reasonable Doubt
D: George King; W: Ewart Brooks; P: Gabriel Pascal; LP: Ivan Brandt, Nancy Burne.

Robber Symphony, The
D: Freidrich Feher; W: Friedrich Feher, Anton Kuhl, Jack Trendell; P: Robert Wiene; LP: Oscar Asche, Webster Booth, Hans Feher.

Second Bureau
D: Victor Hanbury; W: Reginald Long, Charles Robert-Dumas (novel), Ákos Tolnay; P: John Stafford; LP: Bruno Barnabe, Leo de Pokomy, Fred Groves.

Secret of Stamboul
D: Andrew Marton; W: George A. Hill, Noel Langley, Richard Wainwright, Dennis Wheatley (novel – *The Eunuch of Stamboul*), Howard Irving Young; P: Richard Wainwright; LP: Valerie Hobson, James Mason, Kay Walsh.

Show Flat

D: Bernard Mainwaring; W: George Barraud, Cecil Maiden (play), Sherard Powell, Martha Robinson (play); P: Anthony Havelock-Allan; LP: Billy Bray, Max Faber, Miki Decima.

Sporting Love (part)

D: J. Elder Wills; W: Ingram D'Abbes, Stanley Lupino (play), Fenn Sherie; P: H. Fraser Passmore; LP: Stanley Lupino, Laddie Clift, Eda Peel.

Such is Life

D: Randall Faye; W: Brandon Fleming; P: Brandon Fleming, Reginald Gottwaltz; LP: (No information)

Sweeney Todd: The Demon Barber Of Fleet Street

D/P: George King; W: Frederick Hayward, H.F. Maltby; LP: Tod Slaughter, Stella Rho, John Singer.

Vandergilt Diamond Mystery, The

D/P: Randall Faye; W: Margaret Houghton; LP: Elisabeth Astell, Bruce Seton.

Wake Up Famous

D: Gene Gerrard; W: Basil Mason; P: John Stafford; LP: Fred Conyngham, Gene Gerrard, Nelson Keyes.

Wings Over Africa

D: Ladislau Vajda; W: Ákos Tolnay; P: John Stafford; LP: Joan Gardner, Ian Colin, James Harcourt.

Wolf's Clothing

D: Andrew Marton; W: Evadne Price, Brock Williams; P: Richard Wainwright; LP: Claude Hulbert, Gordon Harker, Lili Palmer.

1937

Academy Decides

D: John Baxter (no other information)

Auld Lang Syne

D/P: James A. Fitzpatrick; W: W.K. Williamson; LP: Andrew Cruickman, Christine Adrian, Richard Ross.

Bells of St Mary's, The

D: Redd Davis; W: W.K. Williamson; P: James A. Fitzpatrick; LP: Kathleen Gibson, Sylvia Marriott.

Double Exposures

D: John Paddy Carstairs; W: Gerald Elliot; P: George King; LP: George Astly, Ivor Barnard, Frank Birch.

Elder Brother, The

D: Frederick Hayward; W: Anthony Gibbs (novel), Dorothy Greenhill; P: George King; LP: John Stuart, Majorie Taylor, Basil Langton.

For Valour

D: Tom Walls; W: Ben Travers; P: Max Schach; LP: Tom Walls, Ralph Lynn, Veronica Rose.

House of Silence

D/P: R.K. Neilson Baxter; W: Rowan Kennedy, Paul White; LP: Tom Helmore, Jenny Laird.

It's Never Too Late to Mend

D: David MacDonald; W: H.F. Maltby (dialogue), H.F. Maltby (script), Charles Reade (novel); P: George King; LP: Tod Slaughter, Jack Livesey.

Last Adventurers, The

D: Roy Kellino; W: Dennison Clift; P: H. Fraser Passmore; LP: Niall McGinnis, Roy Emerton, Linden Travers.

Last Rose of Summer, The

D/P: James A. Fitzpatrick; W: James A. FitzPatrick, W.K. Williamson; LP: John Garrick, Kathleen Gibson.

Merry Comes to Town

D/P: George King; W: Evadne Price (story), Brock Williams; LP: Zasu Pitts; Guy Newell, Bernard Clifton.

Mr Stringfellow Says No

D: Randall Faye; W: Randall Faye, Brandon Fleming; P: Brandon Fleming, Reginald Gottwaltz; LP: Muriel Aked, Claude Dampier, Kathleen Gibson.

Overcoat Sam (aka 'Sunshine Ahead')

D: Wallace Orton; W: Geoffrey Orme, Con West; P: John Baxter; LP: Eddie Pola, Betty Astor, Leslie Perrins.

Return of a Stranger

D: W. Victor Hanbury; W: Reginald Long, Ákos Tolnay; P: John Stafford; LP: Griffith Jones, Rosalyn Boulter.

School for Husbands

D: Andrew Marton; W: Frederick J. Jackson (also play), Austin Melford, Gordon Sherry; P: Richard Wainwright; LP: Rex Harrison, Diana Churchill.

Screen Struck

D: Lawrence Huntington (no other information)

Song of the Road

D: John Baxter; W: Gerald Elliott; P: John Baxter; LP: Tod Slaughter, Davy Burnaby, Bransby Williams.

Talking Feet

D: John Baxter; W: Jack Francis (story), H. Fowler Mear, Geoffrey Orme (story); P: John Baxter; LP: Hazel Ascot, Jack Barty.

Thunder in the City (part)

D: Marion Gering; W: Robert E. Sherwood, Aben Kandel, Ákos Tolnay; P: Alexander Esway; LP: Edward G. Robinson, Luli Deste, Nigel Bruce, Ralph Richardson.

Ticket of Leave Man

D/P: George King; W: H.F. Maltby, A.R. Rawlinson; LP: Tod Slaughter, John Warwick, Marjorie Taylor.

Under a Cloud

D/P: George King; W: Gordon Francis (story), M.B. Parsons; LP: Edward Rigby, Betty Ann Davies.

Wake Up Famous

D: Gene Gerrard; W: Basil Mason; P: John Stafford; LP: Fred Conyngham, Gene Gerrard, Nelson Keys.

Wanted

D/P: George King; W: H.F. Maltby, Brock Williams (play); LP: Finlay Currie, Billy Bray, Stella Bonheur.

When the Poppies Bloom Again
D: David MacDonald; W: Evadne Price; LP: Nancy Burne, Jack Livesey.
Wife of General Ling
D: Ladislau Vajda; W: Peter Cheyney (story), Dorothy Hope (story), Reginald Long, Ákos Tolnay; P: John Stafford; LP: Griffith Jones, Valery Inkijinoff.

1938

Ask a Policeman (part)
D: Marcel Varnel; W: Marriott Edgar, Sidney Gilliat (story), Val Guest, J.O.C. Orton; P: Edward Black; LP: Will Hay, Moore Marriott, Graham Moffatt.
Dream of Love, A
D/P/W: James A. Fitzpatrick (seventeen-minute short)
George Bizet, Composer of Carmen
D/P/W: James A. Fitzpatrick; LP: Dino Galvani, Peter Gawthorne.
John Halifax, Gentleman
D/P: George King; W: Dinah Maria Mulock Craik (novel), A.R. Rawlinson; LP: Hugh Bickett, Billy Bray, Roddy McDowall.
Kate Plus Ten
D: Reginald Denham; W: Jeffrey Dell, Jack Hulbert, Edgar Wallace (novel); P: Richard Wainwright; LP: Jack Hulbert, Genevieve Tobin, Felix Aylmer.
Life of Chopin
D: James A. Fitzpatrick (no other information)
Old Bones of the River (part)
D: Marcel Varnel; W: Marriott Edgar, Val Guest, J.O.C. Orton; P: Edward Black; LP: Will Hay, Moore Marriott, Graham Moffatt.
Old Iron
D/P: Tom Walls; W: Ben Travers; P: Richard Ainley, Cecil Parker, Tom Walls.
Second Best Bed
D: Tom Walls; W: Ben Travers; P: Max Schach; LP: Tom Walls, Greta Gynt, Davy Burnaby.
Sexton Blake and the Hooded Terror
D/P: George King; W: Pierre Quiroule (story – *The Mystery of Caversham Square*), A.R. Rawlinson; LP: George Curzon, Tod Slaughter, Greta Gynt.
Silver Top
D/P: George King; W: Gerald Elliott, Dorothy Greenhill, Evadne Price (story); LP: Brian Buchel, Betty Ann Davies, Polly Emery.
Stepping Toes
D: John Baxter; W: Barbara K. Emary (story), Jack Francis (story), H. Fowler Mear; P: John Barter; LP: Hazel Ascot, Enid Stamp-Taylor.

1939

Chinese Bungalow, The
D/P: George King; W: A.R. Rawlinson, George Wellesley; LP: Jane Baxter, Robert Douglas, Kay Walsh.
French Without Tears
D: Anthony Asquith; W: Ian Dalrymple, Anatole de Grunwald, Terence Rattigan; P: Mario Zampi; LP: Ray Milland, Ellen Drew, Roland Culver.

Riding High
D: David MacDonald; W: H. Fowler Mear; P: George King; LP: Mae Bacon, Billy Bray, Kathleen Gibson.

Spy for a Day
D/P: Mario Zampi; W: Ralph Block, Anatole de Grunwald, Emeric Pressburger, Tommy Thompson, Hans Wilhelm; LP: Douglas Wakefield, Paddy Browne, Jack Allen.

Stars Look Down, The (part)
D: Carol Reed; W: A. Coppel, A.J. Cronin (also novel), J.B. Williams; P: Michael Redgrave, Margaret Lockwood, Emlyn Williams.

Closed to film production during the Second World War

1946

London Town
D/P: Wesley Ruggles; W: Val Guest (additional dialogue), Siegfried Herzig, Elliot Paul, Wesley Ruggles (story); LP: Sid Field, Greta Gynt, Petula Clark, Kay Kendall.

Piccadilly Incident (W.H./Shepperton)
D: Herbert Wilcox; W: Vivian Ellis, Nicholas Phipps, Florence Tranter (novel); P: George Maynard, Herbert Wilcox; LP: Anna Neagle, Michael Wilding.

Shop at Sly Corner, The (W.H.)
D/P: George King; W: Reginald Long, Edward Percy, Katherine Strueby; LP: Oskar Homolka, Derek Farr, Muriel Pavlow.

While the Sun Shines (W.H.)
D: Anthony Asquith; W: Anatole de Grunwald, Terence Rattigan; P: Anatole de Grunwald; LP: Barbara White, Margaret Rutherford, Joyce Grenfell, Ronald Squire.

White Cradle Inn (W.H.)
D: Harold French; W: Basil Mason, Lesley Storm; P: A.E. Hardman, Ivor McLaren, Mary Pickford; LP: Ian Hunter, Michael Rennie, Anne-Marie Blanc.

1947

An Ideal Husband
D/P: Alexander Korda; W: Lajos Biró, Oscar Wilde (play); LP: Paulette Godard, Michael Wilding, Diana Wynyard.

Bonnie Prince Charlie (W.H./Shepperton)
D: Anthony Kimmins; W: Clemence Dane; P: Edward Black; LP: David Niven, Margaret Leighton, Jack Hawkins, Finlay Currie.

Courtneys of Curzon Street, The
D: Herbert Wilcox; W: Nicholas Phipps, Florence Tranter (story); P: George Maynard, Herbert Wilcox; LP: Anna Neagle, Michael Wilding.

Man About the House, A
D: Leslie Arliss; W: Leslie Arliss, John Perry (novel), J.B. Williams, Francis Brett Young (novel); P: Edward Black; LP: Margaret Johnston, Dulcie Gray, Kieron Moore.

Mine Own Executioner (W.H.)
D: Anthony Kimmins; W: Nigel Balchin; P: Anthony Kimmins, Jack Kitchen; LP: Burgess Meredith, Dulcie Gray, Kieron Moore.

1948

Anna Karenina (W.H./Shepperton)
D: Julien Duvivier; W: Jean Anouilh, Julien Duvivier, Guy Morgan, Leo Tolstoy (novel); P: Alexander Korda; LP:Vivien Leigh, Ralph Richardson, Kieron Moore.

Call of the Blood
D: John Clements/Ladislau Vajda; W: John Clements, Robert Hichens (novel), Basil Mason, Ákos Tolnay; P: Steven Pallos, John Stafford; LP: Kay Hammond, John Clements.

Fallen Idol, The (W.H. / Shepperton)
D/P: Carol Reed; W: Graham Greene, Lesley Storm (additional dialogue), William Templeton (additional dialogue); LP: Ralph Richardson, Michele Morgan, Bobby Henrey.

Night Beat (W.H.)
D/P: Harold Huth; W: Guy Morgan, T.J. Morrison, T.J. Westerby; LP: Anne Crawford, Michael Horden, Sid James.

Spring in Park Lane
D/P: Herbert Wilcox; W: Alice Duer Miller (book – *Come Out of the Kitchen*), Nicholas Phipps; LP: Anna Neagle, Michael Wilding, Tom Walls.

Winslow Boy, The (W.H./Shepperton)
D: Anthony Asquith; W: Anatole de Grunwald, Terence Rattigan (also play); P: Anatole de Grunwald; LP: Robert Donat, Cedric Hardwicke, Margaret Leighton, Kathleen Harrison.

1949

Britannia Mews
D: Jean Negulesco; W: Margery Sharp (novel), Ring Lardner Jr; P: William Perlberg; LP: Dana Andrews, Maureen O'Hara, Sybil Thorndike, Diana Hart.

Elizabeth of Ladymead
D/P: Herbert Wilcox; W: Frank Harvey (play), Nicholas Phipps; LP: Anna Neagle, Hugh Williams.

I Was a Male War Bride (W.H./Shepperton)
D: Howard Hawks; W: Henri Rochard (story), Charles Lederer, Leonard Spigelgass, Hagar Wilde; P: Sol C. Siegel; LP: Cary Grant, Ann Sheridan.

Last Days of Dolwyn, The (W.H.)
D/W: Emlyn Williams; P: Anatole de Grunwald; LP: Edith Evans, Emlyn Williams, Richard Burton.

Saints and Sinners (W.H.)
D/P: Leslie Arliss; W: Leslie Arliss, Paul Vincent Carroll; LP: Kieron Moore, Christine Norden.

Small Back Room, The (W.H.)
D: Michael Powell; W: Nigel Balchin (novel), Michael Powell, Emeric Pressburger; P: Michael Powell, Emeric Pressburger; LP: David Farrar, Katheen Byron, Jack Hawkins.

That Dangerous Age
D/P: Gregory Ratoff; W: Gene Markey, Illa Sugutchoff (play); LP: Ronald Adam, Elizabeth Allan, Peggy Cummins.

Third Man, The (W.H./Shepperton)
D: Carol Reed; W: Graham Greene (story), Alexander Korda (story), Graham Greene (screenplay); P: Carol Reed, Alexander Korda, David O. Selznick; LP: Orson Welles, Joseph Cotton, Alida Valli, Trevor Howard.

1950

Angel With the Trumpet, The
D: Anthony Bushell; W: Clemence Dane, Karl Hartl, Ernst Lothar (novel), Franz Tassié; P: Karl Hartl; LP: Eileen Herlie, Basil Sydney, Oskar Weiner.

Black Rose, The
D: Henry Hathaway; W: Thomas B. Costain (novel), Talbot Jennings; P: Louis D. Lighton; LP: Tyrone Power, Orson Welles, Jack Hawkins; Cecile Aubrey, Michael Rennie.

Circle of Danger (W.H./Shepperton)
D: Jacques Tourneur; W: Philip MacDonald; P: Joan Harrison, David E. Rose, John R. Sloan; LP: Ray Milland, Patricia Roc, Marius Goring.

Cure for Love (W.H.)
D/P: Robert Donat; W: Robert Donat, Albert Fennell, Walter Greenwood (play), Alexander Shaw; LP: Robert Donat, Renee Asherton, Thora Hird, Dora Bryan.

Curtain Up (W.H.)
D: Ralph Smart; W: Jack Davies, Philip King (play), Michael Pertwee; P: Robert Garrett; LP: Robert Morley, Margaret Rutherford, Kay Kendall.

Elusive Pimpernel, The
D/P/W: Michael Powell, Emeric Pressburger; LP: David Niven, Margaret Leighton, Cyril Cusack, Jack Hawkins.

Flesh & Blood
D: Anthony Kimmins; W: James Bridie (play – *A Sleeping Clergyman*), Anatole de Grunwald; P: Anatole de Grunwald; LP: Richard Todd, Glynis Johns, Joan Greenwood.

Gone to Earth
D: Michael Powell; W: Mary Webb (novel), Michael Powell, Emeric Pressburger; P: Michael Powell and Emeric Pressburger; LP: Jennifer Jones, David Farrar, Cyril Cusack, Sybil Thorndyke.

Happiest Days of Your Life, The (W.H. – part)
D: Frank Launder; W: John Dighton (play), Frank Launder; P: Sidney Gilliat, Stephen Harrison, Frank Launder, Mario Zampi; LP: Alastair Sim, Margaret Rutherford, Joyce Grenfell, Guy Middleton.

Into the Blue (W.H.)
D: Herbert Wilcox; W: Pamela Bower, Nicholas Phipps, Donald Taylor; P: Herbert Wilcox, Michael Wilding; LP: Michael Wilding, Constance Cummings.

Lost Hours, The (W.H.)
D: David MacDonald; W: Robert S. Baker (story), Steve Fisher, John Gilling, Carl Nystrom (story); P: Robert S. Baker, Monty Berman; LP: Mark Stevens, Jean Kent, John Bentley.

Mudlark, The
D: Jean Negulesco; W: Theodore Bonnet (novel), Nunnally Johnson; P: Nunnally Johnson; LP: Irene Dunn, Alec Guinness, Andrew Ray.

My Daughter Joy
D/P: Gregory Ratoff; W: Irene Nemirowsky (novel), William Rose, Robert Thoeren; LP: Edward G. Robinson, Peggy Cummins, Richard Greene.

Night and the City
D: Jules Dassin; W: Austin Dempster, Jo Eisinger, Gerald Kersh (novel); P: Samuel G. Engel;
LP: Richard Widmark, Gene Tierney, Googie Withers.

Seven Days to Noon
D: John Boulting; W: James Bernard (story), Roy Boulting, Paul Dehn (story), Frank
Harvey; P: Roy Boulting; LP: Barry Jones, André Morrell, Hugh Cross.

State Secret (W.H.)
D: Sidney Gilliat; W: Sidney Gilliatt, Roy Huggins (novel); P: Sidney Gilliat, Frank
Launder; LP: Douglas Fairbanks Jr, Jack Hawkins, Glynis Johns.

Wonder Kid, The (W.H. / Shepperton)
D/P: Karl Hartl; W: Gene Markey; LP: Bobby Henrey, Elwyn Brook-Jones, Oskar Werner.

Wooden Horse, The
D: Jack Lee; W: Eric Williams; P: Ian Dalrymple; LP: Anthony Steel, David Tomlinson, Leo
Genn.

1951

African Queen, The (W.H.)*
D: John Huston; W: C.S. Forester (novel), James Agee, John Huston; P: Sam Spiegel; LP:
Humphrey Bogart, Katharine Hepburn, Robert Morley.
*Contrary to popular belief, this feature was not filmed at Shepperton. Only post
production and a very few pick-up shots were completed there – after the main cast had
left the production.

Lady Godiva Rides Again
D: Frank Launder; W: Frank Launder, Val Valentine; P: Sidney Gilliat; LP: Stanley Holloway,
Alastair Sim, Diana Dors, Joan Collins, Dennis Price, Googie Withers.

Lady with the Lamp, The
D/P: Herbert Wilcox; W: Reginald Berkeley (play), Warren Chetham Strode; LP: Felix
Aylmer, Anna Neagle, Sybil Thorndike, Michael Wilding.

Late Edwina Black, The (W.H.)
D: Maurice Elvey; W: David Evans (additional dialogue), David Evans (screenplay), Charles
Frank (screenplay); P: Ernest Gartside; LP: David Farrar, Geraldine Fitzgerald, Roland
Culver.

Pandora and the Flying Dutchman
D/W/P: Albert Lewin; P: Joseph Kaufman; LP: James Mason, Ava Gardner, Nigel Patrick.

Tales of Hoffman, The
D/P: Michael Powell, Emeric Pressburger; W: E.T.A. Hoffmann (stories), Jules Barbier
(libretto), Michael Powell, Emeric Pressburger, Dennis Arundell; LP: Moira Shearer,
Ludmilla Tcherina, Robert Helpmann.

1952

An Outcast of the Islands
D/P: Carol Reed; W: Joseph Conrad (novel), William Fairchild; LP: Ralph Richardson,
Trevor Howard, Robert Morley, Wendy Hiller, Kerima.

Beggars Opera, The
D: Peter Brook; W: Denis Cannan, Christopher Fry, John Gay; P: Laurence Olivier, Herbert
Wilcox; LP: Laurence Olivier, Dorothy Tutin, Stanley Holloway.

Circumstantial Evidence
D: Daniel Birt; W: Allan MacKinnon; P: Philip Brandon; LP: Rona Anderson, Patrick Holt.

Cry, The Beloved Country
D: Zoltan Korda; W: Alan Paton, John Howard Lawson; P: Zoltan Korda, Alan Paton; LP: Sidney Poitier, Joyce Carey, Canada Lee, Charles Carson.

Derby Day (W.H.)
D: Herbert Wilcox; W: Arthur Austen (story), John Baines; P: Maurice Cowan; LP: Anna Neagle, Michael Wilding, Googie Withers.

Gift Horse, The (W.H.)
D: Compton Bennett; W: William Fairchild, Ivan Goff (story), Hugh Hastings, Ben Roberts (story), William Rose; P: George Pitcher; LP: Trevor Howard, Richard Attenborough, Sonny Tufts.

Holly and the Ivy, The
D: George More O'Ferrall; W: Wynyard Browne, Anatole de Grunwald; P: Anatole de Grunwald; LP: Ralph Richardson, Celia Johnson, Margaret Leighton, Denholm Elliott.

Home at Seven
D: Ralph Richardson; W: Anatole de Grunwald, R.C. Sherriff; P: Maurice Cowan; LP: Ralph Richardson, Margaret Leighton, Jack Hawkins.

Mr Denning Drives North
D: Anthony Kimmins; W: Alec Coppel; P: Anthony Kimmins, Stephen Mitchell; LP: John Mills, Phyllis Calvert, Sam Wanamaker.

Sound Barrier, The
D/P: David Lean; W: Terence Rattigan; LP: Ralph Richardson, Ann Todd, Nigel Patrick.

Trent's Last Case
D/P: Herbert Wilcox; W: E.C. Bentley (novel), Pamela Bower; LP: Michael Wilding, Margaret Lockwood, Orson Welles.

Twice Upon a Time (W.H./Shepperton)
D/W/P: Emeric Pressburger; LP: Pat Baker, Alanna Boyce, Margaret Boyd.

Who Goes There?
D/P: Anthony Kimmins; W: John Dighton; LP: Nigel Patrick, Valerie Hobson, Peggy Cummins.

1953

Appointment in London
D: Philip Leacock; W: Robert Westerby, John Wooldridge; P: Aubrey Baring, Maxwell Setton; LP: Dirk Bogarde, Ian Hunter, Dinah Sheridan.

Beautiful Stranger
D: David Miller; W: Carl Nystrom, Robert Westerby; P: Maxwell Setton, John R. Sloan; LP: Ginger Rogers, Herbert Lom, Stanley Baker.

Captain's Paradise, The
D/P: Anthony Kimmins; W: Alec Coppel, Nicholas Phipps; LP: Alec Guinness, Yvonne de Carlo, Celia Johnson.

Folly to be Wise
D: Frank Launder; W: James Bridie, John Dighton, Frank Launder; P: Sidney Gilliat; LP: Alastair Sim, Elizabeth Allan, Roland Culver.

Intruder, The
D: Guy Hamilton; W: John Hunter, Robin Maugham, Anthony Squire; P: Ivan Foxwell; LP: Jack Hawkins, Hugh Williams, Dennis Price, George Baker.

Laughing Anne
D: Herbert Wilcox; W: Pamela Bower, Joseph Conrad (novel – *Between the Tides*); P: Herbert Wilcox, Herbert J Yates; LP: Margaret Lockwood, Forest Tucker, Ronald Shiner.

Man Between, The
D/P: Carol Reed; W: Walter Ebert (novel – *Susanne in Berlin*), Harry Kurnitz; LP: James Mason, Claire Bloom.

Moulin Rouge
D/P: John Huston; W: John Huston, Pierre La Mure (novel), Anthony Veiller; LP: Jose Ferrer, Zsa Zsa Gabor, Maureen Swanson.

Profile
D: Francis Searle; W: John Gilling, John Temple-Smith (story), Maurice Temple-Smith (play); P: John Temple-Smith, Francis Edge; LP: John Bentley, Kathleen Byron.

Red Beret, The
D: Terence Young; W: Sy Bartlett (screen adaptation), Richard Maibaum, Frank S. Nugent, Hilary St George Sanders (novel); P: Albert R. Broccoli, Irving Allen; LP: Alan Ladd, Leo Genn, Susan Stephen, Harry Andrews.

Ringer, The
D: Guy Hamilton; W: Lesley Storm, Val Valentine, Edgar Wallace (play); P: Hugh Perceval; LP: Herbert Lom, Donald Wolfit, Mai Zetterling.

Single-Handed
D: Roy Boulting; W: C.S. Forester (novel – *Brown on Resolution*), Valentine Davies; P: Frank McCarthy; LP: Jeffrey Hunter, Michael Rennie, Wendy Hiller.

Story of Gilbert and Sullivan, The
D: Sidney Gilliat; W: Leslie Baily (book – The Gilbert and Sullivan Book), William S. Gilbert (operettas), Sidney Gilliat, Vincent Korda; P: Frank Launder, Sidney Gilliat; LP: Robert Morley, Peter Finch, Dinah Sheridan, Maurice Evans.

They Who Dare
D: Lewis Milestone; W: Robert Westerby; P: Aubrey Barring, Maxwell Setting; LP: Dirk Bogarde, Eric Pohlmann, Akim Tamiroff.

1954

An Inspector Calls
D: Guy Hamilton; W: Desmond Davis, J.B. Priestley (play); P: A.D. Peters; LP: Alastair Sim, Jane Wenham, Brian Worth, Bryan Forbes.

Aunt Clara
D: Anthony Kimmins; W: Kenneth Horne, Noel Streatfield (novel); P: Anthony Kimmins, Colin Lesslie; LP: Ronald Shiner, Margaret Rutherford, A.E. Matthews.

Bang, You're Dead
D/P: Lance Comfort; W: Ernest Borneman, Guy Elmes; LP: Jack Warner, Derek Farr, Veronica Hurst.

Beat the Devil
D/P: John Huston; W: James Helvick (novel), Truman Capote, John Huston; LP: Humphrey Bogart, Jennifer Jones, Robert Morley.

Belles of St Trinians, The
D: Frank Launder; W: Sidney Gilliat, Frank Launder, Ronald Searle (also cartoons), Val Valentine; P: Frank Launder, Sidney Gilliat; LP: Alastair Sim, Joyce Grenfell, George Cole.

Colditz Story, The
D: Guy Hamilton; W: William Douglas-Home (dialogue), Ivan Foxwell, Guy Hamilton; P: Ivan Foxwell; LP: John Mills, Eric Portman, Lionel Jeffries, Ian Carmichael.

Devil Girl from Mars
D: David MacDonald; W: James Eastwood; P: Edward J. Danziger, Harry Lee Danziger; LP: Hugh McDermott, Hazel Court.

Eight O'Clock Walk
D: Lance Comfort; W: Gordon Harboard (story), Guy Morgan, Jack Roffey (story), Katherine Strueby; P: George King; LP: Richard Attenborough, Cathy O'Donnell, Derek Farr.

Green Scarf, The
D: George More O'Ferrall; W: Gordon Wellesley; P: Albert Fennell, Betram Ostrer; LP: Michael Redgrave, Ann Todd, Leo Genn.

Heart of the Matter, The
D: George More O'Ferrall; W: Ian Dalrymple, Graham Greene (novel), Lesley Storm; P: Ian Dalrymple; LP: Trevor Howard, Elizabeth Allan, Denholm Elliott.

Hobson's Choice
D/P: David Lean; W: Harold Brighouse (play), Wynyard Browne, David Lean, Norman Spencer; LP: Charles Laughton, John Mills, Brenda DeBanzie.

It's a Great Day
D: John Warrington; W: Michael Pertwee, Roland Pertwee; P: Victor Lyndon; LP: Ruth Dunning, Edward Evans, Sid James.

Josephine and Men
D: Roy Boulting; W: Nigel Balchin, Roy Boulting, Frank Harvey; P: John Boulting; LP: Glynis Johns, Jack Buchanan, Donald Sinden, Peter Finch.

Malaga
D: Richard Sale; W: Robert Westerby; P: Mike Frankovich; LP: Maureen O'Hara, Macdonald Carey, Guy Middleton.

Prince Valiant
D: Henry Hathaway; W: Hal Foster (comic), Dudley Nichols; P: Robert L. Jacks; LP: James Mason, Janet Leigh, Robert Wagner, Victor McLaglen.

Raising a Riot
D: Wendy Toye; W: Ian Dalrymple, James Matthews, Hugh Perceval; P: Ian Dalrymple, Hugh Perceval; LP: Kenneth More, Shelagh Fraser, Ronald Squire.

Teckman Mystery, The
D: Wendy Toye; W: Francis Durbridge, James Matthews; P: Josef Somlo; LP: Margaret Leighton, John Justin, Roland Culver.

1955

Carrington VC
D: Anthony Asquith; W: John Hunter; P: Teddy Baird; LP: David Niven, Margaret Leighton.

Cockleshell Heroes, The
D: José Ferrer; W: Bryan Forbes, George Kent (story), Richard Maibaum; P: Phil C Samuel; LP: José Ferrer, Trevor Howard, Dora Bryan.

Constant Husband, The
D: Sidney Gilliat; W: Sidney Gilliat, Val Valentine; P: Frank Launder, Sidney Gilliat; LP: Rex Harrison, Cecil Parker, Kay Kendall.

Deep Blue Sea, The
D/P: Anatole Litvak; W: Terence Rattigan; LP: Vivien Leigh, Kenneth More, Eric Portman, Emlyn Williams.

End of the Affair, The
D: Edward Dmytryk; W: Lenore J. Coffee; P: David Lewis; LP: Deborah Kerr, Van Johnson, John Mills.

Gentlemen Marry Brunettes
D: Richard Sale; W: Mary Loos, Richard Sale; P: Richard Sale, Robert Waterfield; LP: Jane Russell, Jeanne Craine.

Geordie
D: Frank Launder; W/P: Frank Launder, Sidney Gilliat; LP: Alastair Sim, Bill Travers.

Good Die Young, The
D: Lewis Gilbert; W: Vernon Harris, Lewis Gilbert; P: Jack Clayton; LP: Laurence Harvey, Richard Basehart, Joan Collins.

I am a Camera
D: Henry Cornelius; W: John Collier; P: Jack Clayton; LP: Julie Harris, Laurence Harvey, Shelley Winters.

Kid for Two Farthings, A
D/P: Carol Reed; W: Wolf Mankowitz; LP: Celia Johnson, Diana Dors, David Kossoff, Joe Robinson.

Man Who Loved Redheads, The
D: Harold French; W: Terence Rattigan; P: Josef Somlo; LP: Moira Shearer, John Justin, Gladys Cooper.

Private's Progress
D: John Boulting; W: John Boulting, Frank Harvey; P: Roy Boulting; LP: Richard Attenborough, Dennis Price, Ian Carmichael, Terry-Thomas.

Storm Over the Nile (part)
D: Zoltan Korda, Terence Young; W: R.C. Sherriff; P: Zoltan Korda; LP: Anthony Steel, Laurence Harvey, Mary Ure, Ian Carmichael.

Summer Madness
D: David Lean; W: H.E. Bates, David Lean; P: Ilya Lopert; LP: Katharine Hepburn, Rossano Brazzi.

They Can't Hang Me
D: Val Guest; W: Val Guest, Val Valentine; P: Roger Proudlock; LP: Terence Morgan, Yolande Donlan, Ursula Howells.

Three Cases of Murder
D: Wendy Toye, David Eady, George More O'Ferrall; W: Sidney Carroll ('You Killed Elizabeth' segment), Ian Dalrymple ('Lord Mountdrago' segment), Brett Halliday ('You Killed Elizabeth' story), Somerset Maugham ('Lord Mountdrago' story), Roderick Wilkinson ('In the Picture' story), Donald B. Wilson; LP: Orson Welles, John Gregson, Elizabeth Sellers, Alan Badel, Zena Marshall.

1956

Admirable Crichton, The
D: Lewis Gilbert; W: Vernon Harris, Lewis Gilbert; P: Ian Dalrymple; LP: Kenneth More, Diane Cilento, Cecil Parker, Sally Ann Howes.

Baby and the Battleship, The
D: Jay Lewis; W: Richard De Roy, Bryan Forbes (additional scenes and dialogue), Gilbert Hackforth-Jones, Jay Lewis; P: Anthony Darnborough, Jay Lewis; LP: John Mills, Richard Attenborough, Michael Hordern.

Charley Moon
D: Guy Hamilton; W: Leslie Bricusse, John Cresswell; P: Colin Lesslie; LP: Max Bygraves, Dennis Price, Shirley Eaton.

Dry Rot
D: Maurice Elvey; W: John Roy Chapman; P: Jack Clayton; LP: Ronald Shiner, Brian Rix, Peggy Mount.

Extra Day, The
D/W: William Fairchild; P: E.M. Smedley-Aston; LP: George Baker, Richard Basehart, Jill Bennett.

Green Man, The
D: Robert Day; W/P: Frank Launder, Sidney Gilliat; LP: Alastair Sim, George Cole, Terry-Thomas.

Hill in Korea, A
D: Julian Amyes; W: Ian Dalrymple, Ronald Spencer, Anthony Squire; P: Anthony Squire; LP: George Baker, Harry Andrews, Stanley Baker, Robert Shaw, Michael Caine.

Iron Petticoat, The
D: Ralph Thomas; W: Ben Hecht, Harry Saltzman; P: Betty Box, Harry Saltzman; LP: Bob Hope, Katharine Hepburn, Robert Helpmann.

Loser Takes All
D: Ken Annakin; W: Graham Greene; P: John Stafford; LP: Glynis Johns, Rossano Brazzi, Robert Morley.

Manuela
D: Guy Hamilton; W: Guy Hamilton, Ivan Foxwell, William Woods; P: Ivan Foxwell; LP: Trevor Howerd, Elsa Martinelli, Donald Pleasance.

March Hare
D: George More O'Ferrall; W: Paul Vincent Carroll, Allan MacKinnon, Gordon Wellesley; P: Albert Fennell, Bertram Ostrer; LP: Peggy Cummins, Cyril Cusack, Terence Morgan.

My Teenage Daughter
D/P: Herbert Wilcox; W: Felicity Douglas; LP: Anna Neagle, Sylvia Syms, Wilfrid Hyde-White.

Passionate Stranger, A
D: Muriel Box; W: Muriel Box, Sydney Box; P: Peter Rogers; LP: Margaret Leighton, Ralph Richarsdson.

Richard III
D/P: Laurence Olivier; W: Colley Cibber (textual alterations), David Garrick (textual alterations for his production of the play), William Shakespeare; LP: Laurence Olivier, Cedric Hardwicke, Ralph Richardson, John Gielgud.

Sailor Beware
D: Gordon Parry; W: Falkland L. Cary, Philip King; P: Jack Clayton; LP: Peggy Mount, Cyril Smith, Shirley Eaton, Ronald Lewis.
Secret Tent, The
D: Don Chaffey; W: Jan Read; P: Frank Bevis, Nat Miller; LP: Donald Gray, Andree Melly, Jean Anderson.
Three Men in a Boat
D: Ken Annakin; W: Hubert Gregg, Vernon Harris, Jerome K. Jerome (novel); P: Jack Clayton; LP: Jimmy Edwards, David Tomlinson, Laurence Harvey, Shirley Eaton.

1957

Behind the Mask
D: Brian Desmond Hurst; W: John Hunter; P: Sergei Nolbandov, Josef Somlo; LP: Michael Redgrave, Tony Britton, Venessa Redgrave.
Birthday Present, The
D: Pat Jackson; W/P: Jack Whittingham; LP: Tony Britton, Sylvia Syms, Jack Watling.
Blue Murder at St Trinian's
D: Frank Launder; W: Sidney Gilliat, Frank Launder, Val Valentine; P: Frank Launder, Sidney Gilliat; LP: Terry-Thomas, Joyce Grenfell, Joyce Grenfell, Lionel Jeffries.
Bonjour Tristesse
D/P: Otto Preminger; W: Arthur Laurents; LP: Deborah Kerr, David Niven, Jean Seberg.
Fortune is a Woman
D: Sidney Gilliat; W: Sidney Gilliat, Frank Launder, Val Valentine; P: Sidney Gilliat, Frank Launder; LP: Jack Hawkins, Arlene Dahl, Dennis Price.
Happy is the Bride
D: Roy Boulting; W: Roy Boulting, Jeffrey Dell; P: Paul Soskin; LP: Ian Carmichael, Janette Scott, Cecil Parker, Terry-Thomas, Joyce Grenfell.
King in New York, A
D/W/P: Charles Chaplin; LP: Charles Chaplin, Maxine Audley, Jerry Desmonde.
Long Haul, The
D/W: Ken Hughes; P: Maxwell Setton; LP: Victor Mature, Gene Anderson, Diana Dors.
Lucky Jim
D: John Boulting, Roy Boulting; W: Patrick Campbell, Jeffrey Dell; P: Roy Boulting; LP: Ian Carmichael, Terry-Thomas, Jean Anderson.
Saint Joan
D/P: Otto Preminger; W: Graham Greene; LP: Richard Widmark, Richard Todd, Anton Walbrook, John Gielgud.
Second Fiddle
D: Maurice Elvey; W: Mary Cathcart Borer (story), Robert Dunbar (also story), Allan MacKinnon; P: Robert Dunbar; LP: Adrienne Cori, Thorley Walters, Richard Wattis.
Seven Waves Away
D/W: Richard Sale; P: John R. Sloan; LP: Tyrone Power, Mai Zetterling, Stephen Boyd.
Smallest Show on Earth, The
D: Basil Dearden; W: John Eldridge, William Rose (also story); P: Sidney Gilliat, Frank Launder, Michael Relph; LP: Virginia McKenna, Bill Travers, Peter Sellers, Margaret Rutherford.

Story of Esther Costello, The
D: David Miller; W: Charles Kaufman; P: Jack Clayton, David Miller; LP: Joan Crawford, Rossano Brazzi, Fay Compton.

Town on Trial
D: John Guillerman; W: Ken Hughes, Robert Westerby; P: Maxwell Setton; LP: Charles Coburn, John Mills, Barbara Bates, Derek Farr.

1958

Carlton-Browne of the FO
D: Roy Boulting; W: Roy Boulting, Jeffrey Dell; P: John Boulting; LP: Terry-Thomas, Peter Sellers, Thorley Walters.

Danger Within
D: Don Chaffey; W: Bryan Forbes, Michael Gilbert, Frank Harvey; P: Colin Lesslie; LP: Richard Todd, Bernard Lee, Michael Wilding, Richard Attenborough.

Horse's Mouth, The
D: Ronald Neame; W: Alec Guinness; P: John Bryan, Ronald Neame; LP: Alec Guinness, Kay Walsh, Renee Houston.

Jack the Ripper
D: Robert S. Baker; W: Jimmy Sangster; P: Robert S. Baker, Monty Berman; LP: Lee Patterson, Eddie Byrne, John Le Mesurier.

Killers of Kilimanjaro
D: Richard Thorpe; W: Earl Felton, John Gilling, Cyril Hume, Richard Maibaum; P: Irving Allan, Albert R. Broccoli, John R. Sloan; LP: Robert Taylor, Anthony Newley, Anne Aubrey.

Law & Disorder
D: Charles Crichton; W: T.E.B. Clarke, Patrick Campbell, Vivienne Knight; P: Paul Soskin; LP: Michael Redgrave, Robert Morley, Joan Hickson, Lionel Jeffries.

Life is a Circus
D: Val Guest; W: Val Guest, Len Heath, John Warren; P: E.M. Smedley-Aston; LP: Bud Flanagan, Chesney Allen, Shirley Eaton.

Man Upstairs, The
D: Don Chaffey; W: Alun Falconer; P: Robert Dunbar; LP: Richard Attenborough, Bernard Lee, Donald Houston, Virginia Maskell.

Orders to Kill
D: Anthony Asquith; W: Paul Dehn, George St George; P: Anthony Havelock-Allan; LP: Eddie Albert, Paul Massey, Lillian Gish.

Silent Enemy, The
D/W: William Fairchild; P: Betram Ostrer; LP: Michael Craig, Laurence Harvey, Dawn Addams.

Tread Softly Stranger
D: Gordon Parry; W: George Minter, Denis O'Dell; P: Denis O'Dell; LP: Diana Dors, George Baker, Terence Morgan.

Truth About Women, The
D: Muriel Box; W: Muriel Box, Sydney Box; P: Sydney Box; LP: Laurence Harvey, Julie Harris, Diane Cilento, Eva Gabor, Mai Zetterling.

Whole Truth, The

D: John Guillerman; W: Jonathan Latimer; P: Jack Clayton; LP: Stewart Granger, Donna Reed, George Sanders.

1959

Angry Silence, The

D: Guy Green; W: Michael Craig, Bryan Forbes, Richard Gregson; P: Richard Attenborough, Bryan Fobes; LP: Richard Attenborough, Pier Angeli, Michael Craig, Bernard Lee.

Friends and Neighbours

D: Gordon Parry; W: Talbot Rothwell, Val Valentine; P: Bertram Ostrer; LP: Arthur Askey, Reginald Beckwith, Jess Conrad.

Idle on Parade

D: John Gilling; W: John Antrobus; P: Harold Huth; LP: William Bendix, Anthony Newley, Lionel Jeffries, Sid James.

I'm All Right Jack

D: John Boulting; W: John Boulting, Frank Harvey; P: Roy Boulting; LP: Peter Sellers, Terry-Thomas, Richard Attenborough, Ian Carmichael, Dennis Price.

Jetstorm

D: Cy Raker Endfield; W: Cy Raker Endfield, Sigmund Miller; P: Steven Pallos; LP: Richard Attenborough, Stanley Baker, Diane Cilento.

Left, Right and Centre

D: Sidney Gilliat; W: Sidney Gilliat, Val Valentine; P: Frank Launder; LP: Ian Carmichael, Alastair Sim, Patricia Bredin.

Model for Murder, A

D: Terry Bishop; W: Terry Bishop, Robert Dunbar; P: Robert Dunbar, Jack Parsons; LP: Keith Andes, Hazel Court, Michael Gough.

Mouse That Roared, The

D: Jack Arnold; W: Roger MacDougall, Stanley Mann; P: Carl Foreman, Jon Pennington, Walter Shenson; LP: Peter Sellers, Jean Seberg, William Hartnell.

Mummy, The (part)

D: Terence Fisher; W: Jimmy Sangster; P: Michael Carreras; LP: Peter Cushing, Christopher Lee, Yvonne Furneaux.

Next to No Time

D/W: Henry Cornelius; P: Albert Fennell; LP: Kenneth More, Betsy Drake.

Our Man in Havana

D/P: Carol Reed; W: Graham Greene; LP: Alec Guinness, Burl Ives, Maureen O'Hara.

Room at the Top

D: Jack Clayton; W: Neil Paterson; P: John Woolf, James Woolf; LP: Simone Signoret, Laurence Harvey, Donald Wolfit, Donald Houston.

Subway in the Sky

D: Muriel Box; W: Jack Andrews; P: Sydney Box, Patrick Filmer-Sankey, John Temple-Smith; LP: Van Johnson, Hildegard Knef, Cec Linder.

Suddenly Last Summer

D: Joseph L. Mankiewicz; W: Gore Vidal, Tennessee Williams; P: Sam Spiegel; LP: Elizabeth Taylor, Katharine Hepburn, Montgomery Clift.

Tarzan's Greatest Adventure
D: John Guillerman; W: Berne Giler, John Guillermin; P: Harvey Hayutin, Sy Weintraub; LP: Gordon Scott, Anthony Qualye, Sean Connery.

Third Man, The (television series)
Series One was produced at Shepperton, comprising thirty-nine thirty-minute episodes in total.
D: John Ainsworth, Julian Amyes, Anthony Bushell, Paul Henreid, Arthur Hiller, Robert M. Leeds, Iain MacCormick, David Orrick McDearmon, Cliff Owen, Paul Stanley; W: various; P: Bernard Coote, Leslie Gilliat; LP: Michael Rennie, Jonathan Harris, Rupert Davies.

1960

City of the Dead, The
D: John Moxey; W: George Baxt, Milton Subotsky; P: Max Rosenberg, Milton Subotsky, Donald Taylor; LP: Patricia Jessel, Dennis Lotis, Christopher Lee.

Cone of Silence
D: Charles Frend; W: Jeffrey Dell, Robert Westerby; P: Aubrey Baring; LP: Michael Craig, Elizabeth Seal, Peter Cushing, Bernard Lee.

Dead Lucky
D: Montgomery Tully; W: Maurice Harrison, Sidney Nelson; P: Ralph Bond, Robert Dunbar; LP: Vincent Ball, Betty McDowall, John LeMesurier.

Entertainer, The
D: Tony Richardson; W: Nigel Kneale, John Osborne (also play); P: Harry Saltzman; LP: Laurence Olivier, Brenda DeBanzie, Roger Livesey, Joan Plowright.

Expresso Bongo
D/P: Val Guest; W: Wolf Mankowicz; LP: Laurence Harvey, Sylvia Syms, Cliff Richard, Yolande Donlan.

Faces in the Dark
D: David Eady; W: Ephraim Kogan, John Tully; P: Jon Penington; LP: John Gregson, Mai Zetterling, John Ireland, Tony Wright.

Flesh and the Fiends, The
D: John Gilling; W: John Gilling, Leo Griffiths; P: Robert S. Baker, Monty Berman; LP: Peter Cushing, June Laverick, Donald Pleasance.

French Mistress, A
D/W/P: Roy Boulting; LP: Ian Bannen, Robert Bruce, Jeremy Bulloch, Michael Crawford.

Grass is Greener, The
D/P: Stanley Donen; W: Hugh Williams, Margaret Williams; LP: Cary Grant, Deborah Kerr, Robert Mitcham.

Greengage Summer, The
D: Lewis Gilbert; W: Rumer Godden (also novel), Howard Koch; P: Victor Saville, Edward Small; LP: Kenneth More, Susannah York.

Greyfriar's Bobby
D: Don Chaffey; W: Robert Westerby; P: Walt Disney, Hugh Attwooll; LP: Donald Crisp, Laurence Naismith, Duncan Macrae.

Guns of Navarone, The
D: J. Lee-Thompson; W/P: Carl Foreman; LP: Gregory Peck, David Niven, Anthony Quayle, Stanley Baker, Anthony Quinn.

Hands of Orlac, The
D: Edmond T. Greville; W: John Baines, Edmond T. Gréville; P: Steven Pallos, Donald Taylor; LP: Christopher Lee, Mel Ferrer.

Horsemasters, The
D: William Fairchild; W: William Fairchild, Ted Willis; P: Walt Disney, Hugh Attwooll; LP: Janet Munro, Tony Britton, Donald Pleasance.

Mysterious Island
D: Cy Raker Endfield; W: John Prebble, Daniel B. Ullman, Crane Wilbur; P: Charles H. Schneer; LP: Michael Craig, Joan Greenwood, Herbert Lom.

Nearly a Nasty Accident
D: Don Chaffey; W: Jack Davies, Wally Veevers, Hugh Woodhouse; P: Betram Ostrer; LP: Jimmy Edwards, Kenneth Connor, Shirley Eaton.

Night We Got the Bird, The
D: Darcy Conyers; W: Darcy Conyers, Ray Cooney, Tony Hilton; P: Darcy Conyers, Brian Rix; LP: Brian Rix, Dora Bryan, Ronald Shiner.

Offbeat
D: Cliff Owen; W: Peter Barnes; P: E.M. Smedley-Aston; LP: William Sylvester, Mai Zetterling, Anthony Dawson.

Pure Hell at St Trinian's
D: Frank Launder; W: Frank Launder, Sydney Gilliat, Val Valentine; P: Frank Launder, Sidney Gilliat; LP: George Cole, Joyce Grenfell, Cecil Parker.

Queen's Guards, The
D/P: Michael Powell; W: Simon Harcourt-Smith, Roger Milner; LP: Daniel Massey, Raymond Massey, Robert Stephens, Ursula Johns.

Spare the Road
D: Leslie Norman; W: John Cresswell; P: Victor Lyndon; LP: Max Bygraves, Geoffrey Keen, Donald Pleasance.

Surprise Package
D/P: Stanley Donen; W: Art Buchwald, Harry Kurnitz; LP: Yul Brynner, Mitzi Gaynor.

Suspect
D/P: John Boulting, Roy Boulting; W: Nigel Balchin (also novel – *A Sort of Traitor*), Roy Boulting, Jeffrey Dell; LP: Tony Britton, Virginia Maskell, Ian Bannen, Peter Cushing.

Tarzan the Magnificent
D: Robert Day; W: Robert Day, Berne Giler; P: Sy Weintraub; LP: Gordon Scott, Jock Mahoney, Lionel Jeffries.

Trunk, The
D/W: Donovan Winter; P: Lawrence Huntington; LP: Philip Carey, Dermot Walsh, Julia Arnall.

Tunes of Glory
D: Ronald Neame; W: James Kennaway; P: Colin Lesslie; LP: Alec Guinness, John Mills, Dennis Price, Kay Walsh, Susannah York.

Two-Way Stretch
D: Robert Day; W: Len Heath, John Warren; P: E.M. Smedley-Aston; LP: Peter Sellers, Lionel Jeffries, David Lodge, Bernard Cribbins.

Unstoppable Man, The
D: Terry Bishop; W: Terry Bishop, Alun Falconer, Paddy Manning; P: John Pellatt; LP: Marius Goring, Harry H Corbett, Lois Maxwell.

Weekend with Lulu, A
D: John Paddy Carstairs; W: Ted Lloyd, Val Valentine; P: Ted Lloyd; LP: Bob Monkhouse, Leslie Phillips, Shirley Eaton.

Yesterday's Enemy
D: Val Guest; W: Peter R. Newman; P: Michael Carreras; LP: Stanley Baker, Leo McKern, Guy Rolfe, Gordon Jackson.

1961

Barber of Stamford Hill, The
D: Casper Wrede; W: Ronald Harwood; P: Ben Arbeid; LP: John Bennett, Megs Jenkins, Maxwell Shaw.

Day of the Triffids, The
D: Steve Sekely; W: Philip Yordan, John Wyndham (novel); P: George Pitcher; LP: Howard Keel, Nicole Maurey, Kieran Moore, Janette Scott.

Day the Earth Caught Fire, The
D/P: Val Guest; W: Wolf Mankowitz, Val Guest; LP: Edward Judd, Janet Munro, Leo McKern, Michael Goodliffe.

Dentist on the Job
D: C.M. Pennington-Richards; W: Hazel Adair, Hugh Woodhouse, Bob Monkhouse; P: Betram Ostrer; LP: Bob Monkhouse, Kenneth Connor, Shirley Eaton, Charles Hawtrey.

Foxhole in Cairo
D: John Moxey; W: Leonard Mosley (also novel); P: Steven Pallos, Donald Taylor; LP: James Robertson Justice, Adrian Hoven, Fenella Fielding.

Frightened City, The
D/P: John Lemont; W: Leigh Vance; LP: Herbert Lom, Sean Connery, John Gregson, Alfred Marks, Yvonne Romain.

Girl on the Boat
D: Henry Kaplan; W: Reuben Ship, P.G. Wodehouse (novel); P: John Bryan; LP: Norman Wisdom, Millicent Martin, Richard Briers.

Golden Rabbit, The
D: David MacDonald; W: Gerald Kelsey, Dick Sharples; P: Barry Delmaine, Jack O. Lamont; LP: Timothy Bateson, Maureen Beck, Dick Bentley.

Hair of the Dog
D: Terry Bishop; W: Tony Hawes, John O'Gorman (story); LP: Alison Bailey, Reginald Beckwith, Harold Goodman.

HMS Defiant
D: Lewis Gilbert, Frank Tilsley (novel), Nigel Kneale, Edmund H. North; P: John Brabourne; LP: Alec Guinness, Dirk Bogarde, Maurice Denhan, Nigel Stock.

Information Received
D: Robert Lynn; W: Berkley Mather (story), Paul Ryder; P: John Clein, George Maynard; LP: Sabine Sesslemann, William Sylvester.

Innocents, The

D/P: Jack Clayton; W: William Archibald, Truman Capote; LP: Deborah Kerr, Meg Jenkins, Pamela Franklyn, Michael Redgrave.

It's Trad, Dad

D: Dick Lester; W: Milton Subotsky; P: Max Rosenberg, Milton Subotsky; LP: Helen Shapiro, Craig Douglas, Acker Bilk, Arthur Mullard.

Kind of Loving, A

D: John Schlesinger; W: Keith Waterhouse, Willis Hall, Stan Barstow (novel); P: Joe Janni; LP: Alan Bates, Thora Hird, June Ritchie.

Kitchen, The

D: James Hill; W: Sidney Cole, Arnold Wesker (play); P: Sidney Cole; LP: Carl Mohner, Mary Yeomens, Tom Bell.

Man of the World (television series)

D: Harry Booth, Anthony Bushell, Charles Crichton, Charles Frend, David Greene, John Llewellyn Moxey, Jeremy Summers; W: Ian Stuart Black; P: Harry Fine; LP: Craig Stevens, Tracy Reed, Graham Stark.

Nothing Barred

D: Darcy Conyers; W: John Chapman; P: Brian Rix, Darcy Conyers, LP: Brian Rix, Leo Franklyn, Naunton Wayne.

On the Fiddle

D: Cyril Frankel; W: Harold Buckman, R.F. Delderfield (novel); P: S. Benjamin Fisz; LP: Alfred Lynch, Sean Connery, Cecil Parker, Wilfrid Hyde-White, Kathleen Harrison.

Only Two Can Play

D: Sidney Gilliat; W: Bryan Forbes, Kinsley Amis (novel); P: Leslie Gilliat; LP: Peter Sellers, Mai Zetterling, Kenneth Griffith.

Over the Odds

D: Michael Forlong; W: Rex Howard Arundal (play), Ernest Player; P: Alec C. Snowden; LP: Marjorie Rhodes, Glenn Melvyn, Cyril Smith, Esma Cannon.

Painted Smile, The

D: Lance Comfort; W: Jane Baker, Pip Baker; P: Tom Blakeley; LP: Liz Fraser, Kenneth Griffith, Craig Douglas.

Prince and the Pauper, The

D: Don Chaffey; W: Mark Twain (novel), Jack Whittingham; P: Walt Disney, Hugh Attwooll; LP: Guy Williams, Laurence Naismith, Jane Asher, Nigel Green, Donald Houston, Sean Scully, Peter Butterworth.

Road to Hong Kong, The

D/P: Melvin Frank; W: Norman Panama, Melvin Frank; LP: Bob Hope, Bing Crosby, Dorothy Lamour, Joan Collins, Robert Morley.

Sentimental Agent (television series)

D: Harry Booth, John Paddy Carstairs, Harold French, Charles Frend; W: Ian Stuart Black; P: Harry Fine; LP: Carlos Thompson, Burt Kwouk, Clemence Bettany, John Turner.

Take Me Over

D: Robert Lynn; W: Dail Ambler; P: William McLeod; LP: The Temperance Seven, John Paul, John Rutland.

Two and Two Make Six

D: Freddie Francis; W/P: Monja Danischewsky; LP: George Chakiris, Janette Scott, Alfred Lynch.

Valiant, The
D: Roy Baker; W: Giorgio Capitani, Franca Caprino, Willis Hall, Robert Mallet (play – *L'Equipage au complet*), Keith Waterhouse; P: John Penington; LP: John Mills, Robert Shaw, Ettore Manni.

War Lover, The
D: Philip Leacock; W: Howard Koch, John Hersey (novel); P: Arthur Hornblow Jr; LP: Steve McQueen, Shirley Anne Field, Robert Wagner, Michael Crawford.

1962

Amorous Prawn, The
D: Anthony Kimmins; W: Anthony Kimmins (also play), Nicholas Phipps; P: Leslie Gilliat; LP: Joan Greenwood, Ian Carmichael, Cecil Parker, Dennis Price.

Billy Liar
D: John Schlesinger; W: Keith Waterhouse, Willis Hall (also play); P: Joe Janni; LP: Tom Courtenay, Julie Christie, Wilfred Pickles, Finlay Currie.

Break, The
D: Lance Comfort; W: Jane Baker, Pip Baker; P: Tom Blakeley; LP: Tony Britton, William Lucas, Sonia Dresdel.

Cool Mikado, The
D: Michael Winner; W: William S. Gilbert (operetta – *The Mikado*), Maurice Browning, Michael Winner, Lew Schwartz, Robert White; P: Harold Baim; LP: Frankie Howerd, Stubby Kaye, Mike Winters, Bernie Winters, Tommy Cooper, Dennis Price.

Danger by my Side
D: Charles Saunders; W: Ronald Liles; P: John Phillips; LP: Brandon Brady, Maureen Connell, Wally Patch.

Devil's Agent, The
D: John Paddy Carstairs; W: John Paddy Carstairs, Hans Habe (novel – *Im namen des Teufels*), Robert Westerby; P: Emmet Dalton; LP: Peter van Eyck, Marianne Koch, Christopher Lee, Billie Whitelaw.

Dock Brief, The
D: James Hill; W: John Mortimer (also play), Pierre Rouve; P: Dimitri de Grunwald; LP: Peter Sellers, Richard Attenborough, Beryl Reid.

Doomsday at Eleven
D: Theodore Zichy; W: Paul Tabori, Gordon Wellesley; P: Jack Parsons; LP: Carl Jaffe, Stanley Morgan, Alan Heywood, Jennifer Wright.

Heaven's Above
D: John Boulting; W: Frank Harvey, John Boulting; P: Roy Boulting; LP: Peter Sellers, Isabel Jeans, Cecil Parker, Ian Carmichael, Mark Eden.

Hide & Seek
D: Cy Raker Endfield; W: David Stone; P: Hal Chester; LP: Ian Carmichael, Janet Munro, Curt Jurgens, Kieron Moore.

I Could Go On Singing
D: Ronald Neame; W: Mayo Simon; P: Lawrence Turman; LP: Judy Garland, Dirk Bogarde, Jack Klugman.

King's Breakfast, The
D/W: Wendy Toye; LP: Maurice Denham, Michael Pearson, Larry Bowers, David Warner.

L-Shaped Room, The

D: Bryan Forbes; W: Bryan Forbes, Lynn Reid Banks (novel); P: Richard Attenborough, James Woolf; LP: Leslie Caron, Tom Bell, Brock Peters, Emlyn Williams.

Main Attraction, The

D: Daniel Petrie; W/P: John Patrick; LP: Pat Boone, Mai Zetterling, Yvonne Mitchell.

Mix Me A Person

D: Leslie Norman; W: Ian Dalrymple, Jack Trevor Story (novel); P: Sergei Nolbandov, Victor Saville; LP: No information

Mystery Submarine

D: C.M. Pennington-Richards; W: Hugh Woodhouse, Betram Ostrer, John Manchip White; P: Betram Ostrer; LP: Edward Judd, James Robertson Justice, Laurence Payne.

Night of the Prowler

D: Francis Searle; W: Paul Erickson; P: John Phillips; LP: Patrick Holt, Colette Wilde.

Night Without Pity

D: Theodore Zichy; W: Aubrey Cash; P: Jack Parsons; LP: Sarah Lawson, Neil McCallum.

Sammy Going South

D: Alexander Mackendrick; W: Dennis Cannan, W.H. Canaway (novel); P: Hal Mason; LP: Fergus McClelland, Edward G. Robinson, Constance Cummings, Harry H. Corbett.

Serena

D: Peter Maxwell; W: Edward Abraham, Reginald Hearne, Valerie Abraham (story); P: John Phillips; LP: Patrick Holt, Emrys Jones, Honor Blackman.

Small World of Sammy Lee, The

D/W: Ken Hughes; P: Frank Godwin; LP: Anthony Newley, Julia Foster, Robert Stephens, Wilfrid Brambell.

Station Six-Sahara

D: Seth Holt; W: Bryan Forbes, Brian Clemens; P: Victor Lyndon; LP: Carroll Baker, Ian Bannen, Peter van Eyck, Denholm Elliott.

Stolen Hours (formerly 'Summer Flight')

D: Daniel Petrie; W: Jessamyn West; P: Denis Holt; LP: Susan Hayward, Michael Craig, Diane Baker, Edward Judd.

Two Guys Abroad

D: Don Sharp; P: Ian Warren; LP: George Raft, Diane Todd, David Lawton.

Two Left Feet

D: Roy Baker; W: Roy Baker, John Hopkins, David Stuart Leslie (novel); P: Leslie Gilliat; LP: Michael Crawford, Nyree Dawn Porter, Julia Foster, David Hemmings.

Victors, The

D/P/W: Carl Foreman; LP: George Peppard, George Hamilton, Albert Finney, Melina Mercouri, Eli Wallach.

1963

A Jolly Bad Fellow

D: Don Chaffey; W: Robert Hamer; P: Donald Taylor; LP: Maxine Audley, George Benson, Joyce Carey.

Becket

D: Peter Glenville; W: Edward Anhalt; P: Hal B. Wallis; LP: Peter O'Toole, Richard Burton, Donald Wolfit, John Gielgud, Sian Phillips.

Catacombs (also known as 'The Woman Who Wouldn't Die')
D: Gordon Hessler; W: Dan Mainwaring, Jay Bennett (novel); P: Jack Parsons; LP: Gary Merrill, Neil McCallum, Georgina Cookson.

Comedy Man, The
D: Alvin Rakoff; W: Peter Yeldham, Douglas Hayes (novel); P: Jon Pennington; LP: Kenneth More, Cecil Parker, Dennis Price, Billie Whitelaw.

Dr Strangelove
D: Stanley Kubrick; W: Stanley Kubrick, Peter Southern, Terry George (also novel); P: Victor Lyndon; LP: Peter Sellers, George C. Scott, Peter Bull, Slim Pickens.

Eyes of Annie Jones, The
D: Reginald Le Borg; W: Henry Slesar (story), Louis Vittes; P: Neil McCallum, Jack Parsons; LP: Richard Conte, Francesca Annis, Joyce Carey.

First Men in the Moon
D: Nathan Juran; W: Nigel Kneale, Jan Read, H.G. Wells (novel); P: Charles Schneer; LP: Lionel Jeffries, Edward Judd, Martha Hyer.

Horror of it All, The
D: Terence Fisher; W: Ray Russell; P: Margia Dean; LP: Pat Boone, Erica Rogers, Dennis Price.

It's All Happening
D: Don Sharp; W: Leigh Vance; P: Norman Williams; LP: Tommy Steele, Angela Douglas, Michael Medwin.

A Jolly Bad Fellow
D: Don Chaffey; W: Robert Hamer, Donald Taylor, C.E. Vulliamy (novel); P: Donald Taylor; LP: Leo McKern, Janet Munro, Duncan Mcrae, Dennis Price.

The Long Ships
D: Jack Cardiff; W: Frans G. Bengtsson, Beverley Cross, Berkley Mather; P: Irving Allen; LP: Richard Widmark, Sidney Poitier, Oskar Homolka.

Lord Jim
D/W: Richard Brooks; P: Rene Dupont; LP: Peter O'Toole, James Mason, Eli Wallach, Jack Hawkins, Daliah Lavi.

Matter of Choice, A
D: Vernon Sewell; W: Paul Ryder, Vernon Sewell (story), Derren Nesbitt; P: George Maynard; LP: Anthony Steel, Jeanne Moody, Ballard Berkeley.

Psyche 59
D: Alexander Singer; W: Julian Halevy, Francoise de Ligneris (novel); P: Philip Hazelton; LP: Patricia Neal, Curt Jurgens, Samantha Eggar.

Pumpkin Eater, The
D: Jack Clayton; W: Harold Pinter, Penelope Mortimer (novel); P: James Woolf; LP: Anne Bancroft, Peter Finch, James Mason, Maggie Smith.

Ring of Spies
D: Robert Tronson; W: Frank Launder, Peter Barnes; P: Leslie Gilliat; LP: Bernard Lee, Margaret Tyzack, David Kossoff, William Sylvester.

Saturday Night Out
D: Robert Hartford-Davis; W: Donald Ford, Derek Ford; P: Robert Hartford-Davis, Michael Klinger; LP: Bernard Lee, Heather Sears, Francesca Annis.

Servant, The
D: Joseph Losey; W: Harold Pinter, Robin Maugham (novel); P: Joseph Losey, Norman Priggen; LP: Dirk Bogarde, James Fox, Sarah Miles, Wendy Craig.

Walk a Tightrope
D: Frank Nesbitt; W: Neil McCallum, Mann Rubin; P: Jack Parsons; LP: Dan Duryea, Patricia Owens, Terence Cooper.

Yellow Teddybears, The
D: Robert Hartford-Davis; W: Derek Ford, Donald Ford; P: Robert Hartford-Davis, Michael Klinger; LP: Jill Adams, John Bonney, Victor Brooks.

1964

Allez France!
D: Robert Dhery; W: Colette Brosset, Robert Dhéry, Jean L'Hôte, Pierre Tchernia; P: Henri Diamant-Berger; LP: Pierre Tornade, Pierre Doris, Jean Richard, Catherine Sola, Mark Lester, Ronald Fraser, Diana Dors.

Amorous Adventures of Moll Flanders, The
D: Terence Young; W: Dennis Cannan, Roland Kibbee, Daniel Defoe (novel); P: Marcel Hellman; LP: Kim Novak, Richard Johnson, George Sanders, Lilli Palmer, Angela Lansbury.

Bedford Incident, The
D/P: James B. Harris; W: James Poe, Mark Rascovitch (novel); LP: Richard Widmark, Sidney Poitier, Eric Portman.

Black Torment, The
D: Robert Hartford-Davis; W: Derek Ford, Donald Ford; P: Robert Hartford-Davis, Michael Klinger, Tony Tenser; LP: John Turner, Heather Sears, Raymond Huntley.

Curse of Simba
D: Lindsay Shonteff; W: Brian Clemens, Leigh Vance; P: Richard Gordon, Kenneth Rive; LP: Bryant Haliday, Dennis Price, Lisa Daniely.

Curse of the Fly
D: Don Sharp; W: Harry Spalding; P: Robert L Lippert, Jack Parsons; LP: Carole Gray, George Baker, Brian Donlevy.

Danger Man (television series)
Series Two was produced at Shepperton – twenty-one sixty-minute episodes.
D: Charles Crichton, Don Chaffey, Robert Day, Quentin Lawrence, Philip Leacock, Peter Maxwell, Michael Truman; W: Donald Johnson, Wilfred Greatorex, Louis Marky, David Stone, Marc Brandel, Jan Read, John Roddick, Michael Pertwee, James Foster, David Weir, Philip Broadley, Malcolm Hulke, Ralph Smart, Raymond Bowers; P: Sidney Cole; LP: Patrick McGoohan.

Darling
D: John Schlesinger; W: Frederic Raphael; P: Joe Janni, Victor Lyndon; LP: Julie Christie, Dirk Bogarde, Laurence Harvey.

Do You Know This Voice?
D: Frank Nesbitt; W: Neil McCallum, Evelyn Berckman (novel); P: Jack Parsons; LP: Dan Duryea, Isa Miranda, Gwen Watford.

Dr Terror's House of Horrors
D: Freddie Francis; W: Milton Subotsky; P: Max Rosenberg, Milton Subotsky; LP: Peter Cushing, Christopher Lee, Donald Sutherland, Ursula Howells, Alan Freeman, Roy Castle.

Earth Dies Screaming, The
D: Terence Fisher; W: Harry Spalding; P: Robert L Lippert, Jack Parsons; LP: Willard Parker, Virginia Field, Dennis Price.

East of Sudan
D: Nathan Juran; W: Jud Kinberg; P: Charles Schneer; LP: Anthony Quayle, Sylvia Syms, Jenny Agutter.

Every Day's a Holiday
D: James Hill; W: James Hill, Anthony Marriott, Jeri Mattos; P: Ronald J. Kahn, Maurice J. Wilson; LP: Michael Sarne, John Leyton, Ron Moody, Liz Fraser.

Gonks Go Beat
D: Robert Hartford-Davis; W: Robert Hartford-Davis (story), Peter Newbrook (story), Jimmy Watson; P: Robert Hartford-Davis, Peter Newbrook; LP: Kenneth Connor, Frank Thornton, Terry Scott, Jerry Desmonde.

I've Gotta Horse
D: Kenneth Hume; W: Ronald Chesney, Ronald Wolfe, Larry Parnes (story), Kenneth Hume (story); P: Kenneth Hume, Larry Parnes; LP: Billy Fury, Amanda Barrie, Michael Medwin, Bill Fraser.

Joey Boy
D: Frank Launder; W: Eddie Chapman (novel), Frank Launder, Mike Watts; P: Leslie Gilliat; LP: Harry H. Corbett, Stanley Baxter, Bill Fraser, Reg Varney.

Just For You
D: Douglas Hickox; W: David Edwards; P: Ben Nisbet, Jacques de Lane Lea; LP: Peter Asher, Gordon Waller.

Khartoum (part)
D: Basil Dearden; W: Robert Ardrey; P: Julian Blaustein; LP: Charlton Heston, Laurence Olivier, Ralph Richardson, Richard Johnson.

King & Country
D: Joseph Losey; W: J.L. Hodson (story), A.E. Housman (poem – *Here Dead Lie we Because we did not Choose*), Evan Jones (screenplay), John Wilson (play – *Hamp*); P: Joseph Losey, Norman Priggen; LP: Dirk Bogarde, Tom Courtenay, Leo McKern, Barry Foster.

Night Train to Paris
D: Robert Douglas; W: Harry Spalding; P: Robert L. Lippert; LP: Leslie Nielsen, Aliza Gur, Eric Pohlmann.

Projected Man, The
D: Ian Curteis; W: John C. Cooper, Peter Bryan (story), Frank Quattrocchi; P: John Croydon, Maurice Foster; LP: Mary Peach, Norman Wooland, Derek Farr.

Rotten to the Core
D: John Boulting; W: Jeffrey Dell, Roy Boulting, John Warren, Len Heath; P: Roy Boulting; LP: Anton Rodgers, Thorley Walters, Eric Sykes, Kenneth Griffith.

Sicilians, The
D: Ernest Morris; W: Reginald Hearne, Ronald Liles; P: Ronald Liles, John J. Phillips; LP: Robert Hutton, Reginald Marsh, Ursula Howells.

Space Flight IC-1

D: Bernard Knowles; W: Harry Spalding; P: Robert L. Lippert, Jack Parsons; LP: Bill Williams, Norma West, Donald Churchill.

Tomb of Ligeia, The

D/P: Roger Corman; W: Robert Towne, Edgar Allan Poe (story); LP: Vincent Price, Elizabeth Shepherd, Richard Johnson.

Troubled Waters

D: Stanley Goulder; LP: Tab Hunter, Zena Walker, Andy Myers, Michael Goodliffe.

Witchcraft

D: Don Sharp; W: Harry Spalding; P: Jack Parsons, Robert L Lippert; LP: Jack Hedley, Lon Chaney Jr, Jill Dixon.

Young Detectives, The

D: Gilbert Gunn (no other information)

1965

Casino Royale

D: John Huston, Ken Hughes, Val Guest, Robert Parrish, Joe McGrath, Richard Talmadge; W: Ian Fleming (novel), Wolf Mankowitz, John Law, Michael Sayers, Woody Allen, Val Guest, Ben Hecht, Joseph Heller, Terry Southern, Billy Wilder, Peter Sellers; LP: Peter Sellers, David Niven, John Huston, Ursula Andress, Orson Welles, Woody Allen, Deborah Kerr.

Cul De Sac

D: Roman Polanski; W: Roman Polanski, Gerrard Brach; P: Gene Gutowski; LP: Lionel Stander, Donald Pleasance, Francoise Dorleac, Renee Houston.

Daleks: Invasion Earth 2150 A.D.

D: Gordon Flemyng; W: Milton Subotsky, David Whittaker, Terry Nation (story); P: Max Rosenberg, Milton Subotsky; LP: Peter Cushing, Bernard Cribbins, Ray Brooks, Andrew Keir.

Doctor Who and the Daleks

D: Gordon Flemyng; W: Milton Subotsky, Max Rosenberg, Terry Nation (story); P: Milton Subotsky, Max Rosenberg; LP: Peter Cushing, Roy Castle, Jennie Linden.

Drop Dead Darling

D: Ken Hughes; W: Richard Deeming (novel – *The Careful Man*), Ronald Harwood, Ken Hughes; P: Ken Hughes, Ray Stark; LP: Tony Curtis, Zsa Zsa Gabor, Lionel Jeffries.

Georgy Girl

D: Silvio Narizzano; W: Margaret Forster (also novel), Peter Nichols; P: Otto Plaschkes, Robert A. Goldston; LP: James Mason, Lynne Redgrave, Charlotte Rampling, Alan Bates.

Great St. Trinian's Train Robbery, The

D: Frank Launder; W: Frank Launder, Ivor Herbert; P: Leslie Gilliat; LP: Frankie Howerd, Dora Bryan, Reg Varney, George Cole.

House at the End of the World, The (also know as 'Die, Monster Die!')

D: Daniel Haller; W: H.P. Lovecraft (story), Jerry Sohl; P: Pat Green; LP: Boris Karloff, Nick Adams, Freda Jackson.

Life at the Top

D: Ted Kotcheff; W: Mordecai Richler; P: James Woolf; LP: Laurence Harvey, Jean Simmons, Honor Blackman, Michael Craig.

Modesty Blaise
D: Joseph Losey; W: Evan Jones, Peter O'Donnell, Jim Holdaway; P: Joe Janni; LP: Monica Vitti, Dirk Bogarde, Terence Stamp, Harry Andrews, Michael Craig.

Murder Game (The)
D: Sidney Salkow; W: Harry Spalding, Irving Yergin; P: Jack Parsons, Robert L. Lippert; LP: Ken Scott, Marla Landi, Conrad Phillips.

Night Caller (The)
D: John Gilling; W: Jim O'Connelly, Frank Crisp (novel); LP: John Saxon, Maurice Denham, Patricia Haines, Alfred Burke.

Othello
D: Stuart Burge; W: William Shakespeare; P: John Brabourne, Anthony Havelock-Allan; LP: Laurence Olivier, Maggie Smith.

Promise Her Anything
D: Arthur Hiller; W: William Peter Blatty, Arne Sultan (story), Marvin Worth (story); P: Stanley Rubin; LP: Warren Beatty, Leslie Caron, Robert Cummings, Lionel Stander.

Psychopath (The)
D: Freddie Francis; W: Robert Bloch; P: Milton Subotsky, Max Rosenberg; LP: Patrick Wymark, Margaret Johnson, John Standing.

The Return of Mr Moto
D: Ernest Morris; W: Fred Eggers; P: Robert L. Lippert, Jack Parsons; LP: Henry Silva, Terence Longdon, Sue Lloyd.

Sands of the Kalahari
D/W: Cy Raker Endfield; P: Cy Raker Endfield, Stanley Baker; LP: Stanley Baker, Stuart Whitman, Harry Andrews, Susannah York.

Skull, The
D: Freddie Francis; W: Milton Subotsky, Robert Bloch (story); P: Milton Subotsky, Max Rosenberg; LP: Peter Cushing, Christopher Lee, Patrick Wymark, Jill Bennett.

Spy Who Came in from the Cold, The (part)
D/P: Martin Ritt; W: Paul Dehn, Guy Trosper, John Le Carré (novel); LP: Richard Burton, Claire Bloom, Oskar Werner, Sam Wanamaker.

Study in Terror, A
D: James Hill; W: Donald Ford, Derek Ford, Ellery Queen (novel); P: Henry E. Lester; LP: John Neville, Donald Houston, John Fraser, Robert Morley.

1966

Anne of a Thousand Days
D: Charles Jarrott; W: John Hale, Bridget Boland, Maxwell Anderson (play); P: Hal B. Wallis; LP: Richard Burton, Genevieve Bujold, John Colicos.

Berserk! (formerly 'Circus of Blood')
D: Jim O'Connolly; W: Herman Cohen, Aben Kandel; P: Herman Cohen; LP: Joan Crawford, Diana Dors, Judy Geeson.

Calamity the Cow
D: David Eastman; W: David Eastman, Kerry Eastman; P: Ian Dalrymple; LP: John Moulder-Brown, Elizabeth Dear, Phil Collins.

Family Way, The

D: Roy Boulting; W: Bill Naughton; P: John Boulting; LP: John Mills, Marjorie Rhodes, Hywel Bennett, Hayley Mills.

Fathom

D: Leslie Martinson; W: Lorenzo Semple Jr, Larry Forrester (novel); P: John Kohn; LP: Raquel Welch, Tony Franciosa, Clive Revill, Ronald Fraser.

Half a Sixpence

D: George Sidney; W: Beverley Cross, H.G. Wells (novel – *Kipps*); P: Charles Schneer, George Sidney; LP: Tommy Steele, Julia Foster, James Villiers.

Man for All Seasons, A

D/P: Fred Zinnemann; W: Robert Bolt; LP: Paul Scofield, Wendy Hiller, Susannah York, Robert Shaw, Orson Welles.

River Rivals

D: Harry Booth; W: Michael Barnes, Harry Booth; P: Roy Simpson; LP: Darryl Read, Sally Thomsett, Renee Houston.

Spy With a Cold Nose, The

D: Daniel Petrie; W: Ray Galton, Alan Simpson; P: Robert Porter; LP: Lionel Jeffries, Laurence Harvey, Daliah Lavi, Eric Sykes.

Torture Garden

D: Freddie Francis; W: Robert Bloch; P: Max Rosenberg, Milton Subotsky; LP: Burgess Meredith, Jack Palance, Peter Cushing.

Trygon Factor, The

D: Cyril Frankel; W: Derry Quinn, Stanley Munro, Kingsley Amis; P: Ian Warren; LP: Stewart Granger, Susan Hampshire, Cathleen Nesbitt, Robert Morley.

1967

Danger Route (formerly 'The Eliminator')

D: Seth Holt; W: Meade Roberts, Andrew York (novel); P: Milton Subotsky, Max Rosenberg; LP: Richard Johnson, Diana Dors, Sylvia Syms, Carol Lynley.

Don't Raise the Bridge, Lower the River

D: Jerry Paris; W: Max Wilk; P: Walter Shenson; LP: Jerry Lewis, Terry-Thomas, Jacqueline Pearce.

Duffy (formerly 'Avec-Avec')

D: Robert Parish; W: Donald Cammell, Harry Joe Brown Jr; P: Martin Manulis; LP: James Coburn, James Mason, James Fox, Susannah York, John Alderton.

Girl on a Motorcycle

D: Jack Cardiff; W: Ronald Duncan, Andre Pieyre de Mandiargues (novel); P: William Sassoon; LP: Marianne Faithful, Alain Delon, Roger Mutton.

Great Catherine

D: Gordon Flemyng; W: Hugh Leonard, Bernard Shaw (play); P: Jules Buck; LP: Jeanne Moreau, Peter O'Toole, Zero Mostel, Jack Hawkins.

Hostile Witness

D: Ray Milland; W: Jack Roffey; P: David E Rose; LP: Ray Milland, Sylvia Syms, Felix Aylmer.

Mikado, The
D: Stuart Burge; W: William S. Gilbert; P: John Brabourne, Anthony Havelock-Allan; LP: Donald Adams, Philip Potter, John Reed.

Mrs Brown, You Have a Lovely Daughter
D: Saul Swimmer; W: Thaddeus Vane; P: Allen Klein; LP: Peter Noone and Herman's Hermits, Stanley Holloway, Mona Washbourne, Lance Percival.

Oliver!
D: Carol Reed; W: Vernon Harris, Lionel Bart (play), Charles Dickens (novel – *Oliver Twist*); P: John Woolf; LP: Ron Moody, Oliver Reed, Harry Secombe, Mark Lester.

Salt & Pepper
D: Richard Donner; W: Michael Pertwee; P: Milton Ebbins; LP: Sammy Davis Jr, Peter Lawford, Michael Bates.

1968

Adding Machine, The
D/W/P: Jerome Epstein; LP: Phyllis Diller, Milo O'Shea, Billie Whitelaw, Julian Glover.

Battle of Britain (part)
D: Guy Hamilton; W: Wilfred Greatorex, James Kennaway; P: Harry Satzman; LP: Laurence Olivier, Michael Caine, Trevor Howard, Ralph Richardson, Michael Redgrave, Susannah York.

Best House In London, The
D: Philip Saville; W: Denis Norden; P: Philip Breen, Kurt Unger; LP: David Hemmings, Joanna Pettet, George Sanders.

Birthday Party, The
D: William Friedkin; W: Harold Pinter; P: Max Rosenberg, Milton Subotsky; LP: Sidney Tafler, Patrick Magee, Robert Shaw.

Body Stealers, The (formerly 'Thin Air')
D: Gerry Levy; W: Mike St Clair, Peter Marcus; P: Tony Tenser; LP: George Sanders, Maurice Evans, Patrick Allen, Neil Connery.

File of the Golden Goose, The
D: Sam Wannamaker; W: John C. Higgins, James B. Gordon; P: David E. Rose; LP: Yul Brynner, Edward Woodward, Charles Gray.

Looking Glass War (The)
D/W: Frank R. Pierson; P: John Box; LP: Christopher Jones, Pia Degermark, Ralph Richardson, Anthony Hopkins.

Negatives
D: Peter Medak; W: Peter Everett, Roger Lowry; P: Judd Bernard; LP: Glenda Jackson, Peter McEnery, Diane Cilento, Maurice Denham.

Otley
D: Dick Clement; W: Ian LaFrenais, Dick Clement, Martin Waddell (novel); P: Bruce Cohn Curtis; LP: Tom Courtenay, Romy Schneider, Alan Badel, James Villiers.

Play Dirty
D: Andre de Tooth; W: Melvyn Bragg, Lotto Colin, George Marton (story); P: Harry Saltzman; LP: Michael Caine, Nigel Davenport, Nigel Green, Harry Andrews.

Project Z
D: Ronald Spencer (no other information)

The Reckoning

D: Jack Gold; W: Patrick Hall (novel), John McGrath; P: Ronald Shedlo; LP: Nicol Williamson, Ann Bell, Douglas Wilmer.

Romeo and Juliet

D: Franco Zeffirelli; W: Franco Brusati, Maestro D'Amico, William Shakespeare (play), Franco Zeffirelli; P: John Braborne, Anthony Havelock-Allan; LP: Leonard Whiting, Olivia Hussey, John McEnery.

Smashing Bird I Used to Know, The

D: Robert Hartford-Davis; W: John Peacock; P: Peter Newbrook; LP: Madeline Hinde, Renee Asherson, Dennis Waterman, Patrick Mower.

Till Death us do Part

D: Norman Cohen; W: Johnny Speight; P: Jon Pennington; LP: Warren Mitchell, Dandy Nicholls, Anthony Booth, Una Stubbs.

Touch of Love, A (Formerly 'The Millstone')

D: Waris Hussein; W: Margaret Drabble (also novel); P: Milton Subotsky, Max Rosenberg; LP: Sandy Dennis, Ian McKellen, Michael Coles, John Standing.

Twisted Nerve

D: Roy Boulting; W: Leo Marks, Roy Boulting; P: John Boulting; LP: Hayley Mills, Hywel Bennett, Phyllis Calvert, Billie Whitelaw.

2001: A Space Odyssey (part)

D/P: Stanley Kubrick; W: Arthur C. Clarke (also story – *The Sentinel*), Stanley Kubrick; LP: Gary Lockwood, Keir Dullea, William Sylvester.

Ugliest Girl in Town, The (television series)

Thirty twenty-minute episodes.

D: James Frawley; W: Robert Kaufman; P: Harry Ackerman; LP: Peter Kastner, Patricia Brake, Gary Marshall, Nicholas Parsons.

1969

Cromwell

D/W: Ken Hughes; P: Andrew Donally; LP: Richard Harris, Alec Guinness, Robert Morley, Dorothy Tutin.

Every Home Should Have One

D: James Clark; W: Marty Feldman, Barry Took, Denis Norden; P: Ned Sherrin; LP: Marty Feldman, Shellty Berman, Judy Cornwell, Julie Ege.

Last Grenade, The (formerly 'Grigsby')

D: Gordon Flemyng; W: Kenneth Ware, John Sherlock (novel – *The Ordeal of Major Gribsby*); P: Josef Shaftel; LP: Stanley Baker, Alex Cord, Honor Blackman, Richard Attenborough.

Loot

D: Silvio Narizzano; W: Ray Galton, Alan Simpson, Joe Orton (play); P: Arthur Lewis; LP: Richard Attenborough, Lee Remick, Hywel Bennett, Milo O'Shea.

Mind of Mr. Soames, The

D: Alan Cooke; W: John Hale, Edward Simpson, Charles Eric Maine (novel); P: Max Rosenberg, Milton Subotsky; LP: Terence Stamp, Robert Vaughn, Nigel Davenport.

Oblong Box, The

D/P: Gordon Hessler; W: Lawrence Huntington; LP: Vincent Price, Christopher Lee, Hilary Dwyer.

Promise, The
D/W: Michael Hayes; P: Anthony B. Unger, Henry T. Weinstein; LP: Ian McKellen, John Castle, Susan Macreadie, Mary Jones.

Scream and Scream Again
D: Gordon Hessler; W: Christopher Wicking, Peter Saxon (novel – *The Disorientated Man*); P: Max Rosenberg, Milton Subotsky; LP: Vincent Price, Christopher Lee, Peter Cushing, Alfred Marks.

Severed Head, A
D: Dick Clement; W: Frederic Raphael, Iris Murdoch (novel); P: Alan Ladd Jr; LP: Lee Remick, Richard Attenborough, Ian Holm, Claire Bloom.

Take a Girl Like You
D: Jonathan Miller; W: George Melly, Kinsley Amis (novel); P: Hal Chester; LP: Hayley Mills, Oliver Reed, Noel Harrison.

Three Sisters
D: Laurence Olivier; W: Moura Budberg, Chekhov (play); P: Alan Clore; LP: Laurence Olivier, Joan Plowright, Jeanne Watts.

When Dinosaurs Ruled the Earth
D: Val Guest; W: Val Guest, J.G. Ballard (story); P: Aida Young; LP: Victoria Vetri, Robin Hawdon, Patrick Allen, Patrick Holt.

1970

Cry Of The Banshee
D/P: Gordon Hessler; W: Tim Kelly, Christopher Wicking; LP: Vincent Price, Elizabeth Bergner, Patrick Mower.

Dad's Army
D: Norman Cohen; W: Jimmy Perry, David Croft; P: John R. Sloan; LP: Arthur Lowe, John LeMesurier, Clive Dunn, Ian Lavender, John Laurie, Arnold Ridley.

Day In The Death Of Joe Egg, A
D: Peter Medak; W: Peter Nichols (also play); P: David Deutsch; LP: Alan Bates, Janet Suzman, Peter Bowles, Joan Hickson.

Fright
D: Peter Collinson; W: Tudor Gates; P: Harry Fine, Michael Style; LP: Susan George, Ian Bannen, Dennis Waterman, Honor Blackman, John Gregson.

House That Dripped Blood, The
D: Peter John Duffell; W: Robert Bloch; P: Milton Subotsky, Max Rosenberg; LP: John Bennett, Christopher Lee, Peter Cushing, Denholm Elliott, Ingrid Pitt.

I, Monster
D: Stephen Weeks; W: Milton Subotsky; P: Max Rosenberg, Milton Subotsky; LP: Christopher Lee, Peter Cushing.

Macbeth
D: Roman Polanski; W: Roman Polanski, Kenneth Tynan, William Shakespeare (play); P: Andrew Braunsberg; LP: Jon Finch, Francesca Annis, Martin Shaw.

Puppet on a Chain
D: Geoffrey Reeve; W: Alistair MacLean (also novel), Don Sharp, Paul Wheeler; P: Kurt Unger; LP: Sven Bertil Taube, Barbara Parkins, Patrick Allen.

Scrooge
D: Ronald Neame; W: Leslie Bricusse, Charles Dickens (novel – *A Christmas Carol*); P: Robert H. Solo; LP: Albert Finney, Michael Medwin, Alec Guinness, Edith Evans, Kenneth More.

There's a Girl in My Soup
D: Roy Boulting; W: Terence Frisby; P: John Boulting; LP: Peter Sellers, Goldie Hawn, Tony Britton, Nicky Henson.

Wuthering Heights
D: Robert Fuest; W: Patrick Tilley; P: John Pellatt; LP: Anna Calder-Marshall, Timothy Dalton, Harry Andrews, Julian Glover.

Zee and Co.
D: Brian G. Hutton; W: Edna O'Brien; P: Alan Ladd Jr, Jay Kanter; LP: Elizabeth Taylor, Michael Caine, Susannah York.

1971

Crucible of Horror (also known as 'The Corpse')
D: Victors Ritelis; W: Olaf Pooley; P: Gabrielle Beaumont; LP: Michael Gough, Yvonne Mitchell, Sharon Gurney.

Crucible of Terror
D: Ted Hooker; W: Ted Hooker, Tom Parkinson; P: Tom Parkinson; LP: Mike Raven, James Bolam, Mary Maude.

Fun and Games
D: Ray Austin (no other information)

The Magnificent 6½
D: Peter Graham Scott (no other information)

Mary, Queen of Scots
D: Charles Jarrot; W: John Hale; P: Hal B. Wallis; LP: Vanessa Redgrave, Glenda Jackson, Patrick McGoohan, Timothy Dalton.

Psychomania
D: Don Sharp; Julian Zimet, Arnaud d'Usseau; P: Andrew Donally; LP: Nicky Henson, George Sanders, Beryl Reid, Robert Hardy.

She'll Follow You Anywhere
D: David C. Rea; W: Theo Martin, Peter Newbrook, David C. Rea; P: Peter Newbrook; LP: Keith Barron, Kenneth Cope, Richard Vernon, Mary Collinson, Madeleine Collinson.

Something to Hide
D: Alastair Reid; W: Nicholas Monsarrat (novel), Alastair Reid; P: Michael Klinger; LP: Peter Finch, Shelley Winters, Colin Blakely, Linda Hayden.

Tower of Evil (also known as 'Horror of Snape Island')
D: Jim O'Connolly; W: George Baxt (novel), Jim O'Connolly; P: Richard Gordon; LP: Bryant Haliday, Dennis Price, Jack Watson, Robin Askwith.

Who Slew Auntie Roo?
D: Curtis Harrington; W: Robert Blees, Gavin Lambert, David D. Osborn (story), Jimmy Sangster; P: Samuel Z. Arkoff, James H. Nicholson, Jimmy Sangster; LP: Shelley Winters, Mark Lester, Ralph Richardson, Lionel Jeffries.

Young Winston

D: Richard Attenborough; W: Carl Foreman; P: Richard Attenborough, Carl Foreman; LP: Simon Ward, Anthony Hopkins, Robert Shaw, Anne Bancroft, Jack Hawkins.

1972

Alice's Adventures in Wonderland

D: William Sterling; W: Lewis Carroll (novel), William Sterling; P: Derek Horne; LP: Fiona Fullerton, Michael Crawford, Ralph Richardson, Peter Sellers, Flora Robson, Dudley Moore.

And Now The Screaming Starts!

D: Roy Ward Baker; W: David Case (novel), Roger Marshall; P: Max Rosenberg, Milton Subotsky; LP: Peter Cushing, Herbert Lom, Stephanie Beecham, Ian Ogilvy.

Asphyx, The

D: Peter Newbrook; W: Christina Beers (story), Laurence Beers (story), Brian Comport; P: John Brittany; LP: Robert Stephens, Robert Powell, Jane Lapotaire.

Asylum

D: Roy Ward Baker; W: Robert Bloch; P: Max Rosenberg, Milton Subotsky; LP: Peter Cushing, Britt Ekland, Herbert Lom, Robert Powell.

Bequest to the Nation

D: James Cellen Jones; W: Terence Rattigan; P: Hal B. Wallis; LP: Glenda Jackson, Peter Finch, Michael Jayston, Anthony Quayle.

Boy Who Turned Yellow, The

D: Michael Powell; W: Emeric Pressburger; P: Drummond Challis, Emeric Pressburger; LP: Mark Dightam, Robert Eddison, Helen Weir, Brian Worth, Esmond Knight.

Creeping Flesh, The

D: Freddie Francis; W: Peter Spenceley, Jonathan Rumbold; P: Michael P. Redbourn; LP: Christopher Lee, Peter Cushing, George Benson, Lorna Heilbron.

Day of the Jackal, The

D: Fred Zinnemann; W: Frederick Forsyth (novel), Kenneth Ross; P: John Woolf; LP: Edward Fox, Michael Lonsdale, Terence Alexander, Alan Badel.

Dr Jekyll and Mr Hyde (television series)

D: David Winters; W: Robert Louis Stevenson (story), Sherman Yellen; P: Burt Rosen, David Winters; LP: Kirk Douglas, Susan George, Stanley Holloway, Michael Redgrave.

Follow Me!

D: Carol Reed; W: Peter Shaffer; P: Hal B. Wallis; LP: Mia Farrow, Topol, Michael Jayston, Annette Crosbie.

From Beyond the Grave

D: Kevin Connor; W: R. Chetwynd-Hayes (stories), Raymond Christodoulou, Robin Clarke; P: Milton Subotsky, Max Rosenberg; LP: Peter Cushing, Donald Pleasance, Ian Carmichael, Diana Dors, David Warner.

Hitler – The Last Ten Days

D: Ennio de Concini; W: Ennio De Concini, Maria Pia Fusco, Ivan Moffat, Wolfgang Reinhardt; P: Wolfgang Reinhardt; LP: Alec Guinness, Simon Ward, Adolfo Celi, Diane Cilento.

Homecoming, The
D: Peter Hall; W: Harold Pinter; P: Ely A. Landau; LP: Cyril Cusack, Ian Holm, Michael Jayston.

It's a 2'6" Above the Ground World (aka 'The Love Ban')
D: Ralph Thomas; W: Kevin Laffan; P: Betty E. Box; LP: Hywel Bennett, Nanette Newman, Milo O'Shea.

Jumbleland (television series) (aka 'Anita in Jumbeland')
LP: Anita Harris.

Last Chapter, The
Short film.
D: David Tringham; LP: Denholm Elliott, Susan Penhaligon.

Lovers, The
D: Herbert Wise; W: Jack Rosenthal; P: Maurice Foster; LP: Richard Beckinsale, Paula Wilcox, Joan Scott.

Luther
D: Guy Green; W: Edward Anhalt, John Osborne (play); P: Ely A. Landau; LP: Stacy Keach, Patrick Magee, Hugh Griffith, Robert Stephens.

Tales That Witness Madness
D: Freddie Francis; W: Jennifer Jayne; P: Norman Priggen, Milton Subotsky; LP: Jack Hawkins, Donald Pleasance, Georgia Brown, Donald Houston, Joan Collins.

Wicker Man, The
D: Robin Hardy; W: Anthony Shaffer; P: Peter Snell; LP: Christopher Lee, Britt Ekland, Edward Woodward, Diane Cilento.

With These Hands (aka 'Clinic Exclusive')
D: Don Chaffey; W: Elton Hawke, Kent Walton; P: Elton Hawke; LP: Polly Adams, Vincent Ball, Maria Coyne.

1973

Beast Must Die, The
D: Paul Annett; W: James Blish (story), Michael Winder; P: Max Rosenberg, Milton Subotsky; LP: Calvin Lockhart, Peter Cushing, Anton Diffring, Charles Gray.

Butley
D: Harold Pinter; W: Simon Gray; P: Ely A. Landau; LP: Alan Bates, Jessica Tandy, Richard O'Callaghan.

Craze
D: Freddie Francis; W: Herman Cohen, Aben Kandel, Henry Seymour (novel – *Infernal Idol*); P: Herman Cohen; LP: Jack Palance, Diana Dors, Julie Ege, Edith Evans.

Internecine Project, The
D: Ken Hughes; W: Mort W. Elkind (novel – *Internecine*), Barry Levinson, Jonathan Lynn; P: Barry Levinson; LP: James Coburn, Lee Grant, Harry Andrews.

Soft Beds, Hard Battles
D: Roy Boulting; W: Roy Boulting, Leo Marks; P: John Boulting, Roy Boulting; LP: Peter Sellers, Lila Kedrova, Curt Jurgens, Jenny Hanley.

Tales from the Crypt
D: Freddie Francis; W: Milton Subotsky; P: Max Rosenberg, Milton Subotsky; LP: Joan Collins, Peter Cushing, Ralph Richardson, Patrick Magee.

1974

Brannigan (formerly 'Joe Battle')
D: Douglas Hickox; W: Michael Butler, William P. McGivern, William W. Norton, Christopher Trumbo; P:Arthur Garner, Jules Levy; LP: John Wayne, Richard Attenborough, Judy Geeson, Mel Ferrer.

Conduct Unbecoming
D: Michael Anderson; W: Robert Enders, Barry England (play); P: Michael Deeley, Andrew Donally, Barry Spikings; LP: Michael York, Richard Attenborough, Trevor Howard, Stacy Keach, Christopher Plummer, Susannah York.

Great Expectations (television)
D: Joseph Hardy; W: Sherman Yellan, Charles Dickens (novel); P: Robert Fryer; LP: Michael York, Sarah Miles, James Mason, Margaret Leighton.

Land That Time Forgot, The
D: Kevin Connor; W: Edgar Rice Burroughs (novel), James Cawthorn, Michael Moorcock; P: John Dark; LP: Doug McClure, John McEnery, Susan Penhaligon, Keith Barron.

Lisztomania
D/W: Ken Russell; P: Roy Baird, David Puttnam; LP: Roger Daltry, Paul Nicholas, Ringo Starr, Rick Wakeman, Sara Kestelman.

Man Who Fell to Earth, The
D: Nicolas Roeg; W: Paul Mayersberg, Walter Tevis (novel); P: Michael Deeley, Barry Spikings; LP: David Bowie, Rip Torn, Candy Clark.

Mr Quilp (part)
D: Michael Tuchner; W: Charles Dickens (novel – *The Old Curiosity Shop*), Irene Kamp, Louis Kamp; P: Helen M. Strauss; LP: Anthony Newley, David Hemmings, Jill Bennett, David Warner.

Return of the Pink Panther, The
D/P: Blake Edwards; W: Frank Waldman, Blake Edwards; LP: Peter Sellers, Christopher Plummer, Catherine Schell, Herbert Lom, Burt Kwouk.

1975

Adventures of Sherlock Holmes' Smarter Brother, The
D/W: Gene Wilder; P: Richard A. Roth; LP: Gene Wilder, Marty Feldman, Dom DeLuise, Madeline Kahn, Leo McKern.

The 'Copter Kids
D/P: Ronald Spencer; W: Patricia Lathan; LP: Vic Armstrong, Michael Balfour, Marc Boyle.

Omen, The
D: Richard Donner; W: David Seltzer; P: Harvey Bernhard; LP: Gregory Peck, Lee Remick, David Warner, Billie Whitelaw.

Pink Panther Strikes Again, The
D/P: Blake Edwards; W: Frank Waldman, Blake Edwards; LP: Peter Sellers, Herbert Lom, Lesley Anne-Down, Burt Kwouk.

Sinbad and the Eye of the Tiger
D: Sam Wannamaker; W: Beverley Cross, Ray Harryhausen (story); P: Ray Harryhausen, Charles Schneer; LP: Patrick Wayne, Taryn Power, Margaret Whiting, Jane Seymour.

1976

Jabberwocky
D: Terry Gilliam; W: Charles Alverson, Lewis Carroll (poem as Revd Charles Dodgson), Terry Gilliam; P: Sanford Leiberson; LP: Michael Palin, Terry Jones, Harry H. Corbett, John Le Mesurier.

Marriage of Figaro, The
D: Jean-Pierre Ponelle; W: Pierre Augustin Caron de Beaumarchais (play), Lorenzo da Ponte (libretto); P: Fritz Buttenstedt; LP: Hermann Prey, Dietrich Fischer-Dieskau, Mirella Freni, Kiri Te Kanawa, Maria Ewing.

Queen Kong
D: Frank Agrama; W: Frank Agrama, Robin Dobria, Ronald Dobrin, Fabio Piccioni; P: Virgilio De Blasi; LP: Robin Askwith, Rula Lenska, Valerie Leon, Roger Hammond.

1977

Boys From Brazil, The
D: Franklin Schaffner; W: Ira Levin; P: Stanley O'Toole, Martin Richards; LP: Gregory Peck, Laurence Olivier, Lilli Palmer, James Mason.

Dominique
D: Michael Anderson; W: Edward Abraham, Valerie Abraham, Harold Lawlor (story); P: Andrew Donally, Milton Subotsky; LP: Cliff Robertson, Jean Simmons, Jenny Agutter, Simon Ward, Ron Moody.

Force Ten from Navarone (part)
D: Guy Hamilton; W: Robin Chapman, Carl Foreman (story), Alistair MacLean (novel); P: Samuel Z. Arkoff, Oliver A. Unger; LP: Robert Shaw, Harrison Ford, Edward Fox, Barbara Bach, Richard Kiel.

Four Feathers, The (television)
D: Don Sharp; W: A.E.W. Mason (novel), Gerald Di Pego; P: Norman Rosemont; LP: Beau Bridges, Robert Powell, Simon Ward, Jane Seymour.

Medusa Touch, The (part)
D: Jack Gold; W: John Briley, Peter van Greenway (novel); P: Arnon Milchan, Elliott Kastner; LP: Richard Burton, Lee Remick, Lino Ventura, Harry Andrews.

Prey (aka 'Alien Prey')
D: Norman J. Warren; W: Max Cuff, Quinn Donoghue (story); P: David Wimbury; LP: Barry Stokes, Sally Faulkner, Glory Annen.

Revenge of the Pink Panther, The
D/P: Blake Edwards; W: Frank Walden, Ron Clarke, Blake Edwards; LP: Peter Sellers, Herbert Lom, Robert Webber, Dyan Cannon.

Star Wars: Episode IV (part)
D/W: George Lucas; P: Gary Kurtz; LP: Mark Hamill, Harrison Ford, Carrie Fisher, Alec Guinness.

Superman (part)
D: Richard Donner; W: Mario Puzo, David Newman, Robert Benton, Leslie Newman; P: Pierre Spengler; LP: Christopher Reeve, Marlon Brando, Susannah York, Margo Kidder.

The Strange Case Of The End Of Civilisation As We Know It
D: Joe McGrath; W: John Cleese, Jack Hobbs, Joe McGrath; P: Humphrey Barclay; LP: John Cleese, Arthur Lowe, Ron Moody, Joss Ackland.

1978

Alien
D: Ridley Scott; W: Dan O'Bannon; P: Walter Hill, Gordon Carroll, David Giler; LP: Sigourney Weaver, Tom Skerritt, John Hurt.

Dracula
D: John Badham; W: W.D. Richter; P: Marvin Mirisch, Tom Pevsner; LP: Frank Langella, Laurence Olivier, Donald Pleasance, Kate Nelligan.

Martian Chronicles, The
D: Michael Anderson; W: Ray Bradbury (novel), Richard Matheson; P: Richard Berg, Andrew Donally, Milton Subotsky; LP: Linda Lou Allen, Michael Anderson Jr, Robert Beatty, Bernie Casey.

Murder by Decree
D: Bob Clark; W: John Hopkins; P: Robert A. Goldstone; LP: Christopher Plummer, James Mason, Anthony Quayle, David Hemmings, John Gielgud.

Odd Job, The
D: Peter Medak; W: Bernard McKenna, Graham Chapman; P: Mark Forstater, Graham Chapman; LP: Graham Chapman, David Jason, Simon Williams, Diana Quick.

Saturn Three
D/P: Stanley Donen; W: Martin Amis, John Barry (story); LP: Kirk Douglas, Farrah Fawcett, Harvey Keitel, Ed Bishop.

Thief of Baghdad, The
D: Clive Donner; W: A.J. Carothers, Andrew Birkin; P: Aida Young; LP: Roddy McDowall, Kabir Bedi, Frank Finlay, Terence Stamp, Peter Ustinov.

1979

All Quiet on the Western Front (television)
D: Delbert Mann; W: Paul Monash, Erich Maria Remarque (novel); P: Norman Rosemont; LP: Richard Thomas, Ernest Borgnine, Donald Pleasance, Ian Holm.

Flash Gordon
D: Michael Hodges; W: Lorenzo Semple Jr; P: Dino de Laurentis; LP: Sam Jones, Timothy Dalton, Max von Sydow, Topol.

SOS Titanic (television)
D: William Hale; W: James Costigan; P: Lou Morheim; LP: David Janssen, Cloris Leachman, David Warner, Ian Holm.

1980

Elephant Man, The
D: David Lynch; W: Christopher DeVore, Eric Bergren, David Lynch; P: Jonathan Sanger; LP: Anthony Hopkins, John Hurt, John Gielgud, Wendy Hiller.

Eye of the Needle
D: Richard Marquand; W: Ken Follett (novel), Stanley Mann; P: Stephen J. Freidman; LP: Donald Sutherland, Kate Nelligan, Christopher Cazenove.

History of the World: Part One
D/W/P: Mel Brooks; LP: Mel Brooks, Dom DeLuise, Harvey Korman, Cloris Leachman.

Little Lord Fauntleroy (television)
D: Jack Gold; W: Frances Hodgson Burnett (novel), Blanche Hanalis; P: Norman Rosemont; LP: Ricky Schroder, Alec Guinness, Eric Porter, Connie Booth.

Priest of Love
D: Christopher Miles; W: Harry T. Moore (book), Alan Plater; P: Andrew Donally, Christopher Miles; LP: Ian McKellen, Janet Suzman, Ava Garner, Penelope Keith.

Ragtime
D: Milos Forman; W: E.L. Doctorow (novel), Michael Weller; P: Dino De Laurentis; LP: James Cagney, Brad Dourif, Jeff Daniels, Samuel L. Jackson.

Tale of Two Cities, A (television)
D: Jim Goddard; W: John Gay, Charles Dickens (novel); P: Norman Rosemont; LP: Chris Sarandon, Kenneth More, Peter Cushing, Flora Robson.

1981

Brimstone and Treacle
D: Richard Loncraine; W: Dennis Potter; P: Alan E. Salke, Herbert F. Solow, Kenith Trodd; LP: Sting, Denholm Elliott, Joan Plowright.

Five Days One Summer
D/P: Fred Zinnemann; W: Michael Austin, Kay Boyle (story); LP: Sean Connery, Betsy Brantley, Anna Massey.

Gandhi (part)
D/P: Richard Attenborough; W: John Briley; LP: Ben Kingsley, Candice Bergen, Edward Fox, John Gielgud, Trevor Howard, John Mills.

Hunger (The)
D: Tony Scott; W: James Costigan, Ivan Davis, Whitley Strieber (novel), Michael Thomas; P: Richard Shepherd; LP: Catherine Deneuve, David Bowie, Susan Sarandon.

Pirates of Penzance (The)
D: Wilford Leach; W: William S. Gilbert (operetta), Wilford Leach; P: Joseph Papp; LP: Kevin Kline, Angela Lansbury, Linda Ronstadt.

Winds of War, The (television mini-series)
D/P: Dan Curtis; W: Herman Wouk (also novel); LP: Robert Mitchum, Jan-Michael Vincent, Ali MacGraw, Elke Sommer, Topol.

1982

Gilbert and Sullivan (television series)
Five operettas in the series filmed at Shepperton: *Pinafore, Pirates, Iolanthe, Mikado* and *Gondoliers*.
D: Michael Geliot, David Pountney, Peter Wood; W: Gilbert and Sullivan; P: Judith De Paul; LP: Derek Hammond-Stroud, Gordon Sandison, Peter Marshall, William Conrad, Frank Gorshin, Peter Allen, Clive Revill, Keith Michell, Frankie Howerd, Donald Adams, Gillian Knight.

Hound of the Baskervilles, The (television)
D: Douglas Hickox; W: Arthur Conan Doyle (novel), Charles Edward Pogue; P: Otto Plaschkes; LP: Ian Richardson, Donald Churchill, Denholm Elliott.

Jigsaw Man, The
D: Terence Young; W: Dorothea Bennett (novel), Jo Eisinger; P: Benjamin Fisz; LP: Michael Caine, Laurence Olivier, Susan George.

Keep, The
D: Michael Mann; W: F. Paul Wilson (novel), Michael Mann (screenplay); P: Gene Kirkwood; LP: Scott Glenn, Alberta Watson, Ian McKellen.

Lords of Discipline, The
D: Franc Roddam; W: Pat Conroy (novel), Thomas Pope, Lloyd Fonvielle; P: Herb Jaffe, Gabriel Katzka; LP: David Keith, Robert Prosky, G.D. Spradlin.

Missionary, The
D: Richard Loncraine; W: Michael Palin; P: Michael Palin, Neville C. Thompson; LP: Michael Palin, Maggie Smith, Trevor Howard.

Privates on Parade
D: Michael Blakemore; W: Peter Nicholls; P: George Harrison, Denis O'Brien, Simon Relph; LP: Patrick Pearson, Michael Elphick, Joe Melia, John Standing.

Sender, The
D: Roger Christian; W: Thomas Baum; P: Edward S. Feldman; LP: Kathryn Harrold, Zeljko Ivanek, Shirley Knight.

Sign of Four, The
D: Desmond Davis; W: Arthur Conan Doyle (novel), Charles Edward Pogue; P: Otto Plaschkes; LP: Ian Richardson, David Healey, Thorley Walters.

1983

Bullshot
D: Dick Clement; W: Ronald E. House, Alan Shearman, Diz White; P: Ian LaFrenais; LP: Alan Shearman, Diz White, Mel Smith.

Company of Wolves, The
D: Neil Jordan; W: Angela Carter (story), Neil Jordan; P: Chris Brown, Stephen Woolley; LP: Angela Lansbury, David Warner, Graham Crowden.

Far Pavilions, The (television mini-series)
D: Peter Duffell; W: Julian Bond, M.M. Kaye (novel); P: Geoffrey Reeve; LP: Ben Cross, Amy Irving, Christopher Lee.

Zany Adventures of Robin Hood, The (television)
D: Ray Austin; W: Robert Kaufman; LP: George Segal, Morgan Fairchild, Roddy McDowall, Janet Suzman.

1984

Bride, The
D: Franc Roddam; W: Mary Shelley (novel), Lloyd Fonvielle; P: Victor Drai; LP: Sting, Jennifer Beals, Anthony Higgins.

Doctor and the Devils
D: Freddie Francis; W: Dylan Thomas (earlier screenplay), Ronald Harwood; P: Jonathan Sanger; LP: Timothy Dalton, Jonathan Pryce, Twiggy, Stephen Rea.

Ellis Island (television mini-series)
D: Jerry London; W: Christopher Newman, Fred Mustard Stewart (novel); P: Nick Gillott; LP: Peter Reigert, Claire Bloom, Joan Greenwood, Stubby Kaye.

1984

D: Michael Radford; W: Jonathan Gems (story), George Orwell (novel), Michael Radford; P: Simon Perry; LP: John Hurt, Richard Burton, Susannah Hamilton.

Passage to India, A

D: David Lean; W: E.M. Forster (novel), David Lean; P: John Brabourne, Richard B. Goodwin; LP: Judy Davis, Peggy Ashcroft, Alec Guinness, James Fox.

Reunion at Farnborough

D: Herbert Wise; W: Albert Rubin; P: William Hill; LP: Robert Mitchum, Deborah Kerr, Red Buttons.

2010

D/P: Peter Hyams; W: Arthur C. Clarke (novel), Peter Hyams; LP: Roy Scheider, John Lithgow, Helen Mirren.

Water

D: Dick Clement; W: Dick Clement, Ian La Frenais, Bill Persky; P: George Harrison, Ian LaFrenais; LP: Michael Caine, Billy Connolly, Leonard Rossiter.

1985

Absolute Beginners

D: Julien Temple; W: Richard Burridge, Terry Johnson (dialogue), Colin MacInnes (novel), Don MacPherson, Christopher Wicking; P: Chris Brown, Stephen Woolley; LP: David Bowie, Patsy Kensit, James Fox.

If Tomorrow Comes (television mini-series)

D: Jerry London; W: Carmen Culver, Sidney Sheldon (novel); P: Carmen Culver, Nick Gilliott; LP: Tom Berenger, Madolyn Smith, Liam Neeson.

Link

D: Richard Franklin; W: Lee David Zlotoff (story), Tom Ackermann (story), Everett De Roche; P: Richard Franklin; LP: Terence Stamp, Elizabeth Shue, Steven Pinner.

Out of Africa

D/P: Sydney Pollack; W: Isak Dinesen (memoirs), A.E. Housman (poem – *To An Athlete, Dying Young*), Kurt Luedtke, Errol Trzebinski (book – *Silence Will Speak*); LP: Meryl Streep, Robert Redford.

1986

Cry Freedom

D/P: Richard Attenborough; W: John Briley, Donald Woods (books); LP: Kevin Kline, Denzel Washington, Penelope Wilton.

84 Charing Cross Road

D: David Jones; W: Hugh Whitemore; P: Geoffrey Helman; LP: Anthony Hopkins, Anne Bancroft, Judi Dench.

Hearts of Fire

D: Richard Marquand; W: Joe Eszterhas, Scott Richardson; P: Jennifer Alward, Richard Marquand, Jennifer Miller; LP: Bob Dylan, Rupert Everett.

Princess Bride, The

D: Rob Reiner; W: William Goldman; P: Rob Reiner, Andrew Scheinman; LP: Cary Elwes, Mandy Patinkin, Christopher Guest.

Return of Sherlock Holmes, The (television)
D: Kevin Connor; W: Bob Shayne; P: Nick Gilliott; LP: Michael Pennington, Connie Booth, Shane Rimmer.

Shanghai Surprise
D: Jim Goddard; W: Tony Kenrick (novel – *Faraday's Flowers*), John Kohn, Robert Bentley; P: John Kohn; LP: Sean Penn, Madonna.

1987

Gorillas in the Mist (part)
D: Michael Apted; W: Harold T.P. Hayes (article), Dian Fossey (work), Anna Hamilton Phelan (story), Tab Murphy (story), Anna Hamilton Phelan; P: Terry Clegg, Arne Glimcher; LP: Sigourney Weaver, Bryan Brown.

Lonely Passion of Judith Hearne, The
D: Jack Clayton; W: Brian Moore (novel), Peter Nelson; P: Richard Johnson, Peter Nelson; LP: Maggie Smith, Bob Hoskins, Wendy Hiller.

Poor Little Rich Girl: The Barbara Hutton Story (television)
D: Charles Jarrott; W: C. David Heymann (book) Dennis Turner (teleplay); P: Nick Gillott; LP: Farrah Fawcett, Burl Ives.

White Mischief
D: Michael Radford; W: James Fox (novel), Michael Radford, Jonathan Gems; P: Simon Perry; LP: Greta Scacchi, Charles Dance, Joss Ackland, Sarah Miles.

1988

Bert Rigby, You're a Fool
D/W: Carl Reiner; P: George Shapiro; LP: Robert Lindsay, Robbie Coltrane, Anne Bancroft.

Endless Game, The (television)
D/W: Bryan Forbes; P: Fernando Ghia; LP: Albert Finney, George Segal, Kristin Scott Thomas.

Erik the Viking
D/W: Terry Jones; P: John Goldstone; LP: Tim Robbins, Mickey Rooney, Eartha Kitt, Terry Jones.

Henry V
D: Kenneth Branagh; W: Kenneth Branagh, William Shakespeare (play); P: Bruce Sharman; LP: Kenneth Branagh, Derek Jacobi, Brian Blessed.

How to Get Ahead in Advertising
D/W: Bruce Robinson; P: David Wimbury; LP: Richard E. Grant, Rachel Ward, Richard Wilson.

Mountains of the Moon
D: Bob Rafelson; W: William Harrison, Bob Rafelson; P: Daniel Melnick; LP: Patrick Bergin, Richard E. Grant, Fiona Shaw.

Spooks (aka 'Spies Inc.') (television)
D: Anthony Thomas; W: Jim Hougan, Antony Thomas; P: John E. Levy; LP: Brian Kerwin, Alice Krige, Robert Loggia, Diane Ladd, David Warner.

Strapless
D/W: David Hare; P: Rick McCallum; LP: Blair Brown, Bridget Fonda, Michael Gough.

1989

About Face (television series)
Twelve thirty-minute episodes.
D: John Henderson; W: Carol Bunyan, Chips Hardy, Richard Harris, John Henderson, Ian Hislop, Terry Kyan, Nick Newman, Geoffrey Perkins, Astrid Ronning, Jack Rosenthal, Paul Smith, John Wells; P: Johnny Goodman, John Henderson, Bridget Ikin; LP: Maureen Lipman (various roles).

Back Home (television)
D: Piers Haggard; W: Michelle Magorian; P: J. Nigel Pickard; LP: Hayley Mills, Adam Stevenson, Jean Anderson.

Choice, The (television)
No information

Free Frenchmen, The
D: Jim Goddard; W: Piers Paul Read (book), Ted Whitehead; P: Ted Childs, Yves Pasquier; LP: Jean-Pierre Aumont, Françoise Christophe, Barry Foster.

Killing Dad
D: Michael Austin; W: Michael Austin, Ann Quin (novel); P: Iain Smith; LP: Richard E. Grant, Julie Walters, Anna Massey.

Nuns on the Run
D/W: Jonathan Lynn; P: Michael White; LP: Eric Idle, Robbie Coltrane, Janet Suzman.

Secret Life of Ian Fleming (television)
D: Ferdinand Fairfax; W: Robert J. Avrech; P: Aida Young; LP: Jason Connery, Kristen Scott Thomas, Joss Ackland.

Shell Seekers, The (television)
D: Waris Hussein; W: John Pielmeier; P: Emma Hayter, William Hill, Anne Hopkins; LP: Angela Lansbury, Sam Wanamaker, Patricia Hodge.

Ticket to Ride (television series)
One sixty-minute episode.
LP: Anthony Andrews. Series aborted after pilot.

1990

Gawain and the Green Knight (television)
D/P: John Michael Phillips; W: David Rudkin; LP: Jason Durr, Marie Francis.

Hamlet
D: Franco Zeffirelli; W: William Shakespeare (play), Christopher DeVore, Franco Zeffirelli; P: Dyson Lovell; LP: Mel Gibson, Glenn Close, Alan Bates.

Kiss Before Dying, A
D: James Dearden; W: Ira Levin (novel), James Dearden; P: Robert Lawrence; LP: Matt Dillon, Sean Young.

Manhattan Project (television)
No information

Rainbow Thief, The
D: Alejandro Jodorowsky; W: Berta Domínguez; P: Vincent Winter; LP: Jude Alderson, Briggite Barclay.

Red Dwarf IV (television series)
Six thirty-minute episodes.
D: Ed Bye; W: Rob Grant, Doug Naylor; P: Hilary Bevan-Jones, Rob Grant, Doug Naylor, Justin Judd; LP: Craig Charles, Chris Barrie, Danny John-Jules, Robert Llewelyn, Hatty Hayridge.

Robin Hood – Prince of Thieves
D: Kevin Reynolds; W: Pen Densham, John Watson; P: Richard Barton Lewis, Pen Densham, John Watson; LP: Kevin Costner, Morgan Freeman, Mary Elizabeth Mastrantonio, Alan Rickman, Sean Connery.

Smith and Jones (television series)
LP: Mel Smith, Griff Rhys Jones.

Three Men and a Little Lady
D: Emile Ardonilo; W: Coline Serreau (screenplay – *Trois Hommes et un Couffin*), Sara Parriott (story), Josann McGibbon (story), Charlie Peters; P: Robert W. Cort, Ted Field; LP: Tom Selleck, Steve Guttenberg, Ted Danson.

To Be The Best (television)
D: Tony Wharmby; W: Elliott Baker, Barbara Taylor Bradford (novel); P: Aida Young; LP: Lindsay Wagner, Anthony Hopkins, Stephanie Beacham.

You Bet
Series Four of the LWT gameshow.
LP: Matthew Kelly.

1991

Big Break (television)
BBC gameshow.
LP: Jim Davidson, Tony Virgo.

Blame it on the Bellboy
D/W: Mark Herman; P: Steve Abbott, Jennifer Howarth; LP: Dudley Moore, Bryan Brown, Penelope Wilton, Richard Griffiths.

Bye Bye Columbus (television)
D/W: Peter Barnes; P: Ann Scott; LP: Dan Massey, Simon Callow, Dilys Laye, John Turner.

Chaplin (part)
D: Richard Attenborough; W: Diana Hawkins (story), William Boyd, Bryan Forbes, William Goldman; P: Richard Attenborough, Mario Kassar; LP: Robert Downey Jnr, Anthony Hopkins, Geraldine Chaplin.

Crying Game, The
D/W: Neil Jordan; P: Stephen Woolley; LP: Forest Whitaker, Miranda Richardson, Stephen Rea, Jaye Davidson.

EX TV
D: Paul Seed; W: William Humble; LP: Penny Downie, Geraldine James, Griff Rhys Jones.

Murder Most Horrid (television series)
Six thirty-minute episodes.

D: Bob Spiers, James Hendrie; W: Ian Hislop, Nick Newman, Paul Smith, Terry Ryan, Graham Alborough, Jez Alborough, Ian Brown, James Hendrie; P: Jon Plowman; LP: Dawn French

Pressgang (television series)
Children's drama. Ten twenty-five minute episodes.
D: James Devis, John Hall, Lorne Magory, Colin Nutley, Gerry O'Hara, Bren Simson, Bob Spiers, Bill Ward; W: Steven Moffat; P: Sandra C. Hastie; LP: Julia Sawalha, Dexter Fletcher, Kelda Holmes, Lee Ross.

Red Dwarf V (television series)
Six thirty-minute episodes. See 1990 for credits.

Thomas The Tank Engine and Friends (television series)
Series of five-minute children's programmes.
D: David Mitton; W: Revd W. Audry; P: Britt Alcroft, Robert D. Cardona, David Mitton; LP: Ringo Starr, Michael Angelis.

Under Suspicion
D/W: Simon Moore; P: Brian Eastman; LP: Liam Neeson, Kenneth Cranham, Maggie O'Neill.

Wuthering Heights
D: Peter Kosminski; W: Emily Brontë (novel), Anne Devlin; P: Mary Selway; LP: Juliette Binoche, Ralph Fiennes, Jeremy Northam.

You Bet (television series)
Series Five of the ITV gameshow. See 1990 for credits.

Young Indiana Jones Chronicles (television) (part)
Series of forty-five-minute episodes.
D: various; W: various; P: Rick McCallum; LP: Sean Patrick Flanery, Corey Carrier, George Hall, Ronny Coutteure.

1992

Borrowers, The (television series)
Series One. Six thirty-minute episodes.
D: John Henderson; W: Richard Carpenter, Mary Norton (novel); P: Grainne Marmion; LP: Ian Holm, Penelope Wilton, Sian Phillips, Stanley Lebor.

Calling The Shots (television)
D: Ross Devenish; W: Laura Lamson; P: David Snodin; LP: Lynn Redgrave, Jack Shepherd, Cyril Nri.

Covington Cross (television series)
Thirteen sixty-minute episodes.
D: William Dear, Alister Hallum, James Keach, Les Landau, Francis Megahy, Joe Napolitano, Peter Sasdy, Ian Toynton, Herbert Wise; W: Beverly Bridges, Gil Grant, Dennis E. Leoni, Chris Ruppenthal, Joel Surnow, Nick Thiel; P: Aida Young, Joel Surnow; LP: Nigel Terry, Cherie Lunghi, James Faulkner, Jonathan Firth.

Damage
DP: Louis Malle; W: David Hare, Josephine Hart (novel); LP: Jeremy Irons, Juliette Binoche, Miranda Richardson.

Foreign Affairs (television series)
D: Alan Erlich, Hans Treffers, Ricardo Vicuña; P: Charles Falzon, John de Mol; LP: Gregory Dayton, Antoinette van Belle, Anne E. Curry, George Dayton.

Inspector Morse (television series)
Five sixty-minute episodes.
D: John Madden, Adrian Shergold, Colin Gregg, Antonia Bird, Danny Boyle; W: Danny Boyle, Alma Cullen, John Brown, Julian Mitchell; P: Deidre Keir; LP: John Thaw, Kevin Whately.

Jeeves And Wooster (television series)
Six sixty-minute episodes.
D: Ferdinand Fairfax; W: Clive Exton, P.G. Wodehouse (novels); P: Brian Eastman; LP: Stephen Fry, Hugh Laurie.

Life and Death of Philip Knight, The (television)
D/W: Jeremy Brock; P: Peter Kosminsky, Peter Waller; LP: Daniel Newman, Holly Aird.

Muppet Christmas Carol, The
D: Brian Henson; W: Charles Dickens (novel), Jerry Juhl (screenplay); P: Martin G. Baker, Brian Henson; LP: Michael Caine, The Muppets.

Paradise Club, The (television series)
Twenty fifty-minute episodes.
D: Derek Banham, Gabrielle Beaumont, Lawrence Gordon Clark, Carl Gregg, Colin Gregg, Ken Hannam, Selwyn Roberts, Renny Rye, Richard Standeven, John Watson; W: Murray Smith, Brian Ward; P: Selwyn Roberts; LP: Don Henderson, Leslie Grantham, Barbara Wilshire.

Red Dwarf VI (television series)
Six thirty-minute episodes. See 1990 for credits.

Smith and Jones '92 (television series)
Mel Smith and Griff Rhys Jones' sketch show.

Splitting Heirs
D: Robert Young; W: Eric Idle; P: Simon Bosanquet, Redmond Morris; LP: Eric Idle, Rick Moranis, Catherine Zeta-Jones.

Turn of the Screw
D: Rusty Lemorande; W: Rusty Lemorande, Henry James (novel); P: Jeremy Bolt, Michael White; LP: Patsy Kensit, Marianne Faithfull.

You Bet (television series)
Series Six of the game show, hosted by Matthew Kelly.

You Me and It (television)
D: Edward Bennett; W: Andrew Payne; P: Kevin van Thompson; LP: James Wilby, Suzanne Burden.

1993

Four Weddings and a Funeral
D: Mike Newell; W: Richard Curtis; P: Duncan Kenworthy; LP: Hugh Grant, Andie MacDowell, Kristen Scott Thomas, Simon Callow.

Funny Man, The
D/W: Simon Sprackling; P: Nigel Odell; LP: Tim James, Christopher Lee, Benny Young, Pauline Chan.

Intimate with a Stranger
D: Melanie Woods; W: Roderick Mangin-Turner, Melanie Woods; P: Roderick Mangin-Turner; LP: Roderick Mangin-Turner, Daphne Nayar.

Mary Shelley's Frankenstein
D: Kenneth Branagh; W: Steph Lady, Frank Darabont, Mary Shelley (novel); P: Francis Ford Coppola, James V. Hart, John Veitch; LP: Kenneth Branagh, Robert De Niro, Helena Bonham Carter.

Never Ending Story III
D: Peter MacDonald; W: Michael Ende (characters), Karin Howard (story), Jeff Lieberman; P: Heinz Bibo, Dieter Geissler, Tim Hampton, Klaus Kaehler, Harold Tichenor; LP: Jason James Richter, Melody Kay, Jack Black.

Porgy and Bess (television)
D: Trevor Nunn; W: Dorothy Heyward, DuBose Heyward; P: Greg Smith; LP: Willard White, Cynthia Haymon.

Princess Caraboo
D: Michael Austin; W: Michael Austin, John Wells; P: Andy Karsch, Simon Bonsanquet; LP: Phoebe Cates, Jim Broadbent, Kevin Kline, John Lithgow.

Shadowlands
D: Richard Attenborough; W: William Nicholson; P: Richard Attenborough, Brian Eastman; LP: Anthony Hopkins, Debra Winger, Edward Hardwicke.

1994

Carrington
D: Christopher Hampton; W: Christopher Hampton, Michael Holroyd (book); P: John McGrath, Ronald Shedlo; LP: Emma Thompson, Jonathan Pryce.

Haunted
D: Lewis Gilbert; W: James Herbert (novel), Timothy Prager, Bob Kellett, Lewis Gilbert; P: Lewis Gilbert, Anthony Andrews; LP: Anthony Andrews, Aidan Quinn, Kate Beckinsale, John Gielgud.

Judge Dredd
D: Danny Cannon; W: Michael De Luca (story), William Wisher Jr (story), Steven E. de Souza (screenplay); P: Charles Lippincott, Beau Marks; LP: Sylvester Stallone, Diane Lane, Armand Assante.

Madness of King George, The
D: Nick Hytner; W: Alan Bennett; P: Stephen Evans, David Parfitt; LP: Nigel Hawthorne, Helen Mirren, Ian Holm.

Restoration
D: Michael Hoffman; W: Rose Tremain (novel), Rupert Walters; P: Sarah Black, Cary Brokaw, Andy Paterson; LP: Robert Downey Jr, Sam Neill, Polly Walker.

1995

Hamlet
D: Kenneth Branagh; W: Kenneth Branagh, William Shakespeare (play); P: David Barron; LP: Kenneth Branagh, Kate Winslet, Richard Attenborough.

In the Bleak Midwinter
D/W: Kenneth Branagh; P: David Barron; LP: Richard Briers, Joan Collins, Michael Moloney.

Muppet Treasure Island
D: Brian Henson; W: Robert Louis Stevenson (novel), Jerry Juhl, Kirk R. Thatcher, James V. Hart; P: Brian Henson, Martin G. Baker; LP: Tim Curry, Jennifer Saunders, the Muppets.

101 Dalmatians
D: Steve Herek; W: Dodie Smith (novel), John Hughes; P: John Hughes, Ricardo Mestres; LP: Glenn Close, Joely Richardson, Jeff Daniels.

Othello
D: Oliver Parker; W: Oliver Parker, William Shakespeare (play); P: David Barron, Luc Roeg; LP: Laurence Fishburne, Kenneth Branagh, Irene Jacob.

Sense and Sensibility
D: Ang Lee; W: Emma Thompson, Jane Austen (novel); P: Lindsay Doran; LP: Emma Thompson, Hugh Grant, Kate Winslet.

Wind in the Willows
D: Terry Jones; W: Kenneth Grahame (novel), Terry Jones; P: Jake Eberts, John Goldstone; LP: Terry Jones, Steve Coogan, Eric Idle.

1996

Amy Foster
D: Beeban Kidron; W: Joseph Conrad (story), Tim Willocks; P: Beeban Kidron, Charles Steel, Polly Tapson; LP: Vincent Perez, Rachel Weisz, Ian McKellen.

Borrowers, The
D: Peter Hewitt; W: Mary Norton (novels), Gavin Scott, John Kamps; P: Tim Bevan, Eric Fellner, Rachel Tadalay; LP: John Goodman, Mark Williams, Jim Broadbent, Celia Imrie.

Evita (part)
D: Alan Parker; W: Tim Rice (play – *Evita*), Alan Parker, Oliver Stone; P: Alan Parker, Robert Stigwood, Andrew G. Vajna; LP: Madonna, Antonia Banderas, Jonathan Pryce, Jimmy Nail.

Fairy Tale – A True Story (part)
D: Charles Sturridge; W: Albert Ash (story), Tom McLoughlin (story), Ernie Contreras; P: Bruce Davey, Wendy Finerman; LP: Harvey Keitel, Paul McGann, Phoebe Nicholls, Bill Nighy.

In Love & War
D: Richard Attenborough; W: Allan Scott, Dimitri Villard, Allan Scott, Clancy Sigal, Anna Hamilton Phelan; P: Richard Attenborough, Dimitri Villard; LP: Sandra Bullock, Chris O'Donnell.

London Suite (television)
D: Jay Sandrich; W: Neil Simon; P: Greg Smith; LP: Kelsey Grammar, Michael Richards.

Masterminds
D: Roger Christian; W: Floyd Byars, Alex Siskin (story), Chris Black (story); P: Floyd Byars, Robert Franklin Dudelson; LP: Patrick Stewart, Brenda Fricker.

Mrs Dalloway
D: Marleen Gorris; W: Eileen Atkins, Virginia Woolf (novel); P: Stephen Bayly, Lisa Katselas Paré; LP: Vanessa Redgrave, Natasha McElhone, Rupert Graves.

Rebecca (television)
D: Jim O'Brian; W: Daphne Du Maurier (novel), Arthur Hopcraft; P: Hilary Heath; LP: Anthony Bate, Charles Dance, Faye Dunaway, Emilia Fox.

Shooting Fish
D: Stefan Schwartz; W: Stefan Schwartz, Richard Holmes; P: Richard Holmes, Glynis Murray; LP: Dan Futterman, Stuart Townsend, Kate Beckinsale.

Wings of the Dove
D: Iain Softly; W: Henry James (novel), Hossein Amini; P: Stephen Evans, David Parfitt; LP: Helena Bonham Carter, Linus Roache, Charlotte Rampling.

Gulliver's Travels (television)
D: Charles Sturridge; W: Simon Moore (based on the Jonathan Swift novel); P: Duncan Kenworthy; LP: Ted Danson, Mary Steenburgen, Edward Woodward, Peter O'Toole.

1997

An Inch over the Horizon
D: Robert Young; W: Jack Rosenthal; P: John Goldschmidt; LP: Bob Hoskins, Gemma Jones, Maureen Lipman.

Avengers, The (part)
D: Jeremiah Chechik; W: Don MacPherson; P: Jerry Weintraub; LP: Uma Thurman, Ralph Fiennes, Sean Connery.

Elizabeth
D: Shekhar Kapur; W: Michael Hirst; P: Tim Bevan, Eric Fellner, Alison Owen; LP: Cate Blanchett, Geoffrey Rush, Joseph Fiennes.

King Lear (television)
D: Richard Eyre; W: Richard Eyre, William Shakespeare (play); P: Sue Birtwistle; LP: Paul Rhys, Timothy West, Barbara Flynn.

Lost in Space
D: Stephen Hopkins; W: Akiva Goldsman; P: Carla Fry, Akiva Goldsman, Stephen Hopkins, Mark W. Koch; LP: William Hurt, Mimi Rogers, Heather Graham, Matt LeBlanc.

Parent Trap, The
D: Nancy Myers; W: David Swift, Nancy Meyers, Charles Shyer; P: Charles Shyer; LP: Lindsay Lohan, Dennis Quaid, Natasha Richardson.

Sliding Doors (part)
D/W: Peter Howitt; P: Philippa Braithwaite, William Horberg, Sydney Pollack; LP: Gwyneth Paltrow, John Hannah, Jeanne Tripplehorn.

1998

Alice in Wonderland (television)
D: Nick Willing; W: Lewis Carroll (book), Peter Barnes; P: Dyson Lovell; LP: Robbie Coltrane, Whoopi Goldberg, Ben Kingsley.

An Englishman in New York
D: Matt Lipsey. No other information.

Cleopatra
D: Franc Roddam; W: Margaret George (novel – *Memoirs of Cleopatra*), Stephen Harrigan, Anton Diether; P: Dyson Lovell, Steve Harding; LP: Billy Zane, Timothy Dalton, Rupert Graves.

Elephant Juice (part)
D: Sam Miller; W: Amy Jenkins; P: Amy Jenkins, Sheila Fraser Milne; LP: Emmanuelle Béart, Sean Gallagher, Daniel Lapaine.

Entrapment (special effects)
D: Jon Amiel; W: Michael Hertzberg (story), Ronald Bass, William Broyles; P: Sean Connery, Rhonda Tollefson, Michael Hertzberg; LP: Sean Connery, Catherine Zeta-Jones.

Eugene Onegin
D: Martha Fiennes; W: Peter Ettedgui, Michael Ignatieff; P: Simon Bosanquet, Ileen Maisel; LP: Ralph Fiennes, Toby Stephens, Liv Tyler.

Felicia's Journey
D: Atom Egoyan; W: William Trevor (novel), Atom Egoyan; P: Bruce Davey, Robert Lantos; LP: Bob Hoskins, Arsinée Khanjian, Elaine Cassidy.

Gladiator (part)
D: Ridley Scott; W: David Franzoni, John Logan, William Nicholson; P: David Franzoni, Branko Lustig, Douglas Wick; LP: Russell Crowe, Joaquin Phoenix, Oliver Reed, Richard Harris.

Hilary and Jackie
D: Anand Tucker; W: Frank Cottrell Boyce; P: Nicholas Kent, Andy Patterson; LP: Emily Watson, Rachel Griffiths, Charles Dance.

Love's Labour's Lost
D: Kenneth Branagh; W: Kenneth Branagh, William Shakespeare (play); P: David Barron, Kenneth Branagh; LP: Kenneth Branagh, Alessandro Nivola, Alicia Silverstone, Natascha McElhone.

Mummy, The
D: Steve Sommers; W: Stephen Sommers, Lloyd Fonvielle, Kevin Jarre; P: Sean Daniel, James Jacks; LP: Brendan Fraser, Rachel Weisz, John Hannah.

Notting Hill
D: Roger Michell; W: Richard Curtis; P: Duncan Kenworthy; LP: Hugh Grant, Julia Roberts.

Shakespeare in Love
D: John Madden; W: Marc Norman, Tom Stoppard; P: Donna Gigliotti, Marc Norman, David Parfitt, Harvey Weinstein, Edward Zwick; LP: Joseph Fiennes, Geoffrey Rush, Gwyneth Paltrow.

Simon Magus
D/W: Ben Hopkins; P: Robert Jones; LP: Noah Taylor, Stuart Townsend, Ian Holm.

Sleepy Hollow (part)
D: Tim Burton; W: Washington Irving (story – *The Legend of Sleepy Hollow*), Kevin Yagher, Andrew Kevin Walker; P: Scott Rudin, Adam Schroeder; LP: Johnny Depp, Christina Ricci.

1999

Billy Elliott (formerly 'Dancer')
D: Stephen Daldry; W: Lee Hall; P: Greg Brenman, Jonathan Finn; LP: Jamie Bell, Gary Lewis, Julie Walters.

Blackadder – Back And Forth
D: Paul Weiland; W: Richard Curtis, Ben Elton; P: Sophie Clarke-Jervoise; LP: Rowan Atkinson, Colin Firth, Rik Mayall, Crispin Harris, Simon Russell Beale, Stephen Fry.

Circus
D: Robert Walker; W: David Logan; P: James Gibb, Alan Latham; LP: John Hannah, Famke Janssen.

Don Quixote (television)
D: Peter Yates; W: Miguel de Cervantes y Saavedra (novel), John Mortimer; P: Dyson Lovell; P: John Lithgow, Bob Hoskins, Isabella Rossellini.

End of the Affair, The
D: Neil Jordan; W: Graham Greene (novel), Neil Jordan; P: Neil Jordan, Stephen Woolley; LP: Ralph Fiennes, Stephen Rea, Julian Moore.

Jason and the Argonauts (television)
D: Nick Willing; W: Matthew Faulk, Mark Skeet; P: Dyson Lovell; LP: Jason London, Dennis Hopper, Frank Langella.

Just Visiting
D: Jean Marie Gaubert; W: Christian Clavier, Jean-Marie Poiré, John Hughes; P: Patrice Ledoux, Ricardo Mestres; LP: Jean Reno, Christina Applegate, Christian Clavier.

Kevin and Perry Go Large
D: Ed Bye; W: Dave Cummings, Harry Enfield; P: Peter Bennett-Jones, Harry Enfield, Jolyon Symonds; LP: Harry Enfield, Kathy Burke.

Magical Legend of the Leprechauns, The (television)
D: John Henderson; W: Peter Barnes; P: Paul Lowin; LP: Randy Quaid, Whoopi Goldberg, Roger Daltrey, Colm Meaney.

Maybe Baby
D/W: Ben Elton; P: Phil McIntyre; LP: Hugh Laurie, Joely Richardson.

102 Dalmatians
D: Kevin Lima; W: Kristen Buckley, Bob Tzudiker, Noni White; P: Edward S. Feldman; LP: Glenn Close, Gérard Depardieu, Ioan Gruffudd.

RKO 281 (television) (part)
D: Ben Ross; W: John Logan; P: Su Armstrong; LP: Liev Schreiber, James Cromwell, Melanie Griffith, John Malkovich.

Women Talking Dirty
D: Coky Giedroyc; W: Isla Dewar; P: Helena Bonham Carter, Eileen Atkins, Gina McKee.

2000

Bedazzled
D: Harold Ramis; W: Larry Gelbart, Harold Ramis, Peter Tolan; P: Trevor Albert, Harold Ramis; LP: Brendan Fraser, Elizabeth Hurley.

Bridget Jones's Diary
D: Sharon Maguire; W: Helen Fielding, Andrew Davies, Richard Curtis; P: Tim Bevan Jonathan Cavendish, Eric Fellner; LP: Renée Zellweger, Hugh Grant, Colin Firth.

Calling, The
D: Richard Caesar; W: John Rice, Rudy Gaines; P: Bernd Eichinger, Martin Moszkowicz, Norbert Preuss; LP: Laura Harris, Richard Lintern, Francis Magee.

Conspiracy
D: Stanley Tucci; W: Loring Mandel; P: Nick Gillott; LP: Kenneth Branagh, Stanley Tucci, Colin Firth.

Chocolat
D: Lasse Hallstrom; W: Joanne Harris (novel), Robert Nelson Jacobs; P: David Brown, Mark Cooper, Kit Golden, Leslie Holleran; LP: Juliette Binoche, Johnny Depp, Alfred Molina.

Crush
D/W: John McKay; P: Lee Thomas; LP: Andie MacDowell, Imelda Staunton, Bill Patterson.

Dog Eat Dog
D: Moody Shoaibi; W: Moody Shoaibi, Mark Tonderai; P: Amanda Davis; LP: Mark Tonderai, Nathan Constance, David Oyelowo.

Endgame
D/W: Gary Wicks; P: Gary Jones; LP: Daniel Newman, Corey Johnson, Toni Barry.

Killing Me Softly
D: Chen Kaige; W: Sean French (novel), Kara Lindstrom; P: Michael Chinich, Joe Medjuck, Lynda Myles; LP: Heather Graham, Joseph Fiennes, Ian Hart.

La Tour Montparnasse Infernale
D: Charles Nemes; W: Kader Aoun, Ramzy Bedia, Eric Judor, Xavier Matthieu; P: Christian Fechner; LP: Eric Judor, Ramzy Bedia, Marina Foïs.

Mummy Returns, The
D/W: Steve Sommers; P: Sean Daniel, James Jacks; LP: Brendan Fraser, Rachel Weisz, John Hannah.

Not I (short film)
D/P: Neil Jordan; W: Samuel Beckett; LP: Julianne Moore.

Possession
D: Neil La Bute; W: A.S. Byatt (novel), David Henry Hwang, Laura Jones, Neil LaBute; P: Barry Levinson, Paula Weinstein; LP: Gwyneth Paltrow, Aaron Eckhart.

Spy Game
D: Tony Scott; W: Michael Frost Beckner, David Arata; P: Mark Abraham, Douglas Wick; LP: Robert Redford, Brad Pitt.

Unconditional Love
D: P.J. Hogan; W: Jocelyn Moorhouse, P.J. Hogan; P: Jocelyn Moorhouse, Jerry Zucker; LP: Kathy Bates, Rupert Everett.

2001

About A Boy
D: Paul Weitz, Chris Weitz; W: Nick Hornby (novel), Peter Hedges, Chris Weitz, Paul Weitz; P: Tim Bevan, Robert De Niro, Brad Epstein, Eric Fellner, Jane Rosenthal; LP: Hugh Grant, Toni Collete, Nicholas Hoult.

American Embassy, The (television series)
Six sixty-minute episodes.
D: John David Coles, Stephen Cragg, Stephen Surjik, Andy Tennant; W: Kip Koenig, Lori Lakin, James D. Parriott, Michael Sardo; LP: Arija Bareikis, David Cubitt, Jonathan Cake.

Anita & Me

D: Metin Hausayn; W: Meera Syal; P: Paul Raphael; LP: Sanjeev Bhaskar, Kathy Burke, Lynn Redgrave.

Being April (television)

D/W: Pete Lawson; P: Deborah Jones; LP: Pauline Quirke, Nicholas Gleaves.

Below

D: David Tuohy; W: Lucas Sussman, Darren Aronofsky, David Twohy; P: Sue Baden-Powell, Michael Zoumas; LP: Olivia Williams, Dexter Fletcher, Jason Flemyng.

Bend It Like Beckham

D: Gurinder Chadha; W: Gurinder Chadha, Paul Mayeda Berges, Guljit Bindra; P: Gurinder Chadha, Deepak Nayar; LP: Parminder Nagra, Keira Knightley, Jonathan Rhys-Meyers.

Combat Sheep (television)

D: Dominic Brigstocke; W: Tim Firth; P: Robert Howes; LP: Steve Coogan, Ronni Ancona, Mark Williams.

Dirty Pretty Things

D: Stephen Frears; W: Steven Knight; P: Robert Jones, Tracey Seaward; LP: Chiwetel Ejiofor, Audrey Tautou.

Doctor Terrible's House of Horrible's (television series)

Six thirty-minute episodes.

D: Matt Lipsey; W: Steve Coogan, Graham Duff, Henry Normal; P: Alison MacPhail; LP: Steve Coogan.

Four Feathers, The

D: Shekhar Kapur; W: A.E.W. Mason (novel), Michael Schiffer, Hossein Amini; P: Paul Feldsher, Robert Jaffe, Stanley R. Jaffe, Marty Katz; LP: Heath Ledger, Kate Hudson.

Gosford Park

D: Robert Altman; W: Julian Fellowes; P: Robert Altman, Bob Balaban, David Levy; LP: Maggie Smith, Michael Gambon, Ryan Phillippe, Clive Owen, Helen Mirren.

Gathering Storm, The (television)

D: Richard Loncraine; W: Hugh Whitemore; P: Frank Doelger, David Thompson; LP: Albert Finney, Vanessa Redgrave, Jim Broadbent.

Glass, The (television mini-series)

D: Philippa Langdale, Patrick Lau, Nicholas Laughland; W: Chris Lang; P: Tom Grieves; LP: John Thaw, Sarah Lancashire, Joseph McFadden.

Heart of Me, The

D: Thaddeus O'Sullivan; W: Lucinda Coxon, Rosamond Lehmann (novel); P: Martin Pope; LP: Helena Bonham Carter, Olivia Williams, Paul Bettany.

Last of the Summer Wine (television series)

Six thirty-minute episodes.

D/P: Alan J.W. Bell; W: Roy Clarke; LP: Peter Sallis, Frank Thornton, Kathy Staff.

Pollyanna (television)

D: Sarah Harding; W: Simon Nye, Eleanor Porter (novel); P: Trevor Hopkins; LP: Amanda Burton, Kenneth Cranham, Aden Gillett.

Shackleton (television)

D/W: Charles Sturridge; P: Selwyn Roberts; LP: Kenneth Branagh, Phoebe Nicholls.

Shipping News, The
D: Lasse Hallstrom; W: E. Annie Proulx (novel), Robert Nelson Jacobs (screenplay); P: Rob
Cowan, Linda Goldstein Knowlton, Leslie Holleran, Irwin Winkler; LP: Kevin Spacey,
Julianne Moore, Judi Dench.
Thomas the Tank Engine (television series)
See 1991 for credits.
Two Men Went To War
D: John Henderson; W: Richard Everett, Raymond Foxall (book – *Amateur Commandos*),
Christopher Villiers; P: Pat Harding, Ira Trattner; LP: Kenneth Cranham, Derek Jacobi,
Phylldia Law.

2002

Black Ball
D: Mel Smith; W: Tim Firth; P: James Gay-Rees; LP: Paul Kaye, Kenneth Cranham, James
Cromwell.
Calendar Girls
D: Nigel Cole; W: Tim Firth, Juliet Towhidi; P: Nick Barton, Suzanne Macki; LP: Helen
Mirren, Julie Walters, John Alderton.
Cheeky
D/W: David Thewlis; P: Trudie Styler, Travis Swords; LP: David Thewlis, Lisa Gordon,
Johnny Vegas.
Cruise of the Gods (television)
D: Declan Lowney; W: Tim Firth, Michael Marshall Smith; P: Alison MacPhail; LP: Steve
Coogan, Rob Brydon, Helen Coker.
Ella Enchanted
D: Tommy O'Haver; W: Gail Carson Levine (novel), Laurie Craig, Karen McCullah Lutz,
Kirsten Smith, Jennifer Heath, Michele J. Wolff; P: Jane Startz; LP: Anne Hathaway, Cary
Elwes, Minnie Driver.
Falklands Play (television)
D: Michael Samuels; W: Ian Curtis; P: Jeremy Howe; LP: Patricia Hodge, James Fox, John
Standing.
Fame Academy (television)
Reality television series.
Harry Potter and the Chamber of Secrets (part)
D: Christopher Columbus; W: Steve Kloves, J.K. Rowling (novel); P: David Heyman; LP:
Daniel Radcliffe, Rupert Grint, Emma Watson, Richard Harris, Maggie Smith.
I Capture the Castle
D: Tim Flywell; W: Dodi Smith (book), Heidi Thomas; P: David Parfitt; LP: Romolo Garai,
Henry Thomas, Bill Nighy, Marc Blucas.
If Only (part)
D: Jil Junger; W: Christina Welsh; P: Jill Gilbert, Jeffrey Graup, Jennifer Love Hewitt, Gil
Junger, Robert F. Newmyer, Jeffrey Silver; LP: Jennifer Love Hewitt, Paul Nichols.
Jack (short film)
D/W: Matty Limpus; P: Francesca Strano; LP: Barry Langrishe.
J.M. Barrie's Neverland (aka 'Finding Neverland')
D: Marc Foster; W: Allan Knee (play), David Magee; P: Nellie Bellflower, Richard N.
Gladstein; LP: Johnny Depp, Kate Winslet, Julie Christie.

Johnny English
D: Peter Howitt; W: Neal Purvis, Robert Wade, William Davies; P: Tim Bevan, Eric Fellner, Mark Huffan; LP: Rowan Atkinson, Natalie Imbruglia.

K19: The Widowmaker (part)
D: Kathryn Bigello; W: Louis Nowra (story), Christopher Kyle; P: Kathryn Bigelow, Edward S. Feldman, Sigurjon Sighvatsson, Chris Whitaker; LP: Harrison Ford, Liam Neeson.

Last of the Summer Wine
See 2001 credits.

Life of David Gale, The (part)
D: Alan Parker; W: Charles Randolph; P: Alan Parker, Nicholas Cage; LP: Kevin Spacey, Kate Winslet, Laura Linney.

Love Actually
D/W: Richard Curtis; P: Tim Bevan, Eric Fellner, Duncan Kenworthy; LP: Hugh Grant, Bill Nighy, Keira Knightley.

Mindhunters
D: Renny Harlin; W: Wayne Kramer, Kevin Brodbin; P: Cary Brokaw, Akiva Goldsman, Robert F. Newmyer, Susan E. Novick, Jeffrey Silver, Rebecca Spikings, Scott Strauss; LP: Val Kilmer, Johnny Lee Miller, Christian Slater.

My House in Umbria (television)
D: Richard Loncraine; W: William Trevor (novel), Hugh Whitemore; P: Ann Wingate; LP: Maggie Smith, Ronnie Barker, Timothy Spall.

Robot Wars (television series)
Forty-five-minute episodes hosted by Craig Charles.

Second Nature (television)
D: Ben Bolt; W: E. Max Frye; P: Lars MacFarlane, Craig McNeil; LP: Alec Baldwin, Powers Boothe, Louise Lombard.

Sons and Lovers (television)
D: Stephen Whittaker; W: Simon Burke, D.H. Lawrence (novel); P: Suzan Harrison; LP: Sarah Lancashire, Hugo Speer.

Sport Relief
BBC charity fundraising programme.

State of Play (television mini-series)
D: David Yates; W: Paul Abbott; P: Hilary Bevan-Jones; LP: David Morrissey, Bill Nighy, Polly Walker.

Strange (television)
D: Joe Ahearne; W: Andrew Marshall; P: Marcus Mortimer; LP: Richard Coyle, Ian Richardson, Samantha Janus.

Sylvia
D: Christine Jeffs; W: John Brownlow; P: Alison Owen; LP: Gwyneth Paltrow, Daniel Craig, Jared Harris.

To Kill a King (aka 'Cromwell & Fairfax')
D: Mike Barker; W: Jenny Mayhew; P: Kevin Loader; LP: Tim Roth, Dougray Scott, Olivia Williams.

Walking with Cavemen (television series)
Four thirty-minute episodes.
D: Richard Dale, Pierre de Lespinois; W: Michael Olmert; Host: Professor Robert Winston.

Wondrous Oblivion

D/W: Paul Morrison; P: Jonny Persey; LP: Sam Smith, Emily Woolf, Delroy Lindo.

2003

Alexander (part)

D/W: Oliver Stone; P: Moritz Borman, Jon Kilik, Thomas Schühly, Iain Smith, Oliver Stone; LP: Colin Farrell, Angelina Jolie, Val Kilmer, Anthony Hopkins.

Bridget Jones II: The Edge Of Reason (part)

D: Beeban Kidron; W: Richard Curtis, Adam Brooks, Andrew Davies, Helen Fielding; P: Jonathan Cavendish, Eric Fellner, Tim Bevan; LP: Renée Zellweger, Colin Firth, Hugh Grant.

Five Children and It

D: John Stephenson; W: E. Nesbit (novel), David Solomons; P: Lisa Henson, Nick Hirschkorn; LP: Kenneth Branagh, Zoë Wanamaker.

Harry Potter and the Prisoner of Azkaban (part)

D: Alfonso Cuaron; W: Steve Kloves, J.K. Rowling (novel); P: David Heyman; LP: Daniel Radcliffe, Emma Watson, Rupert Grint, Fiona Shaw.

Last of the Summer Wine (television series)

See 2001 credits.

Life and Death of Peter Sellers, The

D: Stephen Hopkins; W: Roger Lewis (book), Christopher Markus, Stephen McFeely; P: Simon Bosanquet; LP: Geoffrey Rush, Charlize Theron, Emily Watson.

Poirot (television)

D: Andy Wilson; W: Agatha Christie (novels), Kevin Elyot; P: Margaret Mitchell; LP: David Suchet.

Shaun of the Dead (part)

D: Edgar Wright; W: Edgar Wright, Simon Pegg; P: Nira Park; LP: Simon Pegg, Kate Ashfield, Nick Frost.

Stage Beauty

D: Richard Eyre; W: Jeffrey Hatcher; P: Robert De Niro, Hardy Justice, Jane Rosenthal; LP: Billy Crudup, Claire Danes, Rupert Everett.

Thomas the Tank Engine

Two series. See 1991 credits.

Thunderbirds (part)

D: Jonathan Frakes; W: William Osborne, Michael McCullers; P: Matk Huffam, Tim Bevan, Eric Fellner; LP: Bill Paxon, Brady Corbet, Ben Kingsley.

Troy

D: Wolfgang Peterson; W: David Benioff; P: Wolfgang Petersen, Diana Rathbun, Colin Wilson; LP: Brad Pitt, Orlando Bloom, Eric Bana.

Wimbledon

D: Richard Loncraine; W: Adam Brooks, Jennifer Flackett, Mark Levin; P: Eric Fellner, Liza Chasin, Jennifer Flackett, Mary Richards; LP: Kirsten Dunst, Paul Bettany.

U Get Me (television)

Children's BBC television programme.

Young Visitors, The (television)

D: David Yates; W: Patrick Barlow; P: Christopher Hall; LP: Jim Broadbent, Hugh Laurie, Bill Nighy.

2004

Batman Begins
D: Christopher Nolan; W: David S. Goyer, Christopher Nolan; P: Larry J. Franco, Charles Roven, Emma Thomas; LP: Christian Bale, Morgan Freeman, Michael Caine, Liam Neeson.

Born and Bred (television series)
Series Three was produced at Shepperton.
D: David Tucker; W: Chris Chibnall, Dan Sefton, Robert Shearman; P: Chris Clough, Phil Collinson; LP: James Bolam, Michael French, Richard Wilson.

Closer (part)
D: Mike Nicholls; W: Patrick Marber; P: Scott Rudin, Cary Brokaw, John Calley; LP: Jude Law, Julia Roberts, Clive Owen, Natalie Portman.

Crust, The
Television programme.

Hitchhiker's Guide to the Galaxy, The (part)
D: Garth Jennings; W: Douglas Adams, Karey Kirkpatrick; P: Gary Barber, Roger Birnbaum, Jonathan Glickman, Nick Goldsmith, Jay Roach; LP: Martin Freeman, Mos Def, Bill Nighy.

Last of the Summer Wine (television series)
See 2001 credits.

Mrs Henderson Presents
D: Stephen Frears; W: Martin Sherman; P: David Aukin, Laurie Borg, Norma Heyman; LP: Judi Dench, Bob Hoskins, Will Young.

Poirot (television)
D: Simon Langton; W: Nick Dear; P: Margaret Mitchell; LP: David Suchet, Edward Fox, Lysette Anthony.

Russian Dolls
D/W: Cedric Klapisch; P: Matthew Justice, Bruno Levy; LP: Lucy Gordon, Kevin Bishop, Audrey Tautou.

Sahara
D: Breck Eisner; W: Thomas Dean Donnelly, Matthew Faulk, Josh Friedman, James V. Hart, Joshua Oppenheimer, John C. Richards, John Richards, Mark Skeet, David S. Ward; P: Mace Neufeld, Stephanie Austin, Howard Baldwin, Karen Elise Baldwin; LP: Penélope Cruz, Dayna Cussler, Delroy Lindo, William H. Macy.

Silent Witness VIII (television series)
D: various, including: Bill Anderson, John Duthie, Coky Giedroyc; W: various, including Stephen Brady, Michael Crompton, Richard Holland, Dusty Hughes; P: Tony Dennis, Diana Kyle, Graeme MacArthur, Nick Pitt, Anne Pivcevic; LP: Amanda Burton, William Gaminara, Emilia Fox.

2005

As You Like It
D: Kenneth Branagh; W: Kenneth Branagh, based on the William Shakespeare play; P: Simon Moseley, Judy Hofflund, Kenneth Branagh; LP: Sacha Bennett, Brian Blessed, Jonathan Broadbent.

Bridge, The (short film)
D: Richard Raymond; W: Ludwig Shammasian; P: Mark Young, Richard Raymond; LP: Andrea Corr, Leonard Fenton

Da Vinci Code, The
D: Ron Howard; W: Akiva Goldsman; P: Brian Grazer; LP: Tom Hanks, Audrey Tautou, Ian McKellen, Paul Bettany.

Land of the Blind
D/W: Robert Edwards; P: John Avnet; LP: Ralph Fiennes, Donald Sutherland, Lara Flynn Boyle.

Love & Other Disasters
D/W: Alek Keshishian; P: Alek Keshishian, Virginie Silla; LP: Orlando Bloom, Brittany Murphy, Gwyneth Paltrow, Dawn French, Stephanie Beacham.

2006

Atonement
D: Joe Wright; W: Christopher Hampton; P: Paul Webster; LP: Keira Knightley, James McAvoy, Romola Garai, Brenda Blethyn.

Black Book (Zwartboek) (part)
D: Paul Verhoeven; W: Gerard Soeteman, Paul Verhoeven; P: Jeroen Beker, San Fu Maltha, Frans van Gestel, Teun Hilte; LP: Carice van Houten.

Goal 2: Living the Dream (part)
D: Jaume Collet-Serra; W: Mike Jefferies; P: Matt Barrelle; LP: Kuno Becker, Alessandro Nivola, Anna Friel, Stephen Dillane, Rutger Hauer, Frances Barber, Sean Pertwee.

Golden Age, The
D: Shekhar Kapur; W: Chris Emposimato, Michael Hirst William Nicholson; P: Tim Bevan, Eric Fellner, Jonathan Cavendish; LP: Cate Blanchett, Coral Beed, Morne Botes, Christian Brassington.

Hannibal Rising (part)
D: Peter Webber; W: Thomas Harris; P: Tarak Ben Ammar, Dino De Laurentiis; LP: Gaspard Ulliel, Rhys Ifans, Aaron Thomas.

His Dark Materials: The Golden Compass
D/W: Chris Weitz, based on the Philip Pullman novel; P: Deborah Forte, Bill Carraro; LP: Nicole Kidman, Daniel Craig, Dakota Blue Richards, Eva Green.

Inkheart
D: Iain Softley; W: David Lindsay-Abaire; P: Cornelia Funke, Barry Mendel, Diana Porkony; LP: Helen Mirren, Brendan Fraser, Jim Broadbent, Rafi Gavron, Andy Serkis, Eliza Bennett.

Jam and Jerusalem (television)
D: Mandie Fletcher; W: Jennifer Saunders; P: Jo Sargeant; LP: Jennifer Saunders, Dawn French, Sue Johnston, Joanna Lumley.

Jonathan Toomey
D/W: Bill Clark; P: Tom Mattinson; LP: Aran Bell, Tom Berenger, Clare Burt, Benji Compston.

Magic Flute, The
D/W: Kenneth Branagh; P: Pierre-Olivier Bardet; LP: Joseph Kaiser, Amy Carson, René Pape, Lyubov Petrova.

Mutant Chronicles, The

D: Simon Hunter; W: Philip Eisner, Ross Jameson; P: Edward R. Pressman, Tim Dennison; LP: Thomas Jane, John Malkovich, Ron Perlman, Sean Pertwee, Devon Aoki.

2007

The Golden Compass

D: Chris Weitz; W: Chris Weitz, based on the Philip Pullman novel; P: Bill Carraro, Deborah Forte; LP: Daniel Craig, Nicole Kidman Eva Green, Kevin Bacon.

Last of the Summer Wine (television series)

See earlier entries.

Cranford (television)

D/P: Sue Birtwistle; W: Sue Birtwistle, Susie Conklin, Elizabeth Gaskell, Heidi Thomas; LP: Judi Dench, Imelda Staunton, Michael Gambon.

A Dying Breed

D/P/W: Katharine Collins; LP: James Oliver Wheatley, Luke Cameron, Lourdes Faberes.

Half Broken Things (television)

D: Tim Fywell; W: Alan Whiting; P: Ray Marshall; LP: Penelope Wilton, Daniel Mays, Sinead Matthews.

Love in the Time of Cholera

D: Mike Newell; W: Ronald Harwood, based on the novel by Gabriel García Márquez; P: Scott Steindorff; LP: Benjamin Bratt, Gina Bernand Forbes, Javier Bardem.

Stagknight

D: Simon Cathcart; W/P: Simon Cathcart, Robert Mercer; LP: J.C. Mac, Harry Athwal, Martin Bayfield, Simon Cathcart.

2008

Burlesque Fairytales (part)

D/W: Susan Luciani; P: Lindsay McFarlane; LP: Stephen Campbell Moore, Jim Carter, Lindsay Duncan, Barbara Flynn.

Gladiators (television)

D: Chris Power; P: Louise Whalley; LP: Kirsty Gallacher, Ian Wright.

Harry Potter and the Half-Blood Prince (part)

D: David Yates; W: Steve Kloves (based on the book by J.K. Rowling); P: David Heyman; LP: Daniel Radcliffe, Emily Watson, Rupert Grint.

Moon

D: Duncan Jones; W: Nathan Parker; P: Nicky Moss, Trudie Styler, Stuart Fenegan; LP: Sam Rockwell, Kaya Scodelario.

The Boat That Rocked

D/W: Richard Curtis; P: Tim Bevan, Eric Fellner, Richard Curtis; LP: Philip Seymour-Hoffman, Kenneth Branagh, Gemma Arterton, Bill Nighy.

The Young Victoria

D: Jean-Marc Vallée; W: Julian Fellowes; P: Sarah Ferguson, Tim Headington, Graham King, Denis O'Sullivan, Martin Scorsese; LP: Emily Blunt, Rupert Friend, Paul Bettany.

Thomas the Tank Engine and Friends (television)

Series Twelve.

P: Britt Alcroft; LP: Michael Angelis.

Bibliography

Alexander Korda – A Biography, Paul Tabori (Oldbourne, 1959)

A Cast of Shadows, Ronnie Maasz (Scarecrow Press, 2004)

Halliwell's Film Guide (Harper Collins)

Always Look on the Bright Side of Life, Robert Sellers (Metro, 2003)

Tell Them I'm on my Way, Arnold Goodman (Chapmans, 1993)

So You Want to be in Pictures, Val Guest (Reynolds & Hearn, 2001)

Still Dancing, Lew Grade (Fontana, 1987)

A Lifetime of Films, Michael Balcon (Hutchinson 1969)

Confessions of an Actor, Laurence Olivier (Coronet, 1982)

Mr Strangelove, Ed Sikov (Pan, 2002)

Flickering Shadows, John Mitchell (HMR, 1997)

Amicus, Allan Bryce (The Dark Side)

David Lean, Kevin Brownlow (Faber and Faber, 1996)

British Film Studios, Patricia Warren (Batsford, 2001)

Sherlock Holmes on Screen, Alan Barnes (Reynolds & Hearn, 2002)

J. Arthur Rank and the British Film Industry (Routledge, 1994)

Sam Spiegel, Natasha Fraser-Cavassoni (Little Brown, 2003)

Flashback, George Pearson (George, Allen & Unwin, 1957)

Modern Men of Mark, Mrs Stuart Menzies (Herbert Jenkins, c.1918)

Million Dollar Movie, Michael Powell (Mandarin, 1992)

Blondie, Ewan Southby-Taylor (Leo Cooper, 1998)

The Making of the African Queen, Katharine Hepburn (Alfred A. Knopf, 1987)

An Open Book, John Huston (Da Capo, 1994)

The Films of Sean Connery, Lee Pfeiffer and Phil Lisa (Citadel, 1993)

Fred Zinnemann: An Autobiography (Scribners, 1992)

The Pinewood Story, Gareth Owen and Brian Burford (Reynolds & Hearn, 2000)

The Gimmick Man, Albert J. Luxford with Gareth Owen (McFarland, 2002)

A Life through the Lens, Alan Hume with Gareth Owen (McFarland, 2004)

Shepperton Studios: An Independent View, Derek Threadgall (BFI, 1994)

Christopher Lee: The Authorised Screen Story, Jonathan Rigby (Reynolds & Hearn, 2001)

Korda, Britain's Only Movie Mogul, Charles Drazin (Sidgwick & Jackson, 2002)
In Search of the Third Man, Charles Drazin (Methuen, 1999)
An Autobiography of British Cinema, Brian McFarlane (Methuen, 1997)
Charmed Lives, Michael Korda (Random House, 1979)
Shepperton Studios Annual Reports (various)
Screen International (various)
Kinematograph Weekly (various)
David Blake Archive (interviews from late 1980s onwards)
The Boulting Brothers/British Lion Archives
When the Snow Melts, Cubby Broccoli (Macmillan, 2000)

Other books by the same author:

The Pinewood Story: The Authorised History of Pinewood Studios
Gareth Owen with Brian Burford
Reynolds & Hearn Ltd (2000, 2002, 2006)

The Gimmick Man
Albert J. Luxford with Gareth Owen
McFarland & Co Inc (2002)

Roger Moore: His Films and Career
Gareth Owen and Oliver Bayan
Robert Hale (2002)

Alan Hume: A Life through the Lens
Alan Hume with Gareth Owen
McFarland & Co Inc (2004)

Pictures & Premieres
Harry Myers, John Willis and Gareth Owen
Robert Hale (2007)

My Word is My Bond: the Autobiography of Roger Moore
With Gareth Owen
Michael O'Mara (2008)

Other titles published by The History Press

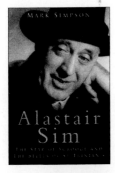

Alistair Sim: The Star of 'Scrooge' and 'The Belles of St Trinian's'
MARK SIMPSON

The only biography of Alastair Sim, this book is supported by extensive researc including information from people who worked on film sets with Alastai material from the theatre museum archives and original reviews from theatr magazines and newspapers. It also includes interviews with over thirty of hi fellow actors including Sir Ian McKellen, Ronnie Corbett and Stephen Fry.

978 0 7509 4966 8

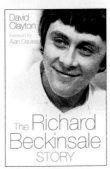

The Richard Beckinsale Story
DAVID CLAYTON

This is the first biography of the much-loved seventies actor Richard Beckinsale who died on 19 March 1979 at the age of thirty-one. It looks back at one of th biggest stars of that decade through the eyes of family, friends and colleagues. Th Richard Beckinsale Story is an uplifting, but ultimately sad, tale of the life an death of a great talent. It is the compelling story of a man destined for greatnes but ultimately cut down in his prime.

978 0 7509 5061 9

Suburban London Cinemas
GARY WHARTON

Through the medium of old photographs, programmes and advertisement Suburban London Cinemas provides a fascinating look at the history of cinema going in and around the capital during the last century. Illustrated with 10 images, this well-researched and informative volume will delight all those wh have fond memories of visiting some of London's long-since vanished cinema as well as those that still remain in some form or another.

978 0 7509 4953 8

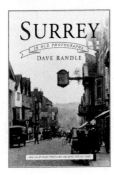

Surrey in Old Photographs: From the Judges Postcard Archive Collection
DAVE RANDLE

Judges Postcards have been celebrating the British landscape for over a hundr years. Their archive now covers a century of change and this book draw on it to present a superb selection of images of Surrey's past. The quality Judges' photography combined with the author's informative and entertainin commentary provides a surprisingly comprehensive introduction to the count

978 0 7509 4161 7

Visit our website and discover thousands of other History Press books.

www.thehistorypress.co.uk